JASMINES
From Egypt Branches
Forever

Tale of a growing child

Complete Second Edition (Black & White)
Written between 2008 and 2018

All ye faithful of the world

"Fear not them which kill the body, but are not able to kill the soul: But rather fear him which is able to destroy both soul and body in hell"
Mathew 10:28

Rafik G. Baladi

Individuals, please order this book online at most retail shops
Retailers: https://www.ingramcontent.com/retailers/ordering

© Copyright 2018 Rafik G. Baladi. Also, protected by:
Canadian Intellectual Property Office (Industry Canada)

All rights reserved to author. No part of this publication may be reproduced, stored in a retrieval system, or transmitted, in any form or by any means, electronic, mechanical, photocopying, recording, or otherwise, without the written prior permission of the author.

isbn: 978-1-7751-501-0-7 (sc)   Black & White Interior
isbn: 978-1-7751-501-1-4 (hc)   Black & White Interior
isbn: 978-1-7751-501-2-1 (e)   Electronic Format
isbn: 978-1-7751-501-4-5 (sc)   Color Interior
isbn: 978-1-7751-501-3-8 (hc)   Color Interior

Reviews

This testimony reveals its author's experience with Egypt, from a unique and factual perspective, recounting warm and overwhelming moments of grief and joy; of pain and human victory. His style as a storyteller is tender but electric. It spirals far back to Egypt's glorious days and forward to her last sixty years of struggles. It depicts vast similarities in the absurdity of human marginalization, from homeland, to school and workplace, including his own recent suffering from corporate politics. It is a beautiful, genuine, and romantic fairy tale of human survival, rich with history and spirituality. It is based on true events. "Just as a living tree loses its aging fruits to its rich soil.", says the author, "so, too, has Egypt lost many of her jasmines but for different reasons. It lost them because of social and political insensitivity." These jasmines had to leave their mother's bosom because of the shifting social climate and because of their shades, passions, and roots. Overseas, they continued to flourish with their gentle scents. Beautiful things happen to them; things that revitalize the souls. But the absurdity of intolerance broke in the homeland; it broke out of proportions, between 2010 and 2018. Hope continued to prevail. In the meantime, the hero of the book, finally, reunites with his Egyptian childhood love at the age of 59, overseas.

Gehan Sabry:

Founder, Publisher and Editor in Chief
"Cross Cultures" magazine, Kitchener, Ontario (Canada).

Reviews

This is a touching comparison of the life and times of an Egyptian immigrant and the baffling cultural history of a great civilization. The author draws a curious parallel between the life of an often occupied nation and the life of a man coming to terms with and rising above personal assaults. A must read which offers important spiritual insights and tries to make rational sense of the struggles which torment both individuals and nations. Thoroughly enjoyable and thought provoking.
Joanne Davies, Entrepreneur, Montreal.

Cofounder Bezanson & Davies Ltée,
Montreal, Canada

This book recounts glimpses of life in ancient and recent Egypt. It's about tolerance and openness to other cultures and other Peoples, beautifully expressed throughout his memoires.

Perry Greenbaum

Writer of:
Seeing the World as I do.

Alexandria historic sea panorama (AD 2009)
Founded by Alexander the Great in 334 BC
Formerly, The town of Rakouda and Rakhotis

Atheneus – Alexandria's 1958 Waterfront
High tea house with music quintets, far left (in 2008)

Dedications

In loving memory of my angel brother 'Kamal'
And of my beloved parents
'George Baladi and Laurice Nicola-Baladi'

Well-done, brave and loving servants of God
Thank you for teaching me
Honesty, justice and survival

- - - - -

To Laila, my beautiful, loving and tender wife,
You are everything I hoped for to live and move forward
Thank you for helping me stand again

To Gloria, my only sister and caring witness
…in this rich journey of life

Disclaimers

While this story is based on true events, almost none of the names used for its living characters are real and some of the names of places in Canada, mentioned in this story are not always authentic; they may have been modified. Any similarities in any of such names are simply a coincidence and are not meant to depict any person or place in particular, whatsoever.

While several portions of this story are based on historical facts and certain of its characters are genuine historical figures, mentioning them is not meant to reflect any views of its author or publisher. They are presented to provide a far more comprehensive portrait of Egypt (for the sake of this biography and its hero), than otherwise perceived by the reader.

The health and medical information, ideas, and suggestions contained in this book are not intended for use as reference or substitute for professional advice. Before following any suggestions contained in this book, you should consult your personal physician or health professional. Neither the author nor the publisher shall be liable or responsible for any loss or damage allegedly arising because of any use or application of information and suggestions in this book.

For Mother

(Our angel)

In recognition to

The Greek Orthodox Patriarchate of Old-Cairo (The ancient Roman fortress of Babylon) for its valuable time and guidance during our interviews in 2009;

…for providing us with priceless knowledge and for giving us access to both some of the shelters of the Holy Family in old Cairo (amongst others) and to its mystical underground halls, relics and remains of Egyptian Christian Martyrs, across the centuries, since the first century after Christ.

Clerics at the countless historical Islamic, Fatimid and Maméluke Mosques and cemeteries, visited in Cairo, for their valuable information, kind and generous access to their places of worship, presented in this book and thereafter.

The clerics at Sinai's Monastery of Saint Catherine the Martyr (of Alexandria), for their valuable time during my interviews, with them and for their leadership; Saint Catherine was persecuted under the Roman Emperor Maximus and killed in Alexandria during the third century after Christ.

The Supreme Council of Antiquities of Egypt; (Islamic and Coptic Monuments Sector) for its priceless efforts to uphold presence and access to various other historical and holy Jewish, Christian and Islamic sites (in historical order) presented by the author in this book and thereafter. Thank you for giving us access to The Holy Family's third shelter in Egypt (At the Sycamore Tree Grotto and the holy well) amongst others.

Citadel of Saladin (Salah-el-Din El-Ayoubi) AD 1176-1183

Citadel of Sultan Mohamed Ali AD 1805-1848

Jasmines from Egypt Branches Forever
Tale of a growing child

(Complete Second Edition)

1951 - 2018

Introduction

PART 1

Chapter 1
Before my September-2008, retreat in Magog - 1

Chapter – 2
Before my September-2008, retreat in Magog - 2
Mother, my rock, fifty-five years earlier 1

Chapter – 3
Before my September-2008, retreat in Magog - 3
Mother, fifty-five years earlier 2

Chapter 4
Who Drove the Flowers Out of Their Roots?

Chapter 5
My ancestors' immigration to from the Levant

Chapter 6
My Mother's Early Years with Dad

Chapter 7
Egypt, the Dwindling Golden Years

Chapter 8
Who Drove the Egyptians Out of Egypt?
A chronological sequence of vital information

Chapter 9
Scents of Jasmine and Seeds of Fear
Fifty-five years earlier, childhood; home and school

Chapter 10
Breeding the Seeds of Fear!
The Departures!

Chapter 11
The Retreat—1
Today, by Lake Memphre-Magog

Chapter 12
The Retreat—2

Chapter 13
Passions and Roots-1
Snapshots of our childhood

Chapter 14
Passions and Roots - 2
Alexandria and Ras-el-Bar (Mes Amours)

Chapter 15
Passions and Roots-3
Sinai, Mon Amour

Chapter 16
Passions and Roots—4
Bending the Barriers of Tradition

Chapter 17
Passions and Roots—5
Struggling Toward My Adulthood

Chapter 18
Passions and Roots—6
My Brother, Camille, the Cool and Loving—1

Chapter 19
Passions and Roots—7
My Brother, Camille, the Cool and Loving—2

Chapter 20
Passions and Roots—8
Turning Points

Chapter 21
Passions and Roots—9
The Last Summer – Building character

Chapter 22
Passions and Roots—10
The Day I Said Farewell to Camille

Chapter 23
Passions and Roots—11
The Day the Sun Went Down

Chapter 24
Return to Life without Camille
Papa, Mon Amour

Chapter 25
After the Storms

Chapter 26
The Retreat - 3
Return to the Present

Chapter 27
Return to Work—1

Chapter 28
Return to Work—2

Chapter 29
Return to Work—3

Chapter 30
The Break in Egypt—1

Chapter 31
The Break in Egypt—2

Chapter 32
The Break in Egypt—3

Chapter 33
The Break in Egypt—4

Chapter 34
Return from Vacation

Chapter 35
The Wedding and the Family

Chapter 36
Cutting the Umbilical Cord

Chapter 37
Four Weeks to Go
A Shade from Sixty Years

Chapter 38
Return to Egypt for winter and the Unbelievable

Chapter 39
The Following Three Months in a Turbulent Egypt

Chapter 40
Reflections and Resolutions — Across the Atlantic

Chapter 41
A Breath of Fresh Air ... Gentle Breezes from the Past
The day following our return to Montreal

Chapter 42
Reflections and Resolutions by the Lake

Chapter 43
The Day the Sun Came Back

Chapter 44
Egypt 2013-2016 the Eternal Cradle of Civilization
And the Immoral Struggle for Power

Chapter 45
A dark dawn in January
Mother, my eternal angel

Saint Marc Cathedral Alexandria, Egypt
Christian See of Alexandria and Africa

Opening Statement by the author

Societies are made of people; people make societies. When people die, societies may continue if those who died are acknowledged and continue to be represented, such as through their findings, descendants and national institutions.

When we wipe out the findings of our fellow citizens, we diminish our societies. So too are they fractured when their members are alienated and rid of both their independence and right to choose. So too are those who are alienated by intolerance or by mind control, fractured and limited from putting their marks unless they fight the fight with faith and fellowship; with carriage and character. It is all about inclusion and exclusion, not about life and death. It is about compassion, truth, love, justice and peace.

Rafik Baladi

Introduction by Bernie (*Bernard Malvoun*)

He found himself falling into a mood bordering despair; one with a severely fractured self-esteem, so he decided to take a break, leave his hometown of Montreal (Quebec, Canada), and drive to Quebec's Eastern Townships. He picked the city of Magog, only a two-hour drive eastward, and he stayed there for a few days, in retreat. He had left me several index cards that contained his diaries to review, promising to start a book one day. Therefore, I used them to compile my thoughts in this introduction, to the best I could, to prompt him to start writing it soon.

The last time I saw him was a few days ago, on September 3, 2008; we had some drinks after work, minutes away from my office, and I clearly noticed his shaking voice and pale face. He was struggling to pose as a man in control. A well-groomed, fifty-seven-year-old Caucasian with gray hair and deep green eyes, Raphael had been coping with peer bullying and petty office resistance for over four years (since September 2004). Previously, between 1993 and 1997, he had worked within a similar negative environment for another hotel, in Montreal's north-side city of Le Soleil. It was at this former hotel that I met him, first, as his client. Staff of both hotels, knew each other since they worked for the same industry and the same hotel chain.

In between working at the two hotels, he worked on his own as a consultant for hotels across the cities of Montreal and Ottawa (Canada), while generating some stable but modest income from a side job at a call center, as he waited for his business to grow. He stayed in Ottawa for four years between 1999 and 2003, where he secured a studio in an upper floor right in the heart of Ottawa's bustling and old center. He had sworn not to work for hotels after 1997, but he did again in 2004, with this current assignment, after his business as a consultant slowed-down. So far, he says, he has exceeded all business targets and expectations at both Montreal hotels. He thinks of himself as a creative, daring, visionary, and tenacious hotelier in Montreal.

His story with violence, he says, spirals back to his school years. Raphy (Raphael) considers himself a survivor of social marginalization since childhood. He witnessed endless moments of marginalization, isolation, and intolerance in his homeland of Egypt before he immigrated to Canada- that targeted him and others. These will unfold, later. But for now, his mind is racing as he struggles to find some light in his tired and manipulated mind.

Over the past few months, Raphy (Raphael) had been plunging into a total breakdown and was struggling to overcome it by taking grip of his state of mind, at times through lengthy meditation and others through heavy medication. He had barely survived his earlier somber work experience for the same reasons. They had drenched him with mind games, manipulation, and control until he resigned in 1997. I was his client in both hotels and his friend just after he served my son's Bar Mitzvah devotedly, at the first hotel. I noticed his grief even then. Between the two hotel assignments, of four years each, there was a period of eight years, in which he suffered fluctuating moods disorder because of the effect of his former work environment, at Le Soleil. These caused him such trauma, that he was unable to cope with the challenges of his own business as consultant. Now, at this hotel, he has become a target of further bullying and corporate hurt. His refined manners did him more harm than good

He used to tell me, "When they know enough about you, they will pierce your mind, and start to anchor your weaknesses to their own benefit (just like a ship's anchor). After this, they will pace you, (befriend you) with the objective of controlling you and leading you (stretching you) and then claim, that they *care about you.* Several of his peers would, secretly serve, as management agents. Then they will tell you words like *you are a good man, you are an honest man,* because they recognize that honesty and goodness are part of your virtues. And, by doing so, they manage to pace with their target employee or executive member and win him or her over, as a trusted friend, after they have anchored and locked it (their target) in their fist. Slowly, as they pace with their target, they will lead her and drive her to an unimaginable volume of work and hours, stating that ... *you are our man or woman*. Hence, they will turn him or her into a [pawn with no identity] at an inequitable salary, using their control tactics to underpay their staff's vast professional experience or stretch her to produce more. All the while, they will still claim that they are helping her and, occasionally, reinforce new anchors of memories (many times painful) to make sure he is locked in their grip sometimes, even, to coerce their prey to resign, or not to leave. ...and guess what? They will drive their target to a point of undue hardship and to a possible irreversible damage."

Raphy told me that as of the first day, he could pick up moods from staff's eyes; vicious moods and vibes. This, he told me, was one of his vices as well as one of his strengths. In other words, Raphy was able to pick up other people's moods in multiple instances. "This is good and bad," he said. It was good because he became far more empathetic than others did, and so he could nurture relationships and profitable ventures simply by choosing the right topics and their wording to suit others. Call it public-relation skills or vision.

However, it was also hurtful because it could influence his mood if he associated himself with it and felt responsible for easing other people's grief- turning his empathy into sympathy. Even more, he could sometimes sense work teams feeling threatened by his ability to *look through*.

Raphy has worked for hotels and airlines all his life. To date, in 2008, he has accumulated a total of eighteen years of international airline and tourism experience and another twenty within hotels, between the Middle East, Europe, South America, and Canada.

Raphy arrived in Canada with his family in August of 1987, at the age of thirty-six. He came with his seventy-two-year-old mother, his thirty-seven-year-old sister, Nora, her husband, and their two lovely kids: eight-year-old boy, and four-year-old girl. They moved from Cairo where they all lived in one home, a villa with two floors. They landed in Montreal and stayed in two separate apartments for one and a half years. He stayed in one with his mother, Laurice, and his sister stayed in another with her family (on the higher floor) until his mother moved with his sister's family when they bought a house two years later (1989). Raphael moved with them, at their request for the first year, while sharing costs, and then moved out.

Raphy is a holder of higher diploma in Hotels from Cairo and a BA in Mass Communication from the AUC (American University in Cairo), with a minor in Drama and Modern Theatre. He loves theatre and considers himself a scholar of masters of modern theatre, such as Stanislavsky, Chekov, Ibsen, Gorki, Pirandello, and Arthur Miller.

On the private side, he loves music and plays the piano passionately. His musical foundation is classical, and he loves playing songs by Glenn Miller, Cole Porter, Ray Charles, Frank Sinatra, and others. But he also writes beautiful music for imaginary film themes, theatre, and documentaries. He does this either for his favorite instrument, the piano, or for the whole orchestra on sheet music.

After writing his music partitions, he plays his music (violin, cello, piano, flute, etc.) dubbing each instrument, one on top of the other, on his multi-instruments music keyboard, apparently worth $8,000, just as if it were an orchestra. Of course, his music keyboard, otherwise known as music workstation, has a bank of over four hundred sounds and instruments. He even writes the music as inspired, for various instruments, far from home with no access to real instruments. It could happen on the subway, in a public bathroom, or even in the staff cafeteria. He keeps one or two sheets of music paper, folded, in his pocket to make sure he never loses a passing tune.

Raphael was born in the city of Port-Said, in Egypt in 1951, six years after World War II was over, three years after

Israel was founded, and one year before the Egyptian revolution of 1952 ousted the king of Egypt and demolished the ruling family's reign after it had lasted for 150 successful years. He talks of himself as a "Post-WW2 casualty." His mother is half-Greek from the Dodecanese Greek Islands and half-Syrian from Damascus, and his dad is half-Greek from Turkey and half-Egyptian. Earlier, in the fifties, he was not one of the stronger school kids and many times, could not defend himself from bullies. His soccer team friends protected him, for a while.

He has been living in the province of Quebec, Canada, for twenty-one years, this day in 2008. He is the second child to his dad, George, and his mom, Laurice. His parents married in 1949 when his dad was sixty and his mom was thirty-three; yes, with a difference of twenty-seven years. It was a love marriage. Their first child was Nora, Raphael's sister. She was born in Cairo, and then Raphael was born one year later. In 1958, Camille, Raphael and Nora's younger brother, was born, still in Cairo, when Raphy's dad was sixty-nine and his mom was forty-two- with a twenty-seven years age gap.

In his current assignment at the hotel, his health gradually declined because of the office environment. This led him to severe burnout, depression, and all that comes with the package: excruciatingly painful gastric attacks, nausea, vomiting, tears, chills and loss of energy. Recently, these attacks grounded him for two and three full days, every week. He was unable to lift his back from the sofa where he laid stretched, throbbing from abdominal pain and swallowing acetaminophens. He would recover on the third day and head back to work, pale but ready to forget the past and eager to start all over, only to fall again, the following week.

Raphael regularly sought to protect himself from the malicious intent he saw in other people's choice of words, looks, and moods. He felt alienated because of other people's looks of indifference that froze him and isolated him; he felt neglected by the silence of many. At this point, I will leave him tell you his story.

Part 1

Chapter 1

Before my September-2008, retreat in Magog – 1
*Reflections between today's office snipers and
Yesterday's childhood bullies*

In September 2004, I applied for the position of Director of Sales at the North Side Hotel in Montreal after having spent eight years between Montreal and Ottawa running a home business and an earlier four years working for Le Soleil Hotel between 1994 and 1997, in another suburb of Montreal. My experience at Le Soleil Hotel was less than rewarding and, by all means, detrimental to my health because of office violence, ambiguity and corporate politics.

Today, in September 2008, four years after I signed my offer at the North Side Hotel, I realize that I have been just as hurt and turned into casualty of corporate bullying, at this last hotel, as I was, earlier at Le Soleil. I am drained and drenched. I need a break and some space to reclaim my broken esteem.

I went to visit Bernie *(Bernard)* my friend and client at the first hotel, for tea. Bernie and his Wife, Milena where people from the old school; gentle and caring. They were high profile people in the Aerospace industry. Both are immigrants like me: Bernie, fifty-five in 2008, five-feet eight inches high, slightly stout, white complexion and bald while Milena, an elegant woman, is five years younger, with a European look and a conservative well-styled brown hair.

At tea, I told them that my four years' experience, at this last hotel 'North Side' was no different from the Le Soleil's; just as hard to cope with and unfulfilling for one's career aspirations and, even, identity.

"As you know, I have a wealth of over 360 cards that I filled across the years, simply by listening to my mother as she recounted her description of Egypt's rich social cohesion prior to and during the post-war era (WW2) in Egypt, followed by Egypt's subsequent disintegration, in view of rising shades of *Social Dissonance*. Such *dissonance* hovered as a continuing consequence of the persisting Cold War. I witnessed it, and it shaped me. I want to write something and include office practices in my story."

"Are you feeling alright?" said Milena.

"No, actually very tired, almost broken, again. Nothing has changed and although I kept my word not to lose my soul, my health was seriously damaged. I am furious and determined to find the underlying cause that led me to it. [I said] I will take a few days in Magog to think, peacefully and to hit two birds with one stone. First, I want to rest, and then, I want to identify the source of the psychological tactics I keep experiencing now in 2008, just as I did at Le Soleil between 1994 and 1997, especially after I had succeeded in reversing all crumbling business trends to tangible profits. I continue to feel turned into casualty of intense guilt and public scoffing. Now, all this painful bloating, vomiting, panic, sweat, chills, tears, and excruciating backaches, is proof that something is wrong. I need to return to nature and be ready for Divine intervention to cleanse my soul, for some genuine love and Divine guidance. I believe that Magog (a Canadian eastern township), during this September foliage season, surrounded by its Abbey of Saint Benoit (Saint Benedict) on the Lake, will help me reclaim my soul and regain some energy. I need it so much!"

"Then, go and rest Raphy. It will do you good. Milena and I went to Magog several times. You will love its nature."

"I will Bernie. You know; workload does not bother me; it is not the resistance that I encounter that bothers me; it is when resistance turns into intolerance and when peer pressure turns into bullying and abuse. I experienced many of these sentiments as a child, as you know, and am used to it."

"So what triggered it, this time?" asked Bernie.

"You know, just let me give you some examples of what I go through, at this hotel. I started working for *North Side Hotel*, with no hand-over from anyone; no introduction to the sales department, to any files, customer base, records, documents, spreadsheets, or even a twenty-second statement from my general manager defining my objectives or giving me a chance to look at the business plan's requirements so that I could set my own action plan, accordingly. There were no records of previous trends—nothing, nothing at all; simply four hundred dusty paper files hanging on four grey dusty drawers. In no time, I had to define my target clients, update the customer base that lay hanging on these drawers for so many years and transfer them to a brand new Database program, mostly by myself within three months of extra hard work, amidst harsh resistance from existing young staff and management indifference. Nevertheless, we did it, all together, and I was fortunate to have influenced all figures, reversing all trends and exceeding any achievements that this hotel had ever had, in less than nine months, if at all by refining the market mix and raising the yield per market segment and bedroom per night.

Words and slurs by young and lazy team-members would haunt me for four years and management distance would leave me all by myself in the battlefield. It is not right, and these corporate tactics and such management incompetence, should end. They defeat all declared values by labor, civil, and human standards. One feels so lonely when this happens."

A few of my peers scoffed at my social status as a single male, making extremely hurtful and suggestive comments. Some even labeled me because I cared for my elderly mother and sometimes for my interest in buying tickets for theatre and music shows in downtown Montreal [...Going to have lunch with *Mamina*, Raphy?] one of them would mumble, mockingly.

Bernie, do you know what keeps me alive in the middle of all this harshness—all the violence, the absurdity of intolerance, this teaming-up, this exile? It is when I can escape all of this and reemerge with a beautiful tune, a song, a short poem, or even a home-baked loaf of bread, standing in my shorts and T-shirt, and humming the tune I hear on the radio with love, until I find the love of my life! This is when I reclaim life, as it should be; it is when I celebrate it and refuse to let my spirit crumble. It is keeping me sane, so far."

"So go, and have some fun"

Previously, between 1994 and 1997
(Eight years after I arrived as immigrant)

One day in 1995, at *Hotel Le Soleil* in Montreal, I had only started to work a few months before preparing to set down the business objectives of this hotel. Being who I was then, a thin 44 years old person, a little flamboyant with my appearance, well dressed, well shaved and mannered, I had to start my research for trends in the hotel's dusty files to set some business objectives for the market plan for 1995. This started in September of 1994 and I had to set some new creative and effective tactics to reverse the crumbling trends of the hotel that had been looming in the 'Red' for over three years. However, to reverse sliding trends is far more difficult than to push an already existing rising trend in order to acquire incremental growth.

I had already started feeling the negative and slack work environment, from day one. Suddenly, one of those days, I clearly felt I was a target of slimy looks and gazes by a few who did not want to accept change or to join the plan- mostly the four members my manager asked to me to lead. My office was huge (450 square feet, *40 square meters*). One day, during one of our weekly meetings, there was a dark discussion. Incidentally, I had ordered a tray of muffins and tea, from the kitchen for our meeting.

"Folks, let us set the plan together; we need to meet."

"And why don't you do it by yourself; that's not in our job description. They told us that they will get us someone to go on the road."

"Look…" I said, "I will go when I know what I am going after. You have been here for many years and have vital knowledge of this hotel, its competition, strengths and weaknesses. I am new and am able to overlook the portrait as a superficial gazer who just wants to drive the business plan; and I have vast airline and hotel experience from overseas. By the way, I will go on the road; and so will many of us. That is my job. Let's pick a day were the five of us can meet for three hours."

"Why don't you just use the plan we have always had and go on the road instead of bossing us all?" Said a 30-year-old married, young and brown-haired person from my own homeland of Egypt. She was five feet six tall, well dressed and her hair was always elegantly styled. We do not need muffins; we need you to produce, produce, produce! She was addressing me defiantly, sitting back on her chair and almost capturing the reaction of her peers with the corner of her right eye. She paused and so did I.

"Why do I feel you take me as an outsider, Amy? Are we going to work together? Then give me one reason why the tactics of the last four years have not yielded much? Why are we soaking in misery? Why do we not add just a few new community-based programs to gain the sympathy of the four hundred corporations surrounding us? There must be something our competing hotels do?"

"Why don't you ask them?" said one 45 years old married guy; a bit of a flirt, well built, tall, good-looking, of brown curly hair and certainly arrogant. He turned his face to the girl who questioned me earlier and smiled, in a scoffing manner as if he meant to support her. I sensed the direction of the meeting and chose neither to crumble nor to shout. I held myself and said, sternly:

"Why didn't *you* ask them for the past four years, Sami?"

"Oh yes? *Said Amy* …and now you pick at him although you are here to lead. And how can you lead if you talk like this?" I wanted to answer: *You started* but I would have seemed defensive.

"Sami, let us do just that; you and I. We will split the eight neighboring hotels into two. You take four and I will take four. Let us walk through their lobby this week, pick some vibes and discuss them in the next meeting!"

"What is it you don't like about Sami, *said Amy, defiantly, and she paused… and then she threw a verbal bullet, a hateful one*…is it because he has the looks of a real male?" She stared at me, waiting to watch my reaction. (Previously, I was bullied, as a schoolchild, with similar innuendos). To be honest, my pulse rate rose, I sweat and heard a persistent pounding mechanical whistle in my ears, one I had always heard every time I was driven into such dark confrontations, just as the sound we hear in Emergency Rooms, with machines connected to our dear ones. I needed a booster and my lips turned dry and wide. I thought I saw mother urging me to strike back, as she always did, when I was a child, forty years, earlier.

Suddenly, I recalled an incident, at school in the fifties that made me, for the first time in my short life as a child, perceptive of people's harsh innuendos, dark state of mind and cold tone of speech. It was not different from what happens in a typical workplace, these days, by corporate snipers or petty peers; or was it just me? This is a brief description of that incident; this darkest moment of my life, which marked me and shaped me until this day. That morning, I entered school sensing negative vibes. I reached my class for the first lesson, one of my teachers (a robust, tall and dark *structure*) took a shot at me, as I was reading extracts from a beautiful medieval Arabic soliloquy. The soliloquy was charged with reflections and I was touched by its emotions as I read my part. And this cost me a lot of hurt. I was alienated; he bullied me in class in front of all my colleagues when he threw a vicious remark at me. He said in Arabic *"Yalla Ya Helwa,"* meaning, *"Come on, lollypop."* …and to say, that I read it properly according to a few of my classmates who, even, called it beautiful. To top it, the manner in which he said it, made me feel coveted and embarrassed about my non-mainstream Egyptian complexion. Suddenly, my pulse rate rose, I sweat and heard a persistent pounding mechanical whistle in my ears; as the one we would hear in Emergency Rooms. This was a hurtful pattern of labeling that I had been exposed to, repeatedly. It went back so many years I was horrified, and this teacher succeeded in breaking my heart. He managed to alienate me from my classmates to whom I wanted so much to belong. I had my reasons and they went back to 1957 and, later, as noted, just a few pages, further ahead. After this, I was frozen and could not dare to turn my face to see if any of my colleagues was laughing. However, thankfully, I did not hear it. Instead, a few went to the headmaster to report the teacher, taking my defense. Emile, Ahmed, Roland and Stephan were the ones who did so. That day, I went home, and I felt so guilty and different. I locked myself in the bathroom to sob and did not tell anyone of my grief. I looked at myself in the mirror and cursed my looks. I would pray for hours asking for peace and rest at heart. That day, I returned from school and told mother all about it. As usual, she threw my head in her lap and urged me to strike back, in future similar situations. Overall, I was convinced there was something wrong with me, and I started to hate my stupid looks. Alas, it hit me at my last two places of work in Montreal *Hotel Le Soleil* and the current *North Side Hotel* that I had to change and not to expect others to do so.

    Then I turned it back at Amy and said in a stern, hollow and controlled voice: "There is no point in continuing our meeting with such distrust on all sides. I am disappointed at our tone of aggressiveness, Amy, and insist that we must find a way to refine our relationships" They all stared at me as I stood proud and I added "Who will come with me for our first tactic; the Competition Research? I need someone."

    A Czech young man said, "I will". I was hoping he did. And we planned our competition-canvassing tactic for the following day. Amy had been working for fifteen years in this hotel and had demonstrated a hostile attitude with me since I started. I think she felt intimidated by me although I had repeatedly had coffee with her at the hotel and spoken of the future. I learnt later, that her father was a close business friend of my elder cousin who had immigrated to Montreal, before 1987.

I went back home after work, that day in 1995, rested a little and visited my mother who, at seventy-nine, was still working as an evening administrator at a neighboring music school. I waited for her to finish her shift and drove her back to my sister's home. On our way, we stopped for a glass of wine and cheese at a famous city-bistro. I told her what happened earlier with a teary eye.

"Did you cry?"

"No"

"Shout?"

"No; I controlled my emotions and deflected the argument but I heard that sound again"

"Which?"

"The pounding hospital machine beeps"

"Your eyes are wet"

"Only because you are next to me, ma; I am at ease doing so. Do you remember? I promised you when I used to return from school to keep my tears dry, until I saw you" Her eyes turned red, she smiled lovingly and clutched my hand in the bistro. Then I drove her to her home, hugged her and moved out to return to my apartment.

"Stay for dinner", she said

"No mom; my sister must be tired and you too; even I; I have some stomach cramps. I love you mom"

"And so do I, my beloved son; drink some chamomile tea with honey."

Despite my success stories with this hotel, my public speeches, my travels and my being a well-respected and looked upon hotelier in Montreal, I felt I was starting a career chapter, in Canada, I did not feel comfortable with. Something did not smell right. I felt I was scrutinized on every move and question with no team participation; simply scrutiny and criticism from members of an old workplace culture or even from my own circle of relations. However, resistance is typical in the work field and inquisitiveness is a detriment in our own social circles. In addition, if one shared her thoughts with a few, they would label her as *sensitive* or *paranoiac*. What arrogance; what little care!

My superior, the General Manager who was French from Quebec told me once:

"Don't change things; I have been at this hotel for five years."

"Monsieur Legault, before each move I make I tell you, don't I? Let me know what you want from me, and I will do it. Besides, only yesterday you questioned why I was not more firm with my staff. Market penetration tactics need to change, sir! What do you want me to do, and I will comply?"

"Don't lecture me. You know, you are too soft spoken and your mannerism does not fit the team" I felt he slashed me and I held my breath, again, so as not to burst out. Then, he said:

"Are you happy with us?" …and I gazed, disappointed but not surprised at such style of corporate snipers! That sound came back haunting me, again.

After four years at Le Soleil, I broke and started a home business for a while until I could start again. I resorted to building a portfolio of 5-7 one-hundred room hotels and provided them with market advice while earning a monthly retainer without being on their payroll or part of their full-time working hours. I picked my hotels in the two provinces of Quebec and neighboring Ontario, between the cities of Montreal, Three Rivers, Ottawa, Kingston, Belleville, Toronto, Mississauga and Hamilton. I would only deal with the hotel manager and keep replacing my portfolio hotels, each time we reached the objectives. I generated some modest income but could no longer sustain the long drives and soon my rising cramps and violent abdominal pains blew-up out of all proportions. I took a few months break and started over with this North Side Hotel as Sales and Marketing director, in October 2004.

It is important to mention that my Manager at the earlier hotel, Le Soleil, Monsieur Legault was the business partner of a

Canadian Egyptian from the same age group of fifty-five, of the same height (five feet-seven, *1.68 meters, approximately*) which is relatively short. Both of them were so cold, solid, even wicked and had controlling eyes. Monsieur Legault had short dark curly hair with very little white; his partner, Mr. Zinky, (who liked to call himself Doctor Zinky) was bold but wore a wig with brown hair and artificial streaks of grey hair, indicating 'structured candor and character'. He had no significant educational degree. In fact, he was already fired, twice, from Montreal Hotels, as Hotel Manager (his only two short assignments as Hotel Manager), because of his aggressive and invasive ways with staff and union. Apparently, one day he refused to meet the union leader who wanted to approach his hotel staff (Mr. Zinky's). By law, he had to; instead, he ran after him in the lobby with a rifle. Mr. Zinky lost his job and the union assumed the staff. They (Monsieur Legault and Mr. Zinky) had a side business, which they called *International Neuro Linguistic Programming Institute in Canada*; a bit of a hoax; I always thought. This is, of course, a well-known and researched academic subject, by various, scholars since WW1. As for this venture, it has its own niche. He picked his business audience from a select group of medium sized hotel Managers, and his target audience, from citywide hotel employees "whom he meant *to develop*". Their declared objective was team building but their inhibited tactics were many times manipulative; the rest theatrical. So says the title of their business, until it crashed ten years later, following which Mr. Zinky returned to Cairo, Egypt where he started a similar business from his home's basement.

    In fact, I remember that one day in August of 1994, just after my Job interview, Monsieur Legault introduced me to Mr. Zinky who arranged for a meeting with him at his office (home basement, in Montreal). He was sitting by his desk on an elevated chair and he invited me to sit (sinking) in front of him on a deep, soft and comfortable leather armchair. I felt, that day, he was draining my energy as he peeped in my eyes from up to down, condescendingly.

A few months, later, after I had taken the job, I went to his place. Again, Mr. Zinky opened the door, looked me in the eyes, almost penetrating my mind and led me to his basement. His looks were scary and invasive. He did not offer me anything to drink and sat on his solid high wooden chair while asking me to sink on this cozy, low leather love seat, barely the height of his stomach.

"Come with me I will train you to be a certified Nero Linguistic Programmer"

"For what purpose" I asked

"So that you can program your staff, shape them and lead them; this way you can control your operation"

"I don't understand, Mr. Zinky"

"Doctor; Doctor Zinky"

I paused

"First you gather information on your staff, even personal information, and then if they resist you there is a way of using this information, intelligently, to drive your department." He paused and reiterated, pompously and loudly, in a broken English accent "Information is power!"

"You mean a means to empower them?"

"No, just force them to reach your objectives. You apply pressure."

Something seemed wrong… "You mean persuade them through quelling, crushing and compulsion? How can I reach my objectives if I claim I can see everything through my eyes and hear everything through my ears? This will limit my chances to what only I can perceive; it will decrease productivity instead of multiplying it, instead of using available eyes, ears and brains."

"This is leadership and team building!" he said.

"How can you build courage and character when you take away initiative and independence?" *Abraham Lincoln had made this famous quote in 1863.*

"Leadership; leadership"

"You mean compulsion and coercion!" I swiftly hit back.

"I can break you and rebuild you" he replied.

Suddenly, I heard those sounds and started sweating. "No thanks, I said. I am an hotelier and I manage by objectives, the old-fashioned way. I trust people," I said respectfully.

I bowed my head and left. Mr. Zinky used an expensive wig since he had no hair. Most of his published subject matter or presentations, I believe, were copied (with no academic thesis) from earlier prominent researchers. To me, they were true academic builders of self-esteem, helpers of fractured families and builders of work-teams. I mean, authors like Seymour, O'Conner, Bandler, Grinder and others. After I left the room with Mr. Zinky behind me, I felt uncomfortable and was gasping for air; I had lost enormous energy. I took my car and drove back home.

The following week while I was passing by mother before going home (where she stayed with my sister and her husband), I was asked to stay for a bite with a few relatives. I did and after supper, the doorbell rang and Mr. Zinky came in. He knew my family (not my mother).

"What the hell does this man want?" I thought to myself. "My only problem with his approach, let alone his invasive looks, is the following. He wants to crush all the progress and character that I have built throughout my life, one layer over the other, year after year, to have me start all over; to start within a concocted cage that he has planned for me (he and whoever is with him). Unfortunately for him (them), I swore not to allow a few psychopaths or hunters rebuild me to fit their narcissistic sculpture and to derail me from pursuing my own dreams. Unfortunately, for me, as you will see, my resistance worked but at a high cost".

Tea and cakes were served and while everyone was interacting, he told me "I want you to come back to my office we have a lot to discuss"

"...for what Mr. Zinky?" I replied.

"Doctor please; [he shouted at me], I said Doctor Zinky" and he looked me in the eye. I nodded, respectfully and turned my head to mother exploring hers. She in turn, turned her head left and right, indicating that she had nothing to do with him.

"Listen to him (said a relative of mine); listen well, he helped his wife and other people, before."

"What help; I don't understand; what is asked of me"

"You are weak and you speak in a non-traditional male tone; you are soft and a little lost, sometimes. I can help you be a better person (while still, piercing my eyes with his invasive looks)." (I did not know then that he was no doctor; simply a psychopath. Anyway, I did not want to nurture his ego.)

"I am very well, thank you. I do not want help and I don't appreciate your condescending tone in my mother's home." I said firmly.

"All I want is to help you be a better person. You must ask yourself what more can I do every single day, to be a better person. What more can I do than the day before. I can help you improve yourself. We just have to go back, together and start from the very distant past"

My energy was slipping away, and then "What is this? Is this a game? Do you want to use me as a model *gene pig* for your career development business, to boast about me?"

"Hey stop this, a little respect to Dr. Zinky" said a relative of mine who was present, to me"

"It is not your call, Sami," I said.

"You are scared!" intervened, Mr. Zinky.

"Just go for one hour in his office, (said another relative) he helped many people. He will fix you!"

The Emergency Room sounds started hitting me violently, my lips got wider and dry, I sweat and shouted to my relative: "It is not your call; Really!" I turned my head to Zinky and said:

"I hear you are a man of God… So why do you do this? I am not comfortable with your innuendos and will not come" Then, he swiftly turned his eyes to his cell phone and pretended he missed a call from his daughter, and left in fury.

After that, there was a lot of sulking in my family's home- except for mother. She told them all "Leave him alone. You never told me that you will engage in such conversations with Raphy."

She left to the kitchen and I followed her for a few minutes, said "thank you mommy", hugged her and left home, slamming the gate-door, without saying good night to my family. I was short of breath.

Immediately after, I went to a giant bookstore and bought myself some self-help books to protect myself from psychopaths. Among these was *Introducing Neuro Linguistic Programming* by Joseph O'Connor and John Seymour, *Seven Habits of Highly Effective People* by Stephen R. Covey and *The Power of Your Subconscious* by Joseph Murphy. My research helped me rigorously; thanks to them.

During and following WW1 and WW2 military heads viciously used these tactics with their prisoners of war. Many corporations applied them, thereafter.

For four years working for this hotel, until 1997, the hostile language never ended- even if a few faked fellowship during staff parties. By Mid-1995, a career consultant and 'System Analyst' joined the management team. The owner from Connecticut hired him. There was rising conflict between the owner and Monsieur Legault, the manager. Eventually, the System Analyst replaced the French manager from Quebec (Monsieur Legault) who was the partner of this Egyptian Canadian Team-Builder. The atmosphere was still dark and the pettiness did not end until, finally, I left towards the beginning of 1997. They stretched me to work seventy hours a week and, this burnt me. I was so weak and heartbroken with the staff and peers games. I understood, later, that Mr. Zinky was manager at this hotel during the eighties and that he had established close relations with the current staff. It is funny when one ponders in these situations; we contemplate ourselves and start asking questions as to why all this has to happen! …and I asked myself, repeatedly, these questions. Then I realized that I had forgotten why I ever immigrated to Canada ten years earlier. Many of the staff members had arrived to Canada from Egypt, much earlier, as immigrants. Were they, too, trained to become Neuro Linguistic Programmers or, if I may, Psychopaths?

In January of 1997, I had had enough and I received a call from a general manager of another hotel in Montreal claiming that he heard good things about me and that he wanted to add me to his team. Frankly, I was not sure if this was a set-up by my current general manager at Le Soleil to get rid of me, or not. So I resigned from *Le Soleil* and accepted the new offer, only for two months until I decided to, finally, start my business and then, I fled to Ottawa, in May 1997, which is less than two hours drive from where my mother stayed with my family (in Montreal).

Just before moving to Ottawa; to be specific, in April 1997, three months after I had resigned from Le Soleil, Monsieur Legault returned as its manager. He called me on my cellular phone whose number one of my relatives gave him; he called to invite me to attend a seminar presented by his friend, Mr. Zinky the former manager of this hotel and self-declared Career Consultant in a downtown banquet hall. Unfortunately, I did. After his presentation, he called on two or three persons on stage to display how they had *conquered some of their fears and phobias*.

Then, in front of an audience of over eighty corporate heads and Montreal hotel veterans, who were his guests and target audience, and out of absolutely nowhere, he called me out on stage, by my name ... just like that, in public, and with no pre-advice! I dragged myself, (as if I was holding a ton of stones over my shoulders), with my gray hair, tired complexion, double jaw and overweight, towards him. I pushed myself upstage only to be slammed by this man's words.

He told his audience, in a pompous, arrogant and condescending manner, referring to me: "Ladies and gentlemen, here is Raphael. Here is the man I talked to you about for so long; he has overcome his fears and is now free to lead a small team! Let us applaud him, come on." He was gaining market share with this audience at my expense and he had to have been involved with the mind games that happened to me at Le Soleil. I did not know the extent of what he told them about me, previously, and was discouraged. I was frozen, numb, and heartbroken. I looked at him, bent my head down in utter defeat, started sweating, and had some chills. Instantly, I heard those haunting mechanical sounds of that typical hospital emergency room. Then I pushed myself with extreme difficulty toward the end of the platform and walked down its stairs, feeling so little and cheap, while the audience was clapping for me, flamboyantly. Then, I caught the eyes of a few members of this audience, refusing to smile and looking at me with respect, almost disapproving of this cheap and cruel make-belief scene. As for him, I knew that he had achieved his objective of acquiring market share at my expense. He seemed heartless and narcissistic. By next morning, my stomach cramps had started.

    This incident reminded me, once more, of my classroom experience in the fifties, when my teacher called me Lollypop, publicly. It was no less horrifying! Moreover, these few spectators, who refused to clap, looking at me supportively, reminded me of Emile, Ahmed, Roland and Stephan who held my back at the headmaster's office. Looking back to my school years, at the age of 12, I resorted to music and started piano, harmony, and theory lessons while continuing to train with my friends from the AMC's (Anglican Mission in Cairo) soccer team. This time, I was alone. Soon, I left for Ottawa to start my business.

    The highlights of my four years stay in Ottawa were securing a studio apartment on the upper floor of a *posh* commercial shopping strip, overlooking bistros and cafés. On the same floor, there were two other studios, similar to mine. They were occupied, one by a retired government clerk and amateur poet (James), and another by a professional wood carver (Guy). We shared a common hall of 180 square feet (16 square meters), a small one that had two chairs and a table, where we would come across each other, as we walked in or stepped out.

Another highlight was my having joined the senior choir of a Presbyterian church in the famous Glebe area, footsteps from where I lived. I was so well treated, welcomed and appreciated with this community and, eventually, joined their Mission and Service Committee. We delivered three major productions: Brahms Requiem, the Choral Prelude of J. S. Bach's Passion Music according to Saint John and the Choral Finale by Bach's Passion Music according to Saint Matthew. I participated with endless projects, bazaars and outdoor activities. It was *Heaven, I realized I was accomplishing what I had immigrated for,* and living a life, I have always lived, as a child, youth and, later, adult with my family and circle of friends at Saint Michael Church next to my childhood home. I would walk for hours by the Ottawa Riverside Panorama-Way, minutes from my studio church. I would take pictures of sunrise and sunset and return to my studio playing my electronic keyboard or composing music. It is all that my heart desired in life and, of course, to be next to mother, until I found the girl, meant to be. That is it, nothing more. It became another glorious highlight of my life in Ottawa.

While staying in Ottawa I would drive to Montreal to visit my mother three or four times a month for a couple of days but would always return to Ottawa as if it were my real home. Mom was strong and independent then; she was eighty-four. Of course, my abdominal attacks persisted, in Ottawa, just as well, but I always managed to stand up on my feet, with a hopeful and earnest heart.

Once or twice a week, I invited my two neighbors to listen to my music, I would prepare some snacks, cheese and crackers and they would bring some wine. They called me the Maestro, while one of them was a sixty-seven years old, thin, Scottish poet (James), with long white hair and the other was a French wood-carver (Guy), fifty years old, with brown hair. It was quite a Bohemian set-up and such a rewarding fellowship.

Soon, I started building my portfolio of hotels base, to consult them with marketing and budgeting issues. I generated some income by means of modest monthly retainers but had to supplement my income by means of a stable, if even modest, weekly check. I did this, until I was able to make it to the government as Communication Strategist, while pursing my music. I managed several times to get to the pre-final interview for government offers in Social Marketing, before signing the offer letter, but could not make it through because of a missing reference from Le Soleil Hotel. ... So was I told, clearly, by two of my potential government employers. Someone wanted me back at this hotel. I felt I had become its property.

Finally, I decided to persist but found a junior job at a neighboring Call-Center. The call center I worked for was only fifteen minute away from my studio. I worked only thirty hours a week, to pursue my other priorities. Occasionally, I had a late evening shift, and chose not to drive, if the snow was too deep to handle, on a late winter evening. So, I would take a bus out and connect with another until I reach work. On the way back, I would do the same.

Guy, a woodcarver, had brown hair; he was a little stout, my height and always pensive but funny and even loud. He was a true artist. James was a bit of a Scottish Canadian hippie, thin and five feet eight inches tall, slightly taller than I was. I was only forty-eight years old, then. James was always jovial, bending his head forward, slightly to the right, in reverence and would read-out poetry for hours and hours; even at 3 am. He seemed to me a perfectly content man whom life had wounded. A heavy beer drinker, he would spend most of his pensions by the third week of the month. If he drank too much, he would step out of his studio and sit on a chair in the common hall, reading from Lord Byron or Shakespeare, in a loud tone, as if he was on stage; a truly simple and good man. One day, I asked him, politely, to lower his voice, a little but regretted it, deeply, afterwards

Another day, he (James) saw me stepping off the public bus, returning from my shift at the call center, very late, at night.

I was experiencing an excruciating abdominal attack and my pain was unbearable. I was pushing myself up the stairs to my studio, with difficulty, dreaming of reaching my room. Soon, I noticed that I had forgotten my keys in my studio, that morning and had slammed the door, rhetorically, on the way out. That night, there was no way I could survive with such pain away from my hot shower and painkillers. Interestingly, the most beautiful thing, ever, happened. I saw James pacing in the common hallway.

"James, I am in pain. I have forgotten my keys in my studio and am about to have a heart attack from the pains. May I sit in your living room for a while?"

"Don't even worry about it. Come in" he said.

He led me to his room, filled a bucket with hot water, put salt in the water, undid my bootlaces, removed my socks, rolled my trousers up, and soaked my two legs in the bucket, with his small hands. Then he made me a bowl of soup and gave me some painkillers to abort the pain. In a few seconds, he jumped into my room's window, standing on the top of the roof of the antique shop, below. The temperature was minus thirty degrees and the shop's roof, below, was slippery with pallets of ice hidden under the snow. He managed at last to hold my studio window from outside and forced it open by means of a ripping-bar and sledgehammer. After this, he opened my door from within my studio. I was humbled and reassured. *Little things that I can never forget, throughout my life*, I said to myself! I could not forgive myself for having complained about him reading poetry at 3:00 a.m.! I miss him now, in the midst of my misery, at this heartless hotel. Yes, all through our life, we never forget such incidents that bring forth such good people! They restore our faith in humankind; they become our heroes and our lifelines, even at distance and for many years later!

As for my peers at the Ottawa call center, they were normal people, a little competition but no rivalry, perhaps because our leaders had character. Yea… it was such a pleasure to work with them and to flourish within this environment. They were mostly thirty years younger than I was, and they included me in each social gathering they made. I loved it.

When I lost hope in working with the government, despite the harsh research and hard work that led me to several federal ministers' offices, I knew that the battle with references was not one I could win. Eventually, I decided to return to Montreal to be next to mother and I found this job at the North Side Hotel in October of 2004, which I am sure, had to do with the previous hotel. I had no choice, because mother was getting older. In addition, it drained me, struggling to take grip of my life, and failing to so, for other people's sake, whims and caprices. This was my story, all through my life. It is funny, I always felt like the underdog, and I know I was turned to one by all those who wanted to manipulate me. Who was it? I asked myself and swore to reach some light. Was it those psychopaths and career consultants or could it have been my relatives who pushed me to them, to keep me in Montreal? After all, mom was strong until very recently, and my sister and grandchildren surrounded her. I am still there until this day in September 2008, at the North side Hotel, in Montreal. I miss the choir and church congregation, which I attended for close to four years. I miss them really, too much. They were the best part of my life; the one I always searched for, since my childhood, within a safe church environment, joining its activities and flourishing with its objectives. Of course, it was not my mother, who pulled me, because she told me, before and later. In a sense, I was happy to be back in Montreal, next to her, because I realized that I would regret for good, losing the opportunity to be by her side in her senior years. One thing I know, I lost fifteen years of my life (between 1994 and 2008), struggling desperately to reach my own modest aspirations, my music, theatre, choir, church, nature and good neighbors. I was not keen on bars, outings, suppers. I was just cool and thankful, for the little things, you will see, in my testimony! I wanted to dream, at ease.

These were *flashbacks* of my last fifteen years starting with *Le Soleil Hotel* in 1994 all the way until my current assignment at

North Side Hotel, in September 2008. My retreat in Magog this month would reshape the remaining cycle of my life. It would put me back on track. I promise you.

Picture of the Abbey of
Saint Benoit du Lac, Magog, Québec, Canada
September 2008

Chapter 2
Before my September-2008, retreat in Magog - 2
Mother, my rock, fifty-five years earlier 1

Somehow, the last week I spent in Montreal prior to my September 3 (2008) trip to Magog, made me ponder of these things. I had been seriously pensive and coping with childish resistance, undue rivalry, and dark bullying at my workplace—one that reached a point where I felt I was almost forced to leave my job or, as many casualties of intolerance in this biography, would name it, flee the scene just as many had fled their homeland for ambiguity and marginalization!

I grabbed my paper notebook, where I had scribbled snapshots of this biography, placed it in my briefcase and decided to pick up the rest, forward, in my Magog retreat.

First, here are some lifetime scenes of infinite passions and roots that are absolutely rich and informative before continuing in Magog, Some call it character building; I choose to call it 'Things of life'. I started writing them throughout last year to use them as a solid foundation for what follows. They are mostly based on diary cards that I had filled across my growing years- and there were over three hundreds of them.

Throughout my childhood, I was typically frail. At six, I was thin and blond with honey-green eyes and golden curly hair. My family would tell me that I always had a curious set of eyes. They said, my deep eyes would look toward the clouds in endless pursuit for answers to questions that my family never knew.

In fact, I recall my sitting next to my mother on a Cairo (Egypt) public bus gazing through the window toward the sky; this was in 1956 or 1957, when I was around five. Mother shook my shoulder gently, saying in French, *"Mon enfant, qu'est ce que tu regardes?"* meaning, "My son, what are you looking at?" I replied, "I don't know!" The passenger sitting opposite to us, an elderly well-dressed gentleman, gracefully told mother, in French as well, *"Madame, laissez-le méditer dans la vie; ne prenez pas son espace,"* meaning "Madam, leave him to contemplate life; do not take his space away!"

The following year, in July 1957, my parents took us for our typical six-week summer vacation to Alexandria just two hours by car from Cairo. They booked a holiday apartment in *Mandara* Beach by the Mediterranean, which was then one of Alexandria's prominent and famous beaches. This vacation was so refreshing, as always. My cousins, aunts and uncles surrounded us under two or three umbrellas, almost daily, by the beach. However, to me, it also carries with it dark vibes that make me pensive and more apprehensive of people's perceptions of our looks, thoughts and actions.

In fact, I remember that Mandara Beach in Alexandria had those two-floored cabins with an overtone of white and blue, stretching over one kilometer overlooking the sea, by Alexandria's extreme east beach. This was not far from the port of Abu-Kier, where the battle between Napoleon Bonaparte's fleet and the British fleet under Sir Ralph Abercrombie took place in 1803. Abu-Kier was used by Alexander the Great as docking zone some 330 years before Christ and is known for his (Alexander's) unexcavated underworld of *Heracleion*. Many families or youth would rent one of those Mandara Beach cabins during summer instead of renting an umbrella or even a holiday apartment.

I was wandering alone that day, at seven, walking on the beach toward the two-floored cabins. Then I met three ... three nice people—men, thirty years of age. They asked me if I wanted to have a tour of the upper set of cabins. I said yes. We walked up the staircase to the second floor where there were many cabins, one after the other, overlooking the beach. They even invited me to their cabin, and I remember it had a small kitchenette, fridge, kettle, one double bed, two love seats, a TV, table, and chairs. They closed the door and offered me juice. They kept touching my arms and insisting I should sit. I kept pushing my way out until, finally, after twenty horrible minutes; they opened the door and helped me walk down the stairs. They were very ... very kind. This 1957 vacation was one of my life's pivotal experiences that would make me cautious of how people visualized me; but I was seven and innocent of some people's vulgar intent, till this day.

Another of my life's pivotal experiences was on Mother's Day celebration at school, in 1960. My sister and I were prepared to give our mother her gifts, together with other kids. She had bought them and given them to us, earlier, to present them to her during the celebration. The celebration was at the AMC's (Anglican Mission in Cairo) Rose Garden. Mom was my idol and life's immaculate gift to me; she meant so much to me, especially after dad fell sick with cancer in 1959 and after my 1957 summer vacation in Mandara Beach, Alexandria. Ma was also my supportive rod each time I was bullied at school, by a few relatives and, even later, at workplace.

"*Look into my eyes;* [She would tell me tenderly and reassuringly] *I have immense faith in you my son. Some people are bad and others are good. With bad people raise your head and leave the scene if they are many and stronger than you are. Because that does not mean they are wiser. If you can strike back, go ahead; if not, leave the scene with grace my son. Their day will come. You will see.... In any case, you are master of yourself and you just have to think of yourself as the master of such a scene, despite all odds; I will send you positive vibes.*"

The time came to honor our mothers. A few students went first. Then came my sister Nora's turn to give her gift, and everyone applauded our mom just as they did the other moms. Then I ran, frail as I was, holding my box of gifts that was wrapped with a burgundy ribbon. The gift itself was a cream-colored rectangular box, about six inches wide and four long. It was about 1.5 inches thick. Inside the box was a set of three lavender soaps from Yardley of England, each wrapped in off-white, soft tissue paper and separated from the other by a thin, dark plastic bar, that mom had bought from *Boots* store in London the year before. As I rushed toward the mounted stage, I stumbled on the floor, fell and bruised my knees. My knees bled a little. The box flew open, and the soap bars and plastic separators fell out. I was horrified and panicked.

One of my teachers, Ms. Abboud, a stout fair-haired Palestinian woman, five feet and five inches tall and extremely kind, rushed to help me. She was about forty-five years old. She looked at me firmly and reassuringly, mostly lovingly. Then she patted my shoulder and encouraged me to move forward. "Go ahead my boy, you are OK; here [*and she gathered the soap and its wrappings and placed them back in the box*] …go my Raphy, slowly and hug your dear mom" …I continued, running, limping a bit and hoping not to miss the opportunity of giving Mom her gift. I did it "Happy Mother's Day mama" and she bowed down to hug me. I grabbed her waist and threw my head in her tummy. I was blessed with a feeling of fulfillment. Mom grabbed me and thanked me and I returned back to my seat with the crowd; and so did mom with the panel."

Ms. Abboud was my most beloved teacher at school. I loved her for how she was kind to me, how she let me talk in class, and how she encouraged me to read loudly or ask questions. She taught me between 1958 and 1963. She was a wonderful and loving single woman, originally from Palestine. She had moved to Egypt in 1948.

On another occasion, while still reflecting on my school at the Anglican Mission in Cairo during the fifties, I remember some glimpses of the remaining missionaries before they returned to England and before my school had shifted, completely, to Egypt's new mainstream, with inclination to the Eastern Block and to Egyptian Pan-Arabism. In the fifties (and before), under the missionaries the students were split into three groups—Jews, Christians, and Muslims—each in their own shelter so as to start the day with worship.

One day, in the late fifties, the headmaster asked me to lead the Christian group in the school's old chapel with the Lord's Prayer. In the middle of the prayer, I changed one or two of the original verses from, "… and forgive us our trespasses as we forgive those who trespassed against us," to "… forgive us our trespasses as you taught us to forgive others".

One of my teachers, a priest from England, stopped me and rebuked me in front of the whole assembly. "Don't change the Lord's words," said the teacher.

"I did not mean to; I just did not want to lie because I am not always capable of forgiving".

After this, the headmaster reprimanded me for having changed the words of the prayer and he put me on probation for two weeks. I also received a punishment for not forgiving others. "If you cannot forgive others, then you are not a good Christian," said the teacher.

"But I am trying. It is not that I do not want to; I am only asking for the help of God to do so. I did not want to pretend that I was able to forgive, all the time, I am sorry; I will not do this again."

The headmaster ordered me to stand in the school's main courtyard during the big break in front of all the students, teachers, and staff. He told me to wear a sign saying: *Detention*. In fact, he told me to stay silent and not to open my mouth for one full hour. My teacher, Ms. Abboud, defended me to the headmaster's office and returned to me, thirty minutes later, asking me to go with her to her office for the rest of the lunch break. I did so, and cried to her, while she helped me and gave me her lunch. "If I were God, I would trust you and not this teacher, because you spoke from your heart, my son."

"Ms. Abboud…"

"Yes, my son"

"You know that there a few kids who beat me, call me rude names and push me, repeatedly?"

"Of course I know; I know everything. This was a tough year for you, my boy"

"I want them to stop, can you help me? You know I have become wisely selective with my choice of schoolmates. Most of the main stream, not all of them, could be mean and would label me, touch me or bully me after your English class, if

I read poetry or, at music class, if I sang... The Arabic poetry teacher does not want to spare me with similar comments in class. He called me *lollipop*."

"First of all, I know of this teacher and he will leave at us at the end of this term. In addition, my boy, it is because you read well; from the heart and you sing so well! I told your mother, repeatedly, how good you are (she really did). Now, if they are jealous it is because they cannot do like you; and then, they turn wicked. But I will handle this and keep an eye on them."

Soon she introduced me to a select group of senior colleagues who would stand by me if I were excluded from school assemblies, pushed during a picnic or simply patronized by the stronger or rude guys...

Some of my typical darker days at school was when I'd start the day by walking through the school gates, sign-in and walk with extreme caution through the frequently hurtful schoolmates who would rebuke me until I reached my favorite spot, next to the elder kids who really did not threaten me. By the time, I would reach my spot and sit on my favorite wooden bench my morning could be one of hell and fury. A few of my mean schoolmates could be standing on the side gazing at me and scrutinizing me, as I walked with my thin white legs and in my shorts. They would do so, incessantly, to the extent that I would walk sweating and drenched from this unwanted load of hurt until I sat down, on a deck, for my morning snack. One or two would shout at me '*Yasso Raphy*' (hey Raphy, in Greek-knowing that I had Greek roots) and then giggle stupidly. I would hear a strange sound in my ear; I would hear constant intermittent beeping. A couple would steel my snacks, every now and then or, even, throw them on the dirty playground. I still remember their names, until this day in 2008. I would walk away holding my head up as much as I could (just like mom told me), wondering if there was anything on my forehead that recounted my morbid Alexandria beach memories or whether I just looked so stupid and different.

'Hey, defend yourself pal. Come on, come on, push me... Push Me," they would shout.

"I would continue to walk away until they'd grab me, kick me and bully me or, until someone came to my rescue.

Usually, the prefects who were actually friends of the bullies would intervene only if they are passing by: "Hey cut this out; that's enough..." They would push the idiots away.

One day, three caring and very kind schoolmates rushed to me and pushed these bullies away. One rushed to the headmaster to make a decisive move. He did and the headmaster mentioned it in the following morning's parade: *'This morning, two of your schoolmates were put on probation and disciplined. They will report to school two successive weekends and will remain on detention until 5 pm on schooldays for two weeks."* The supportive schoolmates, who had reported the bullies to the headmaster, came to me after parade and invited me to have lunch with them, that day at the school cafeteria. Their names were Armen, an Armenian Egyptian, Roland, an Egyptian Jew and Ahmed a Muslim Egyptian. These were three of the select group of supportive friends, to whom Ms. Abboud had introduced me. They had formed a senior soccer team and wanted to add me as a center-back player, though three or four years older than me, around fourteen or fifteen. They told me this with a few other good people of the same age group, during lunch. They had spoken with a senior student {Mustafa) who was ready to coach me; the sports teacher (*Monsieur* Henry) would help Mustafa. I was so excited...." Mustafa told me:

"No one will hurt you from now on; you will be one of us and we will play soccer and have fun... OK?"

"Yes, yes... Thank you so much... I will be there"

They laid out the training hours and we started playing within ten days.

We played other teams at school and joined in citywide competitions called *The Triangular Sports,* in reference to three city school boards sports. This made me feel very important.

However, the first soccer game I played went well for the first half time. Five minutes after the second half, had started I was able to abort an attack on our goalie simply by creating panic in our penalty area. The audience was clapping for me, rigorously, and our goalie hugged my shoulders. I felt thrilled. Seconds later, I got kicked and pushed by the center forward of the opposite team and kicked again by another, who used to make my life miserable, earlier, that semester.

Roland and Mustafa rushed to help me but I could no longer continue the game. I was thrilled, though, with the priceless value of camaraderie, and raised my head, again not knowing that I was bleeding. Slowly, I felt part of something strong and nurturing, that I could cling to for a while. Soon my soccer team friends would become my lifetime friends, and their families, the friends of my family.

In 1963, I started the habit of writing ideas and little sketches of my childhood events, in the hope of documenting them one day under the title *'The absurdity of alienation'*. In 1997, I drafted the beginning of this testimony and even called it: "*I nailed the budget; who's playing with my mind!*" Today, in 2008, I am finally able to start my long hoped-for testimony. I will find the right title for it.

Chapter 3
Before my September-2008, retreat in Magog
Mother, my rock, fifty-five years earlier 2

It is early January of 2008. As I look back to the mid-1950s, I read my notes and write my thoughts.

During the first four years of WWII, my mother, Laurice, worked as Public Relations Officer for the RAF (Royal Air Force) Commission, which was based in Cairo, Egypt. She then moved to Force-133 in 1945, in Cairo, and then, again, she moved to Europe for one year to join the newly emerging United Nations. She joined the UNRRA (United Nations Relief and Rehabilitation Administration) in Tirana, Albania, as Administrative Officer.

It had become my passion to listen to mother's stories since preparatory school. Equally, I had developed the habit of recording her stories on small research cards, the type a student uses for a thesis, so as not to forget them. I did this with other incidents I encountered in life. As to my earliest card, I filled it in 1964 and I started giving all cards titles, shortly after. Of course, as I grew older, I filled cards with true stories that I, too, experienced during the fifties but that I had not documented then.

When mom worked during the war for the RAF in Cairo, Egypt, she worked close to prominent war gurus such as Sir Winston Churchill, Field Marshal Bernard Law Montgomery, Wing-Commander Gallagher, Air Marshal Arthur William Tedder, Master Violinist and RAF soldier, Yehudi Menuhin, and so many more. She engaged in conversations with all of them on various occasions. Throughout her assignment, many of the officers delegated to her, the management of onsite business meetings, the planning for outdoor group luncheons and dinners, or even securing reservations at the glorious old Cairo Opera for "the big ones," as she named them to me.

She also worked close to Squadron Leader Hugo Ringgold and Marshal Waverly. I know, because I would write the names, then, in the sixties and early seventies as she recounted her stories. Many of these military personnel were involved with art. For example, Squadron Leader Hugo Ringgold was apparently the Cairo Symphony Orchestra Director during WW2.

Throughout the war, soldiers of the RAF Commission in Cairo were allowed to have a break; they were permitted to roam the streets of Cairo and have some fun. Mother told me that a few soldiers would be late coming back to their dormitories every now and then. "A few were disciplined if they did so," she would say. Once, a British soldier described by Laurice (mom) as a *handsome young man* came late with his friends after spending a long evening in the streets of Cairo, probably *chasing the girls*. He was a violin virtuoso and his superiors asked him to play the violin, in concert, for the staff on the following evening as a punishment for his delay. He did, and mother listened to him in awe. The soldier turned-out to be the Master Violinist Yehudi Menuhin.

In 1946, mother accepted an offer to move from the RAF Force-133 in Cairo, Egypt, to the UN headquarters in Tirana, Albania, before her parents died in Egypt. I would listen to her endless war stories, sometimes too graphic and other times traumatic, on all sides of the war, let alone the seemingly ambiguous distribution of relief supplies. The United Nations Relief and Rehabilitation Administration (UNRRA) was established by agreement of forty-four nations in November 1943. Operations ended in the latter part of 1946, with the termination of the last staff appointment by March 31, 1946. The purpose of the UNRRA was to "plan, coordinate, administer, or arrange for the administration of measures for the relief of victims of war in any area under the control of any of the United Nations through the provision of food, fuel, clothing, shelter, and other basic necessities, medical and essential services." The UNRRA provided billions of US dollars of rehabilitation aid and helped about 8 million refugees.

Of course, it is very difficult for mother to remember now, in 2008, should I ask her for more details. Anyway, as long as she smiles to me every morning and evening, I am blessed. I do not want more, other than her good health and happiness. In addition, when I receive the first published copy of my book, I will show it to her, together with the dedication page, mentioning her name in bold. She is my best friend.

Because of the atrocities of that period, together with the dark atmosphere of post-war changes of power and the Cold War, the UN encouraged its staff, including mom, to move to the south of Italy for RR (Rest and Recreation) trips of a week or so, every now and then, before they returned to their UN camps in Albania. She was a beautiful and attractive young woman, half-Greek and half-Syrian, a graceful mix between Joan Crawford and Ingrid Bergman, the iconic actors, with a Mediterranean touch.

In October 2008, she will celebrate her ninety-second anniversary, and only two years ago, she celebrated her ninetieth anniversary in Montreal. My sister and I invited various nieces and nephews, children of mom's four sisters as well as their children. We invited them to my sister's big home where she (mother) lives with my sister's family, next-door to my apartment. Many flew from Washington DC, New York, San Francisco, Toronto, Ottawa, Paris, Haifa and Ramallah (The Holy Land), and Cairo (Egypt). The house was packed, and she was everyone's queen.

All through my life, especially after school, my cousins and their children recognized me as the *storyteller* of the family, whether at family gatherings, picnics, suppers, or tea parties. My family and friends knew that I kept records of events related to family members, close and distant, of grandparents and even great-grandparents. Over the years, I had developed records of family trees for each of my parents' sides. During that party (Mom's ninetieth birthday), mother became the center of attention. After all, she was and still is the last living girl of the five sisters who gave birth to multiple generations and who were actual descendants of the great Syrian martyr, Saint Joseph George Mouhanna Haddad Firzli of Damascus and Antioch (One of the Five Sees of Christianity: Alexandria, Antioch, Rome, Jerusalem and Constantinople). Saint Joseph was assassinated while preaching at the historical Al-Mariameih Church (Church of Maryam or Mary). I took the younger generation to the basement and told them all sorts of stories. During this reunion, there was so much love and such overwhelming passion in the air that no one wanted to leave before 1 a.m. Mother was shining with joy, and there was genuine affection to all and from all of the family.

After a good hour of storytelling recounting my airline experience in the seventies and early eighties, I left the young generation and went back upstairs to greet the guests, especially those who had arrived from out of town. They had drinks and took many pictures. A few guests helped cook some Egyptian, Lebanese, and Greek specialties, and life was flowing in the house through people's eyes, words, gestures, and hugs, all around our beloved mom (their mothers' last living sister) just as it was in Egypt's glorious days of the fifties, sixties and early seventies. We all made a toast for the departed. It included Mom's sisters, their husbands and parents of many of the guests. It was, truly a grounding experience.

Every morning, to this day, in January of 2008, I pass by her, just next door to my apartment, before driving down to the hotel or in the evening on the way back. I knock at her door, and then I open it with my key. For a few seconds, I have haunting ideas. Then I take a breath, mention God, knock again, open, and step inside my sister's house. I gently shout to mom: "Hi, Lora!"' (This is how I nickname her.) She replies, 'Hi, honey.' After that, everything settles down. Those few seconds of terror vanish, and I see her smiling to me, coming down the wooden stairs, or waving to me from her seat at the kitchen, shining at me with her love. We have our coffee and I rush to work. In July 2012, I published the first edition of this book and showed it to her. I showed her the cover page, dedication with her name shining as my mentor in life and invited her to my book signing, with her sitting as queen, next to me. This testimony is the same but it covers five more years of passion and progression.

    If it is in the evening, I pick her from the shopping mall next-door, drive her back home, fix us both two little drinks while watching TV and nibbling on some crackers and almonds. After this, I have supper with her, hug her, and return to my apartment, next door, after everybody has returned from work, pub or gym.

Chapter 4
Who Drove the Flowers Out of Their Roots?

It is still early January of 2008.
As I look back to the mid-1950s,
I read my notes and write my thoughts.

Back in 1946, when my mother, Laurice, returned to Cairo from her assignment with the UN in Albania, she stayed at her parents' home in Cairo for a while, just until they passed-away, within one year. In 1947, the husband of her third eldest sister, Denise, called both her and her sister Lydia (fourth in line, before mother) to invite them to move into their home in Ramallah (Holy Land), until both remaining sisters had married and were settled with their husbands. He was a remarkable family man, and by all means, my hero. Mother got married in 1949.

The 1948 war between the newly emerging state of Israel and its neighboring Arab countries ended with Israel's victory and with the dispersion and migration of millions of Palestinians who used to live there, for thousands of years. These dispersed refugees experienced endless suffering, which had its inevitable impact on Egypt and other neighboring countries.

At the same time, in Egypt and ever since my childhood (starting at the age of seven in 1958), I witnessed how the Egyptian revolution toppled King Farouk in 1952 and abolished a highly righteous and productive Royal Dynasty that lasted 150 years (though of Turkish origins).

This period followed other stories of unimaginable pain and sorrow covering WWII, the Holocaust, and the dispersion of 4.5 million Palestinian refugees. All these events shaped me as I witnessed them during my growth. Therefore, the sum of the tragedies of WWII, the dispersion of millions of Palestinians, the abolishing of Egyptian monarchy, and the introduction of a new (untrained) regime led to inevitable repercussions within the period of Egyptian social and political changes. It became an indispensable and inseparable backbone to my testimony. I will need to outline it, though, modestly, as this story of passions and roots, moves along.

In addition, the repercussions of the sudden abolishment of the Egyptian monarchy added a dark side to a life that I witnessed since my early childhood, at school and in the streets of Cairo. The Egyptian social mosaic was crumbling due to the inevitable effects of the *Future Shock* generated by the 1952 revolution, the new regime's subsequent shift to radical socialism and to the undermining of prominent Egyptian communities. They were communities of colorful roots, and they founded Egypt over the centuries: Pharaohs, Jews, Copts, Arabs, Greeks, Turks, Italians, Christians, Muslims, Armenians, Germans, Austrians, Swiss, Belgians, Albanians, French, English, Poles, and others (in historical order). Millions of them lived in Egypt and in other countries in the Middle East. In the mid-fifties, I could still taste the soul of the previous 150 years of social, cultural, and economic stability in Egypt; a cultural energy I fail to describe. I still remember it as I write this testimony, fifty years later. It was only in 1959 (at the age of eight) that I started sensing the effects of the 1952 coup and the rising socialist regime. In addition, the lengthy Cold-War environment following WW2 overshadowed the people of Egypt and the region, including me. It took more than ten years for the solid Egyptian structure to crumble, with no expertise or good will to rebuild it.

So, with the political changes in the Holy Land, together with President Nasser's dream to end the British rule of Egypt in 1954, the toppling of Egyptian monarchy, and the introduction of the new young group of Egyptian Revolutionary Officers (under President Mohamed Naguib and, later, Nasser), there were mixed emotions that drove the mainstream Egyptians to disbelief and confusion. The society was distraught. I witnessed these, as well. The sum of all these changes inevitably sparked a social conflict that derailed many, and led to intimidating those innocent Egyptian ethnic communities, who had built Egypt for centuries or, at least, to undermining them. The reason for this was that, to the mainstream Egyptian, thriving and honorable minorities in Egypt were inevitably associated with the (*bad*) West that had overlooked the dispersion of millions of hurting Palestinian refugees after the formation of the state of Israel, which was not true. These minorities, just like mainstream Egypt, were hurting for the Palestinian refugees and contributed to various social programs to ease their grief. Moreover, Egypt's need for funding to save thousands of Egyptian lives from floods in the Egyptian city of Aswan was a pressing priority for the people, at that time. Therefore, these 100 percent Egyptians of diverse cultural backgrounds turned to targets of intolerance by the new mainstream of Egypt that was receiving no assurances from the West (during the Cold War) to the extent of expulsion of the Jews. The new ruling party overlooked the protection of diverse Egyptian ethnic communities and left them alone to face apprehensive mainstream Egypt. Confrontation was inevitable. Equally, the long-standing Egyptian corporation-heads that had staffed tens of thousands of Egyptians, across the years, were under pressure and fled. I do not recall any social marketing campaign that would foster cohesion between segments of Egypt. It was the contrary. "We will get your money..." etc...I witnessed that, too, and still remember the mood and vibes. In a few words, I thought that it was the government's indifference, which nurtured the rising internal dissonance.

Fear and hurt hovered between Egyptians, with absolutely no recourse to justice, dignity and order. I present to you, throughout these pages, my testimony about the absurdity of social intolerance in general, how it hit members of my family and friends in Egypt, in particular, how it affected my life, and how I coped with it, until this day in 2008.

During those difficult days in the fifties, between 1956 (when I was five) and 1967, I could not recall a time when the West (England, France, and the United States) courted the Arab world, judiciously, realistically and sufficiently to calm its rising fear and anxiety, before it turned to chaos. This courtship meant a lot to me and could have made a lot of difference to win Egypt over to the West. Alas, some public relations homework was indispensable, and its absence (on both sides) was at least partly decisive for what followed.

Equally, the rising Pan-Arabism under the Egyptian new regime of 1952 added fresh fuel to peoples' rising emotions on all sides. The only time I remember when the West stood firm to resolve the rising tensions in the Sinai peninsula was when a great man dared to speak and to take a firm stand toward a *fair* and *equitable* peace solution for the Suez-Canal crisis. That person was the Honorable Lester B. Pearson, representing Canada at the United Nations Security Council. He presented his peaceful solution for the Suez Canal crisis of Egypt in 1956, which earned him the Noble Prize. This topic shaped me too and I explain it in some detail, at the right moment, later on.

To add insults to injuries, and in the early fifties (specifically 1954), there was the famous Operation Susannah also known as *Pinhas Lavon Affair*, planned by the new state of Israel's security service *Mossad*. Its objective was to carry out bombings and other acts of sabotage in Egypt with the aim of creating an atmosphere of panic in which the British and American opponents of British withdrawal from Egypt would find grounds to gain the upper hand and block the British withdrawal that President Nasser had long contemplated. The operation started for a while with little casualties but failed with the 1954 attempt to assassinate President Nasser in Alexandria. Nasser was furious and ordered the jailing of several Egyptian Jews that the Israeli *Mossad* had recruited to execute Israel's failed covert operation to destabilize Egypt. At the same time, various Muslim-Brothers members were said to share the same aim (that of toppling Nasser); they attempted to assassinate him as he delivered his 1954 speech in Alexandria. Of course, the mainstream Egyptian Jews of Egypt had nothing to do with this covert operation. The hurt of the new state of Egypt persisted. Egypt had long been a target of coercion by foreign invasions, far before the birth of Christ.

This is not a historical book; it is just a bit of this and a touch of that, every now and then, across the first few chapters because I witnessed it and I want to share its rich background information with the world before I make my testimony and before the hero can make his point. In fact, it is about the casualties of alienation and those who barely managed to survive it.

After the next few chapters, the story unfolds into a lovely experience, my own (Raphy or Raphael), by the lake of Magog. In all honesty, I am referring, also, to the stories of many of my friends and their families who left Egypt, starting in the fifties, because of the turmoil that surrounded the environment of ambiguity and of swift change, whether internally or elsewhere.

It is also about my struggle to make sense of it all and how, even, I was turned into a target of intolerance, for other reasons, but equally into a magnet for love while surrounded by boundless moments of fellowship and camaraderie. It is about our story of human conflict, as children of God, in our different shades and with our diverse interpretations of life, yet united by our unique universality.

Now, the catastrophe of Palestinians continued, and the Arab negative mood toward the West, as I saw it and perceived it since childhood, was growing just like a revolution of rising expectation. Those around me, especially in my homeland of Egypt, were waiting for a solution for this conflict. At the same time, the atrocities of post-WWII and the Cold War continued to haunt everyone and, in many ways, overshadowed the new Diaspora of Egyptian ethnic communities, because of this post-war environment between the East and the West blocks.

The typical conversation on Egypt's streets or cafés would question why the world would condone the expulsion of 4.5 million refugees, when it (the world) had found no record or odor of intolerance to cultural diversity in the Holy Land over the previous two centuries, to justify that. The suffering of Palestinian refugees was immense. Many Egyptians believed that they were unfairly mistreated (to say the least) during the Cold War period, and after, because they had never done anything wrong since AD 1800 to the West, and even before. These were the topics discussed by lay Egyptian audiences and at school.

Starting 1956, for example, hell broke loose. Another chain of cultural intolerance afflicted many local Egyptian Jews, Italians, Greeks, and other sound Egyptian families of diverse cultural roots who had done absolutely nothing wrong to mainstream Egypt or to their homeland of Egypt. What an irony and waste of life! They were alienated, and I saw them leave—just like that, including my own friends from the soccer team; such as Roland, Armen, Stavros and others, who were all my lifelines from school bullies. They kept leaving the country, all the way until 1967 and even later, one after the other, day after day. Many were my friends and others were family members. The world stood still! I felt lonely again, when my soccer team members left Egypt. I continued to feel lonely for fifty years, until today, in September 2008.

This year, I present to you my stories of love and hate, of inclusion and exclusion, of cohesion and alienation. These, stretch to this day in 2008 to include bullying on the street, in school, at work, within some families and some senseless corporations.

The exodus of great Jewish, Greek, Italian Egyptian-thinkers and other community pillars from Egypt followed the 1956 Suez Canal crisis, one year after the other, systematically. I did not understand then why the crisis meant so much. I will explain it, soon, in the book. The conflict rose in the sixties with the shift from private enterprise to public ownership and administration. I remember the mood in Cairo streets, and I am doomed to pick up moods very easily. It has always been my detriment if I allowed myself to engage with it. The repercussions of these crises would haunt Egypt all the way until its turmoil [staged Arab Spring] in 2011, 2012 and 2013 and thereon, took place and throughout which, several sovereign states were set-up, by force and coercion, to implosion, civil wars and tragedies. More than one million were killed and millions of others were wounded and displaced while world media had (oversold) the so-called Arab Spring. Coincidentally, terror groups joined the Arab Spring saga and one could only wonder if it was not intended. Syria, Iraq, Yemen were broken, grievously and millions of more refugees moved around the area or to Europe and North America. The plan was for Egypt to follow. In part two, the testimony will reveal what happened.

Chapter 5

My ancestors' immigration to Egypt
From the *Levant* (East of the Mediterranean)

*Still in spring of 2008. As I look back to the mid-1950s
I read my notes and write my thoughts.*

    Grandma Victoria (my mother's mother), who was financially secure but far from rich came, originally, from Damascus, Syria, and my Grandpa Aristides (mother's dad) had fled Greece (Leros), as a baby, in the late 1800s and early 1900s amid fifty thousand forsaken Greeks, known as the Bellenis Greeks. They fled to Egypt under the leadership of Parissis Bellenis, helper of thousands of afflicted Greeks from the Dodecanese Islands of Greece. Grandpa grew in Egypt and became a kind and successful engineer and a modest supporter of his wife and five girls. His wife, my Grandma Victoria, whose ancestors were originally from Syria, was a wise woman and extremely religious. She was the great-granddaughter of a Greek Orthodox archbishop of several churches in the neighboring cities of Maaloula and Zahla, bordering Damascus, Syria in 1860, that would soon be hit, ruthlessly, by extremist groups, during the Arab Spring time, in 2011 and onwards. His name was Archbishop Joseph George Mouhanna Haddad Firzli of Damascus and patriarch of Antioch (One of the five Sees of Christianity: Alexandria and Africa, Antioch, Rome, Jerusalem and Constantinople- in historical order). He received his Sainthood recently, and his story of martyrdom follows, as well. These two cities were part of Syria then, and they actually border it from present Lebanon. Grandma Victoria's grandfather was the archbishop's son, George. The Archbishop's children, too, moved to Egypt in the late 1800s. They too fled alienation in Syria for Egypt in the 1880s.

    The archbishop became *Saint* for his devotion and resistance to the intolerance of sectors of the Druze and Ismail-Persians that warned him not to preach, at church, in 1860. This story has been passed on across the years to my parents but the Office de Tourisme of Maaloula (Syria) declined to validate it in

2008 when I called it. Greek Orthodox clerics of this region acknowledge his martyrdom in July of each year; and the church commemorates him worldwide, all the way to the Greek-Orthodox Church in the United States.

He was assassinated in Syria on July 9, 1860, became Christian martyr, and so was his congregation of three hundred Christian worshipers, and three thousand other Christians of these cities. They were of Greek Orthodox and Melkite descent. He was assassinated at the church of Al-Mariameih (in reference to Maryam; the Holy mother's passage, north to Ephesus with James son of Zebedee, as he fled to his congregation with his Communion kit. "This is the leader of Christians!" cried the hateful assassins. "If we kill him, we will kill all the Christians!" When he heard these words, Father Joseph knew that his end had come. He took out his Communion kit and partook of the Body and Blood of Jesus Christ. The assassins attacked him with their hatchets, as if they were woodcutters, and disfigured his body. Binding his legs with ropes, they dragged him over the streets until they dashed his body into pieces while they burnt the cities' churches. The church is one of twenty-one ancient churches in Damascus and Maaloula dating back to the days of Christ.

His son, Georges-Khoury (Arabic for Georges-Curé, in French, and *George the priest,* in English), immigrated to Cairo only to marry and give birth to his daughter Maryam, who gave birth to Grandma Victoria (Mom's mother). This was at the same time (in 1883) when my mother's father (Aristides) and his mother Cleo or Kaliope fled the island of Leros in Greece, escaping similar unrest during the Great War for Greece's independence from Turkey. They fled with fifty thousand Greeks to stable Egypt under Khedive Ismail, grandson of Sultan Mohamed Ali and his successor, with the help of their leader Parissis Bellenis. At the same time, thousands of Jews moved from North Africa, Europe, and the Holy Land seeking prosperity in Egypt. They joined other families, who continued

Tale of a Growing Child

to stay in Egypt across the centuries. Egypt was secure and thriving by the end of 1800s until 1952.

You will enjoy reading what I have survived, swinging between intolerance and love, alienation and reconciliation, whether during my childhood and adolescence or later as an adult at my workplace in Montreal.

In 1949, Aunt Kaliope, the eldest of mother's four sisters, introduced her (mom) to my father, who was the brother of Aunt Kaliope's best friend, Aunt Foutini (otherwise nicknamed Aunt Touna, my dad's youngest sister and queen of high-tea receptions). Dad's name was George, and he was still single at sixty years of age. Mom was thirty-three years old and twenty-seven years younger than he was. She fell for him, and hence he became my loving father and idol until this day in 2008. He was born in 1889 and died (in my arms) in 1978.

On October 20, 1949, my parents married in my father's villa in the suburb of Cairo called Heliopolis. Dad's was a two-story villa, in addition to a basement, a roof and huge garden. Originally, dad's family name was Politis. His grandfather's name was *Constantinou Politis*, and he was a Greek from Constantinople (Istanbul), Turkey. He moved to Egypt early 1800. The family background is almost over but necessary to mention so that the story's progress makes sense and reaches its objective.

When mother married dad in 1949, she lived with him in this beautiful Heliopolis villa on the second floor, while my Aunt Isis (dad's sister whom we called Zee) lived on the first floor with both, her adopted son, Neemo, and my dad before he married and moved up to the second floor. Auntie Zee never got married and, in a sense, she had no one but dad and Neemo to cling to in life.

In 1958, Neemo flew to Los Angeles, U.S.A. to pursue his career as a pediatrician. He did not want to risk the new political environment and the questionable future in Egypt. He did very well but my aunt Zee suffered a big blow, after he left her. Of course, Neemo was my cousin, but since my own dad, unlike Neemo's dad (my dad's brother), married at the age of sixty, there was a thirty years gap between Neemo and both, my sister and me. Fortunately, in 1963, my other Aunt Helga, dad's elder sister (my elder cousin Mady's mother) would move in, with Auntie Zee.

In 1964, mother's sister, Denise (who had hosted her together with her husband, after WW2), was diagnosed with brain tumor one year after her soap factory was seized by the new government of Egypt. (She has moved from Ramallah, with her husband, to Egypt during the Israeli-Arab war of 1948) I loved her so much for how she supported my mother, but so too where many business owners broken because they lost their businesses to a new ambiguous and pompous regime. It was not difficult to understand what would happen to my Aunt Denise, and I cried hysterically, when she passed away, because it was my first shock. She meant so much to me and her deep love had showered my mother, across the years. "So, we will never see her anymore, mom?" I asked her in 1963, a few months before she died.

"She will be in heaven, my son and her spirit will be with us. We can pray for her and she will know. She will do the same for us."

St. Joseph of Antioch and Damascus
Beirut 1793 – 1860 Damascus

Chapter 6
My Mother's Early Years with Dad

Still in spring of 2008, as I look back to the mid-1950s
I read my notes and write my thoughts

When Dad and Mum married in 1949, it was an important event for his family and friends, and so was it for my mother's sisters and aunts. It was, in a sense, an organized marriage of respect and love triggered by character rather than infatuation. Dad, Caucasian, five feet nine at the age of 63 (in 1952), with little hair but with such a haughty appearance, was a prominent lawyer, holder of trophies from King Fouad (that I still hold), owner of forty acres of fruits and vegetables, and manager of his land and the lands of his brothers and sisters. As well, he was a full-time executive at the Compagnie de Reforme Agricole d'Égypte (The Agricultural Reform Company of Egypt). He was the eldest of his brothers and sisters and the most counted-on by his mother, Katrina. Grandma Katrina named him George after Saint George who, according to my aunts and uncles, had appeared to her and remained with her while she was struggling to deliver him, in 1889.

Although he was sixty years old when he married Mom in 1949, Dad had great respect for her and appreciation for her looks, wisdom, and business experience. She had enormous appreciation for his knowledge, state of mind, poetic language, and wisdom. She was and still is one of the wisest relics of human nature that I *have ever come* across.

Dad was also a prominent lawyer. He knew the law and applied it wisely. He taught me many aspects of the law when reviewing his cases at home after he came from his full-time job. Egypt applied the Napoleonic Penal Code, mostly starting the early 1800s. It was the foundation of most tribunals across the world, except for countries where the Islamic Sharia law is a moral code of rule derived from the Holy Quran as well as the *Hadeeth,* which recounts the Prophet Mohammad's exemplary code of conduct for Muslims. While Egypt applies the French Penal Law of Jurisprudence in most cases, there are tribunals that exist for complicated Islamic Civil cases in which the Sharia law is applied. This is not the case in some other Muslim countries, such as Saudi Arabia, Pakistan, Afghanistan, and Indonesia. There, only Sharia is applied. Egypt even had its own Jewish Rabbinic Tribunal in Alexandria before WW1.

However, just as Dad included me in his reviews of cases under the French Penal Law, so did he handle a few Islamic-related civil cases that required the application of Sharia law (Islamic divorce, distribution of wealth, etc.) Dad knew the Sharia law very well, and he was one of two Christian lawyers, in Egypt, that were highly revered for advice with such Islamic civil cases.

Perhaps the two greatest founders of Sharia law were Malik Ibn Anas and Ibn al-Shaf'i. Anas established the Maliki School of jurisprudence in the seventh century. Al-Shaf'i was one of Anas's students, and he disagreed with his teacher about the reliability of the *Noble Hadeeth* as a source for the Sharia. To him it was only the moral code of conduct of Prophet Mohamed, peace be on him. Anas felt that it was necessary to trace each Hadeeth from the time of Mohammad through its chain of devout followers of Islam. This concern led Islamic scholars to consider which of the Hadeeth was applicable in recent times and which was not. It also led to debates among scholars as to the proper application of Sharia law.

During my upbringing, in addition to including me in his legal cases, Dad helped me with my homework, far more than I would have liked him to. He was older and wiser than I was. He developed throat cancer in 1958 at the age of seventy, which he treated in 1959. He survived it at the expense of his vocal chords (larynx) and, subsequently, his speech. He could no longer exercise his role as a lawyer; soon he lost his job and ability to run his land shortly after. Alas, he was a heavy smoker.

I felt it would have been hurtful if I declined his help as a mentor while preparing my homework, even though I wanted my space. Interestingly, he was a devout Christian of solid Anglican faith, though the descendant of old-fashioned Greek Orthodox roots from Constantinople (Istanbul), Turkey (fifth and most recent *See* of Christianity). As well, Dad was the chief purser at the neighboring Saint Michael's and All Saints Anglican chapel in Heliopolis, a suburb of Cairo where we lived. Dad used to encourage my sister, brother and I to read the Bible and scripture union.

As I grew, he taught me many verses from the *Holy Quran* and the noble *Hadeeth*. I would ask him why I had to do so, and he would answer "Why not? If you judge that you should not read it because you are Christian, you will not be able to apply the teachings of Christ to love your neighbor. Your Muslim friends could do the same with you. This is a must, and it is nonnegotiable." Then I would do as he said, and he would mesmerize me more and more, with his wisdom. What a good man he was! I loved him so much, and I miss him so much.

Dad also outlined his code of ethics in life, which he wanted me to abide by. "This is how you should lead your life, in the exact order I tell you. If one day you slip for some reason, remember your code and hang on to it again. It will always protect you and no one will ever judge you". Dad's code, in the exact order, became my code, ever since. It goes like this: *Mercy, Truth (whole truth), Love, Justice and Peace*. The first four would always lead to the fifth. It worked very well but a few hated me for it and called me "… too proper"!

In 1961, and following the segregation of private land, property, and industry by the new Egyptian secular social regime under Nasser (a regime that was swiftly drifting to USSR and China for sustenance), dad found it more and more difficult to run his land. Since he lost his voice to cancer, together with his brothers and sisters, he salvaged some acres of land by keeping only the maximum allowed by the regime (five acres per family). They sold the rest to the farmers at nominal prices. Dad was the only one managing all land and its crops for his sisters and brothers. Eventually, he could no longer run the land and sold it, as mentioned. They divided the revenue, equitably.

Not only was Dad counted on by his sisters and brothers and mother, Katrina, who lived for a while in the villa until she passed away, but he was also the moral provider and counsel for his sisters (not brothers) and their children (my cousins). Of course, since Dad was already twenty-seven years older than mom and at least sixty years older than my sister, my brother and I were; there was a huge age gap between us, his three children, and our elder cousins, who were already thirty when we were born, old enough to be our parents.

My cousin Neemo (Uncle Michel's son), whom dad raised with Auntie Isis (Zee) at the villa before dad married mother, had already been rooted in the villa when dad and mom got married in 1949. Neemo was born around 1928. After the wedding in 1949, my mother moved in and stayed with Dad on the upper floor. Neemo must have been twenty-one years old then. He stayed with Auntie Zee on the first floor, as mentioned earlier, and continued to enjoy the beautiful garden for a few years, with his close circle of cousins (my elder ones), until he flew to USA in 1958.

The garden at the villa witnessed numerous parties, suppers, and gatherings, and the villa was truly the social point of encounter for everyone in the family, many years before 1949, but most of all for the Bible Studies that our church priests presided. This persisted for at least twenty years before Dad married Mom and ten years, later.

Before Neemo flew to USA in 1958, much before, Neemo and his generation of cousins spent their childhood playing together in the villa's garden. Then, in 1950 and after mother gave birth to my sister, me in 1951, and my brother (in 1958), things changed. This, too, shaped me since I did not feel part of the elder circle of cousins, whose childhood souvenirs were rooted in our garden, much before I was born.

My Aunt Touna, Dad's sister who was the best friend of my mother's eldest sister, Kaliope, (the one who had set Mother and Dad up), was exceptionally kind to Mother, Dad, my sister, my baby brother, and me. She was adorable and super human to our new family. Auntie Touna would make her typical cookies and send them over to all the family, with the help of her gardener. Moreover, if you send homemade cookies or cakes to someone, in Egypt, you really mean to send a message of peace and love. Besides, she was so proud to share her baked goods with all the family at her tea parties at her villa and garden, not far from ours.

My cousin Mady, who is the daughter of Auntie Helga (dad's third sister), would tell me, as a child, things like "Why don't you go ask your mother?" As if mom was different. She often started with the phrase, "Your mother came into our family …" There was a lot of dry language and intolerance in the air when I was picked to hear statements of the sort. It was easy for me to pick up the negative vibes in her way of speech about my mother or to mother. Of course, this had to break my heart from the age of six all the way to the age of twenty when I put an end to it. My mother felt it, and I felt it for her. Then I started shouting and saying things like "Leave my mother alone. She did nothing to you!" I would turn to mother and tell her, "Don't worry, Mama; I love you so much and will never let anyone hurt you from now on."

"Oh, my tender one," she would say to me and hug me so hard.

Later, in my teens, I felt a little more included by dad's circle of nieces and their families, as compared to the early years of my parents' marriage. I still believe that they were not bad; their words and actions were just so cold and void of soul, sometimes… that is all! I could see my mother's grief but determination to let go each time they made such comments, at least for dad's sake (and they hurt me as I witnessed them, hurt my own mother). There were many times when I would rush to Mother after hearing some of these words and then clutch her lap with my arms and burry my face in her arms, seeking comfort.

Just a recap: Dad's father was Nicola Politis, son of Constantinou Politis, originally from Istanbul. The name of dad's mother was Katrina. His grandfather, Constantinou, worked for Mehmed Ali (Mohammad Ali), founder of modern Egypt in the early eighteen hundreds. Dad's father, Nicola, worked for King Fouad, and my father worked for the Agricultural Reform Company of Egypt under his Royal Highness King Farouk, son of King Fouad I, just until King Farouk was exiled during the Egyptian revolution in 1952. The company was nationalized under Nasser, and Dad continued to work for it until he lost his voice in 1960, for cancer. His boss was a Jew (Mr. Qattawi) who had to leave Egypt in 1961 but who helped Dad financially when he got throat cancer, one year before he was *encouraged* to leave Egypt.

In the meantime, back in 1930, Egypt was reaching unmistakable growth and prosperity in agriculture, translation, culture, art, theatre, and textiles. It had become the world's pinnacle for foreign investment and attracted hundreds of thousands of Greeks, Jews, Italians, Swiss, Poles, Belgians, French, and many others. Of course, many Jews and Greeks had already been living in Egypt and sharing in building it for centuries. During WWI and WWII, many more families of Jewish faith, moved to Egypt. They started their own businesses.

When Mom gave birth to my beloved brother Camille, in January 1958, my sister and I became very protective of him. By that time, Mady (Auntie Helga's only daughter) gave birth to my second cousins, Wael and then his sister Sanaa, who were hardly seven years younger than my sister and me. We loved each other and got along very well.

Chapter 7
Egypt, the Dwindling Golden Years

Still in spring of 2008, looking back at the early years

Back in the forties, Britain was pressuring King Farouk to assign an Egyptian Cabinet under P.M. Mustafa El-Nahhas, who was Britain's choice for WWII and the post-war climate. The king explained that this would not be constitutional because El-Nahhas would have had to be democratically elected and, already King Farouk had his differences with Mr. El-Nahhas. The British High Commissioner in Egypt insisted the king appoint El-Nahhas. The king tried, but El-Nahhas declined the king's offer vehemently, for the same reasons King Farouk had declined it, earlier. The new cabinet would not be constitutional without proper elections. The king contacted the British High Commissioner in Egypt (Lord Lampson) to explain his view. Lord Lampson stormed the Royal Palace in Cairo, Egypt, in 1942 and confronted the king. He did so together with several British soldiers and gave King Farouk an ultimatum to leave Egypt (his country and people). He tried to force him to sign his abdication letter, which the king of Egypt was about to, just until his political advisor intervened and urged him not to.

Young King Farouk did not sign. He stayed in power for hardly ten additional years, just until a group of students called the Revolutionary Freedom Fighters, under Mohammad Naguib and Gamal Abdel Nasser, invaded the Royal Palace in Alexandria, Egypt in July 1952, where the king was spending the summer holidays with his family. They took over the palace and forced the king (at the age of thirty-two), and his family out of Egypt on His Majesty's royal boat (*Al-Mahroussa*). It was a coup that was regarded peaceful by the Freedom Fighters but that involved firearms and shooting to the extent that the king asked to speak with the representative of Mohammad Naguib, master of the coup. Prime Minister Ali Maher Pasha went out of the Royal Palace in Alexandria to speak with General Naguib and then returned to the king, trembling and sweating. The king said he would cooperate but that he had two conditions. *From King Farouk's memoirs:*

> "Your Majesty," told me Prime Minister Ali Maher, trembling and in great grief, "they want your abdication in favor of your [baby] son by noon, and you must leave Egypt by six in the evening."
>
> "I looked at my watch. It was 10:42 a.m.! Yet I did not feel that I needed one minute to think. I thanked him and said, "Tell them I am ready to sign immediately. But I have two conditions. First, the abdication papers must be formal and constitutional. They must be prepared by lawyers and must contain no abuse", said the king.
>
> "Second, [the king added] the revolutionaries must permit those of my loyal troops who wish to give me full military honors as I depart, do so."
>
> ... Without warning, two officers who were advancing side by side opened fire from the hip with their Bren guns ..."

According to the king and witnesses, there was heavy fighting and shooting during the confrontation between the king and the Freedom Fighters. By six p.m., more than fifty people from the royal family, friends, and nannies had made it to the boat and fled to Naples, Italy. In the meantime, many had died fighting to help the royal family flee, not because of the fire from higher ranks of revolutionaries but from the younger soldiers who were in a state of mess, shooting at the royal family in the hype of the palace insertion with no one stopping them.

The king and his family remained in Italy, where he lived until he died in 1965. He had moved to Monaco for a short while and returned to Italy. While the newly self-appointed revolutionary cabinet under Mohammad Naguib prepared to rule, Naguib kept the monarchy running for another year (1953) under Farouk's son, the baby child King Fouad II, in exile. The Chairman Council of Regency, Royal Prince Mohammad Abdel-Moneim, represented Fouad II in Egypt.

King Farouk loved his people and, according to many historians, was the most beloved king of Egypt from the Mohammad Ali Dynasty that generated ten monarchs, including Farouk and his son, Fouad II. This last remained as king, in exile, from July 26, 1952 (the revolution date) until June 18, 1953, just until the effects of the coup d'état subsided and Nasser assumed his role as president, forcing Mohammad Naguib, master of the coup d'état, aside. Later, Nasser confined Naguib to house arrest.

On June 19, 1953, the Freedom Fighters Movement, under Gamal Abdel Nasser and Mohammad Naguib, took power and abolished the monarchy after 150 years of its reign since it was founded by the Sultan-Wali Mohammad Ali. Nasser became the official president in 1954 and remained so until his death in September 1970, after which Anwar El-Sadat, a far more moderate member of the Freedom Officers, became the second president of modern Egypt and brought back Egypt to the middle. In his memoires, while in exile, King Farouk warned the world about how Russia and Comrade Josef Stalin pointed their fingers at Egypt.

Between the coup d'état under Nasser and Naguib and the second generation of Egyptian leadership under Anwar El-Sadat, in 1970, so much happened. There was a lot that led to the fragmentation of a social mosaic that had existed for hundreds of years, canvassing the broader social link in Egypt, especially in major cities like Cairo, Alexandria, Suez, Port-Said, and Ismailia. It was a canvass that flourished starting with Mohammad Ali, the founder of the Egyptian monarchy in 1805; a canvass that portrayed a fascinating country that attracted families and investors of diverse ethnic and social minority groups and communities that exceeded, by 1952, a million hard-workers (out of a population of about twenty million). They have contributed to shaping a colorful and productive society with a ravishing mosaic of intertwining and interlocking bouquets of initiative, passions, roots, scents and aspirations.

To me, the political shift that followed the abolishing of Egyptian modern monarchy did not seem to allow the smooth transition of existing institutions, health providers, intellectuals, schools, colleges, universities, media, artists, and heritage sites from the former rule to the new one. This destabilized these institutions and their leadership; it triggered confusion and apprehension and even led to defiance and confrontation between the social clusters within institutions and between their new leaders. The soul of the motherland was hurting.

Over the following few years, high-ranked officials pounded the media with inflaming speeches and, later, they nationalized most remaining institutions, while shifting to rigid socialism. During this period, many witnessed the confiscation of land and private property, the segregation of media and the control of thought of Egyptian professors and writers. The cold alliance with USSR under Bregenev on one side and the perceived distance of the West on the other side, overshadowed this period. Many Egyptian Greeks, Jews, Armenians, Italians, Belgians, Poles, Yugoslavs, Czechs felt intimidated by the new mainstream *Children of the Revolution*. It devastated the beautiful canvass that had been woven across 150 years with diverse colors and depths. Ultimately, the canvass started cracking because of the new ideology of Pan Arabism, *declared* justice and unrealized promises.

Then the brain drain started to take place; the fleeing of Egyptian minority groups and past entrepreneurs, the relentless rush of *Exodus* of the *neglected* and so much more.

Then, another million moderate Egyptians, Christians and Muslims, started leaving shortly after the October 1973 war with Israel and after the assassination of President Sadat in 1981. The levels of fear were rising; there was no way to quell it.

Interestingly, when King Farouk died in exile in 1965, his family requested to bury him in Cairo at the El-Refai Mosque with his ancestors from the royal family, but Mr. Nasser and his people declined the request. Friends of the family managed to smuggle the king's remains to Cairo and buried him in a secret location for a few years. When President Sadat took power in 1970, he ordered moving his remains, with all due dignity, to Cairo's El-Refai Mosque. I visited his tomb; that of his father, King Fouad I, and his grandfather, Khedive Ismail and paid my respect. President Sadat loved Egyptians more than his image. (See page 98)

It is important to mention that regardless of which ideology the post-monarchy regime may have had or even promised the Egyptian blue-collars, farmers, and lay audiences to adopt; it left Egypt with a fractured social link and an increasingly crumbling level of trust. While the first part of Nasser's plan to take from the rich was realized, little did the second part of the plan to distribute to the needy, see light. Wealth was confiscated, but it vanished behind the sun, except for some national factories and research projects funded by East Germany, USSR, and China.

When the canvass had cracked the formerly productive and privately owned corporations of textiles, steel, cotton, mega-retail stores, porcelain, and other industries ceased to sustain their levels of growth. Alas, they were no longer run under the leadership of their original owners; they had shifted to younger and less trained government ownership and bureaucracy. Consequently, the original owners, whom nationalization had torn, started fleeing Egypt. Hence, Egypt survived thirty continuous years of brain drain and immigration to the West! Many died of heart attacks and brain tumor. What a waste! Examples of these ruined businesses appear today in 2008 and, later, in 2017: Gatteneo, Salon Vert, Ben-Zion, ADS, Shemla, Sednaoui, Hanneau, À l'Americaine, Groppi, Pontremolli and so many more. They are all gone for good; so are their once thriving employees, now staggering.

In 1958, at the age of 7, and six years after the toppling of King Farouk, I would walk with my dad (at his age of 70) through the neighborhood commercial strip of Heliopolis. It was a fine, rich, classy and pleasurable experience to witness. Coming out of my family's villa, we walked around thirty meters to the right before turning left on the main street, renamed *Al-Thawra*, which means revolution. Formerly it was called *Avenue du Baron*, in reference to *Le Baron Edouard d'Empain* founder of the modern Cairo suburb, of Heliopolis in 1912. The shops were distinctive: Ahmed Plumbing, Zervas the Greek baker, Apodiyakos the Greek grocer, Hajj Mohamed the butcher, Home Made Cakes, the Italian Confectionary and Pastry teahouse, Melham Abu-Diab, the Jewish Maître Charcutier (cold cuts master) and so many more. Most of them were spread on my left side of this modern Heliopolis quarter, called Qurba- stunning in architecture. A few appeared on the right such as Everyman's Bookshop, *Christo* the toy shop and further still *La Compagnie des eaux et électricité d'Héliopolis* and *La Maison Groppi* a glorious and successful Swiss Italian tea-house, confectionary, ice-cream and pastry refuge, since 1908. Slightly to the right was the Greek Catholic Basilica of Saint Cyril and behind it, the Jewish Temple and school of Abraham Betesh which I had visited with my Jewish schoolmates and their parents during Sabbath or Jewish celebrations. Two hundred meters, east, stood the stunning mosque of Sultan Hussein. All buildings were hardly three floors high, colonial and Islamic in genre and by all means gripping with their wrought-iron gates and marble entrances. The street lanterns were pompous and cozy, the vendors were clean and their products were, periodically, inspected by the remaining health and food-inspection employees of the pre-1952 coup, until they all retired or immigrated. After this, these businesses dwindled, particularly, by the late sixties. Finally, another honorable chapter of glorious Egypt was extinguished. I still remember them vividly and passionately. When we finished our shopping dad and I would walk back home re-tracking our footsteps and stay with auntie Zee, for tea, if mother was still at work.

Entrance of the glorious Galleries Sednaoui Stores in 2017
Built in 1911, Khazindar, Cairo

Chapter 8

Who Drove the Egyptians Out of Egypt?
A chronological sequence of vital information

The 1952 Revolution

The Egyptian revolution team that surrounded President Nasser and Nasser himself had not had sufficient training in governance as the king and other members of his cabinet had, through countless education and training in Europe. They inevitably drove the media and education syllabi to the new regime's values and sometimes at the expense of the state of mind of the children, their initiative and independence, the growing youth, and, consequently, the whole of Egypt, for years, until it broke, forever. During that time, a completely new generation's right-of-choice was impeded because of selective and compulsive education and media! The gap between the old and the present was growing very fast.

The New Canvass

The new mainstream changes influenced the new generation of Egyptian youth. This affected, too, the well-rooted ethnic communities, their groceries, clubs, sports teams, schools, and cultural centers. The portrait that was once cohesively canvassed for more than 150 years with colors, shades, passions and roots ceased to sustain itself as the sum of the previous seven thousand years of Egyptian passions and roots, had survived for so long. Its colors faded, and its thread dried out and cracked. The new could not rekindle the old; it could no longer notice the remaining existing present and learn to live next to it. These rich cultural remnants of the past were devastated and heartbroken. There were decreasing numbers of citizens from the beautiful past to hand over the flame of culture and heritage to the newly born.

Eventually, casualties of such social change felt alienated and soon started leaving their land *to fit in another*.

In the meantime, as I grew up to the age of nine, I felt the need to cling to my soccer-team friends who were my refuge from bullying and means to nurture my self-esteem. Here are just some of their names: Armen, Vahan and Stefan (of Armenian roots from Turkey and Syria), Ahmed, Haitham, Sami and George (Egyptians) Roland Lévi (son of my mother's friend, Auntie Lucie). There were also, Emile (Egyptian of Jewish faith whose grandparents had moved to Egypt among other immigrants from Europe in the early 1900s), Bruno (Italian), Stavros and his sister Karina (Greek) and a few more. Roland and Haitham played as center forward; I was center back with Vahan. Our first game was in 1960 and we ended second. We continued playing for three years and our parents would invite us to each other's houses for cake, tea and a Black & White home-projected film (sometimes, a naughty film) for as long as they remained in Egypt, all the way until the 1967 war with Israel. On other days, we attended the Armenian Club celebrations or the Jewish Feasts, both next door. Of course, we never missed the Easter procession at the Greek Orthodox Diocese, two kilometers, away from home. My new circle of friends made me feel safe and secure. Sadly, in 1964, the soccer team was completely disintegrated and I was left with enough bullying at school to have me move to another school.

Briefly:

The British in Egypt

In 1954, one year after President Nasser assumed his full role, he ended the British occupation of Egypt that had lasted 150 years. The occupation had started in 1803, with Napoleon Bonaparte's invasion of Egypt in 1798, at which time the British intervened to help Mohammad Ali repel the French army. Sultan Mohammad Ali was only the *Wali* (governor) of Egypt under the Ottoman Empire just until he declared himself viceroy and ruler of Egypt in 1805 with the consent of the Ottoman Sultan Mahmud II, in exchange for a yearly financial bail. However, the British stayed and never left. Later, the French remained in Egypt not with tanks and soldiers but with thinkers, historians, linguists, and builders until the turn of the century in 1900 and later.

The French in Egypt

The French contributed to building modern Egypt immensely and helped turn it into a citadel of culture, agriculture, marine and international investment, under the command of Count Ferdinand De Lesseps of France, among others. In 1855, following the concession of Viceroy Said Pasha, son of Sultan Mohammad Ali, and Khedive Ismail, son of Viceroy Ibrahim Pasha (Son of Sultan Mohamed Ali), Ferdinand De Lesseps led the construction of the Suez Canal of Egypt, the Royal Cairo Opera, and two prominent Cairo bridges. He did this in cooperation with Gustave Eiffel, builder of the famous Tower of Eiffel in Paris.

De Lesseps had read the *Description of Egypt* by engineer Le Père, who was one of sixty French *savants* (thinkers) who had accompanied Napoleon Bonaparte in 1798 in his campaign in Egypt. He continued, while Egypt was still under British rule.

The Suez Canal

When Britain failed to force King Farouk of Egypt to abdicate in 1942, the British High Commissioner and his troops in Cairo turned their back on King Farouk as Nasser ousted him in 1952's coup d'état. They did not help him. In 1954 (nine years after WWII), Nasser pressured the remaining British soldiers and politicians to leave Egypt, and the tensions with Britain were rising; in the meantime, Nasser's good relations with USSR and China were building up!

In 1956, President Nasser was encountering world resistance with his refusal to let Israeli ships pass through Egypt's Suez Canal- given the dispersion of millions of Palestinian refugees. The canal was and still is a masterpiece of strategic navigation. It connects the tip of the left cone of the Red Sea to the Mediterranean, hence connecting the Indian and Pacific Oceans (from the south) with the Mediterranean Sea and the Atlantic Ocean (at the north) and on to the world. Obviously, it suited all trade from Australia, the Asian subcontinent, the Mediterranean and Africa, on to Europe and the Americas (and vice versa). According to Herodotus, the Greek historian (484 BC–425 BC) and father of Western history, the Suez Canal had already been built in 600 BC, and the same waterway stretched over 1,000 stadia (114 miles). It took the lives of 120,000 Egyptians then. Over the years, Egypt referred to this waterway as Ptolemy's Canal. Over the centuries, still, as the Red Sea receded and its coastline was getting farther and farther from the Bitter Lakes of Sinai, together with the River Nile that was filling up with silt, Ptolemy's Canal was dwindling. Two hundred years later, AD20, Queen Cleopatra tried to restore and revive it, but in vain. Over the next eight centuries years, the Suez Canal was successively modified, destroyed, and rebuilt, repeatedly until the Abbasid Caliph al Mansour (C. AD 750) put it out of commission (one hundred years after the Arab Conquests of Egypt took place).

In 1798, Napoleon's rising interest in finding the remnants of an ancient waterway passage that connected the Red Sea to the Mediterranean westward to the Nile led him to summon archaeologists, scientists, cartographers, and engineers to scour the area. They recorded their findings in their famous *Description d'Égypte* (*Description of Egypt*). None-the-less, this did not work. They could not reconstruct it. Later, Napoleon contemplated the construction of another modern, north-south canal to join the Mediterranean and the Red Sea. Unfortunately, he abandoned his project after the preliminary survey erroneously concluded that the Red Sea was 10 meters (33 feet) higher than the Mediterranean. This would have made a locks-based canal too expensive and very long to construct. The Napoleonic survey commission's error came from fragmented readings mostly done during wartime, which resulted in incomplete calculations.

Finally, in 1854 and until 1856, Count Ferdinand De Lesseps obtained concessions from Viceroy Mohammad Said, second son of Mohammad Ali, to construct a new canal in the city of Suez. It would connect the tip of the left cone of the Red Sea, northward to the Mediterranean, during the rule of Mohammad Said Pasha. The present Suez-Canal was built between 1858 and 1869. It is said that somewhere between twenty-seven thousand and fifty-five thousand Egyptian workers lost their lives while constructing the Suez Canal. They had constructed it under forced labor, violence, slavery, and threats induced by Britain and Viceroy Mohammad Said. France perceived more and more that Ferdinand De Lesseps, whom they regarded as a rival, intimidated Britain. When Khedive Ismail, grandson of Mohammad Ali and son of Viceroy Mohamed Said, assumed his role as ruler of the homeland, he worked passionately with the French to accomplish this project among various other cultural and industrial projects. He said his famous phrase around AD 1871: "My country is no longer in Africa; we are now part of Europe. It is therefore natural for us to abandon our former ways and to adopt a new system adapted to our social conditions."

Now, while England was occupying Egypt since 1803, it was indifferent towards the harsh treatment of Egyptian workers between 1858 and 1869 in the Suez Canal. It was indifferent to their slavery, their undue hardship, and meaningless deaths, not to mention the inexistence of compensation packages to their bereaved families. All this reached a point where De Lesseps sent a letter to the government of Britain, condemning it and asking it to intervene to denounce forced labor and slavery. Most of all, De Lesseps asked Britain to show some remorse to the families of the deceased. The same thing had happened during the construction of the British Railway System of Egypt and Palestine, a few years earlier, when thousands of forced Egyptian workers were enslaved to the point of death during its construction. There was no compensation to their families.

Count Ferdinand de Lesseps was born on November 19, 1805 in Versailles, France. His family was for a long time involved with French diplomatic service. At age nineteen, having concluded his law studies, he was appointed *French ambassador to Lisbon*. He served in Tunis later with his father, until 1832 when his father died.

Then he went to Egypt where he had already befriended the Viceroy Mohammad Said (son of Sultan Mohammad Ali). He rushed to Cairo, and soon the construction of the Suez Canal under De Lesseps's command began, as soon as the Suez Canal Maritime Company (*Compagnie Universelle du Canal Maritime de Suez*) was formed in 1858. The excavation lasted eleven years. The grand opening with luxurious ceremonies took place in 1869 under Khedive Ismail (*Emperor Ismail*, Nephew of Mohamed Said Pasha), who was a master of international relations and founder of Egypt's modern culture.

The Cairo Opera House had been built to celebrate the inauguration of the Suez Canal in 1869; and Giuseppe Verdi, the Italian musician, had been commissioned by Emperor Ismail to write *Opera Aida* to perform it in the new Cairo Opera House for the first time. This Opera House is a smaller replica of the glorious *Opera di Scala*, in Milano). Khedive Ismail invited Empress Eugenie of France for its inauguration. De Lesseps became a hero and Emperor Ismail presented him with many decorations. *Opera Aida* was later premiered again in the *Opera di Scala* of Milano and then later in Cleveland, Ohio. I visited them both (and, earlier, the historical Cairo Opera, repeatedly).

Until 1956, (four years following the Egyptian revolution), ships would still pass through the Suez Canal (*Compagnie Universelle du Canal Maritime de Suez*) with no royalties to the Egyptians. Ferdinand De Lesseps had leased it from Egypt for ninety-nine years, starting in 1855, so that he could turn it into a profitable private business and retain all passage royalties in favor of investors and shareholders, including him. In fact, foreign intervention reached a point where in 1936 even Britain took control of the canal in an inequitable treaty with King Abbas II, grandson of Viceroy Abbas I and nephew of King Fouad I (Father of King Farouk). This compromised the interests of many existing foreign investors and shareholders. It also continued to undermine Egypt's rights to autonomy over its canal and to any rights for its enslaved martyrs, builders of the canal. This pivotal controversy would lead the land to endless feuds, for the following six decades.

In 1948 and a few years prior to the 1956 Suez Canal crisis, King Farouk surrounded himself with Egyptians, Italians, Jews, and other Egyptians of ethnic background for advice and consultation over top national issues. In 1949, for example, he imposed a blockade on Israel ships passing through Suez Canal after the hardships that Palestinians encountered between 1947 and 1948. This blockade lasted until the 1973 October War (Yom Kippur War), except for a short period between 1951 and 1952, after intense pressure by the British.

The king of Egypt (Farouk) had asked for assurances that Israel would not displace Palestinians or force them to leave their land. He was under pressure himself. When he did not get a favorable response, he imposed the blockade on Israel's ships through the Suez Canal and repudiated the Anglo-Egyptian treaty of 1936 under Prime Minister Benjamin Disraeli. This treaty gave control to Britain of the canal, thus reinstating the earlier legitimate, ninety-nine-year lease that Khedive Ismail signed with France, and reinforcing the rights of foreign shareholders. Britain was infuriated and started pressuring him to abdicate. He refused.

In 1954, Britain agreed to Nasser's request to withdraw its troops after 150 years of British occupation, Britain withdrew.

Just before, and in 1948, Britain withdrew its occupation of Palestine and ceded it to the state of Israel.

The Suez Canal Crisis

Nasser had tried to reclaim ownership of Egypt's canal since he took office in 1953. In the meantime, in 1956, the United Kingdom and the United States withdrew their pledge to support the construction of the Aswan Dam (south of Egypt) due to Egypt's shift toward the USSR and to Nasser's recognition of the new communist regime of China under Mao Tse-tung. Nasser's regime was in need of funding to build the Aswan Dam to save lives and land. Then, the Egyptian President Gamal Abdel Nasser wasted no time and made quite a daring and forceful decision when he could not get funding from England, France, or the United States.

He nationalized the canal on the anniversary of the end of the ninety-nine year lease that France had imposed in 1855. He did this in order to secure its revenue to finance the Aswan dam project that would save hundreds of thousands of acres of agricultural land and lives from floods. He wanted to save lives and crops, as well as to fund Egypt's struggle for independence. The building of the Aswan Dam was equally vital for the protection of Abu Simbel and Philae, ancient Nubian Monuments, from the threat of destruction by the rising waters. (Nuba is located south of the Egyptian historical city of Aswan, just Between Egypt and north of Sudan.) These monuments were declared world heritage sites by the UNESCO (United Nations Educational Scientific and Cultural Organization). Nasser nationalized the canal in 1956, following its ninety-nine years of operations without a penny of revenue from its royalties to Egypt since the beginning of its construction in 1855 by thousands of Egyptian martyrs.

The nationalization of the Suez Canal provoked the famous Suez Canal Crisis, a crisis that enraged the world to an extent of unimaginable proportions. Immediately, in 1956, the UK, France and Israel declared war on Egypt, only eleven years after the Second World War had ended. The intention was for Israel to lead a ground invasion and for the Anglo-French intervention to provide air and marine support, just until all three resolved the crisis and reclaimed control of the Egyptian Canal. All hell broke loose with the war against Egypt, also known as the Tripartite Aggression.

The war started on October 29, 1956, and ended on November 6, 1956. I remember very well those days. I was five years old, and dad grabbed my sister, mother, Auntie Zee and I, away from our villa that was only one hundred kilometers away from the action. Other family members rushed and joined us at the villa. There were cousins and aunts on both family sides (dad's side and mom's, as well). Within less than one hour, we fled the villa using five or six cars, out of the danger zone, and drove to my dad's family farm before they sold it. We made it to the farm in one and a half hours.

In no time, the world sensed the gravity of the Tripartite Aggression of Egypt. However, it took almost a week for anyone to agree to intervene and for the triangular troops to halt their crawling across Sinai and on to Cairo. The tension was rising, and the UN was unable to come out with a solution at first.

Distraught by what was happening, one person stood solid in the UN assembly, offering a viable plan for immediate peace. The U.S backed him immediately. Again, this was in 1956, eleven years after WWII, amid endless war tribunals and in the heart of a ruthless post-war conflict. His resolution was both fair and strategic. It was the Secretary of State for Foreign Affairs of Canada, the late Hon. Lester B. Pearson. He stood firmly in the UN headquarters to promote his initiative, which called for an international UN peace force that would stay in Sinai and that would withdraw only after the Israeli troops had withdrawn. In other words, he called for a United Nations Emergency Force to police that area, thus permitting the invading nations to withdraw with a minimum loss of face. This is exactly what happened. The occupation ended in March 1957. I had the privilege of meeting Senator Landon-Pearson, who was Hon. Lester B. Pearson's daughter-in-law (wife of his son, Geoffrey Pearson) forty-six years later (in 2001), in Ottawa. She had delivered a speech covering children and youth priorities in Canada. At that time, she was Prime Minister John Chrétien's Advisor for Children and Youth Affairs in Canada. I spoke with her for a few minutes about the 1956 Suez Crisis before and after her inspiring speech.

Immediately in 1956, the United States (under late President *Dwight D. Eisenhower*) backed the Honorable Canadian Secretary-of-State *Pearson's* motion and put financial pressure on the UK, France and Israel to withdraw their troops from Sinai, which they did. The Hon. Lester B. Pearson was granted the Nobel Prize in 1957 for having saved a catastrophe. He became Prime Minister of Canada between 1963 and 1968 and one of my few eternal political idols.

In October 1964, Egypt accepted £4.3m (Egyptian pounds) from the United States (One Egyptian pound, then, was almost equal to 2.25 US dollars) along with a £5m grant from UNESCO (United Nations Educational Scientific and Cultural Organization) to save the Nubian Monuments of Abu Simbel and Philae. In 1968, the temple and other monuments were removed and reassembled on a higher platform. In 1971, the High Dam was inaugurated, one year after President Nasser, who had fought passionately to conclude it, had died. It cost Egypt £300m, with no waste of lives.

Over the seventeen years following the 1956 crisis, the area would witness two harsh wars: The Arab-Israeli War of June 1967 and the October 1973 Yom Kippur war. The state of Egypt was fractured and President Sadat realized that he had to start rebuilding his country. He bravely signed the peace treaty with Israel in 1978. By that time many Egyptian entrepreneurs, intellects, artists and minority groups had had enough. They left for good, including the families of my soccer team. President

Sadat worked hard to reassure the families that had fled, and to encourage them to return, and he did it honorably.

This was an indispensable breakdown of Egypt's modern history. This history shaped me, my generation, other generations, and Egypt's historic twists and turns between the West and the East, with war and peace, with love and hate. It would not be right to judge the marginalization, immigration and exile of Egyptian communities between 1956 and the 1980s without stretching one's depth of knowledge to capture available factors and historical events far back, so that our portrait can be complete and our evaluation can become judicious as opposed to judgmental. In fact, I wanted to draw a comprehensive breakdown of facts, as best as I could visualize them, and may truth and error grapple!

Al-Hassan and El-Rifaii Mosques
Resting place for monarchs and figureheads

Chapter 9
Scents of Jasmine and Seeds of Fear
Fifty-five years earlier, childhood; home and school

The villa where we lived in Heliopolis-Cairo was built of brick in 1920. It stood on a small street that was hardly three hundred feet long and twenty-four wide. This Street's name is Osiris (an ancient God to the pharaohs; God of the Underworld or Death). Our villa was in the middle of the street with one house on our right and another on our left. There were three medium-sized buildings on the opposite side of our pavement. In front, was the telephone company of Heliopolis, a two-floored villa to its left, and a two-floor Colonial-Islamic condominium to its right occupying our street's corner (Osiris) and the main street formerly named Le-Baron Street and later renamed El-Thawra Street (Revolution Street). On the left side of El-Thawra Street, we would find the shopping strip I mentioned earlier, to the right, the great Mosque of Sultan Hussein and the Castle of Le Baron d'Empain. El-Thawra Street continues beyond the Mosque of Sultan Hussein and the Castle of Le Baron d'Empain until it reached the city of Suez, one hundred and one kilometers, further east, (towards Sinai and Israel). All six buildings on our little street (Osiris) were built by and for members of the team of Le Baron d'Empain, founder and architect of Heliopolis between 1906 1920 and so were its Cairo Electric Railways and Heliopolis Oases Company.

Osiris St. (Childhood villa middle left. With El-Thawra Street behind

*El-Thawra (Le Baron) Street, facing commercial strip
Osiris Street, just behind and to the left 2008*

*El-Thawra (Le Baron) Street
Facing Le Baron's Palace and City of Suez 1962
Osiris Street, just behind and to the right*

El-Thawra street, featured two thousand feet of cafés, food outlets, clothes, shoes, and household stores and two churches, the ravishing Saint Cyril Basilica and, (not far), Saint Michael and All Saints Anglican Church where I used to pray. Not far, still, lay the beautiful mosque of Sultan Hussein (mentioned above) and a breathtaking synagogue of Vitali Madjar on Komanos and El-Masalla Streets that was also known as the Sephardic school of *L'école Abraham Betesh*.

The temple and school was built in 1928, and I entered them occasionally when I met my friends Roland (*Auntie Lucie's son*), and Emile in 1959 and the early sixties, together with their parents ready to have Sabbath dinner at their homes, footsteps away. After the peace treaty with Israel (around 1978-80), I received former friends of mine from Haifa, Israel. They were Egyptians, and I had them visit their own school *Abraham Betesh*. I will never forget how they contained their tears as they stood watching its gates, in 1980, twenty years after they had left Egypt. In 2008, I could only sneak a side-street shot.

École (School) Abraham Betesh. Tip seen in middle left
Also known as Templi Vitali Madjar AD1928

Over the years, my sister, my brother and I, would make a habit of running in the garden and of picking up fruits that had fallen from the trees. There were two mango trees in our garden.

It also had two olive trees, one sweet orange tree, one naval orange tree, one Seville orange tree, a Mediterranean jasmine tree, and two Indian jasmine trees. There were also two rare tropical fruit trees (*Sabbouta*) that tasted more like papaya but looked like guava. Olive trees were my responsibility because, over the years, my family counted on me to marinate (loads) of green olives. As for mother, she made us endless delicious orange marmalade using the garden's oranges. She also made semi cooked chewy Seville orange peels. She would slice the oranges in four, empty them, fold each peel, and sew it with two stitches. Then she would soak them in lots of sugar and some orange juice and keep boiling them until the sugar turned into syrup and then, the peels turned into something close to chewy marmalade. She let them dry overnight, and in the morning, she sprinkled them with granulated sugar. At this stage, they were ready to devour as a finger delicacy, while orange scents filled our home. The garden had a lot to offer!

All around our garden's fence, other scents filled the air. We had mimosa bushes mixed with Bougainvillea that produced flowers of divine scents, scents that we captured walking in to the garden and out of it, and even while at home, upstairs with the windows open. There were lilies, clover, roses, pansies and much more. The jasmine trees had a say, too, and so did the orange blossoms, and lilies in spring; a true mosaic of scents (until the oranges were ready to eat in fall)!

I remember walking through the villa's main gate with my sister, through the garden, backwards to the staircase and up to the first floor (in the early sixties), once our school bus had dropped us at the villa's entrance. If it was in spring, the smell of the orange blossoms would invigorate my senses with a divine scent of nature announcing the birth of life; the birth of oranges; the birth of vines and grapes. Then, by end of June, I would smell the honey coming out of the tip of the mangoes all over the two trees. Their branches were sticky because of the sweet dew that dripped from the head of each mango as it slowly came to life. In fact, I would touch the tip of the mango with my fingers, at the age of six or seven, and put them on my lips, tasting the sweetness of the unborn mango's honey. Then there was the Mediterranean jasmine tree, those romantic Indian jasmine trees and the white lilies, hypnotizing my senses and making me wonder why I could not be like them—ready to start all over again every spring; ready to cover my barren hands and legs with leaves of life; ready to bring forth joy to all those around me. I would feel ready for a rebirth despite the dark environment of ambiguity, absurdity, and alienation, surrounding my childhood.

Soon, I would walk through the garden to the orange blossom trees and to the Mediterranean jasmine trees, since they were not much higher than I was. I would bow down to smell them. I would even cuddle the trees' tiny branches and softly put my lips on their leaves, whispering a warm air of gratitude and acknowledgment, as I smelt their lovely white produce. I wanted to kiss the branches many times but was afraid my neighbors would judge me, should they watch me, doing so. Then I would leave them in peace without hurting them. My brother and I would spend some time every now and then by the jasmines, to reenergize, especially during our mellow moments or before exams.

If some of the tiny blossoms or jasmines fell on the ground, my brother and I would pick them up gently, climb to the second floor where my family lived, and then stick them, one by one, softly, on our *Pique Fleures*. This was really a crystal vase, with the shape of half a circle, the base lying flat on the tea table, and the top turning all around with its circumference facing the ceiling. It had tiny little holes all over, each, only wide enough to hold a few drops of water and just one of those graceful orange blossoms or jasmine flowers that would have fallen off its branch. A few minutes later, though, we would reconsider the mini-vase and return the fallen jasmines to the soil. After all, they would die with their mother's roots, next to her and be reborn again, the following year. Equally, the mother would be next to them as they faded away.

The Guava and Sabbouta fruits had a similar look but different smell; so did the mangoes, oranges, and olives, of course. They would start tickling my nostrils by mid-June all the way, until they were ripe in August or September. Then we would reap their produce, celebrate life, and share them with our family and neighbors. When Camille was born in 1958, he joined in, and by 1962 or 1963, we started having such fun in the garden and contemplating its festival of life.

Many times, we would pass by Aunt Zee and Aunt Helga (my second aunt, dad's sister and Mady's mother) on the way up to our second floor from the villa's main gate, inwards. We always cheered them on our way in and out, and they always gave us some delicious homemade cinnamon-buns, cookies, or candies. We seldom went up to the second floor through the garden's back entrance and up its cold staircase. It was always through my aunts' floor.

In 1956, when I was five and my mother had so many friends, far more diverse than Dad's church congregation which was only a five-minute walk from our home. Mom's friends were Syrians (since she was of Syrian descent from her mother's side), Greeks (her father's side), Jews, Italians, Muslims, Armenians, and Belgians from several social communities and clubs. We used to have so much fun in the garden or up in our guest's room.

She never invited more than four or five of her friends at a time, and it was such a pleasure and an overwhelming experience to hear them talk with their *old-school* mannerism and reverences. Aunt Lucie Najjar and her husband Uncle Joachim Levi were the parents of my school friend, Roland and his baby brother Davido. They, too, were of Jewish faith and would bring their decadent and famous yogurt and honey homemade cake sprinkled with powdered sugar. Then there was Aunt Olga (100 percent Greek) and Uncles Vassili and Panayiotis, also Dad's sisters, Auntie Zee and Auntie Helga (when she moved in with Auntie Zee in 1963, leaving her daughter Mady), as well as my beloved Auntie Touna, Dad's sister, too. She lived in the neighbourhood.

On other occasions, Mom would invite her sisters and their husbands; dad, Auntie Zee and Auntie Helga, would invite their sisters and brothers. The younger generations would join in too, and the villa would be full of people from both families, Mother and Dad's. Of course, during Christmas and Easter celebrations, the crowd was much bigger. Auntie Zee and Mom would become good friends during these occasions, and they would cook together. Overall, it was a happy, healthy, and genuine childhood, as it was with all of those who were born just after the war, eager to mend the grief that the war and the shift in Egyptian ruling powers had inflicted on most!

Oh, I will never forget those sandwiches, finger food, cheeses (while we could still find them), crackers, and trays of cold cuts for gatherings of four to six guests. If there were more than six guests, such as in the bigger parties, there would be Mediterranean cooking of all sorts!

Even with the 1954 independence from British colonialism and rule, things were still stable, life was manageable, and the *Future Shock* had not yet struck hard. However, when Britain and the United States withdrew their offer to help fund the construction of the Aswan High Dam, in response to Nasser's recognition of the People's Republic of China, during the height of its tensions with Taiwan, President Nasser was forced to nationalize the Suez Canal to reclaim its ownership and generate income, as mentioned earlier.

Then there was the famous Suez Crisis in 1956, followed by the social reforms programs that transferred ownership of private businesses to the new ruling party, with the intention of turning it into public ownership.

The new regime was swiftly turning to the left block while engaging in fiery Pan-Arabism programs that crossed all lines of nobility and respect to Egyptians of diverse cultural roots. This triggered the inevitable brain drain. It hit me how people could panic so much and leave so quickly, sometimes within twenty-four hours, leaving behind their lifetime family memories, vases, curtains, their cutlery! It was then that I started to capture the inevitable vibes of exile and alienation, of uprooting and marginalization, especially with people around me, including myself.

While Nasser was an idealist and an avant-garde with sufficient stomach to nationalize the canal, to end colonialism, and to dare to hope, he weakened and succumbed to his distant advisors. They made him distant from the reality of the Egyptian streets. They thrived on the West's failure to court Egypt at a time it needed it most, while Israel would receive its courtship in a manner that many regarded as inequitable. This was just the topic, then, at Cairo and Alexandria cafés with lay Egyptians. "What did we do wrong to them to deserve such treatment?" said one person to another in a grocery shop in the early sixties. I heard it, and retained it, ever since.

Egyptian families of diverse cultural roots started packing up their select belongings and leaving their land in 1957, and by 1965, 80 percent of those hundreds of thousands, even the first million and more, had left the land. Yet, amid all those ambiguities and neglect of such prominent and good families, several government officials could see through and feel the hurt in the hearts of the neglected.

Although they could do little to restore what was slipping away from Egypt's social structure, these few officials did a lot to help departing families leave, with as many belongings as they could, without stirring the climate and alerting authorities. They succeeded in many ways. I remember their stories, and I loved the love-love relationships between the departing and their helpers from the new regime, whether at the airport or at the Home Office. Unfortunately, the damage was done, and the canvass had cracked into bits and pieces. There was no way that the remaining Egyptians could paint another canvass all by themselves when there was no cohesive canvass available, if even a cheap new reinvented canvass, to paint, collectively; let alone the hardship of the departed to start a new life overseas!

One family after the other left the land, and the whole pattern was taking a crumbling domino effect. The current state of life, then, made it so difficult for many Egyptians living in Egypt, to set their own aspirations and projections and to uphold them.

Over and above all this, came the state of nonchalance and slackness by mainstream public service providers, including health services, schools, government institutions, firefighting teams, food safety, and quality control. Messy issues were getting more and more entangled within the new trends, with people's rising expectations in Egypt and with the crumbling hopes of youth. Finally, with no cohesive environment, the inevitable happened: labeling by many, and terrible fear by so few. The new regime split the country's social mosaic.

Childhood family Villa, Heliopolis, Cairo – 1985

Chapter 10
Breeding the Seeds of Fear

The Departures

In 1956, I had just ended my kindergarten years, together with my sister, at the Maria Ausiliatrici Italian School of Dominican rite. The school was in Heliopolis, just a five-minute walk from our home. I learnt to play the piano at this school, but one of the nuns made me hate it and I stopped one year later. Then, in 1957, my sister and I moved to attend preparatory school at AMC (Anglican Mission in Cairo), which was of Anglican rite and which followed (among a few other religious and educational institutions in Egypt, the Church of England) or the Franciscan Rite. We always started our day with the new National Anthem of the new Egypt, followed by prayers to suit all three faiths, Christians, Muslims, and Jews—each in a dedicated room. Then we would start classes. Several of our teachers were English. My sister was at the same school as mine, but at the girl's college, separated from the boy's college by means of a beautiful garden, called the Rose Garden. AMC was a good ten minutes away from home by car.

My English teacher, Rev. Frank Randall (I hope I spelt his name right) from Henley, England, would listen to me when I spoke in class and always said something kind and energizing to me. One day, he told me: "Raphy, you will be a prominent scriptwriter if you pursue your talent and love for drama." By 1959, the new regime asked many of my English and French teachers as well as those of nation-wide schools to leave Egypt, hence adding more absurdity to my rising curiosity about selective change, while disrupting my intellectual curiosity.

Reverend Randall would visit my parents at home with his wife, Auntie Samia (Palestinian), together with members from the congregation of Saint Michael's and All Saints Chapel (next door in Heliopolis), which still runs under the Church of England, till this day in 2008. They would visit us with others from the highest Ecclesiastical Anglican authority in downtown

Cairo, Egypt, among whom was Canon Spencer. At *All Saints Cathedral* in downtown Cairo, I used to hear various organ recitals and cantatas for Bach, Handel, Telemann, and Scarlatti. In Heliopolis's chapel, Auntie Samia's brother, Raja, was our chapel's youth leader for afternoon midweek Bible studies and for the evening campfires at the chapel's side garden. We would have roast beef and Cheddar cheese sandwiches smothered with butter and pickles, of course, after discussing the assigned scripture. It was such a joyful and enriching experience.

Late in 1959, a friend of my mother, fifty years old, tall, well-groomed, extremely good-looking woman with hazel eyes and blonde hair, came to visit us. She rolled her hair and turned it over her head, slightly to the right. She clipped it, elegantly, to the right side of her head by means of a small broach, which hoed a little white artificial rose.

Her name was Auntie Lucie Najjar. She was an Egyptian Jew with over four generations of roots in Egypt. Her husband *Joachim Diab Lévi*, was a *Maître Charcutier in* Heliopolis, Cairo (Master of Fine Cold Cuts) and an Egyptian Jew, as well. His shop's name was *Melham Abu-Diab* (Abu-Diab's meats). I remember clearly; he sold sausages, cold cuts, smoked meat and much more. Auntie Lucie's father was a cellist at the Cairo Symphony Orchestra (CSO) during the days of King Fouad in 1926 and, later, his son, King Farouk.

Auntie Lucie was the mother of my Soccer Team friend, Roland and his baby brother Davido. She was a well-spoken French linguist, not to mention her excellent command of Arabic and Hebrew. I could listen to her speak French with my mother for hours and would watch her and smell her classy perfume as she smoked her favorite Egyptian cigarettes, *Matinée* while sitting with Mom in our balcony. She smoked them with such grace and class. Oh, and Mom would brew a small pot of Greek/Turkish coffee, which, until this day, I find immensely challenging to handle without shaking. The coffee was boiled, strong, and delicious, capable of destabilizing the untrained coffee drinker.

That day in 1959 or, even later, in the early sixties, (if my memory does not fail me), she rang the doorbell, and Auntie Zee was standing next to her, upstairs, at our doorstep, of the villa's second floor (from the stairwell). She had seen her walk through the villa's garden entrance and invited her to pass through her (Auntie Zee's) residence on the first floor up, through the stairwell, to our floor, rather than leave her walk through the back garden. Besides, Auntie Zee had met her a few times over the years and knew her well. I was somewhere between seven and nine years old, then, and to be closely precise, it had to be between 1959 and 1961, a few years following the 1956 Suez crisis. When I saw her, I jumped over to kiss her, as I always did with my uncles and aunts. Only this time, I sensed such sadness and horror in her face, in her mood and her eyes! I bent my face forward and to the right and then, took one-step back, as if to withdraw in order to leave her to her space. She cuddled my neck and walked with me to our living room, followed by Auntie Zee.

"*Est-ce-que maman est là, Raphy?*" she asked, (which meant *is Mother here?*)

"*Oui, tante Lucie.*" I replied, and Auntie Zee went inside our kitchen to fetch Mom.

After the reverences and hugs and just as the coffee pot came out of the kitchen with cookies from Auntie Zee's pantry in the lower floor, up, to our living room, Auntie Lucie broke out in such emotions yet with such restraint, her eyes were flooding but she was not sobbing. Then, she spoke in French, gracefully but with a shrugged and nasal voice:

"We are leaving, Laurice!" she said.

"I don't understand. Who is leaving?" said Mom.

"Joachim [her husband], the kids, and I …"

"Leaving Egypt?" screamed Mom, with Auntie Zee patting her lap to console her.

"Yes, leaving Egypt … for good. They knocked at our door and ordered us to leave."

Then there was silence for a few seconds, and I was picking up the mood and the genuine drama in our living room. The post Suez-Canal crisis effect had started. I heard beeping sounds in my ears.

Auntie Zee said, "Who did? And when are you leaving, Lucie?"

"Thursday morning. The ruling party wants all Jews out," she said.

"This Thursday, after tomorrow?" asked Mom.

"Yes." She sighed. "I need to leave some valuables behind that I cannot sneak in my bag. We are taking two bags only but are leaving the furniture and precious articles."

"You're leaving your rosewood living room?" said Mom.

"Yes, and the vases and the carpet. I would like you to have it, Laurice."

"No, no, please," said Mom. "No Lucie. I cannot do this. Not you, not with you."

"What's wrong with it?" said Auntie Lucie.

"You know, we keep hearing these stories … and now you tell me," Mom paused, "oh my sweetheart and soul, I cannot believe it! It is horrible. I will miss you, Lucie."

"Yes … and me too. So, will you take it?" she asked Mom, imploringly.

"No, I can't, Lucie. I do not know how to do this with you. I will buy one of the three rosewood tea tables. That's what I can afford."

"Take the three," she said. "Take the whole guest set. I do not want any money. I understand. I just don't want to leave my valuables in the hands of anyone I don't know!"

"My darling, I cannot. I do not have the money. George [my dad] has been developing malicious growths in his throat and is not generating much income now, especially with the fast-growing shift to radical socialism and the threat of losing our land to the state. He does not take new legal cases and is on paid leave from the company until he is able to stand up. You know I do not work and there are the three kids. Let me buy one, just one table."

"It is not for the money, Laurice. I don't want these people to fill their households with my lifetime furniture." She broke down in tears. "I want you to keep them. Please, please! How much can you pay for the small table?"

"…Fifteen pounds." (One Egyptian pound was equal to $2.25 US then.)

"Then it is all yours, my Laurice, my darling, and you get to keep the three tables, the two vases and the bronze lady with opaline hat. Do you want me to be in tears on the plane knowing that someone strange took them? Send me someone to pick them up after seven tonight. And if you think of taking anything else, just let me know!"

They both stood up, and I moved to sit next to Auntie Zee in terror, unable to make sense of all of this. Hence, the absurdity of change and alienation was growing, and my anguish, from it all, was rising.

"Let me walk you down," said Mom to Auntie Lucie, and I heard them sobbing on the stairs.

I rushed to the balcony and looked down at Auntie Lucie as she walked out of the villa's main gate, while her husband was waiting down in his car. *"Au revoir, Tante Lucie!"* I shouted.

"Au revoir, mon ange!" she said lovingly. *Farewell, my angel.*

I never saw her again. I never knew where she went, and Mom never spoke of her again until 1980 or 1981 when she sent mother a postcard of her children and grandchildren. They had moved to Paris and then to Sao Paolo, Brazil. In 1979, Uncle Joachim passed away.

In the following few months, hundreds of thousands of fractured middle-class families had evacuated Egypt, and the new pompous state-owned media students did very little to dissuade them from leaving. This, split families apart, and many lingered behind for a few years to clear up their assets before joining the rest of their families overseas. Some succeeded in doing this and others failed. The panic persisted for over fifteen years. Among those who left was my Uncle Constantine (Dad's brother). He was forced to leave because he could no longer keep his job as Dean of Philosophy, Psychology, and Social Sciences at the University of Alexandria. Alas, he was a well-spoken liberal.

By 1977, President Sadat had locked the riddle of the remnants of the communist regimes, dismantled power groups, and started building for hope, growth, and life for all. He gave assurances to Egyptians of diverse cultural roots, who had immigrated between 1956 and 1976 to return to their lands. He was eager to compensate them and to help them reestablish themselves in Egypt.

Twenty years before, and a few days after Auntie Lucie left (1959), Mom called on us for a Family Council. She did those every now and then. One day she called upon us, and we met in the main dining room. That day, in 1958, Mom spoke of the situation on the streets of Cairo and other cities. She asked us to be careful when we spoke and never to touch political issues. She urged us to be careful not to hurt our friends and people of ethnic backgrounds. She said she expected us to deal with others as good Christians and not to be swayed by any thoughts of hate or intolerance. Mom said that she knew that "our government counted on us to uphold justice and not to be swayed by negative talk". Of course, I could sense she was downplaying the unwanted pressure imposed by the new political environment of the sixties. Mom never spoke badly about any member of the new regime, and she really wanted us not to fiddle with stuff we could not handle.

By 1965, 80 percent of the initial ethnic and brain drain had taken effect. The rest stretched over the following ten years. Nowadays, emigration persists in thousands, just like any country in the world, but not for cultural reasons (though religious *dissonance* in Egypt is active and alive).

At school, during the sixties, I remember the day our French teacher, Monsieur Balaband, told us: "So, my young ones, it is very important that we force ourselves to overcome any feelings of hate or fear. We are a classroom of three diverse cultures and faiths. Do not allow yourselves be swayed by the challenges of our evolution, and let us continue to love one another. This will be our secret and our code of honor."

To me, all of those who left Egypt were fruits of a tree, rich in history, values, and knowledge. To say that the fruits dwindle with change was fair and unfortunate. Yet, we all knew that Egypt was a tree that would continue to branch and turn over its leaves year after year, just like my favorite jasmine tree and the orange-tree blossoms had, in our garden. The question was how could we nurture its branches, revive its soil, and remove the bad roots so we would continue to harvest its fruit for all those who lived on its land, just as we had for thousands of years. How could we nurture its branches if we took away the tree's freedom to spread love; how can we do it if we do not learn how to plant it, collectively and in fellowship. After all, we all eat from it. More than that, we had to help this rich tree by assuming our roles so that she would lay there happy and content. Egypt needed a break to reinvent herself again, and again, and again, over the centuries and forever, just as she has always done.

In fact, it was in Egypt that the Holy Family sought refuge, until Herod, the inventor of infanticide, died. Several of the Holy Family's caves, shelters, and wells in Egypt are still there to witness all this; so is the well of Moses in old Cairo and so are the human remains of Jacob's Jews in Goshen-Damietta, Egypt! There, the remains of Joseph, son of Jacob, stayed interred for over four hundred years until Moses moved them with him, during the great Exodus, to Sachem in the Holy Land! It was in Alexandria that the Gospel of Saint Mark was translated from Hebrew to Greek in the year AD 150. It was Saint Mark who spread the word into Egypt in AD 40, just as Saint Paul the Apostle did in his voyages heading north to Asia Minor and Europe. Christ's Egyptian followers have grown and multiplied ever since the preaching of Saint Mark in Egypt, to the extent that in the early years of Christianity in Egypt (first century), many Christian martyrs chose to give their lives to God, than to compromise Christ for the Romans. They defied the terrible period of Christian persecution perpetuated by Decius and Valerian of the Roman Empire between 249 and 260 and, a few centuries later, under a few Arab rulers, following the Arab Conquests of Egypt in AD 641-3, resenting coercion.

It was in Egypt that her monks set the first monastic rituals of our planet and put them to practice. This was in an Orthodox temple called the *Deir Mar Antonious* (Monastery of Saint Anthony of Egypt). It was built around AD 356 on the mountain of Al-Qalzam in the city of Zaafarana by the Red Sea, five hundred kilometers south of the city of Suez and less than fifty kilometers east of the ancient city of Thebes (now known as Luxor). However, while it may have been St. Anthony who founded the monastic way of life by inspiring others around the globe, his disciples Amathas and Macarius affirm that Paul of Thebes (Luxor, Egypt) was said to have been the originator of the practice. He was born in AD 248 and died in AD 343. Saint Anthony had heard of him and looked for him in the desert, not far from his (Saint Anthony's) chapel only months before Paul died. This latter gave Saint Anthony his monastic secrets and record of his devotion.

Back in 1930, there were at least seventy-five thousand Egyptian Jews in Egypt, and the numbers reached eighty-six thousand in 1948. However, I believe that this was an underestimation. I got other numbers from a few rabbis in synagogues of Cairo and its outskirts, during the seventies, who showed me some of their records from their libraries. The numbers I got were such that there had to be at least 150,000 over the last two centuries (specifically from 1750). There were far more Jews, in Egypt, at the birth of Christ until the Islamic invasions under Amr Ibn-El-Assi between AD 641 and 644, than after WW2. Many did not leave with Moses (some twelve centuries before Christ) and chose to stay in their land of Egypt. Traditionally, only twenty percent of the Jews of Egypt left with Moses during the Exodus. One of the most prominent recent names I could trace in my recent research was the Qattawi family (amongst others), one of whom dad worked for. He had given an order to pay a check to dad when he developed throat cancer in 1959. Dad would treat his cancer in London, England, at Saint Mary's Clinic. Dad received the check, and Mom called Monsieur Qattawi to thank him for his generosity and kindness. Dad lived for another twenty years and Monsieur Qattawi left Egypt in 1960, one year after he had given dad the check to for his treatment.

Overall, the *Future Shock* in Egypt broke the mosaic and cracked a canvass of over 150 years of multicultural diversity, interaction, priceless interdependence, indescribable growth and interdenominational maturity. As for the former cultural interdependence, soul and homeland character, I thought, we can easily bid it farewell, for now. Many of those who left overseas longed for their motherland, even to this day in 2008; they longed for it, the way they knew it so many years ago, with all its diversity; all its tolerance, including me.

Right now, in 2008, Montreal, I am truly tired! I am preparing myself for my retreat in the city of Magog, after years of corporate bullying, similar alienation as that of the homeland and exile. I am seeking to reclaim my freedom and independence from mind games and corporate coercion.

Monastery of St. Anthony of Egypt AD 356
Rebuilt across the centuries
The actual chapel is further, beyond the entrance
Father of worldwide monastic rituals

Chapter 11
The Retreat—1
Today, by Lake Memphre-Magog

It is Thursday morning in Magog on September 11, 2008. I am sipping my tea and eating my cheese roll at my motel's restaurant. It is a blessing to be in Quebec's Eastern Townships, surrounded by such beautiful lakes and valleys, small homes and alleys, by villagers and families.

Already, in a few hours, I cleaned my state of mind, a little, from the horror of my last six months at the North-Side hotel, where a few have marginalized and bullied me to leave. Last week, this pressure reached a point where few of my peers and superiors shifted to a new level of hurtful comments, some of which were "old man" and "silly, silly, old man" and "You are at the end of your career; your junior employee will take over from you soon" to make my life miserable, so as to leave. (This is in addition to public bullying, rivalry, and passive-aggressive treatment; which is typical of a dark corporate culture.) Last week, I heard one of my support team-members make this comment: "Raphy, who will be your date for the Christmas party; your mom?" I gazed into his eyes with intense power and pity for his classless joke. Of course, they did this to deplore me, and they failed because I sustained the hurt but decided to seek refuge in this week's divine retreat. I had developed the habit of having a bite with my lovely but ailing mother at lunch break, a few blocks away from my office and my apartment.

The best way to calm down, I thought, was to return to nature. "If they broke me, they cannot break my spirit," I said to myself. Hurting is one thing; loving life is the opposite. Magog is breathtaking, as I discover it with you. Only two hours east of Montreal by car, Magog stands out as a lovely hamlet of stunning beauty, little hills, alleys, waterfronts of various lakes (sometimes extensions of lake Memphre-Magog), little houses, dining places, and boutique hotels. The original inhabitants of this land are the Abenaki Indians; they date back to the period prior to 1600. After the French settlements that started in AD 1608, many American *British loyalists* moved up from USA to

Canada (following the United States independence of 1776). Later, another tide of immigrants arrived from Ireland to Magog, with Britain's acquisition of Northern Ireland in 1850. Some of them were Catholic Irish and others were victims of the great Potato Famine of Ireland in 1840. These, too, fled from their homeland, just as many Egyptians did, but for different reasons.

The motel (*pension*), I am staying at is on Merry Street, facing one side of Lake Memphre-Magog, and is only separated from it by the twenty-four feet wide *Merry Street*. I would walk out from my twelve-room motel, turn right on Merry for fifty feet, and would find myself on Rue Principale's intersection (perpendicular to Merry) where some of the city's café, shops and restaurants are located across five hundred feet to the right; and Rue Principale's Panorama Lake-walkway, runs to the left (of Merry Street).

The Motel in Magog, Québec

If I am standing in my motel room on the second floor, looking through my window (which is just on top of the motel's main entrance on Merry Street), I will capture Merry Street first, and then the humungous lake of Memphre-Magog, which, from my window, looks close to a rectangle. Merry Street would be the east tangent of the rectangle-shaped lake. Rue Principale that intersects with Merry Street stretches to the right of my window and the lake and is parallel to it, representing the right tangent of the rectangular lake. This means that if I were exiting my motel and heading North, on Merry Street (right) to Principale Street; instead of walking toward the right on Rue Principale through the cafés and restaurants, I would cross Merry Street and walk on the left pavement (the panorama route) of Rue Principale. This panorama route is parallel to the lake and, of course, to its right.

The right tangent of Lake Memphre Magog
Seen from my window in 2008

From my window, I could also see the distant left side of the lake that is several kilometers wide but could not capture its end. Ideally, it would be parallel to Rue Principale and its panorama walkway but on the extreme left. Hence, the

Principale Street side was the right tangent of the rectangle, and the far left end of the lake was the left tangent of the rectangle displaying distant, hazy hills, trees, sky and fog.

Both right and left tangents of the lake led to a main street called *Chemin des Pères* (Street of the Fathers, meaning monks) beyond the deep lake if I were to stand watching it from my window. *Chemin des Pères* is parallel to Merry, but at the other end of the lake. The Abbey is on *Chemin des Pères,* up to the far left.

Yesterday, I walked down to Merry Street and moved a few steps to the right with a cup of cappuccino. Then I crossed Merry Street to its waterfront and turned left on rue Principale's stunning panoramic sidewalk. The lake was on my left. As I walked further ahead on this sidewalk (heading to *Chemin des Pères),* with my back to my motel, I saw a green park on my right side, stretching all the way up, parallel to the lake and its sidewalk. The park displayed wooden benches and tables every twenty feet, still on my right side. It spread for four kilometers ahead. It was fifty feet wide (left to right), where tables and benches spread, for quite some distance, upwards. All this led to *Chemin des Pères* that turns left beyond the lake to the Abbey (Monastery of Saint Benedict by the Lake). On my right, where the benches were located, stacks of maple trees surrounded the tables. Some of their leaves had started turning brown already, and others ginger. A few leaves, had already dried up and fallen on the wet soil.

Then, I sat by one of the benches and went into a trance. I took several deep breaths and started gazing at the portrait while folding my arms toward my chest to protect myself from the chilly September day. The sound of the falling leaves kissing the moist lawn as they touched it, the smell of the wet ground, the sensation of the fresh but dark fall breeze, the wet ground, the intertwining gray clouds and sunny cracks appearing in the sky uncovering glimpses of blue every now and then—it all engulfed me. Now I see the seagulls floating in front of me, slightly to my left, in sets of two, four, and eight; they are floating over the gentle ripples of the lake and lifted by its romantic waves, often swinging gracefully to the left and then to the right, depending on where the fall wind and its subsequent water-tide leads them. All of this almost completed the portrait, but something else awed me. These seagulls were free; they danced ballet and married nature. They did so in fellowship as I watched them hoping to be part of their own portrait, part of something that surrounded them, simply by dancing on its canvass. This, reminded me of how I used hop on the playground, fifty years earlier, with my soccer-team friends, in our villa's garden or during Bible studies.

Across the green lawn to my right, I chose a wooden bench adjacent to a rectangular wooden table, typical of the ones we use in picnics, with family or friends. I sank on one of them and breathed deeply, filling my belly with clear air while lying on my right side, until I flew up to the clouds. It took me no more than a few moments of struggling to overcome the fragments of the past few years. Somehow, though, my eyes were fixed on the lake, and I decided to elevate myself to the level of clouds. I think I did so. Another dimension of nature had lifted me from my bench and liberated me from my thoughts, from my zone. It gently delivered me to the boundless sky, not with the saints but up in the arms of infinity, free of all boundaries and labels and absorbed by a timeless rainbow. Then I saw it all from up there; I saw the lake, the trees, the other side of the lake, the hills, the shy sun cracking through the September clouds, intermittently. Then I flew and became part of the clouds, part of nature. Then I became nature.

Content as I felt to have perceived myself as nature, after having extinguished it from my life for so long, I knew I had to go back again to discover more. I descended to my bench and noticed that my cappuccino cup was empty. Earlier this morning (at 7:30), I had a tea and some cereal at the hotel's tiny and pleasant restaurant.

My motel has an overtone of wood. Going down to the breakfast lounge on the wooden staircase over two floors, and smelling fresh homemade coffee, was a pleasure. The women at the reception desk just ahead and to the left of the lobby's door smiled at me. Each time I went for breakfast at this hotel, I would feel important and start "chilling" and *living my life*. I engaged in a few conversations with another person in the food lounge and found that she has a rich baggage of history. Then she took interest in mine, filled her cup, and sat with me in a most professional and friendly manner. I regained some of my lost confidence in a matter of seconds and started my day smiling. Alas, there were still genuine humans around.

It is already 9:40 a.m.; I must leave my bench and go for a snack at a family-owned café on *Rue Principale's* east side and then walk back to the motel, change my sweat pants and shirt to prepare for my visit to the abbey. Eucharist is served at 11:00, and the drive would take me ten minutes on Rue Principale on to Chemin des Pères, and then left for sixteen kilometers upward to the ravishing abbey of Saint Benoit du Lac (Saint Benedict). I walked to the café and then signaled to its young waiter for my snack. "A cappuccino, please," I said in French, "a little strong this time, and a croissant with a slice of cheddar; no butter, please. And could you get me the check, as I must rush." *"Bien sur, monsieur,"* she said, which is *"Certainly, sir."* She did, and then I finished my meal and ran to the hotel to change.

It is now 10:20 a.m. I went to my room, changed my clothes, and grabbed a bottle of cold water for my drive. I had one last look from the window, across the lake, from right to left and then deep inside, behind it, uphill toward the abbey until I could clearly spot it.

The abbey was situated exactly twenty kilometers away from my motel. In other words, I would have to pick my car from the motel, make a quick right on Merry Street and a quick left on Rue Principale, and then drive for about four kilometers parallel to the lake on its right side. I drove four kilometers on rue Principal until I saw a sign that said *Abbey St. Benoit du Lac* that pointed left to the hilly street called Chemin des Pères (Route of the Priests) and drove up for about sixteen kilometers before reaching the abbey. While driving uphill and looking left, I noticed the other side of the lake and spotted Merry Street and my motel. I continued driving, half-dreaming as I went uphill, looking at the trees and the lake to my left while turning my head occasionally to the gorgeous set of hillside houses to my right, interrupted by one or two country boutique hut-style restaurants every now and then. I got to the front of the abbey at 10:53 a.m., seven minutes before mass and the Eucharist celebration. Every morning at eleven, the monks throw a feast of prayers, monitions, and Eucharist. Every evening at six, they throw another mass for meditation, adoration, and Gregorian chants.

When I reached the abbey, I parked my car on the right side of the little hill facing the monastery's front gate, two hundred feet before it, and walked through the alley toward the breathtaking divine site. I saw seven or eight monks walking solemnly across the monastery's main gate. Then, I came across local families, farmers, wives, husbands, and children, senior citizens, some with wheelchairs, all around me, heading toward the monastery's gate. I got that feeling of *déjà-vu*; I felt at home, in my birthplace many years ago, as if I was entering Saint Michael's and All Saints Chapel in Heliopolis, Cairo, Saint Cyril's Basilica in Qurba Square, Heliopolis or, later, at the Basilica of our *Lady of Lourdes* in France which I had visited with mother in the eighties. Only this time the congregation was made of local families. Villagers have taken the habit of seeking nourishment in the Eucharist, while in fellowship with others, right in the soothing arms of nature.

Of course, there were quite a few others like me, searching for peace and solace. I forced myself through the dispersed, humble crowd onto the monks before getting to the iron gates. I bowed my head with a little smile to two of the monks whose faces crossed mine on the way in. They did not react; they were in another world. They were serene and in a divine state of preparation for the feast. I smiled again, with restraint, turning my head forward to the gates and through them.

As I entered, I noticed a few doors to the left and right of the wall facing the main gate from inside, and a few others to the left and right of the actual wall of the gate where I stood. The monks used them, mostly, as offices, dormitories, registration booths, and a small library. *Of course, the bulk of monks and retreaters' dormitories stood elsewhere.* To the extreme left of the wall facing the main gate was a hallway that was intriguingly mystical and solemn. It indicated, in French, *Paroisse*, meaning Parish. Just before the hallway, and to its right, I saw a staircase leading to one or two floors below. I saw a sign, indicating *canteen* where the monks sold the products they manufacture: varying from different types of cheese, honey, maple syrup, recordings of their chants, candies, chocolates and so much more. This I visited on my last day. Right now, I had to rush through the hallway, on my left, to get to the parish and join the feast.

The hallway was almost 180 feet long and fifteen feet wide. Going through the hallway to the parish, its left wall had windows every twenty feet that overlooked the glorious lake, preceded by trees and agricultural fields and followed, at distance, by Rue Principale. To the right was another wall that bore the portrait of various monks that had led this community since its creation and some history in French and English.

Benedictine Monk Dom Paul Vanier built the monastery on the original chapel of 1912. It was the Benedictine Community of Saint Wandrille of Belgium, which had commissioned him. This Benedictine community originated from France that exiled it in 1901 by anticlerical laws in France.

The monastery was built in homage to Saint Benedict (Saint Benoit), who was born in Nursia, a small town in Umbria, Italy, around AD 480. He went to Rome to pursue his studies. However, the corruption of student life then led him to separating himself from the mob and to seeking refuge in God within solitude, in a grotto close to the present city of Subiaco, Italy. In AD 529, he had to leave with a few disciples to build the first Benedictine Monastery in Mount Cassino, Italy, under pressure. There he set down his liturgy for a monk's life, following earlier monastic rituals that were inspired from the earliest monastic disciplines of the Monasteries of Saint Anthony of Egypt in AD 356 and previously, Saint Paul of Egypt in AD 248. Saint Benedict died in 547. In the year 817, the monastic reforms were set, based on the *Rules for Monks* that Saint Benedict had laid out; this is why he is considered the Patriarch of the Monks of the West.

Over the centuries, the Rules of a Monk's Life according to Saint Benedict developed and flourished. Benedictines, followers of Christ according to Saint Benedict, found joy in searching for God, worshipping Him in seclusion and adoring Him in peace and penitence. Following the French Revolution, Benedictine life flourished in 1833 in *Solesmes*, France, under Dom Prosper Guéranger but, soon, disappeared in France and moved to Belgium.

Upon his arrival in Canada, from Belgium, Dom Vanier received the blessings, support, and approval of the Bishop of Sherbrook, the neighboring city to Magog. Five monks were chosen to assist him, four French from the exiled community of Saint-Wandrille in Belgium and one French Canadian. It was under Dom Léonce Crenier, from 1931 to 1944, that the monks of Saint Benoit Du Lac grew in all respects and became a true monastic community.

In 1935, Saint-Benôit-du-Lac became an autonomous house. In 1938, the monks decided to build a monastery and on September 23, 1952, the monastery was raised to the status of an abbey, and the Right Reverend Dom Odule Sylvain was elected as the first abbot of Saint-Benoit-du-Lac.

God blessing the project, the monks were able to celebrate the solemn dedication of their church on December 4, 1994, on the eighty-second anniversary of its foundation. On May 20, 2006, the Right Reverend Dom André Laberge was elected third abbot of Saint-Benoit-du-Lac.

The abbey has now been expanded to its present state. It features beautiful hallways, dormitories, and a library, let alone vast fields of agricultural and animal produce.

While the highlight of Dominican monastic life is based on penance and devotion, so is the highlight of Benedictine monastic life based on obedience and silence. These are manifestations of humility, which is an important virtue in a monk's spiritual character. Saint Benedict devoted a long chapter of his life to it. He compared our life in this world to a ladder that the Lord, having respect to our humility of heart, raises up to heaven.

One of its gripping marvels is, the endless hallway of colored small mosaic tiles not exceeding one square inch, starting from the gates of the abbey and leading to the door of the parish. I walked through it, having read the inscriptions to my right briefly, and then later in detail. As I entered the parish of the abbey, I noticed its high ceilings, arcades, and thick walls. The echo of every single move or breath was another of its rich experiences. I sat down in the parish and bowed for a few seconds. Then I rose and saw about forty monks coming in and spreading themselves into two groups across the altar, one to the left and another to the right.

Mass started. However, it was different. It was solemn, peaceful, and extremely profound. I was not sure, if with all my thoughts, I was fit enough to earn the blessings of the moment. However, looking at the rest humbled me, and I felt human again, rightfully, in search for peace, search for God. The celebration of Eucharist started, with about three hundred people in the parish. I accepted mine with gratefulness and went back to my seat to pray. By noon, the mass was over and the monks started walking out at a very slow pace, in groups of eight at a time, four to the right and four to the left. Each time they did, they bowed to the altar and left the scene from the respective door, whether left or right, and so on until they had all gone. They all wore white.

There was no shaking of hands of monks after mass, just a solemn exit. Then I walked out through the mosaic hallway to the main gate, this time with the windows to my right. I exited the abbey and descended a few marble steps. After descending, I crossed to the hill that was opposite the abbey's gates and to the right of the street where I parked my car. Once I crossed to the hill base, I ascended another set of metal stairs and reached the tip of the hill. I chose a cold and wet table and bench that were facing the monastery and its main gate. It was past noon. Many were preparing to walk or drive back. Some went up the hill, with me, for more soul-searching. The monks were most probably, preparing to have lunch.

A few minutes later, the bells rang. They must have started eating. It was not a very sunny day. The skies were gray, and the ground I had walked on was wet and muddy. My shoes kept drowning a few inches in it, each time I moved my legs. It was quite humid, and my feet were wet. Some sprinkles of dew covered me; it had poured the night before. My wooden table was already humid and just as wet, and so was my notebook as I scribbled these thoughts. I wiped the bench under me, using my hand and a few sheets from my notebook. After all, I was not in jeans; I was in formal gray trousers, a blue striped shirt, and a black midseason blazer. My head was turning cold, and so was my nose.

It was all part of the moment. I had a spare pen with which to back up myself, so as not to lose my thoughts. The following morning, I arrived twenty minutes before the 11:00 a.m. service, so as to settle down calmly, before the service. This way, by coming earlier, I could prepare my thoughts while sitting in the heart of nature, for the feast of penitence at the parish. Tonight, Friday, as well, I will come back, twenty minutes early, for the evening chants. They start at 6:00 p.m. Right now, I am facing the monastery. It is lunchtime. There are several trees around me; a few bushes, and several squirrels slipping through the moist leaves.

There is more movement though; it is not over. Birds are hopping over the remaining green branches, some singing nocturnal tunes, some overflying me, and others picking the remaining red leaves from the fallen trees' branches. They pick them with their beaks, flying around and in between those squirrels as they crawl through the fallen leaves. As well, the birds dip themselves in the refreshing moisture of the ground, dropping the leaves from their beaks, nibbling on some ground-ridden crumbs, picking them up and bursting up to the sky, right into the multi-shaded gray, orange, and red clouds, on this early September evening. Then, I feel that I am doing just the same, leaving my pen, floating between the ground-ridden leaves while lifted with the grace and freedom of those air-born birds, and grounded by the humility and tenderness of these crawling squirrels. The fast-moving clouds are covering me; mesmerizing and rooting me to the center of a universe in action; one I immersed myself into only over the last twenty-four hours. It is dark, though, for an early afternoon. Autumn foliage is but too imminent. I turn my head left, (to the left of the Abbey), staring at the green park at the top of some hills, and gradually slipping downhill; I see small houses that are within a sealed wooden fence. This, too, is monks' land. It must be some of their dormitories.

Further, left and downwards, I capture more land, fruits, and other crops continuing clockwise, from the left of the Monastery, and rightwards behind it all the way to its right fence and forward just to the right side of my table where I parked my car. Beyond those hundreds of acres, starting from my left side runs the sublime lake surrounding the monastery. I moved my head up and forward. I saw the monastery again, but this time I stretched my view to include everything, from left to right. I saw the lake, and then beyond the lake to the far end, the fields around the abbey, the dormitories and the cheese- and food-manufacturing huts, the trees, the bushes, squirrels, birds, the dew, the clouds, and the worshippers scattered all around me.

I breathed for twenty minutes in total seclusion. Then, suddenly, I was no longer contemplating nature. I became part of it again. Then I became nature, just as I did earlier, lifted by divinity, and then I was grounded by humility.

Soon, the post-luncheon bells rang, calling on the monks to pray before they rested. Gradually, I came back to my senses and decided to drive back to my motel.

I did so in ecstasy and awe. Then, I made it to my motel at 2:00 p.m. I parked my car; I changed my clothes for my sportswear and walked back to Rue Principale's sidewalk by the lake with my pen and notebook. I brought a sweatshirt with me and an overcoat in case it rained. Then I stretched over one of the benches and slept for more than an hour, preparing for another walk and for my evening visit to monks' land for the chanting. I needed to relax.

Happy are they who dwell in Thy house:
they still can sing Thy praise!
Happy are those whose strength is in Thee
roads open wide in their hearts!
—Psalm 83, 5–6

Chapter 12
The Retreat—2

It is 8:15 on Friday morning, and here I am having breakfast at the motel's lounge. The plan is for me to do my soul-searching again by Rue Principale's lake-walk before driving up to the abbey for the 11:00 a.m. service and, in the evening, far before the 6:00 p.m. for the chanting service. Last night, I visited the abbey for the evening chants but was tired when I left. I drove to a steakhouse, bought myself a steak and cheese sandwich, and went to my room to eat it with some lemonade, which I had in my fridge. After that, I watched the news and slept early.

By 3:00 p.m. today, I was well rested and able to make it before 5:30 p.m. at the Abbey, thirty minutes before evening mass. The monks were already walking to its gates, just as they were this morning and yesterday morning. This time they were dressed in black, just as they were last night. I learnt, later, that during the Eucharist feast of the morning, they had to wear white and in the evening, black. The atmosphere was getting dark, and the ground was soggy. The weather did not intimidate me, since I decided to live the whole moment again tonight. Minutes passed by, and just before 6:00 p.m., the bells started ringing. I hurried down the metal staircase, crossed the entrance to the abbey, went through its wooden doors, and then across the mosaic hallway to the parish, where I succumbed immediately, with the rest, in adoration before listening to Benedictine chanting.

The following morning, I woke up late for my walk, so I decided to finish my breakfast and rush for my Eucharist mass before returning to buy some lunch and stretch by the lakeside for a couple of hours.

At 12:30, I was back at my motel. I parked the car, made an early checkout for the following morning, bought two sandwiches and a huge tea in my portable thermos flask, and went to sit by the walk side on one of its benches. This was my retreat's grand finale.

After finishing my lunch, I stretched on one of the benches, closed my eyes, and went into a trance but not quite into a full sleep. Somehow, all of this took me back to my dad's small farm, in Egypt during the fifties and the sixties. I remembered the scent of lime and orange trees, good soil, and even manure. Then, in my trance, I heard the sound of the good, old farm lake and the distributer of irrigation water. There was the sound of chickens, squawking and the flapping of their wings. I could even rekindle the smell of their fresh hatched eggs, laying on hay, as well as their waste, as I turned back to the year 1958, around May or June. My baby brother was hardly six months old; there was him, my sister, my parents, Auntie Zee, and me. Then I went into my trance and closed my eyelids.

*Lake Memphre-Magog panorama waterfront
Where I wrote most of this testimony*

Chapter 13
Passions and Roots-1
Snapshots of my childhood

On Christmas week, in December of 1958, my brother Camille was almost one year old. He was a Capricorn, born on January 4, of the same year. My parents were preparing a modest Christmas table and we were expecting a few relatives. Mother did not want to stretch the celebrations because dad had undergone a serious throat operation in England. She returned to Cairo, the month before. Previously, dad would assume the role of Santa, to all of us, and to all his nephews and nieces as we gathered at Auntie Zee's lower apartment, huge balcony and garden.

There were always two Christmas trees at the villa, one on Auntie Zee's floor and another on the upper floor, where mom would teach us how to put together, Christ's manger, with as little as cardboard paper, clay statuettes and talcum powder. By the age of twelve, I, together with my baby brother, Camille, started connecting some wires, 1.5 volts lamps and torch batteries, imported from East Germany, to mount our own manger.

Mom's Christmas table always featured a home roast leg-of-lamb, smothered with good Egyptian red wine presented with steamed vegetables and Mediterranean rice, (cooked in a pot containing diced onions tossed in butter, spices, dried raisins, walnuts and water), spinach patties, salad, and a trout or sea bass fish with homemade mayonnaise and capers, diced gherkins and steamed sweet beet. Mother made delicious trifle and hazelnut-chocolate torte sprinkled with bits and pieces of crunchy caramel for desert. Dad's farm would send us double cream, country bread, free-run eggs and fruits of the season.

As I graduated from hotel school, I would always contribute with one or two dishes and when I joined airlines, I would buy imported wine and liqueur from Italy or Switzerland.

Camille would join me putting the tree together as well as Christ's manger. I would stretch up on a ladder hanging decorations and Camille would help me, standing below the ladder and passing on the pins, bells and lights. Wrapping paper and scotch tape were spread everywhere.

Every year, at Saint Michael Parish, next door, the whole congregation, would engage with two bazaars; one on Christmas and one on Easter. Women of the congregation would display their baked goods, jams or knitwear. Men would stand-up by the sandwich and food booths or, even, games tables. Camille and I started taking over one or two of the games tables in 1967 when I was sixteen and he was nine. He would love it and giggle like an angel as he stood by me. Then, we made popcorn, (occasionally overcooked) using a displaceable flame, casserole and oil. Our Bishop always blessed the event before and after. We always worked in fellowship and our Divine Shepherd was always watching over us. We continued doing so, until Easter 1975. After that, something grievous happened and God chose another plan for our angel brother.

Between the colors of our celebrations, the smell of season delicacies or good food we were only one-step away from Christmas carols. These featured the usual J. S. Bach's *Christmas Oratorio* and Handle's *The Messiah* on Christmas week or J. S. Bach's Passion Music, on Easter and the usual John Stainer's *The Crucifixion*; thanks to our 1946 *Garrard* record player and some 30 long play discs (78rpms) that Auntie Zee kept. Nothing seemed to add more joy to our family's lives, than these naïve, simple and genuine moments of fellowship.

On Christmas Eve, Saint Michael's and All Angels Parish, next door would always feature a choral surprise. On December 23, 1965, I joined the church choir and made my first musical contribution (debut), ever. The choir of our Parish was run under the leadership of its capable Music Director Mrs. Rose Freeman, of Palestinian roots, who had moved to Cairo after the 1948 war with Israel. The parish was packed and a few remaining missionaries from my school, would join. There was always a representative of the Church of England and his family, joining the congregation.

Saint Michael's and all Saints Church in Heliopolis, Cairo

That day, Mrs. Freeman assigned to me the role of Alto for an Aria from JS Bach's Christmas Oratorio. I was fourteen. Her lead singers were the great Mr. Christo (of Greek Orthodox faith) and Mrs. Freeman's husband, Mr. Freeman, an English of Jewish faith whom she had married in Palestine in 1946 as well as Ms. Suzanne Boutros, the English teacher at AMC. We presented excerpts of the stunning *Christmas Oratorio* and Mr. Christos voice roared with an intense flame of faith in our Parish. The peak of his passion was always felt when he sang this Oratrio's tenor aria *Frohe Hirten, eilt, ach eilet*, meaning *Merry shepherds, haste, haste!* These days will never be forgotten!

On Boxing Day, for fifteen years starting 1965, still when I was fourteen, I had developed the habit of visiting my aunts and uncles in Heliopolis for fifteen to thirty minutes each, for a total of about five or six visits. I loved hugging them and acting like a grownup extending my family's Christmas wishes. This, too, made me feel important. I would earn a chocolate, usually a *Japonnaise* (a classy chocolate truffle from

Groppi's Confectionary, filled with caramel and chocolate fudge, and covered with powdered Swiss chocolate, then wrapped in two layers of paper; one silver and the other in a red transparent film). I would also enjoy a *Finikia* (a Greek soft cookie made of orange, cinnamon, juice, and sometimes covered with powdered sugar). This came with a drink of cherry brandy or a little shot of Drambuie. I loved visiting them and I was rebuilding my own character, genuinely.

    Of course, when I was younger (on Boxing Day, too), I would help mom and dad, receiving them and hosting them with mom's French Pastries (Gâteau de Savoyards) and, what not.

    Easter eve, my cousins, brother, sister and I would join in the Easter Procession between several churches of all rites, Copt Orthodox, Greek Orthodox, Roman Catholic, Greek Catholic, Maronite and Anglican (all in the same neighborhood). Our parents would be inside the Greek Orthodox parish attending devotional rituals, prayers and chants. All through the neighborhood surrounding these six churches, the procession would comprise thousands of youth, holding crosses, candles and white flags. We chanted Christ is risen in Greek. This was a Byzantine hymn known to all Christians in the Mediterranean of all faiths. The chant dates back to the 8th century and the voice of celebrants in the procession roared, filling the air. It says in Greek: '*Christos Anesti ek nekron, thanato thanaton patisas, kai tis en tis mnimasi zoin harisamenos*. In English, "*Christ is risen from the dead, trampling down death by death, and to those in the tombs, granting life.*" Neighboring shop owners, of all faiths, would join the celebration and strip bakers would offer pastries and Greek Bagels *Koulouria* all along the shops' gates and across the pavement. The people of Egypt were always united in heart and soul. In fact, all Egyptians solemnly shared their diverse religious celebrations, in fellowship, with immense respect and affection. The cohesion was so beautiful and heartfelt. The procession would last until 2 am and the following morning we would rush for the very early morning Holy Communion.

Papa, Mon Amour

Back to one of those beautiful mornings at dad's farm, in late May 1958, two years after the 1956 Suez Canal Crisis, my mother gathered us, three children, on the balcony of our countryside home. They used to call it in Arabic (*Saraya*), which really is a Turkish attribute for castle. Of course, this was no castle. We just had a hut, a nice hut with a wide wooden deck overlooking fruits and vegetables.

The farmers would bring us fresh cream, milk, honey, corn, rye bread, fresh eggs of the day, and lots of fresh fruit, cucumbers, and tomatoes. Oh how delicious those (over easy) eggs were. I will never forget their genuine taste, to this day, in Magog.

Mom and Auntie Zee helped cook us the eggs and made tea. Soon, we started dipping the bread in eggs, and then in honey and cream, until we had devoured the whole stuff. Mom invited some of the farmers to join us. One of them was Hanouna, a beautiful young villager, daughter of the land supervisor, and another girl who was a friend of hers. Hanouna means *compassionate*. After tidying up, mother called us for one of her family chats.

Mom said to us three children: "Your father has an illness which we must address; he has throat cancer. Now, we heard of a good treatment in England called Cobalt Medical Treatment, and he and I must leave very soon, by mid September, to Saint Mary's Clinic in London. The difficult part is that we have many clearances to obtain from the Egyptian Home Office before we can move. On the other side, this is a very good hospital, capable of making miracles. Auntie Zee will take care of you, and I want you to take care of her, as well. We are all one family, and I count on you to support her; promise?"

My sister was overwhelmed and asked mother: "Are we going to see him when you return?"

"Of course you will, my love," said Mom.

"Okay, Ma, we promise to help Auntie Zee," Nora and I said.

Auntie Zee was holding my brother, Camille, and cuddling him. After all, there was no longer that old sentiment that some members of my father's family had shown, occasionally, to my mother. She loved Camille so much. I looked at Dad and pursed my lips in bewilderment and sorrow.

After that short break at the farm, we all returned to our villa in Heliopolis, Cairo. Mom was trying desperately to keep her calm. She said that she would not change our plans for a month vacation in Alexandria. In the meantime, she was taking daddy to his throat specialist, a well-known and prominent physician in Egypt. Following extensive diagnosis and evaluation, Doctor Mahfouz called Mom one day in June, and I heard her tell him, "Yes, yes … I understand. Thank you. Thank you. Will you prepare me the medical report?" Then she hung up.

"What's wrong, Mommy?" I said.

"Nothing, sweetheart; dad has to go for the operation immediately, and the doctor will prepare a medical report to present to the new authorities so that they allow us to take some money out of Egypt, so that we can give him the right cure." Dad was 70 years old then. (Born 1889)

"Will they understand?"

"I am sure they will, son. They just want to regulate these matters." Mom was bluffing.

"Okay, Mommy!"

Mom prepared for Dad's travel and hers. Dad's workplace gave him a check for his medical costs and some other expenses. Monsieur Qattawi, his superior, had ordered that check. Mom never stopped thanking him. Monsieur Qattawi was the son of a prominent two-time Egyptian Cabinet Minister and President of the Sephardic Jews Association of Egypt. His father was born in Egypt in 1861 and died in Egypt in 1942 (my father would tell me, and I would take notes). His son (Dad's boss) followed his same line of business until he left Egypt in 1961 and resigned as CEO of La Compagnie de *Reforme Agricole d'Égypte* (The Agricultural Reform Company of Egypt). Mom booked Dad's spot at the London clinic for early September that year (1958), a few months before, with the help of the throat specialist.

Now she had to go to the Egyptian Home Office, known as *Mogamaa*, to get the necessary exit visas for her and Dad, as well as permission to leave with sufficient money or money order for the operation and for her stay in London. Under the revolutionary socialist rule, no one could leave Egypt without screening; carrying unauthorized transfers was a felony, punishable by law. Of course, by that time, the new cabinet controlled everything. It was very hard to go through this process. Ultimately, Mom would almost lose patience and break into tears after her endless visits to the *Mogamaa*, day after day, for three, four, and even five hours each time.

On one of those days in late June, and just before we prepared for our month vacation to Alexandria, Mom was doing her routine visit to the Egyptian Home Office and was still asked to return the following morning for more clearances. It was quite a frustrating experience, and she was reaching a point where she felt that there was nothing more to do in order to obtain her clearances. Subsequently, dad would have had to accept his dark fate. On her way out, heartbroken for Dad, she saw a high-ranked officer, a colonel, and I believe his name, was Abdel-Ghaffar Azmy. "He was a childhood friend whom I had not recognized at first," she said, "and we played volleyball in the street with my sisters and the neighbors when we were young." Mom was forty-two in 1958, and Dad was sixty-nine. "I tried to remember his name, and I knew I had seen him somewhere but was not quite sure (she said). He smiled and came forward to me and said in a solid but loving tone, *Laurice*?"

"Yes…" mom said!

"This is Abdel-Ghaffar … Abdel-Ghaffar Azmy, your childhood neighbor. How are you? It has been more than thirty years since we met last, except for when we met at your sister Denise's wedding in 1944. Is that right?'

My mother said to us later, "I was trembling a little, with joy of course, and I think I broke into tears. But I did kiss his hands, not knowing if it was safe to hug an old friend in his place of work, especially one with such a high rank."

He looked at her and stretched his hand conservatively and most caringly. "He grabbed my shoulder," said Mother, "and invited me to his office. Then he called one of the younger members of his team and asked him to get me lemonade and a coffee."

"How are they treating you here?" he asked her.

"It is not easy Abdel-Ghaffar. Besides, it is not their mistake; they are working very hard. It is just that my husband has throat cancer and must undergo treatment in England, to save his life. You know, his physician is Doctor Mahfouz … he gave us all the necessary reports, but we still cannot get the clearances. Also, I can't authorize this check from his work so as to carry it over with me through airport customs." He stretched his hands to take her papers. She handed them over to him, and her lemonade came in, followed by her coffee.

"Everything will be fine," he said. "You live in Heliopolis, I see?"

"Yes!"

"We have to do this right. I live in Heliopolis, too. Meet me at Groppi's Teahouse in Heliopolis at 6:00 p.m. tomorrow and get me all your paperwork. I will solve this; I promise."

Mom said she dropped some tears of relief and clutched his right hand with both her hands. He escorted her to the door, and she returned that afternoon, glittering and full of joy and hope. The next day, she went to meet him at Groppi's and they both spent an hour together discussing the *beautiful past* while reviewing all reports together. The Home Office cleared her papers, by the last week in June of 1958.

"He was a good man and a good son of Egypt," Mother commented to me. It is interesting, when we realize how easy life can be; how beautiful our nations could turn with people like Mr. Abdel-Ghaffar! True, we make societies and not the other way round. It is all about the choice of thoughts, actions, habits and character.

We returned from vacation in early August, and Mom started preparing her final paperwork while Dad was still going to his office to finalize his pending files. He was almost seventy years old then and just did not want to let go.

One day in August 1958, Monsieur Qattawi called my mother urging her to have dad, slow down a little. He said he wanted to hand her another big check for his medical expenses and for his rest.

Around mid-September 1958, my parents left for England. Nora and I started going to school a week later. We both went to the same school, AMC (Anglican Mission in Cairo). Nora, my baby brother Camille, and I moved down with Auntie Zee, and so did our interim nanny from the farm, daughter of the land supervisor, *Hanouna*.

My parents were gone for close to three months. It is exactly fifty years now, and I still remember how my sister and I would go to school every morning and come back every afternoon. Ours was bus was number six. Of course, she would go to the girls' college, and I would go to the boys' school. Every morning we would all meet for the morning parade, and then students would split in three rooms for prayers, depending on their religion, until the school abolished morning prayers for all students. In the beginning, we still had some teachers from the Church of England, although the majority had left Egypt, by 1959.

As for my memories while Dad and Mom were in England, I can remember coming back from school with my sister, in 1958 and jumping over our baby brother, cuddling him, and playing with him sometimes in his pram on Aunt Zee's balcony or in the villa's garden. Then, we would have supper with Auntie Zee and our nanny, do our homework, and prepare ourselves for games in the balcony. TV was not our fun outlet

Tale of a Growing Child

then, though Mom and Dad had bought us a black and white set in 1957 from an Egyptian public sector, manufactured by Soviet and East German technicians.

At that time, my Aunt Helga (dad's other sister) had not yet moved to stay down in our villa with Auntie Zee. She did later in 1963. Mom and Dad came back from England just before Christmas, 1958. Camille was turning one year old. Mom and Dad had a lot of stories, but basically, the Cobalt operation that dad had done, did not work, and "cancer was still galloping" according to Doctor Ledermann's own words (dad's specialist).

They had to go again, after the New Year. Auntie Zee accompanied Dad for this operation. Dad had his larynx extracted completely. Later, Auntie Zee came back, and Mom went again for Dad's remission and voice training. Then they both came back with a happy conclusion. The cancer was gone, and Dad lived for twenty years, though, without his larynx and voice. One could understand him as he whispered without his vocal chords. It was not that difficult, and soon we all adapted. It was not difficult because we wanted to hear him; that is the point, I loved to hear him!

Overall, Dad could no longer work at the Agricultural Reform Company of Egypt since he was way over seventy and his friend Monsieur Qattawi was leaving Egypt for good. To me, it did not make sense that someone as grand as Monsieur Qattawi, who had helped Dad repeatedly, be asked to leave Egypt.

Now, the fact that dad could no longer talk freely in public as he did before impeded his days of glory as a lawyer in Egyptian courts and his roaring leadership at the family farm (his forty acres and those of his brothers and sisters). Then, he withdrew from working as an employee, as a lawyer, and as a property owner. Soon, with the socialist reforms, he divided his land into groups of five acres and sold it, at half its value, before Parliament approved the new 1961 socialist laws of confiscation and nationalization, and applied it. After the socialist laws issued

Tale of a Growing Child

by the People's Assembly (Parliament), no family was allowed to own more than five acres.

In any case, suddenly Dad had lost his business engagement on three fronts within less than one and a half years. To top it, he could not walk in the streets of Heliopolis (Cairo) and interact with friends and shop-owners any longer, because, in a sense, there was a 'hole' in his heart with the disappearance of his voice (Let alone, the real hole in his throat that was covered by some bandage). In no time, he was confined to his house unless we all went out for church, lunch, or some outing. Moreover, even at family dinners, he was alone. I could see it. He was a little isolated and hurt.

Feeble as Dad's challenges forced him to become vis-à-vis his daily life's requirements, he had become so proud and increasingly graceful, nurturing, wise, and deep, far more than he already was. Then, he resorted to teaching us and helping us with our homework. This made him fill his time and helped him reclaim some of his wasted business identity. I sat next to him most, for homework, all the way from 1959 to 1968 when I graduated from high school, and even after that. I did so, less frequently, between 1968 and 1971 at Hotel School, to be more precise. My sister had clearly chosen to handle her own homework and life without his help, since 1960.

Other than Dad's commitment to helping me with my homework and his teaching sessions that started in 1961, he liked to walk down to the shopping district a few minutes from our villa, to buy groceries and fresh fruit, just as he did throughout the twenty preceding years. Dad would enjoy cuddling my baby brother, Camille, and taking him on the pram for short walks around the block or to the shopping district. He would buy fresh fruit, wash it, and then set the table for Mom's return from her new work with the Food and Agricultural Organization of the U.N. It made him enjoy his life, gracefully, the way it shaped him. In many cases, Camille's nanny would walk him with Dad.

As time passed, I grew up perceiving how Dad clung to life without his voice. There were these walks to the shopping district, for which I joined him repeatedly and which I can never forget. There was a day in 1964 when he went to the fruit and vegetable store. He whispered to the vendor with his faint voice, "Chief, I need two kilos of oranges and two of peaches."

The Qurba, Heliopolis, neighborhood (Commercial Strip)
To the left is El-Thawra St., leading to the family's street

The store man (where the shop in red is, now) looked at one of his peers and said, "Did you understand what he said?" Dad did not budge and kept standing straight. I was struggling to contain myself, at thirteen, and not to intervene so as not to sound patronizing to Dad. I looked at him, as I knew he would prefer to repeat the phrase himself.

"I need two kilos of these and two of those."

"God have mercy on you—yes, yes, I understood!" shouted the vendor in a crude manner.

Dad paid for his order and looked at me. I held a bag, he held another, and we walked back home. I held his elbow and said "He is not bad, Pa; he just did not know how to react." Dad looked at me so proudly, lovingly, and appreciated my concern. Then, in his frail voice, he said, "It is okay … it is okay …" And that is exactly how he continued his life until November 1978, when at eighty-nine he succumbed to a cancer relapse and flew to heaven, in my arms.

How dad guided and coached me, continuously, with my homework was not very constructive for my personality, but it did shape my character since I was an active partner, trying to help him cope with his challenges. Those guided homework sessions were becoming increasingly alienating, and I felt that I wanted my space to study and to grow with my peers, independently.

Over the years, I learnt so much from Dad about the Penal Code and with regard to endless cases of abuse and injustice. Dad would always tell me: "Regardless of any truths and errors, justice must always prevail within the law. I fight for justice and you must do the same. I would have liked you to be a lawyer; you would have been a good one." This helped me a lot and stayed with me forever, through my work life.

"Pa, I wish! Maybe I will one day, but now I am all mixed up with how I will pursue my studies."

"Then, make a point of sketching your own code in life, your character. This way, if you slip, you know where to come back and stand-up, again. At least you will seek your own justice, and no one can shake you even if she or he can fracture you, at first. In all cases, remember the four steps leading to peace for all humans: Mercy, The Whole Truth, Love & Compassion, Justice and, ultimately, Peace."

"Okay, Pa, I promise you." This, too, stayed with me for the rest of my life.

My younger brother was getting at an age where he could play soccer with the neighbors and me in the street. Ever since his age of six in 1964, we would play soccer at least two or three times a week in the afternoons. Dad used to love watching us from Auntie Zee's balcony.

Suddenly, Camille became a lovely young child, and he soon joined our school. He even took the same bus. When my sister and I were in preparatory school, he joined the primary school, and he and I would have lunch together in the boys' school cafeteria. Before 1963, I had a lot of Egyptian, Armenian, Italian, Jewish, and Greek friends at school, mostly from the soccer team, just as my baby brother formed his own group, seven years younger than me.

Then one day, in sixties, our soccer team collapsed. Most of its members left for Europe and North America. Gone were my excursions with Roland, Stavros, Emile, Vahan, Haitham and others, to the Zoo, the Armenian Club, the Greek-Orthodox prep school or the backyard of the Sephardic Temple of *Templi Vitali Madjar and Abraham Betesh School,* footsteps from our villa.

On another occasion, and this is truly important to mention because of the rising fear factor overshadowing the day-to-day environment, I was heading to hotel school in 1968, in a public bus, just after the defeat of Egypt in the 1967 Israeli war and amidst a continued state of control that had started in the late fifties. The bus was crowded and I was carrying my books and struggling to stand up and hold one of the bus's high rails. Without noticing, I hit a military official's shoulder and he pushed me back. I shouted at him saying that he hurt my neck, without realizing that he was a military head. He clutched my neck and roared at me saying, "Hey watch it lad; there are three types of citizens in this land; those who support the state, those who want to break it and those who mind their own business; I will show you which of these three you are and he twisted my arm." I sighed and lowered my head and shut-up, as usual.

Fortunately, with music, I still had a solid ground to stand on; I had a fallback zone to cling to, every time verbal slings pierced my heart and each time life's absurdity of violence and indifference to violence, seemed unbearable. In chapter 16, I will mention the influence of my wonderful music teacher, Mrs. Rossi, on my life.

Reflections

Today, as I watch the glorious *Lake Memphre-Magog*, I wonder! I think and ponder… Each day of my life, I walk through green pastures, hills and valleys, slums and roads, school halls or churches and then I end up at waterfronts watching their grandeur. I see water, always water. Why do I keep doing this? Why does water scare me, and why does it awe me, all the same? What is its mystery? Why is it so symbolic to me? It never answers me. It only pulls me through its tides. Then its waves lift me with hope and drop me with no mercy, or floating with no ground, only to face life all by myself.

    Three times did waterfronts mark me; once in 1957, by Mandara Beach in Alexandria, when I was caught in a whirl while swimming with my sister in the Mediterranean. We were both drowning, viciously, but two swimmers pulled us to safety. My sister was pulled out first while I heard her shouting, "My brother; my brother". Then, they pulled me just after that. Then once, at Mandara Beach, walking by the shore and guided by those three men to their cabin. Little did I know that in September 1980, I would drown again at Agamy Beach in Alexandria and at the age of twenty-nine! In this last one, I almost died. I had gone to spend a few hours by the beach of Agamy in Alexandria. I was swimming that day in 1980 and then suddenly- in a fraction of a second, I lost grip of the ground and of the ability to continue to swim or even float. I had sensed I would drown that morning but convinced myself that it was only a false presentiment. I insisted on going to sea. I was about to die, drowning in a vicious whirl, but was saved by a young, good-looking swimmer who brought me to safety. In fact, I was staggering in the deep, groundless, and infinite water for more than thirty seconds, surrounded by angry whirls and tides. The waves were gray at times, and then they turned to white, building up with salt at their edges and with their turbulent and swiftly rotating ripples, receding to the deep. I struggled to pull myself out of the strain but it, rigorously, pulled me further into the

Mediterranean's mysterious horizon and groundless depth. I utterly lost it and knew that I was going; I was preparing to meet God. I was tired and had to let go. Then, a huge wave lifted me and turned me on my back, leaving me facing the sky. I was facing heaven. Those ticking hospital ECG mechanical sounds haunted me, again.

Then, I thought I saw God watching over me, like a silhouette, a flame of light with a tender smiling and compassionate face that vanished, swiftly. Then, I saw many of His angels and then fell down, again, into the water strain. I was quickly losing energy, and my voice was squeaking for help. This whole ordeal must have caught me for over forty horrid seconds. Then suddenly, again, just after I thought I saw God, and in the midst of my battle with death, I heard the voice of a young man swimming to my right, one or two feet back. He was outside of the strain, offering to help me. "Stretch your right arm, just stretch it!" he shouted, almost ordering me. I did but lost touch of his hand and then fell back in the merciless strain. Then, I heard the same voice shouting at me again: "Don't look! Just stretch your right arm. I will get you out. Do it now!" I stretched out my right hand, crying in Arabic, "Have mercy on me, my Lord." The young man clutched my palm with his left hand and pulled me out while thrusting himself backward and to the right by propelling his feet, violently but systematically. He was rowing with his right hand, at the same time. In less than fifteen seconds, we were out of the angry strain; he saved me. He continued swimming toward the shore while wrapping my waist with his warm boney left arm, just until I was able to stand and walk out with him to the beach. I looked at his angelic smile and at his shining, kind face and asked him: "How did you see me?"

"Divine providence," he replied softly, and he turned his head away while smiling to me like a breath of fresh air. I was numb and grateful. Then he disappeared in a flash, just like that. He was my guardian angel. He was! And now, twenty-eight years later, here I am in Magog, taking a nap, again, by the waterfront of Lake Memphre-Magog, in September 2008, rolling the reels of my life story and of my passions and roots, reliving them, all over, always by the waterfront, while un-layering moments of intolerance that I witnessed with my friends, family, neighbors, workplace and myself! Eventually, I will find some meaning to my fascination with it, its ripples and its waves!

Chapter 14
Passions and Roots—2

Alexandria and Ras-el-Bar (Mes Amours)

In the sixties, Alexandria was my family's chosen summer resort, at least every other year, and coincidentally, each even year. Alexandria is situated next to the city of Rashid (Rosetta) at the tip of the left branch of the Nile Delta. This branch pours into the Mediterranean, leading to the Western Sahara. On odd years, we went to another resort called Ras-El-Bar, which means Head of the Waterfront. This last resort is situated at the tip of the right branch of the Nile Delta (leading to the Sinai Desert, eastwards). It, too, pours into the Mediterranean at the city of Damietta. Actually, Damietta and Ras-El-Bar, on the right branch of the Nile Delta are less than fifteen minutes away from each other, just as Alexandria and Rashid are close to each other on the left branch of Nile Delta. While Damietta leads to the city of Port Said, and further to the Sinai Desert, and then, Israel, eastward, so does Alexandria lead to the great Sahara Desert, on to Libya westward! In between Alexandria and Libya lies the Egyptian city of Alamein that witnessed the Battle for Africa between Rommel and Sir Walter Montgomery. In the heart of this city are the mesmerizing WWII Commonwealth cemeteries.

The city of Rashid, on the left branch of the Nile Delta, is also known as the city of Rosetta and is famous for Egypt's two thousand years old Rosetta Stones (196 BC), that were excavated by the French in 1799 and translated by their *savants* (intellects), from hieroglyphics, demotic and Greek.

The city of Damietta, on the other hand, was the center of a thriving Jewish community thousands of years before Moses. Abraham, Jacob, Joseph the Tribe, his sons Manasseh and Ephraim (who were born in Egypt) lived there. They planted fruit, vegetables and essential produce. They produced textiles and other household products. Jacob died in a suburb of Damietta called Goshen. His son Joseph took permission from the Pharaoh to take a few days off to carry him over for burial, next to his father Isaac in the city of Sachem (Nablus) in the Holy Land.

Potiphar, one of Pharaoh's senior officials granted Joseph three weeks to do the job and sent seventy of his staff to help Joseph burry Jacob. Immediately, after, pharaoh chose a wife for Joseph; an Egyptian by the name of Asenath (Genesis 41: 45 and 41: 50-52). They would bear fruit to Menasce and Ephraim, Patriarchs of Israel's tribes. The Jews of Jacob continued to live in Damietta.

Later, Joseph died in Goshen-Damietta (Egypt); he was buried there and his bones remained until Moses carried them with him during his Exodus from Egypt. Joseph knew hundreds of years ahead that a great man of God (Moses) would lead the Jews out of Egypt. He wrote his will asking that man to carry his bones from Goshen to Sachem; he did. Goshen-Damietta holds the word's second oldest Jewish cemetery in the world. Unfortunately, few pay attention to this religious relic.

Alexandria, Mon Amour

Alexandria's cultural mosaic goes back to its founding by Alexander the Great in 332 BC. Previously, under the Pharaohs rule, it was known as the Egyptian townlet of *Kakouda* in ancient Egyptian and, later, *Rhakotis* in Greek. It was a resort filled with anglers and pirates. Later, after Alexander died in 323 BC, his disciple Ptolemy succeeded him. The early Ptolemaists kept it in order and fostered the development of its museum into the leading Hellenistic center of learning (Library of Alexandria) but were careful to maintain the distinction of its population's three largest ethnicities: Greek, Jewish, and Egyptian. At that Time, Alexandria was not only a center of Hellenism, but was also home to the largest Jewish community in the world. The Septuagint, a Greek translation of the Hebrew Bible, the Torah, was produced there. The Ptolemaic Dynasty under Ptolemy the Thirteenth rule (Cleopatra) ended in AD 34, with the decisive battle between Mark Anthony and Cleopatra, on one side and their conquerors, Octavius and Julius Caesar of the Roman Empire, on the other. The Romans ruled Egypt for five centuries, thereon. Arab invasions under Amr Ibn El-Assi conquered Cairo (it was called then, Fussatum, and later Fustat and further, Cairo *Al-Qahira*) in AD 641. He (Amr) captured it after a siege that lasted fourteen months, peacefully, with no record of violence or killing (except with the resistance of Romans and Greeks in Egypt under the Patriarch Cyrus of Egypt, based in Alexandria). Amr Ibn El-Assi was able to write to the Caliph Omar in the Arab Peninsula that he had taken a city containing "thousands of palaces, baths, theatres, places of amusement, dealers in fresh food-oil, and gardens- let alone thousands of Jews and Copts who would pay tribute (*Guizieh*)." *See more at the end of chapter 32.* Amr changed today's Cairo former name from Fussatum to Fustat.

Fustat-Fussatum

To the left: Fustat farmers market and Amr Ibn El-Ass Mosque
Saint George Basilica and Hanging Church, seen far left

Fustat Medieval Islamic Market (Circa AD 1300)

In 645, a Byzantine fleet recaptured the city, but it fell for good under the Muslim control, led by Amr Ibn El-Assi, the following year. Amr Ibn El-Assi captured Alexandria, as well (among other cities). The languages used in Alexandria and the whole of Egypt, in historical order are, Hieroglyphic, Coptic, Demotic (mix of Coptic and Greek), Greek, and Arabic. The Roman Empire preferred to keep Greek as the predominant language and did not attempt to change it. Coptic is still used prominently, to this day, mostly in religious rituals.

Some claim that the Library of Alexandria and its contents were destroyed in 642 during the Arab invasion. Others deny this and claim that the library was destroyed much earlier in the third century, due to civil war in the time of the Roman Emperor Aurelian. Alexandria's historical lighthouse is counted as one of the world's seven wonders, to this day. It was destroyed following an earthquake in the fourteenth century, and by AD 1700, the city was just a small town amid the ruins. In AD 1477, *Maméluke Sultan Qaitbay* built his famous and breathtaking fortress and citadel on top of the ruins of Alexandria's ancient lighthouse to defend Alexandria from foreign assaults. The citadel continues to shine gloriously. (See the back cover)

Egypt remained under Mamèluke and Ottoman rule until 1798. On July 2, 1798, French troops stormed the port of Alexandria (Abu-Kier) under Napoleon Bonaparte, and it remained in their hands until the arrival of the British expedition in 1801. The British won a considerable victory over the French in the Battle of Alexandria on March 21, 1801 (still at the port of Abu-Kier, otherwise, formerly known as Alexander's *historical underworld and unexcavated city of Heracleion*) and then they besieged the city, which fell to them on September 2, 1801. Mohammad Ali, the Ottoman Mamèluke, governor of Egypt, began rebuilding the city around 1810, and by 1850, Alexandria had returned to something very close to its former glory. In July 1882, the city came under bombardment from British Naval Forces who occupied it until the evacuation of all British troops from Egypt in 1954, under Nasser.

In 1801, the British Expedition (under Sir Ralph Abercrombie) had defeated the French expedition (under Bonaparte) that invaded Egypt in 1798. The French, however, never left Egypt. Their intellectual and cultural curiosity led them to constructing the Suez Canal in 1869 and to building the glorious Opera of Cairo, which is a smaller replica of *the Opera di Scala*, in Milano. *Khedive* (Emperor) Ismail inaugurated it in the presence of Empress Eugenie of France and Maestro Giuseppe Verdi, composer of its inaugural opera, *Aida* and, later, *Rigoletto and La Traviata*. In addition, they built two famous bridges in Cairo under the leadership of engineer Gustave Eiffel, builder of the Eiffel Tower of Paris, the railway network of Bolivia, and several other famous worldwide projects. The curiosity of the French also led them to decipher the Hieroglyphic language and to summarize their view of modern Egypt in five volumes on the famous Rosetta (Rashid) Stones, *les cinq tomes de la description d'Égypte*.

The mingling of French and Egyptian bloods in the early and mid-1800s gave birth to some Egyptian beauties with typical blue eyes and shaded Egyptian complexion. I always raved about youth who brought us fresh bread at the doorsteps of our rented resort home in Alexandria or others who sold us fresh sea-fruits in Ras-El-Bar and Damietta, when we went there for vacation.

In the meantime, Alexandria flourished with the rebound of its Egyptian, French, Jewish, Greek, Italian, and Armenian communities between 1830 and 1960, under the modern Egypt that Mohammad Ali founded in 1805. The rebound marked Alexandrian life, city, and coast with its cultural traces, until this day, while retaining relics of the Greek, Roman and Muslim architecture.

One could easily trace this coastal heritage in Alexandria's specialty restaurants, hotels, sport clubs, golf courses, theatres, and its romantic beaches. Many of these had a Roman and Greek imprint at their background streets, alleys, or front view, mingling with the more recent Arabesque architecture. Examples of the old relics are the ancient Roman Theatre, Pompey's Pillar; the new Library of Alexandria built on the remains of the old one. As well, the breathtaking Citadel of *Qaed Bay* built several hundred feet deep in the sea beyond Alexandria's shore on top of the old wondrous lighthouse, which an earthquake demolished in AD 1420. After the British bombarded Alexandria in 1882, the citadel was neglected. In the twentieth century, following several restorations by the Egyptian Supreme Counsel of Antiquities, it was reborn and stands out, breathtaking. What lies under Alexandria; from citterns to alleys of the ancient world, is currently revealing itself, gradually, through worldwide excavations.

And then, there is the glorious Mediterranean shore itself, from one end of the huge city to the other, with its gripping coastal curves, depth of field, golden sandy beaches, occasional rocks a few feet deep, and the mesmerizing smell of sea salt, fish, and iodine.

Then just across its coastal highway, on the opposite side of the sea coast, lay those heritage buildings, apartment houses, villas, mosques, synagogues, churches, and stores. I will never forget, those Greek, Lebanese, and Italian restaurants; those French and English teahouses and pastry shops; those beach shops displaying their colorful beach toys and games (rubber geese, plastic shovels, buckets, etc.,). I remember them since the age of seven; those Arabesque and Mediterranean cafés with their terraces (*Cafés Trottoirs*) offering coffee, rice-pudding, and all sorts of herbal teas; those pastry shops selling their fried homemade honey-balls (Lekoumadis), doughnuts, and pancakes; and those beaches with music terraces and dance clubs that I frequented during my teens; how can I ever forget them?

Earlier, in April this year (2008), I went to Alexandria. I walked through some of its beaches all the way from the king's former Palace of *Mountazah*, which was his summer resort and from where he was deported in 1952, down to the beach of *Maamoura*, further east where I spent three summers, and then to the historical port of Abu-Kier, known as the ancient underworld city of Heracleion.. Then I walked back westward. At Mandara Beach, I stopped at a street called Murdoch, in which many prominent Jewish Egyptian families, since the thirties, lived just as other sectors of Alexandria housed Egyptian Greeks, Italians, Armenians, and so many more communities. Equally, one of the historical streets, three kilometers to its west was *Harat Al-Armen* (Armenians Alley). Another of its beaches was even called *Lazaritta*, a metaphoric attribute given to it by some Alexandrian-Egyptians following the burning of the great Library of Alexandria. Over time, its name slipped to *Mazaritta*.

On Murdoch Street, I saw the house where my Aunt Denise and her husband, Asaad (Palestinian), and my two cousins, stayed in Alexandria and on whose balcony we flew many kites with the neighbors. I remembered how she used to prepare her lasagna trays, her delicious stuffed vine leaves, and those scrumptious roast beef sandwiches with pickled dills and butter, and then carry them over to spend full days by the sunny terrace at her cabin by the beach of Mandara with aunts, uncles, cousins and friends of ours.

The two-floored set of cabins that once existed in Mandara had vanished in 2008 and was replaced by new ones. I was able to identify the spot where the 1957 cabins used to stand. Then I roamed one beach after the other (past Armen Street and Lazaritta) until I reached Alexandria's center (Ramleh Square), still by the coast and not far from the old lighthouse. The buildings, so old and impressive, continued to feature there specialty restaurants and bistros on their ground level. The main highway between the coast and the buildings had been renovated to an extent of beauty and uniqueness that exceeded my expectations. This was in April of 2008, while I was sustaining my repeated drenching abdominal attacks. However, it was a great way out of the portrait of years of corporate and health grief and, perhaps, a chance to witness this glorious city once more, should it ever, God forbid face any violence or natural disasters, again.

Then I saw few of the older teahouses that were built in the 1920s: Atheneos, Triannon, Flukiger, Delices and many more. They all featured delicious fine pastries, snacks, truffles, French Soirées (mini pastries) and Luxury Cakes for all events. My preferred were the cheese, roast beef or ham sandwiches on soft buttered toast, without the rim and then sliced into two triangles and presented with two French mini-dills on the side, on a small stainless steel, oval plate. Many also had a luxurious back entrance that led to their huge display-room full of pastries, cakes, English orange and fruit tea cakes, ice cream, and truffles, on to the front overlooking the Mediterranean coast.

Oh, what a mesmerizing fresh smell of baked goods they carried with their display, as we entered from the back door in the fifties, nurtured by the smell of seawater at the other side of their restaurant. I must have started visiting them at the age of six or seven, because I remember one of those typical days I went to church with my family (in Alexandria). We used to pray at a church called Boulkley Cathedral, not far from these two central cafés: Atheneos and Delices. Traditionally, this would have been the spot where Octavius crushed Marc-Anthony, Cleopatra's boyfriend, terminally, in Alexandria after his earlier victory over him in Nicopolis, Greece, around September, AD 32. Some local Greeks in Alexandria called this part of the city Nicopolis, although I could not trace the authenticity of this romantic allegation. (I will trace it, though). Its modern name is Ramleh (Sandy beaches by the coast of Commercial and historical Alexandria). Anyway, this had to have been the place of the final and decisive battle for Egypt between both warriors. It was followed by the suicide of both Anthony and his lover, Cleopatra the Seventh (The Greatest). Then the Romans conquered and colonized Egypt for five centuries. In the end, after church, we, usually, took a taxi to a restaurant or café. Dad would have had seventy years of age then. One day, we went to Atheneos teahouse and entered through the back door to the pastry display showroom, all the way to the other end, overlooking the coast. The windows, as usual, looked over the seaway drive, which was small in the early sixties. We could look right through them to the sea where five or six big rocks repelled the sea waves splashing all around them. The weeds around them were green and slippery.

The smell of the Mediterranean from Atheneos (the teahouse) revitalized me when I was a kid. It did the same in

2008. I remember there was always a quintet of piano, banjos, cello, accordion, and violin played by one Greek, one Jew, one Pole, and two Alexandrian musicians in their late fifties. They were elderly and always smiled to their audience and made funny gestures with their hands when they were asked for *encores*. Most of their songs were familiar, to many: tangos, foxtrots, and sweet pieces by Hayden and Mozart. They used to play "The Sea" by Debussy, "The Hungarian Dance" by Brahms, lovely tunes like "La Comparsita" and "Jealousy" that my parents had on a 78-RPM disc in Cairo, as well as, "Bessa Me Mucho," "Amado Mio," and many others. I would clap for them hysterically and with such joy. The state of mind of all Egyptians was elevated with intertwining tastes and artistic passions; w*e could easily call it the remains of the beautiful past.*

That day, when I was a kid, they asked me on stage and invited me to play the banjos while the banjo man played the tambourine. I just banged the banjos, not knowing how to count. I loved it and went down to my seat to eat my sandwich and drink my milk with my family in a state of ecstasy, while still gazing at the great Mediterranean Sea and devouring its distinctive scents of salt, iodine and, most of all, infinite history and civilization. (See page 5)

In April 2008, I meant to visit both restaurants (Atheneos and Délices) but could only visit one, on this trip. At Atheneos, the band hand gone, but the layout of this historical teahouse, had not changed much since I saw it last in 1968, forty years earlier. The floor mosaic was still there, statues of Greek gods and goddesses were still hanging around the ceiling, and the mirrors still stood up as before. I decided to keep Délices for a later time.

At Atheneos, I asked for the old silver-plated cutlery, especially the metal ice-cream cups and their squared metal spoons. A young server smiled and asked me to wait. Then he came back with an elderly man, around eighty years of age, another waiter but from the older days. He had gold teeth, a dark complexion, a traditional Egyptian waiter's hat, and a big smile.

He said, "Returning immigrant?"

"Yes" I said, pretending that I was returning from Canada to my birthplace.

"When's the last time you came?"

"Exactly forty years, in 1968. [*I had returned in 1998.*] Were you here then?"

"Yes, I have been here for sixty years!" He smiled, and his eyes were a little wet. "Gaber," he added. "My name is Gaber."

Then, I hugged him and we talked for an hour over tea and cookies while taking pictures in the main tearoom.

He showed me the old cutlery and the ice-cream steel cups that existed in 1957, in the stock room. He then took me to the two old mirrors that used to stand at the back entrance- a concave and a convex mirror. I asked him where Alexandra, Tamvaco chocolate, and candy shops had gone; we used to find them just next door to Atheneos, from the back.

"They're gone. They sold and left thirty-five years ago," he said.

Then, I sighed and shut my eyes for some seconds. After this, I thanked him a lot, and left him a little gift of money, which he furiously returned to me. Then he held my shoulders in an extremely fatherly and affectionate manner. I smiled, shook his hands rigorously, and went on with my walking and reminiscing.

Finally, I passed by one of the last remaining synagogues of Alexandria that was home to the world's largest Jewish community before 1948: Eliahou Hannabi [Elijah the Prophet]. I meant to see Menasce Synagogue (in reference to one of Joseph's two sons: Menasce and Ephraim) but could not locate it in such a short while. I will shortly. (They would move from Damietta to Alexandria and back for their trade. To this day, the street where the Synagogue of Eliahou Hannabi still bears the name *El-Nabi Danial Street* (Daniel the Prophet).

Eliahou Hannabi Synagogue seemed glorious and vibrant with history. The vibes surrounding it bore such intense history, worship, and past community involvement with all its ups and downs, that by closing my eyes, I could feel the past, present, and eternity around me. It was all in the air; I just felt it. I visited my Auntie Rosie, the mother of a former school friend of mine. She is eighty-eight years old and is a Jew who would not leave her birthplace of Alexandria. She told me that Alexandria once held its own Rabbinic Tribunal, a Jewish hospital and its foundation.

According to the Bible, the prophet Joseph and his brothers sought refuge in Egypt to escape the famine and poverty of their homeland in 1600 BC, before Moses was declared, in the book of Exodus, to have freed a big part of his people. "There arose a new king over Egypt, who knew not Joseph." (Exodus 1:8) Similarly, since the late middle Ages, up until the creation of Israel, Jews escaped the hardships and oppression of Europe and headed for the prosperity and tolerance of the Nile. They lived in harmony with their Egyptian cousins, for a great while. However, just as many of the children of Israel fled Egypt in the book of Exodus, so too did Jews and others feel compelled to flee Alexandria, Damietta and other Egyptian cities, in the twentieth century, after the creation of the state of Israel, the 1956 Suez Canal crisis and the shift to Egyptian nationalism.

Ras-El-Bar, Damietta, Mon Amour

Ras-El-Bar, Damietta was and is a small but picturesque port with two waterfronts (the Mediterranean front, north of the huts and residential area, and the Nile front from their backside of these huts, *southwest*). A long but narrow street separated The Nile front from the back of these huts (whose fronts overlooked the Mediterranean Sea). It featured lots of typical resort cafés, restaurants, bakeries, groceries, and a panoramic way, overlooking the River Nile front. The French seemed to have left more genetic traces in Ras-El-Bar and Damietta (on this east axis of the Nile Delta and closer to Suez and Sinai) than they did with Alexandrian population (just west of its west axis closer to the Western Sahara).

I remember some of its cafés that existed on Ras-El-Bar's Nile coast, namely Sorour, Heliopolis, and El-Ferdous. I would ask for my favorite oven-penne with meat sauce and béchamel cream topping. Then I remember a modest military brass band, marching in the panorama way, playing songs from all backgrounds. *This was in the late fifties.*

One day, I saw the famous Egyptian singer *Om-Kalthoum*, whose voice was as divine as that of *Edith Piaf.* She was sitting at a table with her family and friends, just next to ours, overlooking the Nile. All restaurants overlooking the Nile, where about six steps above the muddy Nile coast level (the Nile side). Of course, we entered them from the Panoramic Street side. I saluted her when I was eight, and she smiled. Then, almost every other day, I saw the usual ten or fifteen Orthodox Jews doing their prayers just below the café, in the evening hours on a secluded spot standing on the muddy coast of the Nile (facing it) in their light-colored blue and white gowns. I would wet my slippers and sit on the café's stairs watching them as they prayed by the Nile (Where their ancestors Jacob, Joseph, Menasce and Ephraim would pray). I did it with respect and much curiosity. By 1967, most of them had left Ras-El-Bar and Damietta. Again, I was sensing the harshness of change. The old shops continued to exist for a while: Bassiouny, Balboul, Karkour, Abu-Table, El-Ot-El-Domiaty, and others. I did not have a chance to visit it in April 2008 (Ras-el-Bar and Damietta). I also remember Uncle Pessac (nicknamed *Am-Hammed*) in 1957, or so. He used to sell us the best-roasted nuts in the fifties, by the beach, from a small rectangular glass container, which he carried over his left shoulder. He also carried with him his famous honey-wafers, which he used to call Fresca! He had one leg, only, and walked with a cane. He was a little stout and short; and his eyes carried oceans of stories and memories. At the age of ten, I would befriend these adult worshippers by the Nile, join them at table, earn a milkshake, and ramble about anything.

Ras-El-Bar and Damietta continued to home large multicultural communities until many of them left by 1965 (at least, allegedly). Likewise, many Italian, Greek, and Polish families left Alexandria, during that time. Armenians chose to stay in Egypt, and to engage with all the changes that accompanied the new regime, just as many remaining wise, caring, and hopeful Muslims and Christians did, hoping for the political storms to settle down. I was so proud to have rekindled my memories of Alexandria in this April of 2008, although so much had changed and so many had left! My heartbeat was racing, and my lips were dry, during this visit. I cannot describe it. It was all about my childhood, my roots; the tree's roots!

> *Whom the Lord of hosts shall bless, saying: "Blessed be Egypt my people, and Assyria the work of my hands, and Israel mine inheritance."* - Isaiah, 19:25

Chapter 15
Passions and Roots-3
Sinai, Mon Amour

Snapshot recap and map of Egypt introducing the Sinai Peninsula, ...while still lying down on my bench in Magog, September 2008.

When looking at Egypt's map as a whole and tracing its northern and eastern waterfronts, one would see the Mediterranean running from left (at the borders with Libya) to the right, all the way to Israel. Then, we would notice two perpendicular waterways, running south to north and pouring into the Mediterranean. These two waterways are parallel to each other. First, the Nile River that ends with a V-shaped delta with both of its axis, pouring into the Mediterranean. The second waterway is to its right and parallel to it (running south to north across Sinai Desert). This is the Red Sea. It reaches the Mediterranean, still in form of a V shape delta but with a much, much wider pair of axis. The right one (east axis) reaches the border of Israel, Jordan, and Saudi Arabia, almost touching the Mediterranean, and the left branch (west axis) reaches the cities of Port Said, Suez and Ismailia, which touches and pours right into the Mediterranean by means of the 150 years old and strategic Suez Canal of Egypt, cause of recent wars. One more note; this left axis of the Red Sea (where the Suez Canal stretches) is diagonal to the right axis of the Nile Delta where the cities of Damietta and Ras-El-Bar lay in between. These last two (left axis of the Red Sea and right axis of The Nile Delta) look like a pyramid, with the tip of the pyramid touching the sea. Finally, these last bordering two cities (Ras-el-Bar and Damietta) were traditionally and just until recently, recognized as one of the world's most populated areas by Egyptian Jews, second worldwide to Alexandria. They were home of Jacob son of Isaac, his son Joseph and grandchildren Menasca and Ephraim. Joseph stayed and was buried in Damietta for four hundred years until

Moses moved his bones to the Holy Land, through Sinai, during the Exodus.

 The history of Sinai is vast and rich. For example, the Holy Family crossed Sinai from King Arafat's city in Bethlehem, having fled Nazareth and Herod's determination to kill all newly born male babies. They fled into Egypt through the northern shore of Sinai (Christ, Mary, and Joseph on their donkey, *Babyloon*). The infant Jesus would only set foot on earth, for the first time ever, on the soil of Cairo, Egypt, soon after. Hence, he touched earth in Egypt, and rendered it divine before, even, the Holy Land. (In the first century, Cairo was known as Babylon (with one 'O') and was founded by the Romans. They changed its name to Fussatum and later the name changed to Fustat and then, Cairo or *Al-qahira*). The Holy family fled for Egypt (westwards) on the very land of Sinai that witnessed Moses as he received the Covenant of God and the Ten Commandments, right on Mount Moses in Sinai, on the way to the Holy Land (eastwards). This is five hundred meters away from where Saint Catherine, the martyr of Alexandria, Egypt, had her monastery built by orders of Emperor Justinian I, during his reign (AD 527–565). She was born circa AD 282 in Alexandria. She was persecuted under the Roman Emperor Maximus, who ordered her beheading when the ancient Breaking Wheel failed to kill her. She died a martyr and virgin. Her remains are said to have been transported by an angel to this spot on Mount Sinai, and they were discovered in AD 800, at which time the monastery's original name changed from *The Sacred and Imperial Monastery of the God-Trodden* on Mount Sinai to the *Monastery of Saint Catherine of Alexandria*. In 1996, I visited the monastery and spoke with many of its monks. The monastery holds some of the world's oldest manuscripts and priceless books. It is a UNESCO protected relic.

 It is interesting to note that Saint Catherine was born of an atheist family in Alexandria but that she converted to Christianity when she saw Jesus in her sleep. She wrote about Him: "His beauty was more radiant than the shining of the sun,

His wisdom governed all creation, and His riches were spread throughout the entire world." Under Maximus, various martyrs followed her fate and, later, as Coptic Orthodox faith flourished, Greek and Roman Egyptians followed the route to Christian martyrdom. Under Arab invasions of Egypt, Christian martyrdom continued.

In this land of Sinai, we find fig trees, olive trees, orange, lemon, Clementine and date trees, palm trees, shrubs, thyme, rosemary, oregano, sand, sand dunes, sand storms, wells, remains of war crafts, tanks, used rifles, and so much more spread all across it (let alone remains of war casualties). Nevertheless, we also sense the vibes and the footsteps of our ancestors fleeing oppression, whether from Egypt to the Holy Land or vice versa. We render a sense of immense human waste following the four most recent wars. All this adds to its mystique and to its unexplainable glorious mosaic- its history, tragedies, and successes! That is not to mention the railway tracks. The British had extended the railway network from Port Said, Egypt, to the city of Rafah, on the border with Palestine in 1916. After WWII, the railway survived initially but was cut in three by the 1948 Israeli War of Independence. This was and still is the Glorious Sinai, a melting pot of faith, war, peace, fruits, beaches, and tourism. Those who pass through it will feel its mystical and indescribable energy. It will capture their senses and will never leave them and they will never leave her.

> *And when they were departed, behold, the angel of the Lord appeared to Joseph in a dream, saying, "Arise and take the young child and his mother, and flee into Egypt, and be thou there until I bring thee word: for Herod will seek the young child to destroy him." When he arose, he took the young child and the mother by night, and departed into Egypt and was there until the death of Herod that it might be fulfilled which was spoken of the Lord by the prophet, saying, "Out of Egypt have I called my son."*
> —Mathew 2:13–15.

Chapter 16
Passions and Roots—4
Bending the Barriers of Tradition

Rekindling the beautiful past while still laying on my bench
In Magog (September 2008

In 1967, I was sixteen years old, one year short of graduating from school and enrolling for a diploma or university degree. I was clinging more and more to my music.

One of my former kindergarten teachers at Scuola Maria Ausiliatrice was Mrs. Olympia Rossi, whom I loved and kept in contact with long after I immigrated. In 1965, she was fifty. She was tall, solid, kind and had a short haircut similar to that of Sofia Loren, the Italian actress and movie diva. Mrs. Rossi lived together with her family (husband, her mother, mother in-law and her daughter) in one apartment. They were all pure Italian Egyptians and frequently invited me for supper, counting me as their son. Their house was opposite to my old kindergarten Maria Ausiliatrice and hence hardly seven minutes' walk from my family's home. Mrs. Rossi always held a lit cigarette with her left arm. She smoked it gracefully.

In 1966, when I was fifteen, Olympia Rossi confronted me with her conviction that while I was talented and that I could become a famous film composer if I wanted to, I was too old to play in a concert hall for big audiences. She thought, I could play to medium size audiences without an orchestra and write music for piano and/or orchestra. I loved her so much, and even though my queen was always my mother, until this day, I would call her Mama Oly, short for Olympia. She restored my love for music and self-esteem. She mentored me for twenty years, teaching me piano, harmony, music theory, counter-point and composition, and most of all, she guided me to leading my life, far richer than before.

With music, I had a solid ground to stand on; a fallback zone to cling to every time verbal slings pierced my heart. As for

Mama Oly, she never had an Egyptian passport. Neither did her husband, parents or daughter. She and her husband had lived in Egypt since 1937, at the age of twenty-two when their parents emigrated from Italy to Egypt. However, until 1985, they were not considered Egyptians. What was ironic was that she had coached and seasoned so many Egyptian piano virtuosos in Egypt. Her father refused to join the Italian army to fight in WW2 with Mussolini. My teacher and her family left Egypt, their second homeland, and returned to Sardinia, Italy, in 1985 after having lived in Egypt for forty-eight years. She was a legend in music theory, in teaching harmony and composition. Two years, later, my family and I immigrated to Canada.

After Israel defeated Egypt in 1967, the mood on its streets was somber and this scarred the Egyptians. There was a lot of divide, indifference, and even arrogance displayed by some members of the cabinet who offered no explanation. To top it, the political pressure groups of the time that seemed to me, shameless and irresponsible did little to console us. Nasser was clearly tired and exerted. He had returned *Egypt* unto the *Egyptians*, when he ordered the evacuation of British troops from its land in 1954, reclaimed ownership of the Suez-Canal in 1956 and saved thousands from death by funding the Aswan High Dam. He was young and earnest; he earned the right to be considered hero, despite his grievous *slips and turns*. After 1967, he lost his flame of declared nationalism and unfulfilled promises with which he had posed for many years. Alas, the west was on his back and his circle had failed to support him with integrity.

In June 1968, I graduated from school and did not score sufficient grades to make it to university. This led me to the Hotel School of Cairo that did not require high school grades. I went. I studied kitchen, food menus, nutrition, food costing, hotel management, and other subjects. It was a three-year course, including six months of training. The mood in Cairo was still dark, and hardly anyone wanted to engage with political talk in such uncertain times, especially with the looming shadow of the far-from-credible socialist party of Egypt, the unfulfilled promises and the post war grieving neighborhoods.

In April 1970, I finished my hotel-school theoretical studies and chose to undergo my hotel training outside of Egypt in a five-star hotel, member of the British Hotels and Restaurants Association in Bath, England. Throughout my theoretical studies at Hotel School in Cairo, I used to accept assignments in four- and five-star hotels as assistant Pastry Chef or Rôtisseur (Meats division) or even as waiter at wedding and graduation banquets, and even as night auditor and reception clerk. Therefore, during that time, I earned some money and gained a lot of experience.

My mind was still set on the West, and I found myself a nice training opportunity in Bath, England. I sealed it and worked very hard to obtain my exit visa. (An exit visa was a regulatory tactic that the existing regime had introduced to streamline the exit of enemies of state, important figures, candidates escaping military service, significant intellectual heads, scientists that were considered national property, and others) In other words, I did everything to obtain permission from the Egyptian Home Office to leave. Of course, I was not sure if living in the West was the answer to my concerns but I truly wanted to try; I wanted to make my own informed choices. I did, but for me, nothing compared to my Egypt in its earlier fifties, before its brain drain.

In Bath, I lived for six months and learnt a lot about the hotel industry, whether in kitchen, restaurants, banquet services or as High-Tea Assistant. I loved it. I returned to Egypt in September 1970, a few days after President Nasser died.

During my training, I built many friendships with colleagues of diverse nationalities and had my first relationship with a lovely English-Polish girl named Nicole. I was nineteen then, and my hair was still curly, my eyes were still green, and my skin color as fair as always. I did not feel shy, and she was attracted to me. She was warm and petite, had turquoise-blue eyes, she was a little thin, short and quite attractive. I knew that ultimately we would go to bed together, which, of course, horrified me. I had not overcome my anxieties or succeeded in coping with the injustices that were inflicted on me twelve years earlier in 1957 or, later, by innuendos and public scoffing, at school.

Nicole and I met at the Bier-Keller (Beer Cellar), which was a hot English, Scottish, and Irish pub just across from my hotel and a few steps beyond the Abbey Church in Bath. I had secured a part-time assignment as piano player for three hours, twice a week in its *Wood-Lounge*. Of course, I had to buy some sheet music and acquaint myself with Irish, English, and Scottish folk songs to play at the pub. I made three English pounds an hour and two pints of Worthington beer each night (a reddish and slightly sweet beer, quite prominent in England those days.) I enjoyed being the cheerleader, and this prepared me for my love adventure with Nicole. It started nurturing my broken spirit that was fractured in 1957. My roommates were good people; they left me alone to entertain Nicole to my couch. At first, I wanted to finish with the physical encounter and break the ice, especially since I had not told anyone that I had never slept with a woman before.

It took a few minutes of focusing and appreciation of her tender and feminine body until I could devour her. But she helped me, and I think she knew I had not done this before. In no time, I enjoyed the smell of her skin, the touch of her palms and the look of her eyes searching in mine. Fortunately, everything turned well. I was joyful and walked with my hands in my pockets, almost dancing, whistling in the streets of Bath, whether coming from a grocery shop or going for walks by its waterfront.

"Jolly good, lad [shouted at me one of my kind elderly returning weekenders, over breakfast, while serving him kippers and poached eggs]. He was retired, stout, tall and bold. He spoke with a southern British accent, from Chichister and Portsmouth. You look different; did you win a lottery or are you in love?"

"A bit of both Mr. Westcott" I replied

"You're a good chap, Raphy [added his wife]. I am happy for you"

"Thank you Mrs. Westcott"

"Do you go back to school after training?"

"No Mrs. Westcott; I will go back to Egypt to work for a four or five stars hotel, hopefully by mid-September (1970). Thank you for your interest; it has been a pleasure serving you both"

"It has been our pleasure, too. You tell your parents, they did a good job."

"God bless you Madam" and they left me a tip of fourteen shillings that day (70 pence), which in today's money is five English Pounds, only to serve them breakfast.

My repertoire for the Bier-Keller was growing, and I started learning of emerging new musicians and music bands. Led Zeppelin was starting a year or two before their glorious *Stairway to Heaven,* and I saw them in London, live, with Nicole and my colleague, Steve from the kitchen, as well as his girlfriend. He had an iconic car: a Spitfire by Triumph. Steve would smuggle some fresh roast beef and cheese sandwiches from the hotel kitchen with a few soft drinks, and off we went for our picnic in his awesome car. My hotel training ended, and I started preparing for my return to Cairo in the last week of September 1970.

Chapter 17
Passions and Roots—5
Struggling Toward My Adulthood

Rekindling the beautiful past while still laying on my bench in Magog (September 2008)

During the first week of October 1970, I landed in Cairo after a fulfilling and refreshing six months training in Bath, England, claiming my identity, building friendships, speaking in public, performing music in English pubs and going on retreats with friends to London, Oxford and Henley. We would return back in Bath where we worked, offering to share gas costs with Steve, at my age of eighteen with a twenty years older colleague; hence building character and responsibility, let alone, loving someone I deserved to love and to be loved by, after years of self-loathing.

    My plane landed around 4 p.m. Cairo time, and soon I found myself walking through the hallways of Cairo International Airport. There was a grim atmosphere in the air; airport staff seemed subdued, their looks were hazy, and even the hallway lights were restrained. One could render a sense of lost hope in people's attitude. After all, a few days earlier, the president of the nation, President Nasser, who had won over most Egyptians within a period of eighteen years of reign, building their hopes for a better life, had died. Hence, his departure left the nation in despair.

    I walked out slowly, young as I was (nineteen in 1970), untrained by life, unaware of how to deal with people in such circumstances, and restrained by life's earlier injustices. Luckily, I did considerably well. I shut my mouth and kept a cordial, modest but assertive posture. There was no difficulty, and I was able to exit the airport in less than an hour. My memory fails me, and I cannot remember how I got home (alone in a taxi or with family). The airport was less than a ten-minute drive to the family's villa. The taxi drove on the Airport Road, (formerly

Avenue des Palais) on to the Palace of the Baron D'Empain, and right on Le Baron (El-Thawra) Street and left to the villa.

Over the following two weeks, I lost grip of my political and social views and succumbed to the collective chants of homage, in the streets of Cairo. We chanted to the departed President Nasser of Egypt, the first real Egyptian Head of State since the days of the last Pharaoh 'Nektaneb II' (around 330 BC) who had asked for Alexander the Great's help (on his way down to Asia) to help him in his final attempt to overthrow the Persian Emperor Darius III. He did and, in a sense, the Egyptian pharaoh (who was, incidentally, a warrior) ceded power to the (fair and just Alexander) but saved his people from the Persian occupation, marking the start of a new period in Egyptian history, starting with the Ptolemaic rule for 360 years until Cleopatra, the fourteenth, descendent of Ptolemy, Alexander's disciple, in AD34.

President Anwar El-Sadat was vice president at the time of President Nasser's death. He was immediately nominated president of Egypt, the second president that Egypt had ever had. Mr. Sadat was one of the members of the Revolutionary Freedom Officers Movement that helped Mr. Mohammad Naguib, the leader of the movement with late President Nasser and a few others. He was the one who announced to the nation in 1970 the news of President Nasser's death and of his (President Sadat's) succession. His speech was well balanced. His voice was hollow, and his words were coming out of his mouth, shaken and with great anguish. He tried very hard to hold himself from tears but succumbed to weakness repeatedly, throughout his speech.

Then the nation was facing a question mark, and the power groups were still roaming in the political arena. Mr. Sadat knew he had a load of troubles to handle and various unwanted heads that he had to eliminate. In the interim, there was a lot of talk of laundering by the corrupt bunch from the recent past, the rest were people of high integrity. In addition, the nation wanted a solution for occupied Sinai, for occupied Egypt and for so many unfulfilled promises. President Sadat had a truly harsh start. He played it very wisely, though, and he tried to keep afloat since the first months. Every now and then, we heard of some unwanted head from the past removed from office, for some reason.

The old Opera House, Mon Amour

In 1971 and almost one year after President' Nasser's death and my return from Bath, England, among other crumbling institutions from the glorious past, was the tragedy of the glorious Egyptian Opera House. Khedive (Emperor) Ismail and his guest, Empress Eugenie of France, inaugurated it in 1869. But in October of 1971, it caught fire and was reduced to rubble within hours. It was certainly an ambiguous tragedy. Many referred to it as sabotage. The very opera house that was inaugurated to celebrate the launch of the Suez Canal, constructed by Ferdinand De Lesseps, the very Opera that held the performance of Verdi's *Aida, Rigoletto and la Traviata*, for the first time on the planet, had become extinct. So were all its memories, archives and historical costumes declared gone, and all this because of some bigots. This cultural heritage was a replica of the *Opera di Scala* in Milano, Italy. It had housed over a century of souvenirs, sculptures, crystal chandeliers, priceless curtains, and a library of treasures and music scores! A branch of the Egyptian tree was dismantled and left to dry up to rubbles.

At 07:30 that morning (in October 1971), my piano teacher (Mrs. Rossi) called me at home to tell me that music professor Bellardinelli, then Director of the Cairo Opera Orchestra, had called her to tell her what was happening. He asked her to send him some of her students to try to save what he could from the library. Mr. Bellardinelli had directed the Cairo Opera Orchestra for several seasons. One of the guardians of the opera called him to let him know what was happening, that night. Bellardinelli called another of the music masters in Egypt, master composer and teacher of music theory and harmony, Professor Decaro, whom I knew through Mrs. Rossi (my piano teacher). I even kept some of his compositions that Mrs. Rossi, my teacher, had given me. She was his music disciple. He was a violin soloist. Another tall Italian musician, in his mid-forties, stood next to him. His first name was Renzo, I think. He had a big moustache.

As soon as I hung up with Mrs. Rossi, I dressed, grabbed a taxi, and rushed to the burning opera with sticky eyes and with a face of a living dead who had just woken up from sleep. Bellardinelli, Decaro, many students of music, and I were all by the burning Opera House, all struggling to save what we could of its library. We were more than fifteen.

Bellardinelli was running like a squirrel and roaring at us as a wolf, in broken Arabic *Save the library!* I held his shoulder, took off my sweatshirt and soaked it with some soda drink that I grabbed from a juice stand, covered my face, and rushed inside toward the library. A few students had already preceded me and were handing me lots of music score. They were running back and forth, ahead of me and I handed the scores, in turn, to others that were standing behind me closer to the street. We went back and forth struggling to save what we could from the burning library. Then we could no longer handle the carbon monoxide, and Bellardinelli shouted in Italian: *Enough, enough! Out, right now!*

Cairo's central fire brigade was about eighty feet away from the opera's receiving gate in the back. It was there then; it is there today in 2008. I was told that it had arrived quite late. It was there, too, when I arrived in my taxi. The side of the opera perpendicular to the Opera Square was one third burned, and so were its boutiques and cafés (Bodenstein, Erard, Bechstein, Sacher and others); No one seemed to know where, in the name of justice, was the valuable stuff. There was nothing being salvaged. I did not see any boxes of saved artifacts. I did not see the old crystal chandeliers, carpets, statues, etc. I did not even know whether any of these had ever been saved or not. W*hat a waste of culture* … Luckily, 95% of that priceless library of music score, some original and others first releases; operas by Puccini, Toscanini, Verdi, Mascagni, and so many other modern musicians, was saved by a few music students.

Bellardinelli sat on the pavement, as the morning traffic was building up and the smoke from the Opera's crumbling building, filled the skies of Cairo's centre with one final testimony; a testimony of burning scents of a century old of culture and heritage. He was crying profoundly. Just across the street from the opera, was a popular, modest art casino that featured belly dancing for Cairo's lay audiences. It sold cheap local whiskies and spirits. The name of the Casino is *Uzbakeya* in reference to the ancient district founded around it by Prince Uzbek, the Turkish Mamèluke and disciple of *Sultan Qaitbay* (builder of the Citadel of Alexandria in the fourteenth century). Its manager urged his staff that morning, not to return home after their late night shift. By 9:30, many of its workers were running offering to help us. They shouted: "Give it to me, give it to me! We'll stack it up in the casino!" They ran hysterically back and forth to the casino across the street from the burning opera house, during the morning rush hour; they ran with piles of manuscripts and music scores in intense panic. The one-way traffic apparatus running from left to right, as we crossed (half alive) with our boxes in our hands, came to a halt as Egyptian drivers stopped their cars and taxis, to allow for this salvage operation of Egyptian Heritage, instead of running for their lives or rushing to their offices. In fifteen minutes, we had saved most of the library. They kept them at the casino, safe and sound, for a few days until Bellardinelli, secretly, reclaimed them and stored them at the Italian Cultural Centre of Egypt. Later, the government of Japan financed the building and construction of the new and superb modern Opera Centre of Egypt, in a suburb of Cairo, called Zamalek.

By 1977, a new multi-layer garage replaced the old Opera house. While the old heritage boutiques and cafés that once surrounded the glorious old opera were gone, a new set of boutiques appeared in 2008, surrounding the garage. They featured mobile shops, electricians and plumbers!

These men and women from the casino, the music students, the night shift of the Opera and Bellardinelli were honorable Egyptians by *choice and love*; far more honorable and heritage loving than many officials by birth and profession, cared to demonstrate. Later, we heard that we must have saved over 90or 95 percent of the library, including the copies that Verdi's orchestra had used to perform *Aida* in 1869, for the first time ever and, later, *Rigoletto and La Traviata*. Of course, Verdi's original scores were somewhere in Italy, presumably at the Opera di Scala in Milano.

The loss of the opera was devastating, and the indifference of the authorities was unexplainable! The brain drain and the cultural collapse persisted. Only, this time, a branch from Egypt's heritage was plucked; it was burned alive, for good!

Cairo Historical Opera square 1910

Cairo Opera Square in 2017

Chapter 18
Passions and Roots—6
My Brother, Camille, the Cool and Loving—1

Rekindling the beautiful past while still laying on my bench in Magog (September 2008)

In 1970, my baby brother Camille was a beautiful twelve-year-old lad preparing for his school-move from preparatory to secondary. I was nineteen, and my sister was twenty. He was my friend, and I think I was a mentor to him. Oh, I hope so! We nicknamed him Kamkam ... Between 1970 and 1974 he grew up helping his cousins and friends with their teenage love problems, their homework, and their whims. Camille was a generous person and an academic genius. ...and yes, he was always an 'A' student. He was also a bright and passionate contributor to Saint Michael's bazaars on Christmas and Easter since the age of seven. He made sandwiches with me, folded them, set the food table, prepared the pickles containers, and helped me with my cash box before we delivered the sales returns to the church's purser. It was such fun.

  Between 1970 (at the age of twelve) and 1973, Camille grew up so quickly, and his character started taking the shape of a true gentleman. He helped his friends and cousins and was regarded as the *confidant* by many. He was the Billiards Room good-looking hopper and champion at the Heliopolis Sporting Club's competitions. He was a joy to anyone he added on to his list of friends. Later, in 1974 and 1975 (just after the last war with Israel in 1973), he would spend weeks in Alexandria at Agamy Beach resort and would dance with the girls. One of the outfits he loved most was his white trousers, five inches above his ankle, and his white T-Shirt marked *Agamy-Sandstock 1974*. He would let his long, dark hair grow and fall off his face, sideways, to the left and to the right. *Agamy-Sandstock 1974* was a music fest we attended together with our cousin Wael (Mady's son and Auntie Helga's grandson). Wael and Camille were almost the same age and were very close cousins. It is such a lovely memory, an era and way of life that would never return under such shifting social crossroads.

Earlier in 1970, when I returned from Bath, I worked hard to get myself *'a life'*, *and* to start my career. I worked on my image and forced myself to walk proudly and with confidence. I kept on doing this while smiling and it started to work. Then, in 1971, I secured myself a wonderful job as a Catering Supervisor with Italiana Airlines at Cairo International Airport and stayed there for four years, until I moved to Switzer-Airlines in 1975.

At both workplaces, my peers liked me, and I loved them dearly. I did not find myself out of place and started organizing picnics and BBQs every month and sometimes even twice a month for the team. I loved being the cheerleader, and I learnt a lot in my job. To this day, forty years later, we still meet regularly to have fun. One day, I even prepared a first-class buffet, together with my coach from Italy (*Signor Bauli*) for Mr. Aldo Moro, the Italian Prime Minister. I took a picture with him, and this, gradually, added new layers of confidence to my new self.

By 1972, I had stretched the frequency of my piano and music lessons with my teacher, Mrs. Olympia Rossi, to three per week. My lessons continued until 1985 when she announced that, like others, her family would return to its homeland in Sardinia, Italy. I, too, announced to her my family's intention to immigrate to Canada, especially in view of some religious hate language I would hear, by only a few, on the radio and in Cairo cafés, following the assassination of President Sadat in 1981 by some fundamentalists. Since my return from my training in Bath and obtaining my diploma, I had worked for several deluxe Cairo hotels, but airlines fascinated me most, and I enjoyed handling the food side of the airline industry while at Italiana Airlines. Then, with Switzer Airlines, I moved on to other departments; I moved from passenger handling on to aircraft balance control, VIP handling, stretcher cases (heading for treatment overseas), ticket sales, and general sales until 1987, one month before immigration.

Mrs. Rossi, her husband, Aldo, their daughter, Sylvana, and both their mothers lived in an apartment just seven minutes from my home and one minute from my kindergarten school Maria *Ausliatrice*. Mrs. Rossi, whom I used to call *Mama Oly* until the last moment before she left, was an inspiration to me. For twenty-one years of my life, she coached me with music theory, harmony, counter-point, composition, piano playing, and various orchestral tactics ranging from those of Motet, Palestrina, Bach, Mozart, and Beethoven all the way to Ravel, Debussy, Rachmaninoff, Rimsky Korsakov, and Pieter Tchaikovsky. Music had become my heartbeat and reason to lead my life. This also helped me with my peers at Italiana Airlines and, later, at Switzer-Airlines. Still, there was something missing. It was all right to love music, but it would have been far better not to use it as a means to define myself in my day-to-day life and while interacting with those who accepted me, already. Perhaps I did not have to put so much pressure on myself, for now, to have a girlfriend.

Did I need to do more so that I would build balance and crush the cocoon of social labels in which a few had locked me? Did I really need it in order to impress my friends who already counted on me for cheering, picnics and outings, no, definitely not! Now, I know it was not *a big deal*.

In 1973, I was twenty-two years old. Camille was fifteen. He was brilliant! Just a brilliant 'A' student, preparing for his final secondary school year and about to make a crucial decision in his life as to whether choose high school for a diploma or go to university. This would depend on how well he scored in his secondary school finals, of course.

He was far more independent than I was. The way he used to study on his own, with no coaching by Dad, made him far more assertive than me. In my case, Dad stayed with me when he lost his voice and his job; he would coach me until Hotel School. I had never paid attention to my right to such independence, as Camille has, because I knew how much Dad needed to compensate for his fractured identity, through coaching me. Dad had the habit of pulling my right ear with his left hand, as he sat to my right if I lost focus. Dad was never violent.

Until the end, there was no alternative, left for me, out of which to make new choices and whereby I could add some meaning to my life. The best I could do was plan a moment of gentle confrontation, where I would ask Dad to give me a chance to study on my own, to help me flourish with my own initiative and independence. So, one day, I thought of rubbing my right ear with olive oil so that when I sat to his left for my homework, and if he (as he occasionally did) gently squeezed my right ear with his left hand, it would slip, and I would be free for good. It worked, and he broke in laughter, with no end, and then hugged me. I explained, and he understood; he cooperated gracefully. After that, he no longer coached me, but we would continue our evening socials with cheese, crackers, and drinks while watching the TV together with mom, my two aging aunts who lived downstairs *Zee and Helga*. Almost every evening, he would sit behind me, silently listening to me play the piano, appreciating it. Overall, I sensed that something good was coming very soon. I could just feel it!

Chapter 19
Passions and Roots—7
My Brother, Camille, the Cool and Loving—2

Rekindling the beautiful past while still laying on my bench
In Magog (September 2008)

One day in the spring of 1973—to be more specific, on Easter Monday, Camille and I were standing on our bedroom's balcony. This balcony was at the right side of the villa if I were to stand at the villa's main gate on the street, facing the villa and looking up to the right. This balcony overlooked the three-story building to the right of the villa through our right side of the garden (while still standing down in the street, looking up). The right side of our garden had a mango tree and an olive tree as well as the fence that divided our garden from the neighboring building's garden. Standing in the balcony (on the left end of the villa) facing the opposite side of our villa (the telephone, telegraph and telex company), our neighboring three story building, would be on the left. Of course, just beyond the fence was the main small garden of this building. The residents of the first floor's apartment ideally, accessed it, from their balcony. Needless to say that the families of the three floors would spend hours in the garden, drinking tea or beer and listening to music after working hours and on weekends, with the tenants of the first floor. Furthermore, they would all go up to the third floor's wide roof to reverse tactics and have their BBQs; we were usually invited. So too, were they in our garden every now and then for drinks and Mediterranean appetizers.

So really, this corner was a comfort zone for the five families: the three in our neighboring building and the two in our villa, (our aunties and us). In addition, there was a villa situated just behind our two buildings (not on our street facing the telephone company but on the back street, (Cleopatra Street), parallel to ours. This villa in the back shared our two gardens, making the residents of the three villas one powerful social experience of iconic friendship, love and fellowship.

The family that lived in the backside villa, added life and meaning to our rich, vibrant, interdependent, and socially secure neighborhood. There was never a feeling of loneliness in any of our families that the rest of the neighborhood did not neutralize by fellowship and care. There was never grief following the loss of a family member in one of these six families that the rest of the cluster did not share and comfort by means of warm and abundant love. The significance of such soothing fellowship in such painful moments, such as death in one of the families, and also joy, such as in a wedding or graduation, cannot be matched by any other experience of sharing that I have ever had until this day, even in Canada. It was a heavenly gift, one of true affection between all! To this day, when I fly to Egypt, I visit the old neighborhood. We still meet and celebrate life; whoever is remaining. Overall, it is just as warm and just as cordial, though a few have left us already. We sold our villa in 1995. The new owners, partially, dismantled our former villa while preparing to turn it into an apartment building. However, the city of Heliopolis stopped the dismantling, declaring it a heritage site that once hosted Monsieur and Madame Oziol, allegedly engineers of the Baron during the first war. Until this day, in 2008, construction has not moved an inch, leaving the villa half-broken and leaving its garden almost extinct!

In the early seventies, my brother and I would frequently sit on that balcony, chatting together and exchanging thoughts and glances with our neighbors, to our left. There was a distance, I would easily say, of fifty feet between our balconies, including the side of our garden just below it across the fence to their side of the garden. They were to our left and the telephone exchange in front of us. We could also peep forward, turn our heads to the far left, and see the villa, in the back.

Over the years, our families grew very close. We flourished together; we shared life's joys and hardships. We were like an unshakeable rock, nurtured by our diversity in faith, in color, and cultural background. I do not have the words to describe it; just walking into our small street was already my sanctuary and my joy after a hard day's work. It was a mini replica of the mosaic that made Egypt so strong but was swindled by incompetence and intolerance.

On that Easter Monday in 1973, our neighbors on the first floor were hosting a spring brunch, the typical Easter ritual that Egyptian locals, Greeks, Armenians, Jews, Italians, and others celebrated. Typically, families would meet around 11 a.m. and start setting up the buffet with falafel, beans, colored eggs, lettuce, green onions, celery, olives, cheeses, bread, sardines, herring, cakes, tea, coffee, fruit, and milk. What a celebration of optimism! Egyptians call Easter Monday celebration *Sham-el-Nessim* (Smelling the spring-breeze)

This was exactly what happened that day at the Haqqis' party (the ground-floor neighboring family). They invited all neighboring families to their brunch. Of course, one should not forget to mention the season's orange trees with the exquisite and glittering scent of their blossoming flowers, very close to jasmine, announcing the birth of the actual oranges all around the three houses. In the front, the jasmine trees, lilies, and the pansies concluded the portrait of this spring celebration. Then there were the mimosa bushes and the bougainvillea flowers, the Egyptian clovers, and much more!

By 10:00 a.m., my parents, sister, and Auntie Zee had already moved, next door, helping the Haqqis prepare for Easter brunch. Auntie Helga was in her room, behind her window (just under our balcony), overlooking, comfortably, the action at a distance of twenty feet. She was thin, had white hair and a bit of a wise riot. Camille and I were still on our balcony engaging in a serious discussion and sipping our coffee. We could see them down below fretting with the pots and pans but chose to sit on the balcony and finish our discussion until 11:00 a.m.

On that day, I had finished Hotel School three years earlier and had started working for Italiana Airlines. The catering department was my first assignment with Italiana Airlines. I was also filling my time with music and many times involved with the church bazaar's sandwich stands, games, etc., with the help of Kamkam (Camille).

Of course, I was holding on to my music lessons and writing my own music. I would simply sit in a park or a quiet place and just write. Slowly I was able to refine my orchestral writing, remotely, with no need for instruments. It was another of my comfort zones and an identity booster. Unfortunately, it was equally my social detriment. I was lonely and did not know it. Music, of course, confined me to my world of meditation, which added to my distance from the rest.

Camille was fifteen and getting ready to finish his secondary school certificate. He was determined to get high scores so that he could learn Materials or Mechanical Engineering in a prestigious university. I knew he could do it. Yet, proud as I was of him, he could sense my feeling of emptiness. He did! He could sense it, and I saw it in his eyes. I knew, too, that he was trying in an absolutely noble, humble, and non-patronizing manner to boost my morale and to entice me to what he called that day, *the project*.

"I have a project that I wanted to run by you, Raphael."

"Sure, what's on your mind?"

"You know how you always encouraged me to follow my dreams, despite obstacles?"

"Yes."

"You remember how you always told me I had to fight for my space, so I could think?"

"Of course, Camille"

"You know how you used to tell me that you did not have sufficient space for yourself to make your own choices, undistorted by the family traditions and other things? You know, Raphy! I really mean Pa … his voice, his sickness, and how this broke his pride?"

"Okay …?"

"Raphy, it was not your fault, but you chose to have Dad coach you for years so that he could make up for his broken pride!"

"That's true, Kamkam, but I also helped him with his law suits and prepared many of his arguments. In any case, I had no better options."

"Exactly… This is just what I mean."

"Mean what? You're scaring me." I smiled.

"No, no, Raphy … I mean you love research, writing, and debating."

"Hmmmm," I sighed.

He looked at me in such a shy manner; and was holding himself from breaking. I knew he wanted to tell me something positive, and he sounded so warm, about it.

"Listen, in fall of this year, I will start my last term in secondary school, and I hope I will get the grades needed to get me to Mechanical or Material Engineering."

"What's on your mind, Camille?"

"What's on my mind?" He paused for a few seconds and then threw it at me while struggling to pose, fit and solid. "Join me!" in a cracked voice.

"Join you in what?"

"Secondary school certificate …"

"…How?"

"Come on, Raphael; join me in my final secondary exam. Do yours again! You help me, and I help you."

"For what, Camille… To do what my dear brother"

"You know you can enroll again with the Egyptian Ministry of Education to redo your secondary school exam from home. I mean, you get the syllabus and study at home. The week of the exams, you will go to a public school auditorium and join others and you will do your tests. Look, do it with me; we will study together, you in your program and I in mine. Don't tell anyone. Just keep it our secret. You know that you can make it. You can get enough grades this time to take you to your dream career: political science, journalism, communication, or drama!

You just have to commit, Raphy, and we could both support each other till we get there."

"Me join you, Kamkam?" I said, peacefully and smiling with respect. "I would love to. Also, thank you so, so much for thinking of me! It has been almost six years since I did my last secondary school test and got the horrid grades that took me to Hotel School. Not even tourism! And it's been three since I finished Hotel School and started working for airlines."

"And look where it got you! …Hotel diploma with emphasis on kitchen and restaurants."

"Not good?"

"No, I didn't say that. It is just not making you happy. You look so driven by life, and you must help yourself so that you can be the one to drive your life. You must do sufficient studies to enable yourself to reverse this, somewhat, passive trend that you are going through. Does it make sense? Oh come on, Raphael!"

"It does, but how will I ever start formalities? And if I make it through paperwork and enroll myself, and even if I force myself to get the grades and then actually get them, how will I lock myself for another four or five years and reduce my life to sixteen hours of work and study per day, eight for work and eight for university? And when will I study, when will I sleep, when will I do my music and start living and have fun?"

"Are you having fun now? No, no, I am sorry; I did not mean to be critical. All I wanted to say is that I will be with you and you with me. I told you. We'll help one another just as we are trying now."

"Camille, how will I find time? …time, my brother. The logistics are just not working."

"No they are; and very well too! Remember how you always said, 'When I focus on obstacles, I lose sight of the peak of my mountain, and when I override them, I can at least continue seeing the peak or even dreaming of it'?"

"Yes."

"So, do it! Live your life! Finish it in five years instead of four. It will impact your life."

"And your school friends: *Raed, Sameh, Wael, Ashraf, Hani,* and the rest?"

"What about them?"

"Wouldn't it be more appropriate that you studied with them alone instead of me hanging around you? I mean, having me take away your space?"

"What space? You are part of my space! You are my brother, and I am yours! Besides, who cares, Raphy? Join us sometimes; sit in another corner of the room at others or on the balcony if you want. Drink your tea, and listen to your favorite music. I could join you on the balcony at times … whatever! Just be happy and do it, because this is what you want. You deserve to get it, and you can do it. You should do it. Just take the first few steps, and see. It will be easier to judge, then!"

He paused, and then he continued, "So? Think of what comes with the package! … Stretched opportunities, new friends, new teachers, a fabulous library at AUC (the American University in Cairo) to do your research, new horizons, programs, picnics with new friends, music concerts at AUC's famous *Ewart Memorial Hall theatre.* Come on, Raphy, please. It is a road to an enhanced identity, a road for you to claim the life that you always wanted to but never did. You deserve it, and I deserve to see my brother happy. Please? For me—me and you …"

"You think so?" I mumbled these three words emotionally and expressively.

"I believe so, yes … of course I do …"

"It will be tough."

"Of course but all this will be over, one day, and you will laugh about it. We will help each other." He was almost crying, holding his tears but clearly imploring me.

"I guess I should stop my music then and my piano lessons?"

"No, no, and no; of course not... Just reduce the frequency. Instead of two or three lessons per week, keep it down to one or two, and instead of five courses per semester, take three or four ... even two. And then you will stabilize and live your life, and when all this is over, you will rest as a free man!"

I smiled at him in recognition and with much love. I paused, sighed, and then looked down at the neighbors' brunch. It was almost 10:40 a.m., and I was wondering if they were looking at us or even hearing us. Not quite, but they saw me looking at them and waved for us to come down. I waved and acknowledged it. I said, "Right away." Then I looked at Camille and said, "Okay, I am convinced. You are really persuasive."

"...because you are my brother! You are my friend, my first friend since I was born. Did you know that?"

I pursed my lips and turned red. "Was I really?"

"Of course, always... Didn't you know that?"

"I was afraid you were not proud of me," I said.

"Me? ...Why? Why would I not be? I am telling you now."

"Okay, okay, my good Camille. So, may I hug you?"

"Yes, please. If you want to," he said lovingly and triumphantly. Then there was a moment of silence, and we hugged each other with our eyes shut.

"Just be honest with Pa," he said.

"What do you mean?"

"Let him know that this is your life. You need to have your space; you must have it. Raphy, you must manage your time and your own life. You must be solid and stick to your priorities. Just do not hurt him! You don't want him coaching you again, do you?"

"No, I will be careful not to!" I sighed lengthily. "I will not hurt him. Okay, let us go down for brunch with the rest. I already made my point to daddy, gently last week. Remember, with the olive oil on my ears?"

"Ha ha, yes, I do."

"Thank you, Kamkam," I mumbled quickly before I lost grip of my red eyes. He clutched my arms with support, as if he wanted to tell me he had faith in me. Forever, I was grateful to him; to this day … God keep him with His angels … We rushed down to join the rest.

Chapter 20
Passions and Roots—8
Turning Points

Rekindling the beautiful past while still laying on my bench in Magog (September 2008)

The following morning was a Tuesday; I went for my airport shift at 4:00 a.m., as usual. I had been working for Italiana Airlines for almost three years as catering agent until I was promoted. My new title became Catering Supervisor. My prime objectives were to offload (with my team) all food and drink that we found on the arriving flight; whether it arrived from Rome directly or had stopped in Athens on its way to Cairo. I had to destroy this food with my team, clean the aircraft, disinfect food galleys, coffee and tea containers, and prepare for next day's departure.

Among the things, I offloaded were the containers of food trays so that we could replace the used trays with the fresh ones for the departing flight. I would take the count of the departing flight from my colleagues at the airport station and do my homework to prepare for breakfast trays for all passengers flying to Athens or continuing to Rome (including an additional 10 percent). I would also prepare for the lunch snack for passengers continuing from Athens to Rome and others boarding the aircraft in Athens for Rome.

This would require that I maintained an up-to-date stock of clean cutlery, cups, saucers, sugar, salt and pepper bags, cologne, napkins, fresh cheeses, cakes, and more. In addition, it would require that I maintained good relations with the Cairo Airport Authority's kitchen staff so as to ensure top-of-the-line fresh croissants, rolls, clean omelets and fruits (for breakfast), as well as a pasta or chicken and salad snack for the lunch stretch between Athens and Rome.

The company's airport shuttle would pick up members of the morning shift, early enough to have us ready to set-up the check-in counters by 5:00 a.m. with our cash boxes, excess luggage tickets, and blank tickets for last-minute counter-sales as well as the luggage tags. We would be ready to fly our plane at 7:40 a.m., and I, at that time (for the first three years) would be racing with my support team to lay out 150 food trays. Later, when the DC10 came to life around 1973, we prepared much more than two hundred trays of breakfast and lunch, including vegetarian meals, seafood meals, and diabetic meals. All this continued to nurture my self-esteem and somehow I was jumping on a career of fun and success, throwing behind me years of marginalization.

That day, though, the Tuesday following Monday's Easter brunch and my conversation with Camille, I was enthusiastic and had lots of energy. Camille was right when he told me that I did not realize I was lacking identity. Now I moved from the phase of unconscious incompetence to that of conscious incompetence. This way, I could work on my weaknesses, decisively; I was determined to call the ministry of education. When I finished work that day, I did not go home. Instead, I went to the registrars of my secondary school (English school) and found a woman whom I used to speak to six years earlier when I had graduated from secondary school with a low average. I asked if she knew whom I should contact at the Ministry of Education. She said I did not need to. Instead, she could enroll me at school but as an outside student. Of course, I would pay a fee, but she would get me the syllabus and update me with all changes. I shook her hands and thanked her.

The following week, I stopped by her again, and we started the paperwork. Then she asked me to come by in September of 1973, which I did. In the meantime, I shared my plans with Camille, and he was thrilled. Soon, I spoke with my piano teacher, Mrs. Rossi, as well as Aldo, her husband, and both of their mothers. They were all thrilled and encouraged me not to slow down. They meant a lot to me and, soon, I was forming a new cocoon of trust and friendships. Madame Rossi continued to express her thoughts it would be really late for me to become a piano concert-virtuoso but that I would still be able to play good music for small audiences and for my family (not with an orchestra). Throughout my childhood and early adulthood, I had set myself three difficult pieces of piano to play, (The Impromptu in C sharp minor for Chopin, The second movement of Rachmaninoff's piano concerto number two and J.S. Bach's Italian Concerto). After three years, I surprised her with two of them; Chopin's Impromptu and Bach's Italian Concerto. The third, Rachmaninoff's, I played in 2013, in Montreal (thirty years later). This, however, will follow, later. She also said that I continued to be a good candidate for some of the world's film composers because of my dramatization of music and because of my lyrical music cadences. Soon, we planned to reduce the music courses and decided to blast the summer with theory and harmony, and then stick to piano and composition in fall and winter.

In principle, I clung to Korsakov and Rachmaninoff that summer and did not spare a moment to learn their musical sequences, orchestration techniques, instrumentation, musical intervals, and cadences. Previously, and over the earlier two years, I had already done extensive work on counter-point and polyphony, which were musical traits of J. S. Bach, F. Handel, Georg Telemann, and Luigi Scarlatti (the Baroque family of gurus). Furthermore, Mrs. Rossi intensified her musical dictations to me. She continued to play the piano and had me sit at a distance while writing what she played on empty music score. By time, my fingers were trained to record, on paper, both what I heard on radio or in a car and the music I inspired or invented away from my home. I would do this for any instrument I contemplated in my invention; I would hear the notes I invent and write them on music score for later expansion. That was the best I could do as an amateur but far from being career music professional. It was good enough for me; it still is.

After that, I worked on my self-esteem: my health, weight, cardio, and a little more squash. I dropped from 88 KG (198 pounds) to 74 KG (167 pounds) by Christmas. That year,

1973, Dad had to do a check-up for his larynx and an evaluation of his 1959 larynx and cancer extraction (Earlier in summer). He had to fly to London with Mom. Camille wanted to join them. I asked my boss at Italiana Airlines for airline concessions for them, and he offered Mom and Dad a 90 percent discount and Camille a reduced ticked. They all went and came back two months later, satisfied.

Dad's operation was successful and I felt proud to have assumed my role as a loving son to him and my beloved mother, all by myself.

Camille and I continued our mini-soccer extravaganza in our small street together with kids, parents, and other members of our neighborhood until early winter 1974. I would still go to Mrs. Rossi for my lessons after work, and her typical reception went like this: "Did you eat? You do not look like you did. Come, wash your hands and sit." She would go in her kitchen, get me a bowl of homemade ravioli (from A to Z) in chicken broth (not tomato sauce), and tell me to eat it.

"You'd better try these, *mon ami*. They're to die for!" Aldo would shout.

"It's ravishing, Mama Oly," I would say. "It is gentle and well balanced!"

Her husband would be devouring his cigarette and working on his artisanal products: buttons, leather, and cigarette holders. This is how he made his income. These were such nice, humble, and content people! How did they do it? Why did we let them leave? Why did we not give them their Egyptian citizenship when they used to live in Egypt for more than forty years? The two elderly mothers worked on knitwear to enhance the revenue of their home. During the 1973 war with Israel, and shortly after, these two elderly and brave women donated their knitwear to Egyptian soldiers, in action, through relief centers in Cairo. In all fairness, this was how responsible most Italians, Armenians, Greeks and Syrians of Egypt (amongst others) had always been. Sylvana was their beloved daughter who studied art and home décor.

Soon, I received the syllabus and started preparing my mind to study with my beautiful brother, Camille. On October 6, 1973 (one month after my enrolment), the fourth war with Israel broke out (1948, 1956, 1967, and 1973). Tragedies, loss of lives, fear, and war propaganda on all sides blew up again. The mood was a little more optimistic than after the 1967 defeat. Egyptian soldiers crossed the Suez Canal, seized it, and then reclaimed it. However, the Israeli troops penetrated the army that did so. Then there was a siege, and then a status quo, and then a ceasefire all the way until 1977 and during the time of talks for peace (concluded and sealed in 1978). During the 1973 war, the sounds of the Israeli supersonic air force and that of the Egyptian anti-aircraft artillery were brutal and scary. The action was only 101 kilometers from our villa.

In the meantime, as things slowed down during 1973 and 1974, including tourism, business, and trade, I had much more time to do my homework and prepare for my June 1974 final exam than I thought I would. Camille and I worked together many times, but somehow I felt increasingly comfortable studying on my own on the balcony or with the neighbors on the third floor of the building next-door, since they had a big roof. Grasping information was not a difficult brain function to restore, and my mind was clear. Camille was happy for me; he would smile to me from our balcony as I sat on the neighbor's roof, looking across at him.

At night, I would fix my parents' drinks, cucumbers, and cheese slices as well as some crackers and prepare for their daily TV extravaganza. Dad was getting older, yet he loved those moments of fun, relaxation, and assorted finger food. Auntie Zee, 74, would join us; it was one of her preferred outlets besides Auntie Helga was already too old to move up anymore.

Camille would be studying with his friends and discovering his own life. So, I'd join Dad, Mom and Auntie Zee for drinks and appetizers, while watching TV, filling-in the last stretch of my improvised day before I returned to studying.

In May 1974, I received my invitation to the secondary school tests for June, as well as the secret ID and seat number for the assigned auditorium. The hype was rising, and I knew that I could not afford to lose the battle especially with all eyes fixed at me. Indeed, 84 percent would get me to AUC (American University in Cairo) to study Communication and Journalism, but it was a great battle, a very harsh one; a ruthless one. I kept conditioning my mind. Eventually, I managed my day accordingly, working hours that could not be modified, rest hours, sleep, music lessons, and practice. I was twenty-two years old and had the energy to do it. Dad was proud of me and did not even offer to help. Just before the exams, I pledged at Saint Rita's Church next door, with Camille, not far from Mrs. Rossi's flat and from my former Italian kindergarten school, *Maria Ausiliatrice*. The week of exams was in early June 1974. It started and vanished like a flash. Before each test, I would close my eyes for a few minutes, breathe deeply, and reenergize. After my exams, I unwounded in roughly two or three days with great ease, joy, some fatigue, and immense anticipation for the results.

Then, by early July, the results came out. I rushed on a public bus to the Ministry of Education's assigned open grounds, for the North Cairo School District. This is where my results were posted, together with other out-of-school candidates. At 7:30 a.m., I arrived to the assigned campus and waited at its closed gates with together with hundreds of students. The gates opened at 8:00 a.m., and people flooded to the posted results. There were fifteen to twenty stands for posted results, depending on which letter preceded the secret ID number, which I had received prior to my finals. I reached the postings for my letter in such a rush, and by the time I found it, I was fiftieth in line, or so. Twenty minutes later, I was approaching the board; my heartbeat rose drastically. It was extremely hot, and I could see happy faces and gloomy ones all around.

Suddenly, there were two ahead of me, and then one, and then my turn came. I scrolled the alphabetized listings, hysterically, looking for my name and hoping it was there to start with. My heart was racing again, and I was truly drenched from sweat.

All my family and neighbors seemed anxious to know what I would get, hence, intense scrutiny. However, the most anxious was Camille, out of true love, though. He was verifying his own results, elsewhere, at the same time I was searching for mine. I felt the enormous pressure as I was scrolling down the names looking for mine. I could not find it. Had I flunked? Then my tears and sweat started flooding, and I was really shaking from grief. Suddenly, the young man standing just behind me, waiting to read the posting for his own results noticed me and held my arms. He calmly asked me in Arabic "What is your name?"

"Raphael Politis," I said and showed him my student card.

He was polite and quite concerned. He looked at the results and smiled at me. "Congratulations!" he said in Arabic, which is *Mabrouk*! Then he pointed to my name on a right column of successful students, which meant students who had scored in excess of 80 percent. In my panic, I was looking under the column for 60 percent and 70 percent but not under 80 or 90 percent. I looked again; it was 83.87 percent, not quite 84 percent but far higher than 60 and 70 percent. I had passed and with good grades. Suddenly I was free. I was myself for the first time in my life. I remembered Nicole from Bath and forgot completely about everything else. I hugged the student who helped me and said, *Thank you, thank you*. He too had passed with a good score. We each had a soda, and I said I was going to take a taxi to return to Heliopolis. He rode the taxi, with me, and I dropped him halfway, to my home.

At two o'clock in the afternoon, I entered our home and found Auntie Zee and Auntie Helga (dad's two sisters) sitting on their balcony (in the villa's ground-floor balcony). They were knitting and drinking tea. Then they saw me. As I went up the seven stairs to them, I smelled the roses, jasmine, mangoes, and oranges piercing my senses more than ever. I was rushing to give the news to Dad and wanted to tell him and Camille first. My two aunts were happy for me. Mom was at work.

Then I rushed up to Dad. My door key made some noise, so he rushed to the reception hall looking at me with eyes wide open! "It is good, Pa. It is good this time—83.87 percent!" I kissed his hand with intense love and pride. He hugged me, and at eighty-four years of age, he succumbed to tears. Then suddenly, I heard the door key. Camille had come back. He entered with a big smile. He threw his arms around my neck and looked into my eyes. My two aunties had already informed him of my score. He also pretended he did not know to give me the pleasure of being the one to break the news.

"So?"

"It's good news: 83.87 percent, just less than the 84 percent required by AUC."

"That's wonderful," he said, his voice breaking from emotions. He looked again, wondering …

"Kamkam, it's true—83.87 percent."

"That is just fine. You made it. You made it, Raphy. They should take you."

"Wait a minute, how about you? Did you break all records as usual?" I asked, holding his arms.

"I received 92.1 percent."

"Jesus! Kamkam, this is just brilliant!" I said, screaming with joy, and I hugged him.

"All my class made it," he said.

"Man! So you can go to Materials Engineering."

"Yes and no. I am not sure."

"Why?"

"Maybe I'll do Mechanical Engineering! But, Raphy, they *will* take you at AUC."

"Why do you say that?"

"They should. You have several ways to go about it. First, you work very hard and study so much, which is something they will love. Then Dad's health and how you support him and mom—all this would influence their decision, eventually. Oh, Raphy, I wanted you to do it so much, and you did it!"

"It is only because of you, my best friend, that I did it! Thank you, Kamkam! Remember that day on the balcony last year?"

"Of course, I do. You will see, it is only the start. You made it. We both did. The sun will continue shining on you and on me, and we will always be free."

I looked at him and felt a horrible and grave presentiment. I sighed and said, "Yes, Camille, I know!" Then I paused for a few seconds and looked back at him, gasping for air, heavily. "Okay, Kamkam," I continued, "I'll tell the Rossi's (my music teacher's family), and you tell the neighbors. Shall we party tonight in the garden and call the neighbors, say 8:00 p.m.?"

"Great idea, I'll tell them, and you give the news to Mrs. Rossi and her family."

Mom and Nora came around 6:00 p.m., one after the other, and we were all celebrating our successes and resolutions. Then Camille and I went to Saint Rita and lit two candles. We spent more than ten minutes in deep prayer, giving thanks, and returned home for some fun.

Chapter 21
Passions and Roots—9
The Last Summer – Building character

Rekindling the beautiful past while still laying on my bench
In Magog (September 2008)

By the end of August 1974, I applied to two universities and received notice from AUC that I did not make it for the fall semester (1974) but that the Dean of Students had put my name on the short list for the winter semester (January 1975). Although another university accepted my papers, I chose to wait.

In the meantime, I placed a petition to AUC highlighting the fact that I was working to pay for my studies and that I was taking care of my elderly dad who needed support. Then, I received a call from AUC's registrar inviting me to an interview with the dean of students. The interview went well, and I made my educational and career projections that seemed acceptable by the panel. The next morning, I received a call from the registrar's office asking me to pass by and pick up an envelope. That afternoon, I did so, and this was my Christmas present. The envelope contained my confirmation papers to join the BA program starting the 1974 school year's second semester, which was due to start in January 1975.

Camille was hopping with joy when he found out; he jumped like a baby and kissed my forehead. He told me that he received a scholarship from AUC and that he would join me soon, for the second semester, as well.

Overall, 1974 seemed like a year of high energy levels, expectations, dreams, ups, downs, and rewards. During all this turmoil in the summer of 1974, while soliciting universities and setting foundation and directions for our lives and careers, we took a break in September ('74) and went to our beautiful Alexandria resort of Agamy by the Mediterranean Sea. Camille, Wael, a few other acquaintances, and I went for a musical retreat, which the organizers named *Agamy Sandstock 1974*, but which I called "The last summer." More on this event will follow.

In January 1975, after having revised some of my course schedule and following a conversation with Camille, in which he gave me further advice, I registered my name at AUC Student Council's Social Events Committee, asking to contribute to social events that ranged from picnics to stage productions. My airline experience helped a lot in organizing overseas trips, and so did my appreciation for music, art, and theatre help me in planning for community events.

In March 1975, I started enjoying the healthy atmosphere of knowledge acquisition in classes with various brilliant professors and in fellowship with other students who, though seven years younger than me, engaged with me in various after-class studying sessions. The shades of my life were changing gradually, and so was its smell. A couple of girls over the first two years seemed to have a crush on me. After all, my hair was turning curly and dark brown, and I was beginning to float with life's waves. I did not commit to any of these girls but continued to be counted as an attractive and well-spoken male by quite a few girls.

Later, in the month of March (1975), I was approached by the Social Committee at AUC to play two pieces of piano, totaling a maximum of eight minutes, including the interval between each, at the AUC's Annual Talent Show. This project invited about twenty contestants to a competition of musical, comedy, or poetry talent, performing to an audience of a thousand. At least half of the audience would be actual AUC students and faculty members, and most of the rest were their family members as well as AUC alumni (former graduates). Immediately, I accepted the invitation and prepared to play two pieces of music on the piano and to make a funny sketch on stage. Camille was thrilled when I told him! Over the years, I had become a good performer.

As I grew older, these experiences added more shades to my character, depth of field to my sight, and colors to my spirit.

Then I would meet my small and scattered audiences, later, at the cafeteria or at the fountain area, and sit with them, talking about practically anything!

Toward the end of April 1975, one month before the end of my first semester (the second semester of the school year 1974/5), I had developed the habit of entering into Ewart Hall from the back door, more frequently than I did at the beginning of the semester. This I did between sessions with a tea and a biscuit, and I would fall in trances of thirty minutes, playing a romantic *sonatine* for Schubert or Beethoven or, even, a Gymnopédie Eric Satie. I would just revitalize my soul with the glorious resonating sound of the grand acoustic piano, that marvelous Bechstein piano, unlike many ordinary pianos. The piano produced a sweet and velvety sound that gradually increased in brightness, depth, resonance and volume as one applied more pressure. It was a double-action piano like all Steinways, Bechstein, Baldwin, Yamahas, etc. Anyway, the university's Bechstein had a romantic sound, whispering in its low moments and roaring in its higher ones. Its echo filled the air, almost haunting the auditorium like an orchestra. I would keep the hall dark and leave a gift to its guardian so that he would leave me play, in peace.

For thirty minutes, I would fall into a trance just until I returned to my world. Then, I would cover the keyboard with its embroidered cloth and close its cover. I would pick up my music score and class notes and prepare to walk to the left side of the stage on to its extreme left, down its five steps and on to the door leading to the university's fountain area. On the way out, I would notice five, six, and even ten students of my brother's age (six or seven years younger than me) sinking in the dark auditorium's seats, books closed and eyes shut, as they devoured my song menu of the day.

Their silence made me flourish with joy, and their undeclared applause humbled me greatly. Then, I would smile at them on the way out, and whomever I found closest to the aisle,

I would pat on the shoulder, in acknowledgment, or I would give a *high-five* while smiling.

At least two days of the week, I started my morning shift with Switzer-Airlines at the airport and rushed to the center of the city for my classes. Switzer-Airlines had accepted my application for a career move as a VIP and Customer Service Representative weeks after I started university in January 1975. I had resigned from Italiana Airlines with lots of love and experience.

Of course, by the time I arrived to classes, I was drenched. I certainly seized the opportunity of taking a public bus to university, for an hour, to sleep and pick up some energy and focus. On other days, it was the other way round. I would start an early day at university and end up with an afternoon shift at the airport and return home, beaten by exhaustion, around midnight. It was tough but manageable and Camille never stopped to encourage me to *persist*. *"It will* soon be over and we will start living, my brother". He would say!

My new job at Switzer-Airlines and SNTO (Swiss National Tourist Office) was a true pleasure; I just loved it. The public relations side was wonderful. Over the years, I met various prominent heads, CEOs, government cabinet heads, and even actors like Betty Davies, John Finch, David Niven, Egyptian actress Sanaa Gameel, film director Sir Richard Attenborough, and Mr. Youssef Shaheen, as well as singers, such as Charles Aznavour, Umberto Totzi and Amadeo Minghi.

Later, one day in 1975 or 1976 (my memory fails me), I even had a chance to meet and escort the prominent piano virtuosos and concert players Olga and Xaven Katchadourian (both over seventy years of age, white haired, slightly stout and so classy). They were direct cousins of Aram Katchadourian, the famous writer of *Ballet Spartacus* that stunned world ballet-audiences, including those of the Bolshoi concert hall of Moscow. It is regarded as one of the most sublime ballets, just as Tchaikovsky's *Sleeping Beauty* is. Both *Olga* and *Xaven Katchadourian*, originally residents of Egypt, had moved to the

United States but had a Four-Hand (two pianos) concert in Alexandria, Egypt, the day before I met them at the airport. An Egyptian musician of Italian roots, whom my music teacher, Olympia Rossi, recognized when I mentioned him to her, later, accompanied them. I believe his name was *Renzo* or something like that; I had also seen him standing next to Bellardinelli at the Opera House gates while it was burning in 1971. I remember that day I asked the Katchadourians for some piano advice with Chopin's *'Impromptu in C sharp minor'*, for piano.

"Excuse me maestro [I said to Mr. Katchadourian] how do you play this glorious piece if the score has a different count for each hand; the right one in quarter notes and the left in sixes?"

"You don't count to make them fit. You play the left hand in sixes, repeatedly as arpeggios making them fit well in each bar. You keep doing this for a few minutes until you feel the flow and then, you introduce the right hand in quarters, to fit the bar as well, without trying to relate the right hand to the left one; hence introducing the right hand after you would have already started with the left"

"Do you play music, asked me his sister?"

"Yes; I am a music scholar with a private teacher. I am not a professional musician, though. I am so proud to speak to you.'

"Which level?"

"Three."

"Thank you and best of luck for your future career. We started like you and even played at the old opera house in Cairo ten years ago in 1966."

"Oh this is lovely. Thank you for sharing it. I think I saw the gentleman accompanying you standing next to the Opera's Orchestra Director 'Bellardinelli', in October 1971, as it was burning."

"Where you one of the students who helped save the library?" asked me Renzo.

"Yes, and you smiled to me that day and even gave me a Soda drink, standing next to Bellardinelli"

He smiled and said, "Oh, yes, yes… I remember, now. It was a tragedy but you all worked hard and saved most of it." I was not sure if he really remembered me or if he was just being courteous.

I smiled to all of them in ecstasy shook their hands while overwhelmed with joy and emotions, until they left to their gate.

They gave me what I needed, and I thanked them for it. I was practicing at home to surprise Mrs. Rossi on her birthday, with that piece. Incidentally, that was not my only pianistic whim; I had always hoped to play the second movement from Sergei Rachmaninoff's Concerto number 2, which is a sublime pianistic display of pain and suffering as well as Bach's Italian Concerto in D Minor. I managed to play two of these over the years; the first and last but not the Concerto number 2 for Rachmaninoff; for more than twenty years. Of course, I played many preludes, partitas, sonatinas, waltzes and others for many other musicians, like Bach, Mozart, Beethoven, Schubert, Chopin and many more.

The school year ended by early June 1975, and I was a little freer to resume the previous frequency of my piano lessons. I was ready, though, for a long vacation. Until then, I would brag a little to my office peers about my artistic experiences on stage and to my university colleagues about important heads I had met at the airport, without being too arrogant.

Around early August 1975, Mom, Dad, my sister, brother, and I went for the holidays to Alexandria at our preferred Mediterranean beach of *Agamy*. The resort was quickly filling with lovely cottages, cabins, cafés, bistros, and restaurants. It had only one medical center, one or two super markets, and the central post office, together with the telephone, telegram, and telex complex, all in one building. My parents booked us *Chalet-280* for our summer vacation in Agamy, Alexandria. My sister and I went for a week at first and then returned to Cairo for our jobs (her at the bank and me at Switzer-Airlines). After this, we returned to the resort on separate weekends. Once back to the resorts, we changed attire, wearing our shorts, slippers, and T-shirts like the rest. Nora's weekends were Saturdays and Sundays; mine were Tuesdays and Wednesdays. I was still working at the airport and was waiting for a promotion and transfer to the head office.

Our Chalet-280 was a nice, spacious cottage overlooking the sea that hosted many of my cousins during this vacation, not to mention my dear Auntie Touna, the *cookie master*! Having breakfast together, smelling the sea salt, feeling the mornings' and evenings' fresh breeze, nibbling chips, nuts, crackers, and cheese at night on the balcony while covering ourselves in blankets if it got too windy was a unique experience! Camille, in the meantime, had many university friends picking him up for a dance or dropping him back from a dinner at a restaurant. They would join us and walk out and in at any time.

In August 1975, Camille was seventeen and a half years old. He was five feet nine, dressed like Cat Stevens with his loose shirt falling on his light-colored trousers, and he let his long, curly, black hair roll on his head, sideways (left and right), while split in the middle. It also covered part of his forehead. His eyes were dark brown, and the girls at university and Agamy Beach fell for him. He was so beautiful, proud, and giving to friends, cousins, and others who turned to him for advice. Most of all, he changed my life. These cousins and friends talk to me at least once or twice every month, to this day in September of 2008, thirty-three years since I saw him last. We continue to mention my brother, the angel, the legend!

Chapter 22
Passions and Roots—10
The Day I Said Farewell to Camille

Rekindling the beautiful past while still laying on my bench in Magog (September 2008)

On a sunny Wednesday afternoon, around 3 p.m. (on August 20, 1975), I was preparing to leave Agamy Beach in Alexandria, after having spent my weekend with the family at the seaside cottage, Chalet-280. We were all spread by the sea, under two umbrellas, with several chairs, hay carpets, and some towels, just as we used to with those who left Egypt in the sixties (at Mandara Beach) and others. Dad, mom, Camille, my aunt Touna and friends, were present. My sister was in Cairo preparing to come on her weekend, two days later. I had to be back in Cairo on Wednesday evening to start my early shift on Thursday morning. The aircraft's departure to Zurich was at 6:50 a.m. on Thursday. So I decided to take a taxi from Agamy resort to the central train station in Alexandria and made it on time for the 5:40 p.m. train, so as to arrive in Cairo two hours later on that Wednesday evening.

I had spent a magnificent weekend with the family and had an opportunity to join Camille with his girlfriend Norma and two other couples (friends of his) for an evening beach party the night before. That night, Tuesday, August 19, the evening before my return to resume my shift in Cairo, I returned to the cottage early and joined Mom and Dad on the balcony for the remainder of the evening, and we shared a pot of caraway tea. Camille was still with his friends. I had had my two drinks of beer and could not handle anymore. Then, my parents went to sleep. I packed my bag for the next day's return to Cairo, while Camille was still out with his friends. Then I went back to the balcony, listening to music on an old-fashioned tape deck (top of the line, at that time). My tape had Spanish songs by Joachim Rodriguez, played on the guitar. The set-up was perfect—evening hours, deserted beach, the sound of waves, smell of sea salt, the feel of sand on my face, and the sound of the Spanish guitar. Smoking was a bad habit of mine at that time, and I had not learnt to decline it, not even, after Dad's unfortunate experience with throat cancer. He was a heavy smoker himself. My average daily intake of cigarettes was two packs.

    That night, I sat down on our balcony gazing at the seashore. I replayed my life events, just like with a film reel. Camille seemed to me a perfect brother, and now he had this cute Egyptian girlfriend, Norma, and the year before, Melissa, the hot English girl whom he met in London in 1973, while accompanying mom and dad for dad's throat check-up. Being single was not helpful for me, I thought but I knew that something nice was in store for me. Suddenly, the tape deck turned to the other side all by itself, and I dozed for another thirty minutes in the dark hours of the night. I still remember the smell of the sea that night and the actual sea salt at distance from the shore, the gentle sound of its tiny waves, their looks and those of their glittering ripples, especially at nighttime, struck by the powerful light of the glorious moon, shining on Alexander the Great's shore. It felt humid and was turning pitch black. The balcony's fence was made of typical big, white bricks, in the shape of clumsy trapeziums. You would not need to look far to notice the grayish-lead gypsum fillings between them, and beyond them, the sandy beach, all the way deep down, until the white sand turned wet, into mud, as it blended with the seashore. A few weeds lay across the beach. By midnight, Camille returned from his dinner-dance and joined me on the balcony for over an hour of brotherly chat.

    By 1:30 a.m., I felt tired and decided to go to bed. I rinsed my face- lips and eyes from the sand to get rid of the taste of salt and went to bed. Camille followed me less than one hour later; I heard him go to his bed next to mine, by 2.15 a.m.

    At 10:00 a.m., the following morning, Camille prepared breakfast for him and for me. Dad and Mom were already by the beach. Camille and I each ate two fried eggs for breakfast and tea for the last time before I left Agamy at 3:30 p.m., heading to Alexandria's train station and back to Cairo, as planned.

At eleven o'clock (Wednesday), we finished breakfast. My suitcase was already packed, and I put-on my bathing suit, slippers, and T-shirt. We spent the remaining few hours with our parents at the beach, under the umbrella. Camille's friends passed by and joined us. Then, at 3:00 p.m., we left the family, and Camille decided to escort me to the taxi stand. First, we walked through the golden soft sand of the Mediterranean coast toward the cottage so that I could change my clothes and pick my bag. I put on my jeans and T-shirt (the Agamy Sandstock 1974 concert T-shirt), and so did Camille, but he wore his white trousers that extended a few inches below his knees and above his ankles (a 1970's fashion).

The story behind this T-shirt goes back to September 1974 (the year before) when Camille, Wael, some other friends, and I went for the musical retreat almost at the same spot where we were walking with my bag toward the taxi stand in Agamy (in this August 1975). It was a one-night retreat called *Agamy Sandstock 1974*, which was reminiscent of the famous *Woodstock* Music Fair of 1969. It took place overnight on a lovely September evening in 1974 on a wide-open terrain overlooking the beach in between various distant cottages and close-by to cafés and restaurants, one of which was our beach club hangout, *Chez Georges*. Electric connections were extended from everywhere to the huge, elevated platform for the musicians. That night, I could see all types of instruments, mikes, keyboards, bass, lead and rhythm guitars, cymbals, drum sets, saxophones, and woodwind instruments. There was a mix of over fifteen bands, solo singers, and solo instrumentalists. The crowd was close to five thousand young Egyptian spectators and tourists.

Friends, couples, lovers, and groups started pouring in at 3:00 p.m. that day. By 6:00 p.m., the place was overcrowded, and I remember seeing vendors of soft drinks, chips bags, sandwiches, and cigarettes running through the packed lying audience.

At 7:00 p.m., the evening was taking over from the fading light of the day, and for the first twenty minutes, we heard the sound of loud electric guitar strings and drums filling the atmosphere through the scattered loudspeakers. After these twenty minutes of musical prelude, the master of ceremony stood up to present both performers and the program, which was to end at 7:00 a.m. the following morning.

Then, for twelve continuous hours, save a few intervals, the crowd sank in a hopeful, happy, and enthusiastic youth experience, listening to all sorts of songs. There were English, French, Spanish, Italian, Greek, and Egyptian songs of the sixties and the early seventies. Many of these songs were those by Cat Stevens, Elton John, Paul Anka, Charles Aznavour, Cliff Richard, Gilbert Bécaud, Georges Moustaki, The Moody Blues, Sayed Darwish, Haleem, Pink Floyd, the Beatles, Led Zeppelin, Dalida, Pepino Galiardi, Pepino di Capri, Mamas and Papas, the Monkeys, Vanilla Fudge, and so many more. The performers were great Egyptian musicians: The Black Coats, Les Chats, Les Petits Chats, Stardust, Omar Khairat and his Band, Ismail Hakim, the Mass, and so many others. Sadly, many of these, too, are gone forever, amid harsh change, cultural dissonance and apprehension. Alas, these rich and intertwining cultural portraits could no longer sustain themselves; because there was no longer a solid social canvass that could hold them!

Overall, the atmosphere was close to perfect, that night, except for a few who turned rowdy after having consumed many drinks and loaded cigarettes. Of course, the prominent ambiance was one of friendship, camaraderie, and trust—an Egyptian hippie atmosphere, seeking peace and love after years of hurt and national grief.

The celebration was a sweet, honest, and genuine moment of faith that followed the 1973 war between Egypt and Israel, hoping that there would be no more bloodshed on all sides, no more pain, no more grief, and no more family tragedies. After all, between the 1967 war and that of 1973, hundreds of thousands had perished from the Egyptian side, not to mention from the Israeli, Syrian, Palestinian, Jordanian and other partners. The concert came at a time when nobody knew where Egypt was heading to but exactly where we all wanted it to be, if even for one evening.

We heard one song after the other. Smoke filled the air, and the crowd started succumbing to sleep, right on the sandy floor, some with sleeping bags, and others with hay carpets, and many with woolen sheets. Every now and then, we would stand up, replenish our stomachs with some food or drink, dance a little, sing with the bands, and then stretch again on the ground. Overall, it was a strikingly different experience from that of the earlier, morbid post-war one. We were united with hope.

By dawn, the music started to melt a little while the smell of the September waves was tickling our nostrils. Some of the mellow and romantic songs took over, such as "Concierto Aranjuez" by Joachim Rodriguez, just until we heard the last song during the first few moments of dawn. The Black Coats' keyboardist, Ismail Hakim, played it. He played the first few notes on the piano from Elton John's "Yellow Brick Road," and all the rest of the bands, singers, and instrumentalists went on stage to hum the song. We all joined him in one of the most spectacular musical concerts I have ever witnessed on the Mediterranean beach of Alexandria. We were ecstatic and bought T-shirts marked: Agamy Sandstock 1974, which we still have, to this day.

After that, we left and took a taxi to a third-class motel in downtown Alexandria and plunged into five hours of sleep in a room with dusty beds and ants everywhere. Then, of course, we went for a healthy afternoon meal of sandwiches and cold cuts. We were such a good team of cousins and lifetime friends. However, we made sure to buy our T-shirts, and we wore them the year after, in 1975. I still have mine until this day, and my beautiful brother's in a safe leather bag.

Camille and I were wearing those T-shirts on Wednesday, August 20, 1975, as we headed toward the taxi stand. There were quite a few taxis, and it was still 3:30 p.m. We had enough time for another chat, one last chat with my brother before I went back to Cairo. My heart was feeling heavier by the minute, but I did not know why! It was the same presentiment I had when my brother stood with me in 1973, urging me to pursue a remake of my high-school exams and promising me that the sun would continue shining on both of us. It was a somber presentiment.

As we waited for the taxi, he asked for five Egyptian pounds ($10 US dollars, then) since I was making a decent salary. He wanted to take his Egyptian girlfriend out or something. I declined, just like that! I do not know why … It was my life's worst decision ever, one that would haunt me until that day in September 2008, in Magog, and all the way to my grave. God help me! …after all he did for me.

When I said no, because I barely had sufficient cash to return home in Cairo, should something go wrong, he stood still, proud as always, smiled, and said, "That's all right." Then we hugged each other, he patted me on my left shoulder, then stretched his right arm under my left arm backward, reaching my right shoulder in absolute affectionate and brotherly love.

I clutched him and put his head in my arms, smiled, and said, "Bye-bye for now, my Kamkam." Then I grabbed my bag and moved to the first taxi in line. He turned back, heading to the beach. The sunlight was vivid, and the street was dusty but not sandy like the beach. Of course, it was not very clean. There were trees, all around us, to the left and right of the road; they were fig trees and date trees, all naturally sprung. I was still able to smell the sea and feel its breeze, despite the afternoon heat, but could no longer see the sun as it was far down behind the houses. Then I moved on and opened the taxi door, to enter it.

Suddenly, as I was just about to ride the taxi, I reflected, stood up for a few seconds, and turned my head to notice Camille walking back toward the beach. To my biggest surprise and for some unknown reason, he too stopped and turned back to spot me looking back at him. Then he smiled again, raised his hand up to his mouth, and blew me one last brotherly kiss, a habit he had with all those he loved. This kiss would keep me going until I meet him again, one day. I waved to him and blew back another kiss at him. An hour later, close to 5:00 p.m., I was on the train to Cairo with a heavy heart. I was ready to go home and have my supper. On the train, I looked out through the window and saw that the sky was reddish-gray and the sun was sinking intermittently between the clouds. I still remember the atmosphere of that moment, one of a portrait with a sinking sun preparing to dive into the depth of the sea. My train was air-conditioned and had been imported from a European Eastern-Bloc country some six years earlier with a few other trains for the Egyptian Locomotive Company. It was clean and comfortable. By the time I arrived to Cairo's central station, it was close to 7:30 p.m. I took a cab and arrived home in Heliopolis (where we lived), an hour later.

Chapter 23
Passions and Roots—11
The Day the Sun Went Down

Rekindling the beautiful past while still laying on my bench in Magog (September 2008)

The civil war in Lebanon had broken out in July of 1975 (the previous month), and I read in the local papers that it was one of its fiercest and most destructive civil conflicts across its history. In the Bible, several had predicted its violent turmoil: Jeremiah, Ezekiel, Isaiah, Nahum, Habakkuk, and others.

Habakkuk 2:17 - *The violence done to Lebanon will overwhelm you; the destruction of the beasts will terrify you, for the blood of men and violence to the earth, to cities and all who dwell therein...*

It took close to ten years for the horror of the great war of Lebanon to subside. Many left their homes. None of the war rivals seemed to justify their violence and differences; it was an endless struggle for power. However, God promised Lebanon to flourish again one day.

Isaiah 35:2— *it shall blossom abundantly, and rejoice with joy and singing. The glory of Lebanon shall be given to it, the majesty of Carmel and Sharon. They shall see the glory of the Lord, the majesty of our God.*

So, back to July 1975, my maternal cousins and their father moved to Cairo as soon as the war broke out. Auntie Lydia (the youngest of mom's four sisters) had passed away in 1969 in Beirut by heart failure. Most Lebanese friends and relatives leaving Lebanon, managed their stay in Cairo during its 1975 war, but my parents insisted that our cousin Marcelle (Late Aunt Lydia's daughter) and one of my sister's best friends stay with us at our villa, until we had some idea of what would happen with Lebanon. She stayed in Cairo with her father. Her two brothers had left for Europe.

When Marcelle moved in July 1975, her dad stayed with us only for a few days, and then he moved to his sister's home in Zamalek, a suburb of Cairo, just until Marcelle was able to find a close-by nicely furnished apartment, for both of them. By August 1975 (a few weeks after the great war of Lebanon), Marcelle started to loosen up from the war shock. She would travel to Agamy Beach, Alexandria, to our rented cottage, Chalet-280, with the rest of us. Otherwise, she would share my sister's bedroom when she returned with her from Agamy, until she made her move to her own place with her dad. Furthermore, she was able to secure a good job at an internationally acclaimed advertising company in Cairo by mid-October '75, not far from where my sister worked at the bank.

On Sunday, August 24, 1975, Nora and Marcelle returned from their usual weekend rest at the cottage in Agamy (four days after I had returned from Agamy beach and bid farewell to Camille). At 7:00 p.m. on Monday, August 25, we received a call from our parents in Agamy saying that Camille had fallen sick. My parents thought it was an unknown virus and mentioned that he was increasingly weak. The following day, Tuesday, August 26, after waking up from a horrifying nightmare, which felt like a premonition, mom called again from Agamy Beach in Alexandria to confirm that the doctors had diagnosed Camille's illness as *paratyphoid*. I started to panic, especially after my nightmare and earlier presentiments.

The night before, Monday, August 25, 1975, I went to sleep contemplating travel to Alexandria on whichever means of transportation was available, bus or train (before my parents called for the second time). I went to bed with a heavy heart. I had seen him last on the Wednesday of the previous week when he walked me to the taxi stop. Then, in the middle of the night, I woke up with a haunting dream. I still remember it. I walked through our bedroom (Camille's and mine) toward the bathroom, past the powder room through a corridor, at the end of which was the kitchen. Instead of turning left to the bathroom, or further down, to the powder room I continued toward the kitchen. As I entered the kitchen, I noticed it was flooded with water, almost 1.5 inches deep and leaking out toward the corridor, the powder room, and on to the bathroom. I could not call the plumber at 2:00 a.m. and wanted to get to the source of this leak. *It has to be from the kitchen sink*, I thought, *or else from the main feeder-tube*. My memory fails me now, and I am not sure, if I ever turned the faucet off or if I had found the source of the leak

What I do remember was that I grabbed the old, rusted metal bucket together with some rags, took off my pajamas, wore my shorts and then started mopping the water and squeezing it in the bucket for over an hour. I still cannot recall what time I finished. Eventually, I went to bed after I showered and woke up shortly after my sister's alarm clock rang.

Next morning (Tuesday, August 26), there was no trace of the water, and I found the bucket on the balcony, with no rags. I could not have thrown the rags in the waste bags and carried them down for pick-up. Our kitchen was dry and tidy. So, what happened? I wondered and I still do! God only knows if this really happened or whether it was just a presentiment.

Then came that second call from Alexandria that morning (Tuesday, August 26, 1975), confirming that Camille had contracted paratyphoid and that he was surrounded by my parents and his friends, and this disturbed me greatly. I decided to buy a train or bus ticket to Alexandria, whichever was available, first. I went to the bus station and then downtown to the central train station. The first available was the Thursday morning train, and I thought, then, that it was good enough. I thought that I would make it on time. I bought the ticket and returned to Heliopolis.

Just before entering our villa's gate, that afternoon, I stopped at the telephone/telex/telegram company, in front of our villa and ordered an extended call to my family at the chalet in Agamy. *Cairo's homes were still not connected with long-distance lines at that time*. Moreover, since I would have had to wait over twenty minutes for my turn to make that call, I asked the telephone company to transfer it to my home (just across from it), once it was available, and rushed upstairs so as not to lose incoming calls. After fifteen minutes, I received a phone signal from the telephone company downstairs that transferred me to the telephone exchange in Agamy. Sadly, they advised me that the family at Cabin-280 had all moved out to Alexandria's main hospital (Mouassat Hospital), for emergency. They told me that there was no point in trying to reach the hospital since they would not have had the time to arrive and register anyway. I was wearing a jeans and an orange jersey shirt with no undershirt. I started sweating profusely, and my shirt got wet. Half of my buttons were undone, and I started recapturing the earlier night's premonition. I crossed the street and asked for another extended call after thirty minutes. A few minutes later, Nora and Marcelle returned from work. Then my Aunties Zee and Helga called us three (Nora, Marcelle, and me) down to their apartment on the first floor for prayers. It was typical of them to assume their role as traditional Christian believers.

Camille had been increasingly pensive the last few weeks preceding his ascension to God. His knees were weak, and he would tell me his thoughts about it, yet he would always find the time to ask about my music; my new career chapter and whether I had any "nice adventures" in the midst of his discomfort. He would continue to promise me that I would rest one day and that I would, eventually, start living! His excellence as a brother never ceased to overwhelm me. In the middle of his fatigue, he would not only ask about my job and my music but also slide an insinuation, a subtle but extremely gentle one—pressure, if you will—that it was time for me to fall in love. It was almost as if he took it upon himself to walk me through the whole spectrum of metamorphosis, one-step at a time, with respect and affection, of course. He asked about my love adventures because it was Camille the loving; Camille the great; Camille the beautiful brother!

Later in the evening, we received a call from Alexandria, from the hospital. Mom said that several doctors were evaluating

Camille at the same time and that initial diagnosis showed a dual infection: paratyphoid with possible encephalitis. This is a severe form of meningitis that afflicts the nervous system (cerebral cortex) and that can cripple its prey for the rest of its life or, else, cause loss of life in as little as one and a half days.

On Wednesday, August 27, 1975, I called my superiors at Switzer-Airlines and advised them that I had to make an emergency trip to Alexandria on Thursday (my day-off) and that I would need Friday off to help my parents with my sick brother. I got my two days with no difficulty and they offered to help me with medication if we needed to import it overnight from Switzerland. I was overwhelmed with my bosses' kindness. Their names were Hassan and Adel. Hassan was doing fine until recently in 2016. I would still visit him every time I return to Egypt for holidays. In 2017, he returned to God at the age of 88. In December 2017, I visited his grave to pray for him. Adel, as well, is doing fine and lives with his family in Australia. I saw him in 2017 in Cairo.

For no reason, something drove me to cleaning up our home, tidying the chairs, furniture, and all I could see in front of me. I may have been thinking that they would soon return and that they needed the tidiness. Alternatively, it could have been a subsequent act to my earlier premonition about the kitchen flood. Deep inside, I may have been preparing for the inevitable without really perceiving it. I even cooked two trays of lasagna. I honestly did. Nora came back from work with Marcelle, that Wednesday (August 27, 1975), and we all prayed again for Camille's recovery.

At 7:00 p.m., I crossed over to the telephone company to order three more long-distance calls to the hospital and to have them transferred at our home, just across. By 11:00 p.m., Nora and Marcelle went to sleep, and I watched some TV. Then my calls finally came in, and I was fortunate to receive my connection, with no difficulty, to Camille's room at the hospital. *It was 11:30 p.m.*

Another person answered the phone, and I said "Greetings, is this the room where Camille Politis is staying?" I heard scratching on the phone. "Hello, hello?" I said.

Then I heard the voice of a man responding, most probably his hospital roommate. He said, *"Ya Ellahi, Ya Ellahi,"* meaning, *My God, My God*, in Arabic He sighed, groaned in extreme agony, and then hung up the phone, just like that. I could not take this ambiguity any longer. My anxiety was rising. Therefore, I went down back to the telephone company and asked for three more long-distance calls. I returned home just after midnight. I made tea and waited by the phone, watching some TV.

My calls never came through, but I received another call from an uncle of mine who had stayed with his wife at my family's cottage during their last few days in Agamy. They had accompanied them to the hospital.

"Hello," I replied.

"Raphael it's your Uncle Guiorgui," he said in a serious but broken voice.

"Yes?" I said.

"Raphael, I need you to be strong. There has been a tragedy," he said. I thought something had happened to Dad, who was already eighty-six. Camille was almost eighteen, and I was twenty-four.

I had also had an earlier premonition, some years before, with Dad walking in a major Cairo Street, called El-Geish Street (the Army Street), where I was about to be run over by a public bus, but in which he stood up under the bus and lifted it with both hands, stretching over his head. He was pushing the bus upward, before it fell on me with all its passengers, until I slipped away. In my dream, I rushed to help him, pushed the bus with my right hand over my head, pulled him out with my left hand and then, let the bus settle on the street. After this, I kissed his hand and wished him well. Throughout my life, I have been plagued by presentiments, among which was this week's with the water flooding our kitchen, hinting to me about the beach and waves and, indirectly, about my brother.

"It's your brother, Camille?" said my uncle. "God give you strength. God bless his soul."

"Camille died?"

"Yes," he said. I did not ask how, why, when. Subconsciously, I thought he drowned.

"Whhahhhhhooooow." I sighed, exhaling lengthily and horrified. Then, instantly, the wall clock's pendulum rang 1:00 a.m.

"You have to listen to me, carefully, Raphael."

"Okay."

"I need you to go to the Greek Orthodox Patriarchate in Old Cairo and issue a permission to open the family plot—you know; the one where your dad's mother is buried and Uncle Gabriel. We will be back by 1 p.m. today." It was already past 1:00 a.m., Thursday. "Try to arrange for the funeral service with Monsignor Dionysius at the Greek Orthodox Metropolitan Parish in Heliopolis for no later than noon Friday and then prepare for the burial by 3:00 p.m. at the latest, that Friday."

"All right," I said, beaten and bewildered. I did not wake up my sister and Marcelle. My mind was racing, and I just did not know where to start. I was lonely, then, so lonely ... as always, truly until this day!

Immediately after, I ran five kilometers to my cousin Mady's home (daughter of Auntie Helga and mother of Wael and Sanaa), on foot and rang their doorbell at 2am. I was beaten, breathless and terrified from life. I, still, had not woken up Nora and Marcelle. My cousin Mady's husband (*Wadie*) opened the door. He was a prominent journalist. I told him and while horrified he made a few calls to the national newspaper night shift and we put together an announcement that would appear on Thursday's late morning's edition for Friday service. At 3:00 am, I called the Greek Orthodox Parish in Heliopolis, four kilometers north of our villa, and received confirmation from its secretary that Monsignor Dionysius would lead the funeral service, the following morning (Friday) at 11:00 am. This meant that the burial would take place at 02:00 pm at the Greek Orthodox Cemetery of Saint George in old Cairo (Fustat). I called Wadie to inform him so that he would enforce the obituary. By 4:00 am, I called my cousin Antoine, who is the son of my mother's eldest sister, Kaliope, and told him what had happened. He was shocked and said he would come by to pick me up at 5:30 a.m. to drive me to the Greek Orthodox Patriarchate (not far from the historical cemetery of Saint George in Old Cairo) and back, which would give me time to explain to Nora after she woke up, preparing to go to work with Marcelle. I returned home before 7.00 am.

At 7:00, the alarm clock rang, and a few minutes later, Nora was out of her room, followed by Marcelle. I had opened all the windows and shutters to allow light to come in to comfort her, the best I could. I was truly tired and had had no sleep. Nora and Marcelle walked out of the bedroom. Nora understood what had happened and shouted at me imploringly: "Camille?" I nodded and said yes. She screamed loudly. Most neighbors heard the screaming, opened their shutters and a few started calling, asking for explanations. Marcelle was numb and had already seen sufficient horror in her neighborhood in Beirut since war had erupted a few weeks earlier. I was laughing hysterically, gasping for air but with such a heavy heart.

At 1:00 p.m., the cortège arrived from Alexandria with my parents, my Uncle Guiorgui's, and his wife, Aida, in my uncle's car, followed by the Funeral Home's car. I stood out on the balcony, not knowing what to say. Dad, eighty-seven then, descended from uncle Guiorgui's car, broken and bending forward. Then, mom followed and then, Aunt Aida, uncle Guiorgui's wife). My mother's eyes caught mine, as she looked up at me upwards, standing and horrified, on the same balcony I stood, fifteen years earlier in 1960, to bid Auntie Lucie, farewell, when she fled Egypt. Mom looked up and said, in French *"Tous ira bien, mes enfants, je vous promets,"* meaning, *everything will be all right, my children, I promise you.* By the end of the day, everyone was beaten and lying back on all sorts of couches and sofas. Monsignor Dionysius opened his parish for Camille to spend the night, while performing the rituals and burning some incense. Then it sank into my stomach, and I realized that my beautiful brother, Camille, had died. I would never hug him again.

By late afternoon (Thursday), the phone started ringing endlessly, and close aunts and uncles started visiting us. Our wonderful neighbors followed shortly and so did Father Dionysius come to our home, to bless it and to burn incense in all its rooms. Then, four or five of the shop owners from the neighborhood (of all faiths) passed to pay their respects instantly without waiting for the proper rituals required before burial. They promised to come to church the following day.

Nora's other best friend, Kiera, came that afternoon and stayed for several weeks to support us. I could not cry and tried to induce myself to doing so. I went to my room (Camille's and mine) but did not succeed. By 10:00 p.m., Kiera and Marcelle warmed up the lasagna, and we all forced ourselves to eat a little. All of this happened as explained. The abundance of love that our home experienced that night and even for weeks was vast and immeasurable. Our neighbors from the three-story building, to the left of our villa, us were stunned and stayed with us for close to a week, on a rotational basis.

The following morning (Friday), the sun rose, as usual. We headed to church at 10:00 am. My dear neighbors were all over our villa, helping. We all arrived at church for the ceremony. There were more than two hundred people, one hundred of which, at least, were under twenty; they were his friends and many of our cousins.

Following service, the cortège entered the cemetery around 02:00 pm, and the procession started with over three hundred mourners preparing to put Camille's body to rest while his spirit ascended to heaven. The cemetery bells struck, at 3:00 p.m., Camille's body was lowered to the ground and his spirit ascended to God. At that moment, we were all numbed. A dark brown overcast pushed the sun down behind the dome of the ancient Saint George's Basilica at the entrance of the cemetery. A new chapter started in the dark hours of the night; the unpredictable, the ambiguous future, the frightful knowledge that Camille had gone for good was unbearable. Once we all returned home, our energy levels were gone, and our little angel had flown. He had departed to God. As of then and until I moved to Montreal twelve years later, I visited him (and later, Dad), every month. The cemeteries were located forty kilometers far from home, in the ancient city of Cairo called *Fustat (Fussatum)*.

Gradually after Camille's departure, I pulled myself together, and following one or two gentle notices of reprimand at work that sounded more like boosters than threats, I managed to reground myself. I resumed music, studies, improved my GPA, passed through probation, twice, and even joined the University Drama Group and became the official Yearly Talent show *Master of Ceremony,* for six years.

In November 1975, I played a requiem that I had written for Camille at the University's Ewart Memorial Hall, forty days after his departure. I did this as a thousand students sat silent for twenty minutes while I recounted his childhood and loving nature on the university's Bechstein Grand-Piano. I thought I owed it to him after all he did for me. I rewrote the music for full orchestra twenty-five years later (in 2000), and it remains a very touchy piece. It was aired repeatedly on Canadian classical radio stations since 2010. Its title is *On the Departure of my Beloved Brother*.

And then I realized that the sun should rise again, day after day, if we can only see it—just as it always had during my childhood, after each moment of psychosocial exile or public bullying. Camille's departure was my shock therapy and a far worse shaker than any injustice I had encountered, but it rooted me greatly. It grounded me, and I became very attached to my grieving, mother and my ailing father who would eventually follow Camille in 1978, out of grief and right in my arms.

Despite my heavy schedule, I would prepare supper and drinks almost four nights a week and join Mom and Dad. Auntie Zee would join too. As always, I would go downstairs to call her upstairs, for some finger food, drinks, and TV watching. I would cheer them and buy them fine bottles of drinks every time I returned from a training course in Europe. Life went on as a family but with a low tone of speech and a broken heart to all. After the TV show, I would walk Auntie Zee downstairs and stay with Auntie Helga to recount to her the TV comedy, which we watched, until she slept. She was too old to go upstairs by 1975. Among other things, it kept everyone going until Dad succumbed to a relapse of cancer in 1977 and on November 1, 1978, he departed to Heaven. Auntie Helga followed his departure on December 31 of the year after, leaving Auntie Zee all by herself downstairs, at the age of eighty. Together with Nimo's departure to USA in 1957, dad and Auntie Helga's departure to God subsequently, she had no one but Mady and us who would offer support to Auntie Zee. For me, the horror of losing my brother would haunt me for many years and, of course, would assume Dad's life shortly.

Chapter 24
Return to Life without Camille
Papa, Mon Amour

Rekindling the beautiful past while still laying on my bench in Magog (September 2008)

Gradually, by the end of the first year following Camille's departure, I had improved my GPA and seemed to be excelling in research. At the same time, the drama and theatre group members engulfed me in their projects, and over the years, I was fortunate to take part in major productions by Anton Chekov, Luigi Pirandello, Arthur Miller, Henrik Ibsen, and William Shakespeare.

In one of my extremely emotional performances, I was presenting the soliloquy by Marc Anthony taken from Shakespeare's *Julius Caesar*. I remember I had a small audience of fifty students in a small theatre (Howard Theatre). As I reached the end of my soliloquy, and as I delivered it with genuine anguish to my audience, firmly claiming that it (the audience) was the same as the Roman mob that Marc Anthony had reprimanded for its indifference to Caesar's death, I reached such heights of emotions that my voice roared with pain throughout the hall. I was able to restore my balance and assumed the image of typical Roman royalty while projecting to that small audience in front of me with grace and candor. Suddenly, my eyes were entangled by the tearful eyes of a younger student girl, sitting in the left column toward the middle of the sixth row downwards. She seemed overwhelmed and taken back by the performance. After this, I ended my soliloquy in utter sorrow for Caesar's assassination and for the indifference of Romans to his death. I turned my back to the left, looked down at his make-belief coffin with genuine tears, and exited the small stage.

After a few moments of applause, I walked to the backstage but returned once more for the cheering audience and for one, more, good round of applause. The person whose eyes I caught tearing jumped on the small stage and cuddled my left cheek with her very tiny but warm left hand. Her eyes were still wet, and she rubbed my hair. I blushed and thanked her. I knew her name was Dahlia. This rekindled my ego and love for life. Soon, both she and I developed a warm but short-lived friendship, which, unfortunately we did not pursue. However, I would soon prepare myself to fall in love with a girl called Helen from church. This was in 1981. I never knew why I did not go out longer with Dahlia. She was cute and seemed to love me. She was seven or eight years younger than me, just like the rest of my classmates were. We exchanged notes and studied together at the library, the main cafeteria, or the Fountain Area's main campus. My relation with Helen did not last.

The wealth of friendships and opportunities were due to my having followed Camille's advice to join university. I was still studying, working hard, and playing music, but I craved the second part of his promise, the one where I would finish my studies and slow down to do what I liked most of all: to rest, breathe, and to start enjoying life. The remaining members of my school soccer team witnessed Camille's departure and its effect on me as well as Dad's subsequent departure to God in 1978. Their support was priceless. The rest had flown out of Egypt in the sixties.

My dad's departure was just another blow. It was as destabilizing as that of my brother. Ever since Camille passed away, and following the presentiment, I had in my dream about the kitchen flooding before he died, I dreaded the earlier presentiment I had had. It was the one where I saw Dad standing under a public bus and lifting it with his hand before it fell on my head, to save me.

In late October 1978, I sensed a déjà-vu as dad's health deteriorated. He was gradually withering with grief after Camille left. He had a cancer relapse, twenty years after his larynx extraction and developed skin tumor in 1977. The hole, remaining in his throat following his earlier larynx extraction was starting to clog with mucous, which reduced his ability to breathe freely.

One day toward the end of October 1978, I noticed he was gasping for air and that he was unable to clear his throat (in addition to his galloping skin cancer). He had a tube that he used over eighteen years to clear the mucous in the hole within his throat. But that day, he was very weak, and his relapsing cancer hindered him from clearing his throat and from breathing properly. He could not clear his throat by himself, any longer. He required special medical equipment to ease his restrained breath. I tried to clear his throat for him, but he refused. I persisted until he agreed. I did and used gauze for a few minutes. Finally, he was able to gasp little intervals of oxygen that were hardly enough to keep him going for the day. I grabbed the telephone and called the central ambulance (downtown Cairo) but was told that the fleet remaining in its central headquarters was busy and that it was prayer time for many. I was very hurt. Therefore, I rushed down to Auntie Zee and asked her to stay with Dad until I grabbed a taxi and went to Cairo's Central Ambulance, and implored the available staff for an ambulatory car.

Mother was at her office, still working for the United Nations' FAO (Food and Agriculture Organization). As I arrived in the central ambulance station, I found more than ten ambulance cars parked, and the whole ambulance apparatus seemed frozen and grounded. It could have been worship time or fasting time; I cannot remember, but I was angry.

I saw a paramedic standing in the middle of the ambulance parking lot. I explained what Dad needed. I said he did not need an oxygen mask but a special machine that would suck the mucous from his throat, to permit him to breathe. He explained that he could not influence any of the available drivers and that the ambulance apparatus, at that time, had no such machine.

Apparently, there were only two of these machines available, as he explained. One was at the Italian hospital on El-Geish Street (Army Street in Abbassiya Square), halfway between Heliopolis and downtown Cairo and, and another was two blocks east of the Italian hospital, namely the Greek hospital on El-Geish Street. (The name of the street did not trigger any memories of the earlier premonition I had had.) Then, I looked at him imploringly, searching for his understanding to give clearance for a car. Then I held his elbow with both my hands and said, "Help me, God bless you." I was emotional but restrained.

"What do you want from me?" he said.

"Come and take him to the Greek Hospital, if you please. Could you do this for someone like your father? He is eighty-nine years old."

The paramedic stared at me, almost about to give in. A driver was standing next to him. I offered him and the driver 200 LE (Egyptian pounds), which was worth two months of my salary then (equivalent to two hundred US dollars, at that time).

"Use them as you will, for your costs, yourselves, or for charity; but please help me; we're losing precious time," I said.

The paramedic and the driver looked at each other, nodded at me, and took the money. They went and signed some roster book at a booth just out of their building's main gate. Then they invited me on board their van, and we rushed back to our home in Heliopolis, where Dad was still alive. We moved him on a stretcher to the van and rushed to the Greek hospital on El-Geish Street, where I spent over twenty minutes explaining that he was prepared to wait for a doctor, if these were the rules, but that, until then, he was in immediate need of the machine to breathe. Having managed stretcher cases at Switzer-Airlines, heading for Swiss hospitals, some of which ended joyfully, and some of which returned tragically, I was well experienced with the job. After all, I had done it for two years at the airport. I had celebrated happy conclusions with the families of healed patients, returning from Switzerland. I shared moments of intense grief with the bereaved families; families of those who could not make it back, alive. The paramedic and the driver said they were ready to return to their headquarters. To my utter surprise and heartfelt gratitude, they asked to talk to me on the side, where they handed back to me the two hundred Egyptian pounds that I had given them earlier. They smiled in extreme compassion, and wished Dad well.

"But this was our agreement, and I want you to keep it," I said.

One of them replied, "But you gave us the option of giving it to charity, and there is no better charity than helping an ailing human being. Besides, this is our holy month of fasting, and we have to do our evening prayers soon. So we must meet God with a clear conscience."

I smiled at them in gratitude, wished them blessed fasting, and insisted they kept at least forty pounds. Then I returned to dad. But it was not over. It was only the beginning of the struggle to have him survive. The required machine was in the hospital's storage, and I was told that it had not been used at the hospital for years.

Finally, Dad was moved to a proper stretcher (the hospital's roller-bed) and was placed by the wall in one of its corridors. After a total of thirty minutes of waiting, the machine came. The nurse who got it had it rolling on a mobile tripod. Dad was still struggling to clear his throat, and I was handing him gauze tissues, one after the other, to help him. He would let me do it for him. I collected the used gauze and threw it in the closest bin. Then the nurse and I connected the machine and started attempting to suck the mucous out of Dad's throat. And the inevitable happened. The machine did not work, and my anguish was rising to a level of intense hypertension and despair.

"Is there another machine at this hospital?" I asked, inhibiting my anger. "No, the only one available other than this is at the Italian hospital, two blocks away, on the same street," said the nurse.

"Any idea if it is working?"

"No, I cannot tell."

She seemed concerned and wanted to help. We used the closest phone to call the Italian hospital, but there was no one at the other end who could confirm the functionality of the machine. Dad was looking at me and seemed quite worried for me. He clutched my hand and signaled to me to calm down.

"Pa, I will find a solution; I promise you. I will rush to the Italian hospital and be back in about ten minutes, and then I will move you there."

He nodded his head. I asked the nurse to stay with Dad and gave her a pack of gauze, keeping the rest in my pockets. I begged her to have someone prepare and clean a functional wheelchair for the move. After all, as mentioned, I was trained to handle wheelchair and stretcher cases that boarded our flights and vice-versa. She promised she would prepare one, and I rushed like a flash of light, toward the Italian hospital, through the crowded, disorganized, dirty, muddy, bumpy, and broken pavement of El-Geish Street (Army Street). The street was full of traffic and public buses. I jumped up the hospital's main marble stairs and reached out for a receptionist but could only see two sisters walking out of the chapel looking at me.

"My sisters, help me, if you please, help me. My father is at the Greek hospital and is choking from lack of breath." I said. They rushed to the general manager of the hospital, wasting no time. I looked at him, recognizing him: he was Doctor Azzam Soulaimany, an uncle of my dear neighbor and friend who lived with his family in the villa behind us. I told him about Dad and implored him to help. "Doctor, help my dad please. Do you have this machine?"

"Yes," he said, "and it is working well! Go get Monsieur Georges [my dad], but I have no one to help you transport him here. I will prepare a private room for him. We can discuss details later. This meant I had to walk him down the staircase of the Greek hospital, through two side streets and back, up to the stairs of the Italian hospital.

A minute later, I stood at the Greek hospital's main gate, where Dad was already seated on a wheelchair. I descended backward, pulling dad as he sat on the wheelchair, carefully, right on the sliding pathway on to the street level. In a few seconds, I exited the hospital's fence and started my fifteen-minute journey of hell to the Italian Hospital, walking backward. At all times, I was holding on to Dad, to save him from slipping down or forward from the wheelchair. He did, several times, and his legs would hit the ground with his hips almost falling off the chair. (There were no straps on the wheelchair's leg-rests). I would also wipe his forehead. I stopped several times and pulled him up in the chair so that he would not slip down. I repeated this two or three times. I could not see his facial grimaces, since I was not facing him, but I could imagine how overwhelming this experience must have been for him. In any case, and at all times, I cuddled his shoulders and wiped his forehead repeatedly as I pulled the chair backward, surrounded by army trucks and other vehicles, let alone the atrocities of their dark exhaust and the street's overall debilitating pollution. Suddenly as I pulled his chair down the high pavement, with my back to the side street, toward the last stretch before the hospital, I found Daddy stretching his right hand backward and grabbing the trousers on my right leg forward. He was shrugging his shoulders and moving his head violently, trying to tell me something since he could not talk. I looked to my right and found a public bus full of passengers heading toward us without stopping at the traffic light. I was about to be run over by the bus. He saw it and saved me. A few people ran to help us and gave me a hand in pulling Pa up in the chair and then turning the chair forward. One carried the lower front of the chair holding Dad's legs, and two stood behind the chair, slowly pushing it forward until we made it to the hospital's main gate. I thanked them with intense emotion; and must have been shaking because Dad stretched his two hands and pulled my neck toward his chest to kiss me.

    I suddenly remembered my dream in Alexandria, of 1968 with Dad walking in El-Geish Street, pushing a bus over his head, to set me free, but had long forgotten it. Then, in turn, I clutched him tight, in tears. The three men who were helping us did not stop at this. They stayed with us to bring us up the slope to the hospital's gate, and the two sisters spotted us coming up. Two other male nurses rushed down to pull him up, by orders of Doctor Soulaimany. We finally entered the hospital room, on the first floor toward the right. I thanked the helpers from the street again and raised my right hand toward my heart, in an expression of love and gratitude. Then the nurses moved Dad to the bed. The hospital manager, Dr. Soulaimany, came for a short visit; he made sure the machine was connected and working.

Within a few minutes, I could see Dad breathe peacefully. He was still conscious enough to remove his mucous by himself. Then they stopped the machine when it was no longer needed and showed me how to use it in case I needed to. Later, the hospital's specialist checked dad out, and by 6:00 p.m., things were calm and Dad got some food and juice.

While staying next to dad, upon our arrival to his hospital room on the first night, he succumbed to sleep twice, for several minutes, as we communicated endlessly by whispered word, looks, and holding each other's arms. Our relationship reached its climax of compassion, richness, and love during these first hours at the hospital.

When Camille flew to God two and a half years earlier (1975), a good friend of mine (Nabil), one of my supervisors at Switzer-Airlines told me never to let go of Dad and that, at his old age, he was twice in need of compassion than a middle-aged Dad was, especially after the devastating loss of my young brother. He said, "Don't waste an opportunity to tell him that you love him, while he is alive." His words sank in my mind, and I remembered them as I sat next to Dad that night. After all, today's move to the Italian Hospital must have consumed him.

Soon, I sat with Dad in his small but private bedroom and spoke to him about various topics. He did mention his concerns about the last pension check that, normally, he would receive by mail that week and that, incidentally, required that he went to the ministry of social affairs, personally, to settle a retroactive raise. I promised to go the following day (amid my university hours and work schedule), so as to put his mind at ease, probably, in his final hours with us.

I smiled to him, helped him with his utilities since he was too weak to move out of bed, and kissed his hand, lovingly but with tremendous force so as not to seem condescending. In a sense, I felt I was compensating for my failures with Camille, far as I was from his bed during his last hours. "Good night, Pa," I said. "I will see you in the early morning, before going to resolve the pension changes. See you at 6 a.m." He shut his eyelids and smiled.

I was there next morning at six with his favorite fruit— peeled navel oranges—with salt sticks, a boiled egg and a thermos flask full of English breakfast tea. I left at 8:00 after helping him again and rushed for my courses. Mom joined him later, until I returned at 6:00 p.m. to relieve her.

Upon my return at six, I showed dad an envelope with LE 64 Egyptian pounds, which I claimed came from the pension department. I told him that I went to the Social Affairs Department and showed them my ID as well as his doctor's note mentioning to them that Dad was in remission at the hospital and that he could not move, easily. I told him, "That did it!" I handed him the money, and he asked me to give it to Mom. I promised him I would. It was one of my best decisions ever, even though it was a lie- *a white one*. Actually, I wanted to rest his mind about this issue, even if I had to lie at first and solve it subsequently. I did, later.

Anyway, that night (the second night), we had a wonderful father-son relationship. He would still whisper that night, just as he did for almost twenty years. However, that night, he would run out of breath as he spoke. By the end of the evening, he was running out of energy.

This is a genuine reconstruction of a lovely portion of our conversation that night, on October 31, 1978, after his dinner in bed.

"Pa, how's your energy level?"

He grimaced, smiling and happily acknowledging it was all right.

"I love you so much, Pa, and I will make sure that you are well attended to. Are you breathing well?"

He nodded. He could no longer communicate even by whispering.

"Did you know that they want me to be the Master of Ceremony for next summer's talent show at university?"

He nodded again and signaled for some paper and pen.

I got it for him.

He wrote "Hold on to your music. Never stop." After Camille died, I moved the piano from the family room on to the bedroom, which Camille and I used to share. Dad would sneak in quietly and sit on a chair behind me to listen to me. It made me very proud and content especially when I thought I might have failed him for not having a fiancée. His appreciation for my music made me prouder, as proud as I was when he knew I made it to university.

"I will not, Pa! I will never abandon music. I promise you, and I will finish my university degree, too, I promise."

He nodded again, while smiling, and wrote something else.

"Stand by your mother, and my two sisters."

"I will, Pa. I promise you that I will. This is my oath. Now, rest and be well. I love you, Pa."

At the end of the evening, I could no longer stand the agony of watching Dad struggling to communicate but failing to even whisper, as before. I hugged his head, grabbed it toward my chest, and told him again, "I love you so much, Dad."

"Go home and rest," he signaled to me.

"I will, Pa, but you catch some sleep, and I will sit next to you."

He stretched his hand, asking for mine.

I gave him both.

He clutched my right hand and bent his head forward, with immense difficulty, reaching out to it. I knew what he meant to do and helped him to do it. He kissed my hand. This is an old Mediterranean tradition from father to son (blessings of the father to his son).

"Are you giving me your blessings, Pa?" I smiled with appreciation and a little loving humor and wet eyes!

He nodded again, whistling air through his throat, trying to whisper something.

"Thank you, Pa, thank you. I will pray for God's blessings to you tonight. Okay? And I will see you in the morning, Pa!"

"Go, go," he signaled again with his hand, and he smiled compassionately.

I smiled and said, "Okay, good night, Pa. I'll see you at seven with Mom and Nora!"

My heart was beating vigorously, but I contained my state of emotions. After that, I turned my head backward to catch another glimpse of him, just like Camille did with me three summers earlier at Alexandria's beach resort. Dad acknowledged my smile and then turned his head to the other side while shutting his eyes to sleep. There was an immense load of fear overwhelming me, and I could not stand to confront nature's absurd strikes any longer. But I was tired; I was tired from lack of sleep, too much work, too many studies, no car, a broken heart because of Camille's departure, and a breaking heart because of Dad's age and weakening health. I needed to sleep. At the hospital's gate, there was a taxi dropping off a family of three visitors; I grabbed it and went back home to Heliopolis, showered, and jumped into bed.

The following day (November 1, 1978), my evening shift started at 4:00 p.m., and I had sufficient time to see Dad before seven in the morning with Mom and Nora and then leave at 10:00 a.m. for my classes in downtown Cairo. Both Nora and Mom would go to work late that day and would stay with Dad until I finished my classes and returned to dad the following morning. We left home in Heliopolis (mother, Nora, and me) in Nora's two-door Beatle at 6:15 a.m. and rushed to toward Abbassiya Square and on to El-Geish Street.

My sister had a 1972 yellow Volkswagen Beatle. So, we drove closer to the end of our journey and stalled at the busy Abbassiya Square, just before the hospital. However, there was a square to cross. Then, it all started again; I was dehydrated and started rambling.

Mom said, "Are you okay, darling?"

"No, Mom. I think Dad is calling on us."

"But we will just cross the square and be there in three minutes," said Nora.

"No, something is very wrong; let me go."

"I can't ... we are at a traffic light, and you can only go out from my door."

"Yes you can. Just bend forward and let me slip out behind your seat."

"OK honey, just be careful" shouted mother.

I slipped out of the car while watching-out for the busy traffic, and wiggled my way through the chaotic square, in between cars, buses, and trucks. Then, in a flash, I stormed through the corridor of the ground floor to the fourth room on the right. I pushed Dad's door open and stared at his bed, and there he was looking at me, stretching out his hand. I went to him, grabbed it with my right hand, and wrapped his head with my left hand. I said, "Hi, Papa." He was half-awake. Then he coughed twice and slept in my arms. Dad had gone to eternal sleep, divine sleep, as I was kneeling at his bedside. "Papa ..." I said with my cracking voice, imploring him to wake up.

Mom and Nora (my sister) rushed in, minutes later, and understood instantly. It started all over again; we called our offices; then, followed the preparations, morgue, the paperwork, and the cemeteries! I arranged for the following day's obituary, church, prayers, burial, and the ceremony! After everything was over, I was overwhelmed and beaten with fatigue and emotions.

That night, when it was all over, my good friends from Switzer-Airlines, among other friends from the soccer-team and family members, visited us at home; they stayed with me in a display of mercy, truth, love, justice and peace. To be fair, this did it all; I was humbled and knew that we were all children of God, living in fellowship.

Actually, I cannot forget what compassion that crowd brought to our home and to my bedroom. They were some of my best childhood friends.

They never had a hurtful word or look. They never judged me, and to top it, Switzer-Airline's management was one of immense competence, leadership, compassion, and integrity. That night, I knew it was going to be easier to handle things than with the first blow (Camille's).

I remained with Mother most evenings, preparing the usual cheese and cucumber trays and pouring her favorite drink, just like I did with her and Dad after Camille and even before. Auntie Helga passed away a year later and I would bring auntie Zee upstairs to join mom and me for our evening TV socials. Although Mom was only sixty-four years old then, she was quite vulnerable, and I would hear her loud, deep and troubled breathing pattern, as she slept in her room, next to mine.

Over the next few years, I took mom with me to several European retreats or during my training in Switzerland or Austria. Highlights of our religious retreats were in the Valais (Valley) region in Switzerland, Our Lady of Lourdes in *Lourdes*, France, the Benedictine Abbey of *Disentis*, in Switzerland and, later, with my family to other resorts in Switzerland and Italy. I stood by mom in her battle to replace her two knees in Bern, Switzerland until she could walk again and live, in dignity until and throughout her immigration years in Canada.

One year later, (1981) Auntie Zee succumbed to both Alzheimer's and dementia. We were not aware of such diseases, then. Auntie Zee required immense compassion and care, after all, she had lost dad and Auntie Helga within one year and she would not forget her beloved adopted son Neemo who had left her for USA in 1957. It was a big load for her. Little did I know that Auntie Zee's dementia was only the beginning of another of life's battles! Again, I was overwhelmed with grief for her, and so was my direct family, of course. I graduated in 1981 with BA in Mass Communication, fulfilling my promise to Camille. The struggle to fulfill my oath to Dad with regard to Auntie Zee was starting! It would be a rough battle, let alone her distant nieces throughout her aging years and their lack of care. After all, they had spent their youth in her garden; they were all what remained for her.

Soon, we had to help Auntie Zee all by ourselves; Auntie Isis's (Zee) would start hurting herself, given her rising Alzheimer. She would, for example, burn her food or even jump out of her ground-floor windows, determined to escape, since we had to lock her apartment doors. She would hurt herself to the extent of wounding her face and of bleeding, profusely. If we made it on time, we would reach out for her and bring her back to her flat. Otherwise, we would search for her in the streets of Cairo for hours, sometimes over the night, only to find her in an area of Cairo she would have visited before WWII.

The whole ordeal of terror, horror, and pain would just not stop. It had all started in 1975 with Camille and then daddy and kept pressing until 1984 when Auntie Zee had become a threat to herself and the whole villa.

Having said so, we all had to consume a lot of energy, far more than I thought we could handle between our work, personal priorities (my music), and coping with Auntie Zee's health and human needs, within our work schedule. But her days of glory, hosting her family and nieces in her garden were gone; not so much because of her aging but in view of how she would have done better had these nieces cared to visit her and provide her with what she deserved after all she had done for them in her younger years. They were who she lived for, in the end. Alas, this is life!

The cost of nurses was enormous, and there were none qualified to assist her on her premises. She needed to move to a nursing home, and this was quite a painful experience, for her without the support of her family, nieces and grand nieces and nephews.

By the time Dad flew to God in November 1978, three years after Camille, and the subsequent departure of my auntie Helga (Dad's other sister and auntie Zee's sister and roommate for fifteen years) I had experienced the last of the dreadful moments of family separation that shaped my life until my retreat in Magog, Quebec, Canada, this September 2008. It was the last straw of personal tragedies until I immigrated.

The difficult trial of Auntie Zee dragged all the way from 1980 until 1987, at which time (1987) we had to place her in a senior residence with qualified nursing care. She required surveillance every single minute and needed love each second of the day, failing which, she would run out of her residence and hurt herself, repeatedly.

In 1992, Auntie Zee, still struck by old age and Alzheimer, died in Cairo (while my mother, sister and her family, were in Montreal). She died at Mady's and her husband Wadie's home in Heliopolis, Cairo, with Mady living in Toronto next to her son Wael. Dear Wadie was left all by himself at seventy, to arrange for her funeral and burial. He buried her next to my brother, dad, Auntie Touna the cookie princess, Auntie Helga and Grandmother Katrina in the family's plot. None of her nieces and their children, whom she had long spoilt in the fifties, was present for her burial or even helped pay for the costs. In Montreal, I was under the impression that they had done so and that Neemo had contributed from Los Angeles, with some costs. However, this was not the case. I met uncle Wadie, each time I went to Cairo, after that and he used to gracefully, mention this to me. Wadie is 94, today in 2008, and no one visits him from the family except his daughter Sanaa and a few friends of her brother Wael. (Wael is staying in Toronto, Canada with his wife and kids). Neemo died in Los Angeles in 2014.

Chapter 25
After the Storms

Rekindling the beautiful past while still laying on my bench in Magog
(September 2008)

In 1986, I worked on researching immigration to North America. Canada was my dream and had always been. In the summer of 1986, I flew to Montreal for a test visit, only to return to Cairo and apply for immigration for all of my family and me. I went to the embassy of Canada and secured application forms for all of us, mom, sister, her husband, children and myself. We all lived in the same Villa.

Soon, we cleared our papers and we were ready to liquidate most of what we had. I shipped our best furniture to Montreal (including my 1869 piano that had been with the family for over ninety years, vases and porcelain, carpets and tables, as well as the Rosewood tables that Auntie Lucie had given mother in 1959, and so much more). It was truly a tough job to go through all packing and clearances, by myself; after all, this, I did for mother's household, my sister's family and mine. Unlike other Egyptians of multicultural roots and passions who had almost no chance to transport their belongings, we did; we were fortunate. Many had been forced to leave, but we chose to and had the chance to carry over our memorabilia, finances and most of our furniture with us. The whole ordeal of immigration and paper work was both difficult and lengthy. I never picked up my breath, as I had wanted to. My network of friends in the airlines, packing, shipping and clearance industry, helped my family, and me all he way through.

We planned our travel dates. We split the family into two groups, my sister, her husband and their girl, who was five years old, for July 26, 1987, then Mom, my nephew (who was eight then), and me on August 5. The first group arrived in Canada on July 26, and the second (mine) arrived on August 5 since I had to stay a few more days in Cairo to clear pending matters, family furniture and fiscal obligations.

In no time, we were all ready to explore a new chapter and move on to a new world, seeking safety, social justice, and freedom of thought. Many others joined us in this recent wave of immigration to the West that the assassination of President Sadat and apprehension of neo-fundamentalism, had triggered.

My life in Canada was enriching and fulfilling. First, I was grateful to have made it in one piece with my dear mother who was seventy, then, with my sister, her husband, children and their household. It was the neighbors and corner stores in Cairo and the memories of the Mediterranean and its beautiful waves that I would miss most; but I was excited about my new life in Canada.

Between 1987 and 1989 I was fortunate to start from scratch and to occupy several positions as clerk in a modest travel agency and, then, in a call center until I landed on a position at a six-hundred room hotel (*Le Chateau du Centreville*) as sales representative, in 1989. In 1992, my General Manager promoted me to sales manager, entrusting me with the promotion of our hotel to potential users, conference and convention planners. I dealt with city officials, competing hotels, universities and research centers who booked such events. My relation with these planners was professional, successful and rewarding not as much to *Le Chateau du Centreville,* as to my soul.

Mother would come repeatedly for supper at this hotel and I would be charged 50% of the bill as a staff member. So did my family once or twice. My best moments would be meeting colleagues from the competition every Thursday afternoon after work, for drinks at the neighboring piano bar *Ile de France* where a lady pianist (*Giselle*) played every weekday from 5 to 8 in the evening for a corporate clientele. She would always signal to me to play for fifteen minutes during one of her breaks. I would do so with such joy. Some of the songs I loved to play were What a *Wonderful World, Somewhere over the Rainbow, La Maison sous les arbres* and *La Bohème.* Many of the audience would clap for me as they sat sipping their drinks and I would raise my hand, nod or bow every now and then and return to my table as Giselle ended her break. The bar manager would bring me a free drink and tap my shoulder. It was lovely; I can still feel it.

However, life is not always bright 100 percent. Hotel *Le Chateau du Centreville* was changing owners and I panicked a little because I loved working there. Some of my relatives encouraged me to work for *Le Soleil Hotel* whose previous manager (Mr. Zinky), they knew, too well. This hotel (*Le Soleil*) offered me a position of Director of Sales and Marketing for its one hundred and sixty-room operation, in 1994 but my health broke in 1997 due to its dark work environment. As of then, my life changed. It changed for worse when I accepted to work for this hotel 'Le Soleil' and then, later, in 2004 for the 'North Side Hotel'. In between both assignments, I spent some wonderful years, in Ottawa, building my own business, seeking to build a network of meeting-planners for my home-based business while generating some income in a call center, in the heart of Ottawa. I even tried to solicit career opportunities with the federal government, while, still, in Ottawa.

Throughout my job assignment at Le Soleil hotel between 1994 and 1997, I tried very hard to join a theatre group and to go on stage. Unfortunately, I did not make it to the theatre or music industry at first, but I tried so hard; I joined several auditions and competitions until I was, finally, able to show-case my music, live, in Nashville, Tennessee, in 1998 and 1999 (just before moving to Ottawa) and later, on Canadian airwaves.

Today, in 2008, twenty-one years later, I can easily say that my family and I achieved our primary goals by moving to Montreal, Canada. Yet, with deeper examination and analysis of what human conflict can lead to, in general, even in North America, I decided not to hold responsible any regime for my past and present grief. It is all about character; people have it or they do not. Of course, each one of us has her paradise to achieve and her mountaintop to attain. Right now, I think I am beginning to know what I want, at the age of fifty-seven and after having seen so much in life. I must start by peeling-off my dark years between 1994 and 2008 and cling to the bright ones in Ottawa between 1997 and 2004 and, earlier, of my hotel and airlines career in Egypt and Europe.

What I started to aspire to, when I spoke with Camille on our balcony in 1973 flashed in my memory like a film, during my retreat in Magog. I realize that I have not arrived, totally, there yet. Apart from one fulfilling relationship with a sweet girl from Quebec in 1990 when I worked for *Le Chateau du Centreville*, I had not done much other than whine about workplace injustice. So which is better, living in one's own place of birth, floating or sinking with its restless political climate and conflicting social labels or just shutting-up and working under such difficult changing work conditions of the new millennium, while putting one's health at stake!!

Only in Magog, did I realize that over the last few years, I had allowed myself to be swayed and misled by corrupt thought, peer pressure, bullying and corporate tactics. I was able to peel the layers of my grief all the way back to my experience with child bullying at my school in the fifties. Now, all I need to do is reverse it if I can. Fortunately, I feel a little more rested and will just have to make some decisions as to whether I should continue to work or leave my current dark place of work 'The North Side Hotel'. Only now, it makes sense. I see some light or, perhaps, glimpses of light. Although I am still furious, I am at least free to overlook the portrait; one of what human conflict can lead to; of how corporate mind games and power of systematic suggestion (*Programming*) could restrict one's freedom of choice and independence. However, where do I start? What should I do? Did all this even, happen at all? That is not the point; at least I am free to think, once more! In his *Social Discourse*, *Jean Jacques Rousseau* summed his brilliant thesis as follows: *The individual is unaware of its true will had it not been exposed to absolutely all available alternatives out of which to make its choices or had it not been misled by corrupt institutions.*

Chapter 26
The Retreat - 3
Return to the Present

As I scrolled through the years, lying down on this bench by Lake Memphre-Magog, that afternoon, overlooking the Monastery (Abbey) of Saint Benedict at the far, deep right, it felt cold, and my heart was beating swiftly. It seems that I had been twitching and turning on my bench.

Magog Panorama walk and benches on rue Ptincipale

Suddenly, I felt people pushing my shoulders: "Monsieur, monsieur, vous allez bien? Are you all right?" They must have been trying hard, because I woke up tired and dehydrated. I was still in Magog, on that bench by the lakeside. It was almost 5:30 p.m. I had slept for over two hours. It was a glorious power nap.

Nevertheless, I felt strange ... a little afraid, heavy at heart, and uprooted. As well, it was quite a cloudy afternoon, humid, and somewhat windy. Wow! Moreover, who were these people waking me up? They were from the Quebec Security police.

"Monsieur, est ce que vous êtes intoxiqué?" Meaning, "Sir, are you intoxicated?"

"Non, Monsieur! J'ai pris une grosse sieste, c'est tout." Meaning, "No, sir, I had a power nap, that's all."

"Do you need help going home?"

"No, thanks a lot, sir; I live just there," I said in French, pointing to my motel, to the left. They walked me to my motel anyway, and I felt like a staggering chicken totally spaced out until I crossed to the motel. I thanked them.

Then I went up to my room, showered, and decided to skip the evening chants and go for the late mass at 7:00 and then return for dinner and some drinks. This gave me some time to go for a tea just around the corner. I did so and then hit the road and drove up to Saint Benoit's Monastery. I wanted so much to pray, and in a sense, I felt relieved. One thing I know, I will never have anyone marginalize me again, whether by looks, guilt, allegations, mind games, or intolerance and calculated suggestion—never, ever! My health is not helping me, though, and my recurring abdominal attacks had been harsh, for a long, long, very long while.

I parked my car in the wet and muddy driveway and headed to the abbey with other parishioners. Then I bowed down and plunged into a trance during the ten minutes preceding the prayer service.

Suddenly, the bells rang once, and then another time five minutes later, but I had already made some prayers. I even read, silently, a letter to God that I had written the night before.

Then, the pastor, together with his clergy, stepped in silently and in a most disciplined manner, bowed to the altar, to the congregation, and to each other, and then sat down. After one chant, two readings, and prayers, the pastor read the sermon. The sermon was the highlight of my retreat. The sermon was based on the Gospel of Saint Mathew, chapter 25, vs 31 to 46.

> *31) When the Son of man shall come in His glory, and all the holy angels with Him, then shall He sit upon the throne of His glory: 32) And before him shall be*

gathered all nations: and He shall separate them one from another, as a shepherd divides his sheep from the goats: 33) And He shall set the sheep on His right hand, but the goats on the left. 34) Then shall the King say unto them on His right hand, "Come, ye blessed of my Father, inherit the kingdom prepared for you from the foundation of the world: 35) For I was hungry and ye gave me to eat: I was thirsty, and ye gave me to drink: I was a stranger, and ye took me in: 36) Naked, and ye clothed me: I was sick, and ye visited me: I was in prison, and ye came unto me." 37) Then shall the righteous answer him, saying, "Lord, when did we see thee hungry and fed thee? Or thirsty and gave thee drink? 38) When did we see you a stranger, and took thee in? Or naked, and clothed thee? 39) Or when did we see thee sick, or in prison, and came unto thee?" 40) And the King shall answer and say unto them, "Verily I say unto you, in as much as ye have done it unto one of the least of my brethren, here; ye have done it unto me." 41) Then shall He say also unto them on the left hand, "Depart from me, ye cursed, into everlasting fire, prepared for the devil and his angels: 42) For I was hungry, and ye gave me no food: I was thirsty, and ye gave me no drink: 43) I was a stranger, and ye took me not in: naked, and ye clothed me not: sick, and in prison, and ye visited me not." 44) Then shall they also answer him, saying, "Lord, when did we see thee hungry, or thirsty or a stranger, or naked, or sick, or in prison, and did not minister unto thee?" 45) Then shall He answer them, saying, "Verily I say unto you, in as much as ye did it not to one of the least of among you, ye did it not to me." 46) And these shall go away into everlasting punishment; but the righteous shall dwell into eternal life.

The reading was timely, humbling, comforting, and piercing. I was rooted, once more. I gave thanks, closed my eyes when the service was over, and stayed for another five or ten minutes. Then I rose quietly, bowed, and walked back out of the parish through the colorful mosaic-tiled (slightly chilly) hallways. In a few minutes, I was heading back to my motel, where I parked my car. I walked to the neighboring restaurant for a bite and some tea and returned for a good night's sleep. Then I jumped into bed and slept like a child until I rose next morning and saw the rays of the shy orange sun trying to crack through the gray clouds just outside my window. I rose, slowly, from bed and looked through the window down to the slightly foggy lake one more time before I headed back toward Montreal. On the way back, I stopped by the Abbey and bought some berries, cheese, honey and jam produce from the monks' canteen. It was Sunday, September 14, 2008.

Chapter 27
Return to Work—1

That afternoon, I arrived in Montreal and called Mother, my sister, and her children and then showered and rested at home (next to theirs) for a while. After that, I visited them for supper and brought over some of the monks' cheese, berries, and maple syrup.

By nightfall, I started heading home for a good sleep to wake up rested, for work, the following morning.

"Good night, Ma," I said.

"Good night, my love," she replied.

My return-to-work mood was troubled; after all, I had started writing this testimony in Magog and was determined to finish it while including all the memories I revived before they vanished forever. It was a difficult task to engage in a creative mood while working in the heart of this dark environment.

As I stepped in the hotel at 8:00 the following morning, I sensed a vibe of pretentious camaraderie in its lobby. It felt as if something had been cooking while I was absent for my retreat.

"Hey, Raphy, how's it going?" said one of the girls at the front desk, who resented me because she preferred to see me out and see her younger colleague replace me in sales.

"Always good, Molly... thanks. How is *return to university*?" I said.

"Good Raphy! Really good," she said in a fake joyful tone.

I greeted another young girl from the front desk whose eyes were always expressive and exploring. She was caring and knew all the bullying that I had been going through.

I smiled to her and said, "It's good to see you, Allie."

"So did you have some fun? You seem well and rested."

"Yes, I did, thank you for asking about me. I am pleased to work with people like you."

"How are your abdominal pains?"

"I haven't resolved them yet. But thank you so much for asking, it means so much to me."

I could see a sense of extreme sadness in her eyes, one mingled with respect but not pity. Did she know of something? I breathed heavily and walked through the administration hallway on to the sales office where my eyes caught site of my forty-two years old attractive General Manager, Ronda (of British descent). She was walking to her office with a cup of coffee.

"Good morning, Ronda," I said.

"You will talk to Nadia (my assistant and her friend), as she will explain to you things that I need" …just like that, in a cold and careless manner.

"Sure," I said, assertively but subordinately. I had delivered my business plan and strategic priorities, to her, two weeks earlier after deriving them from her operational plan, but I had not prepared the action plan yet. My heart was racing from fear of further abuse, and I was preparing myself for Nadia's usual loud attitude.

As I entered my office, Nadia was sitting at her desk (just opposite to me). I greeted her and her friend occupying the small space just outside our office where the former Sales Coordinator, used to work. The name of the woman sitting outside was Mandy, and she too was Ronda's (the General Manager) friend. I had this instant sense of discomfort from Ronda's questionable and ambiguous smile. I entered my office, which I nicknamed *the control room*, and was bouncing between the sense of divinity, which I had captured in Magog, and the utter fear of having been tricked by this clan while I was away. "We'll see," I said to myself.

"Morning ladies…"

"Hey, we need to talk," said Nadia, my assistant.

Mandy mumbled, "Good morning."

"I said *good morning*, Nadia," I commented.

"Yes well, good morning, we have a lot of work to do. Ronda needs some reports, and I need you to prepare them for me by the end of this week," said Nadia, referring to the 2009 Action Plan. Theoretically, she was my subordinate.

"Well, listen, if you change your attitude, I will be happy to cooperate. After all, I am your superior. Now please let me settle down, and read my e-mails first. Then we can meet at 10:00 in the restaurant to discuss Ronda's requirements. All right, Nadia?"

"So what is this? You're the one with the attitude," she said.

"Fine, we both are, Nadia, but you started, and neither of us has the right to pick on the other; especially when I have just returned from my few days of well-deserved rest. I need to read my e-mails. Why are you always shouting and banging drawers or slamming the telephone headset in our little office; and now your tone of contempt!" *Such physical maneuvers in the workplace are usually meant to intimidate others; throwing pens on the desk, banging drawers, banging the headset on the telephone console; they are questionable by the Canadian Labor Law.*

"Well then, maybe it is about time you heard my advice and resigned. I am sure Ronda will not say no and will pay you something."

I felt a heavy shovel banging my head and my heart almost stopped. "How dare you. This is none of your business or authority, Nadia. You have to stop this. Stop it right now!"

Then she exploded, mumbling, and ran out of the office to Ronda, who came back in my office, followed by Nadia, shouting at me to go to her office. I did, and she slammed the door as we entered in her office.

"She represents me, and you will not talk to her like this," said Ronda.

"And I represent you, and neither she nor anyone should shout at the other like this," I said. "…besides, this has been overwhelming, Ronda, and very conducive to my declining health, my gastric and abdominal pains. It is also destructive for productivity, and I can no longer function under panic; why? We are doing fine!"

"Well I can replace you in one day, but your family cannot," she said; she honestly said that.

"A threat; a threat, Ronda... Has it really reached that point of apathy? My family cannot replace me, really! First, you leave some careless employees less than half my age; invade my workspace with his childish and invasive innuendos, of last month. Then, if I went on lunch break to help my ailing mother, just next door, to prepare her meal on lunchtime, he throws his slurs on me? To say I start at 7 a.m. and finish at 7 p.m., six days a week? And now, Nadia; it is not right; I work seventy hours a week doing my stuff and helping others until they shape up, so as not to waste opportunities for the company. I am humble about it and do not brag. You leave these kids alone without applying accountability on their less than desirable work habits. I keep waiting for some motivation from you and from the company's *Justin*, the new Director of Regional Marketing, without a *thank you* or *good job*! Now you want to replace me in one day. Did you mean that if I refuse to leave, you would continue to deplore me? Is this what you meant? Honestly, Ronda!"

"Call it what you want, but don't groan in the office. I couldn't care less about your gastric attacks and about your pains," she said.

"What? When did I ever do that? When I am in pain, Ronda, it is only due to the sickening atmosphere of intolerance and isolation in this office and to the lack of disposition of various team members and even management to engage in genuine dialogue, constructive dialogue.

When I am in pain, I inhibit my grief and rush to the toilet to vomit. I throw up my lingering bile fluids during these panic attacks. If it gets too painful, I tell you, and I go home to heal for a day or two. I was not altogether like this when I first started, and I should not go through this, by my thirty years' juniors. This is not the first time you refer to my rising anxiety and grief."

"Don't shout at me; alright? If your health is not well, you should choose other career options elsewhere," said Ronda.

"No, Ronda!" I said, angrily.

There was silence, and she had a cold but venomous look. Then she said, "You are heavy maintenance!"

"Perhaps I have become so, but I must let you know how I feel about it ... Did you know what the most painful thing a man or woman in my state can encounter? It is not the loss of a loved one; it is not the death of his pet or a paycheck; it is this persistent pattern of slurs, threats, looks of indifference, and that tone of arrogance. It is the sum of those little tragedies; those repetitive vexatious comments that keep pounding a human being, consistently, day after day, until they break him or her, just like a shoelace that snaps with no time left and with irreversible damage. Why?"

"Do what you want," she said, giving me the cold shoulder in such a ruthless manner.

I went out of her office, which was just behind the front desk; separated by means of a transparent glass wall. For a second, I asked myself whether last week's retreat had helped me or enraged me. "Maybe a bit of both," I told myself.

As I looked backward with the corner of my left eye, I noticed the front-desk staff watching me through Ronda's window. Then I turned my head slightly, nodded to them with an assertive but modest smile, and walked out to the lobby where there was the coffee and tea machine. I grabbed a tea and turned back, facing the front desk and its staff. They were looking at me again in a concerned but non-invasive manner. I smiled again, wanting to reassure them, or at least those who meant me well. Then, I continued further in the corridor toward my desk, holding myself from breaking apart. In two minutes, I sat on my desk, noticing both Mandy to my right and Nadia opposite to me.

"We will do this meeting at 10:00 a.m., Nadia, in the restaurant, just like I told you. You will let me know what you have." I said these words almost defiantly but showing interest in what she had first said about Ronda's requests.

Again, I finished work at 7:00 p.m. instead of 4:30 because it was the beginning of the season for contracting and bid submissions, for 2009. I did not want to miss it.

On the personal side, my beloved mother had fallen between 2005, and 2008, a total of seven times; she broke her shoulder once, and could only move safely with us or with the morning nurse whom we had contracted for her. All seven times, I took her to the hospital in an ambulatory car and stayed with her overnight! She would only walk with the help of a walker, for now. As a Royal Air Force and United Nations post war veteran, she was entitled to amazing medical and retirement health benefits that covered her senior years. As for me, I was very weak and afraid; I could no longer cope with abuse and hurt, in addition to my devastating abdominal pains; they had become unbearable. I knew, though, that my retreat in the Monastery of Saint Benedict (Saint Benoit) had to bring fruit to my crumbling life. Until then, I was ready for the will of God.

"My Father, if it is possible, let this cup pass from me; yet, not as I will, but as you will." Matthew 26:39

Chapter 28
Return to Work—2

It was impossible to sleep that night, after how vexed I felt by the previous day's return-to-work events and its persistent hovering rotten vibes. I felt as if a bulldozer or a twenty-story building had run over me. I had very little energy and was truly scared, very scared of the unpredictable, of being hurt. I could not see through and had no more projections for the hotel's upcoming year of cutthroat competition amid a ruthless recession and a rising supply of unwanted new hotels-rooms. Alas, I stopped caring!

Of course, we do not stand-alone; we do not walk alone; we are never alone, if we can remember to seek divine guidance. At least, I remembered that, I learnt it in Magog last week, when I started my metamorphosis! I knew that I was called to have my retreat next to the monastery, to worship, to rest and receive peace; so I was not alone; and I am not afraid!

On this Tuesday morning, my second day at work after returning from Magog, I pulled myself together, went to my kitchen, had a tea with toast, honey, and two crackers, then I drove to the hotel's parking lot. I got out of my car, lifted my head straight above my shoulders, took a deep breath and walked through the hotel's lobby with an assertive smile.

Then I saw the faces all over again, the very faces that I could no longer stand, except for the supportive and professional few. I saw my manager's face, nodded to her with a restrained smile, and went right through to my office, only to face Nadia and Mandy. "Morning, ladies," I said as I entered without even looking at them. My face looked like a lime; it was colorless and lifeless! By the end of the day, Nadia told me that I "have to go on the road" for sales. *The ugly pressure was persisting.*

"I will decide about that. I am overwhelmed with projects and can no longer do that, as before. So, I need *you* to go on the road" I said. There was no response, and there was not one single sound in the room, not even the sound of breath or falling paper.

Mandy shouted at me mockingly from the other room "Why don't you go for a swim in the pool to stretch? You will enjoy it; there are a few good looking college boys swimming, now!" She slammed me... *Help me God*, I said to myself. I could not understand where this came from. Inevitably, the sound of beeping rose, persistently, in my eardrum. (We used to host quarterly sports youth competitions for the city arenas).

"Pay attention to your work and don't waste your time craving the boys during work hours' you can do it later," I said. It was hard to pose as a solid boss; but I did and hated myself for acting like a pig.

At 5:00 sharp, I took my coat and left for Bernie. I had not spoken much and kept a professional but cold look all day through. I stopped on the way to buy some flowers for Milena and a bottle of Cabernet Sauvignon. I also brought with me a jar of home-marinated Mediterranean olives, which I had prepared two months before and placed in my car, that morning, well wrapped.

I was really very weary and distant, so I made another stop at a small lounge and had a beer to loosen up. Then I drove across two more blocks until I reached Bernie's home. I parked my car and there was Milena, Ruth (his daughter), Joel, and Michael, their two boys. They greeted me, took my coat, and I could see Bernie standing in the kitchen doing his usual culinary *cauldrons* that always tasted delicious and healthy.

"Bernie, this wine is for you, and, Milena, these flowers are for you. I also got you these green olives. I marinated them from scratch. Wait until the end of December before you open them. I think you will like them."

"Wow," said Milena, "these look nice. What did you put in them?"

"Lime juice, vinegar, oil, lemon peel, sweet red pepper, garlic, celery, salt and little sugar".

"Can't wait to try them," said Milena, "… thanks for the wine and the flowers."

"It is always a pleasure, folks. Thank you for your hospitality and for your friendship."

Bernie finished what he was doing in the kitchen and said that we could have supper in thirty minutes. Milena offered me a drink, and we all sat down to chat. Their dog, Whiskey, is a beauty and is so alive and intelligent. She is a beautiful six years old Golden Retriever. Every time she sees me, she jumps over me and keeps licking my face and neck, endlessly, with such love.

After dinner, we cleaned up the dishes, the children went back to their rooms, and Milena, Bernie, and I went to the living room for tea and coffee.

"So tell us all about it," said Bernie.

"You don't want to spend three days listening, do you?" I said.

"We have no problem," said Milena.

"First, I must apologize," I said, "if I look a little, well, *wiped out* today. I returned to work yesterday, and the inevitable happened."

"What happened?" asked Bernie.

"Corporate trash … you know, as always."

"Tell me about it!" answered Bernie.

"Well, resistance, bullying and intolerance. What can I say, Bernie?" I said.

"No, no, no … let's not go there. Tell me about Magog, I meant!"

"Okay, wait. I will fill my coffee again. Do you want anything?" said Milena.

"Yes, some more tea, please, and I will try one of your brownies," I said.

"I am fine, thanks, Milena," said Bernie. "Will you join me for a cigarillo, Raphy?"

"Yeah… Why not," I said. "Let's have some fun! I will just puff it, though."

"That's what I do, too," said Bernie. "So?"

"Well, just like you said ..."

"Wait for me," interrupted Milena from the kitchen. "I am coming."

Then Milena joined, and we started an endless dialogue, all three of us.

"Well, like you said, folks, it is different. The instant you get off highway 10 East onto the 104, which is Rue Principale (parallel to it), you feel the difference and you can smell fresh air. Just watching the glorious lake, then beyond it, you notice the hills, trees, lights, ducks, pigeons, and geese. If you look on your left, you find those colonial buildings, parks, trees, and restaurants. That is not to mention the smell of fresh immaculate air. Wow! I was blessed."

"That's it?" asked Bernie!

"No. Of course, not, after this, there was the meditation part that sucked me into nature. I wrote notes for my book—endless notes, peeling away years, even decades of injustice, bullying and marginalization. Well, you saw these cards, earlier this year. I used them as a base. Although it was liberating, it drained me considerably. I wrote long dialogues as I remembered them. I watched the lake, the clouds, the trees, the squirrels, the leaves, the colors, and I smelt them and breathed them. I watched divinity, Bernie, and I wrote all about it. Then I became divine again, but for a while."

Bernie looked fixed, interested, even impressed but unshaken. Milena's eyes turned red and wet. Bernie continued to look at me in his appreciative but fixed manner. He smiled to me and said, "I am not religious, but I believe in God. Besides, I am Jewish, although this is not the issue. You speak very well, and I believe that you can write a good book."

"Faith is not religion any more than spirituality is God. However, we are divine creations of God. Thank you, Bern. I want to write this book, and it has gone a considerable way toward taking a solid shape."

"Did you pray?" asked Milena.

"Yes."

"Did you visit the abbey?"

"Repeatedly; you will read about it."

"What happened in August that made you decide to go on retreat?" said Bernie.

"I collapsed and went on a stretcher in an ambulance to the *Montreal's Mercy General*."

"Because of your abdominal attacks?" asked Milena.

"Of course... Well they are also panic attacks, anxiety attacks," I said. "But, mostly because of public abuse by superiors and because of the scoffing I was subjected to by some classless staff and distant management."

"But they were not that violent," commented Bernie. "They would come and go in a day or two every three weeks."

"Yes, but now it has worsened! It hit me every week. I mean it starts with bloating, acidity, grief, sweat, tears, chills, and excruciating cramps and pain in the stomach, bladder, colon, left back shoulder, and then down through my spine. It ends with violent vomit, acid reflux and pain at the bottom of my esophagus, just at the tip of my stomach. Then I throb from lower back-pain and anguish and lean on acetaminophens and anti-inflammatory pills, over intervals of four hours until my pain subsides two to three days later. After this, I am drenched and nauseous from the pills for three days."

"...all this because of work? There must be something else!"

"Yes and no, Bernie... I was not like this when I started. I had almost recovered *from Le Soleil* hotel experience, but my burnout relapsed. In addition, there is something in my esophagus or bladder my physicians cannot spot. Of course, I do not go to the emergency room with every attack, but over the years, I went fourteen times, to emergency, so far; nine on a stretcher, by ambulance. I developed this after my first experience with the Le Soleil hotel. You know that. Ever since then, I ran colonoscopies, gastroscopies, endoscopies, MRIs,

Ultrasounds, X-Rays; over and over and over, again, with no luck."

"Could it be ulcers?"

"I only wish they are, so that I can finally get a cure and kill those pains. And the work environment, let alone the indifference of those you would count on most, does not help."

"Yes," he said. "They made you take antidepressants!"

"Yes they did, given the rising ambiguity which is a systemic tactic of passive bullying; the suggestive conditioning and direct bullying, of course."

"You look tired, Raphy. Really, you look very tired. Do their slurs open up some of your old wounds?"

"...Wounds? ...really Bern, why wounds, what wounds?" I replied defensively.

"Because we all have them, Raphy, and it is okay to feel weak every now and then. After all, they seem persistent and ruthless." I understood what he was referring to but did not even want to consider how far he may have gone with his evaluation. This did destabilize me for a moment though.

"Get out of there. Leave them. They are bad news," said Bernie.

"Screw them. After the, entire research, foundation, and client base and trust I have developed? After all this potential business and wealth of market intelligence that I have founded—leave everything just like that?"

"Leave them! What do you want to prove?"

"How can I do that? I will lose everything if I do so. And I did before; I left the previous hotel before, following a remarkable record of achievements!"

"Well you are already losing your health," said Milena.

"Okay, then you must agree with me that this is coercion," I said.

"You are damn right; it is coercion," said Bernie, "and they have no class or integrity but what can you do? What were they doing before you started?"

"They were eating scrambled eggs and French fries in their offices, with ketchup and toast. They would make their first sales call at 09:30 a.m.; imagine!"

After this statement, I paused for a few seconds, sighed loudly, and breathed deeply. Then, I nodded my head to stretch my neck forward and back, smiled, and went to the kitchen for some more tea.

"Let me boil some fresh water, Raphael. You sit down," shouted Milena.

"Thanks, Milena. So let me go to the toilet, and I will be back. Look, I know tomorrow is Wednesday and you have to go to work. So I will just drink my tea and will leave in fifteen minutes, maximum."

"Okay," said Bernie, "if you want. But come back, as I have to tell you something else."

I did. I came back. Milena joined just after with tea and more brownies.

"Oh these are killers, Milena."

"Eat what you can, Raphy," she said.

"Look," said Bernie, "let us not give you any more grief. You had a great retreat, and you will feel the difference in a few days. You will feel much better if you leave them. They have no HR (human resource) skills or ethics. By the way, did you ever report this to your HR officials?"

"No."

"…why not?"

"I never trusted them! They never talked to me for over four years, despite the growing negative vibes that were floating in our hotel. Was I too proud?"

"No, no. It makes sense, Raphy. You are professional and they hate you for it. You are not rude, but you are short-wired…'

"I HAVE become short-wired, *I interrupted*"

"Yes I know that; I do!"

"Well, Bernie, what do you expect me to do?"

"No, excuse me, Raphy, there is no question about your competence but rivalry is a fact of life and we learn to cope with it. Of course, it needs to be monitored by labor laws. Under normal circumstances, I mean in a company like the one I work for, if something like this happens, management throws the perpetrator of violence out, and acknowledges your rights. Here, when you asked for help, you faced reprisal. They would cut your arms if they could, but they did worse. What I want you to know is that it is impossible that they hired you simply to do this job. You were an interim scapegoat who was looking for a job at a time they had planned to hire someone from within, someone who had no experience, just until you laid down the business plan. They must have known some valuable information about you, which they could use to coerce you; information is power, unfortunately. They kept setting you up, day after day, and then they had the audacity of telling you that you were not a team player, or that you took things personally, or that you had little leadership!" I suddenly remembered Zinky's statement at Le Soleil, in 1994 *"Information is Power"*

"Scapegoat," I asked. "Why use me as scapegoat?"

"But of course! Come on, it is very clear. You are a casualty of a senseless hiring process, among others. You can sue them, and you will win. This is the labor law and the law of the land!"

"And how did the first hotel in Le Soleil know of my insecurities and weaknesses? Who told them? That is the problem; but who, Bernie, Who? …most of all, who passed my history on to this hotel?"

"I have no clue, and I surely understand your frustration. I guess they are all connected; besides, a few of them are connected to your circle of acquaintances and relatives!"

"But that is so private! Is someone after me?" I asked.

"I cannot tell, but, look here, resign take a few months if you can afford it; do some theatre; do your music. It will help you. Do you need money? Do you need some money? Tell me, Raphael. I am serious. I am your friend." He breathed deeply, paused, held my elbows, and gazed in my eyes. "How much do you need?"

"Nothing really, not now," I said. "Not now, Bernie."

"Listen to him, Raphy," said Milena. "Listen carefully; he means it!"

"Let us plan it together," said Bernie. "Just don't get sick. Do not do this, please, Raphy. Your mother needs you, and she has already lost a son in 1975. You and Nora are all she has. Do me this favor! Think about it until the weekend, only until the weekend. Then, let us meet and you can stop thinking all together after this. Tell me how much you need to resign, and I will tell you what I can do; two, three, or four months' worth of salary?"

It was getting late, and I wanted to leave them to rest.

"Thank you. Thank you, Bernie. Thank you, Milena! …Wow, I am a little tired, but I really enjoyed the evening! Thank you so much. I will just go to sleep now and leave you to do the same. Okay, I will think and let you know. I promise you, I will."

"Let us meet for brunch at Marinello's on the weekend for the pasta buffet!" replied Bernie.

"That sounds great. I will call you on Friday. Thanks again, folks. This was a delicious meal and, as always, a great company! I truly love you very much. Take care and sleep tight. A million thanks, again!"

They walked me to the door, and I got in my car and drove back home.

Chapter 29
Return to Work—3

The rest of the week was as dark as it was when I returned on Monday from my retreat. For the remaining three business days, I became the target of persistent and harsh negative comments, cold looks, cold shoulders, as well as destabilizing criticism of my work; they turned me into a staggering scapegoat but my mind was alert at all times.

For example, on Thursday of that week, I closed a difficult sale with a health research company, a key account, and on my way back from the customer's office, I shared the good news with my general manager, humbly, of course. "Don't tell me you went to see the customer with your chipped tooth. Did you?" In no time, I left her office without responding and noticed two staff members controlling their laughs and spotting me from the corner of their eye through Ronda's glass wall. These were members of the older team.

That weekend, I went for brunch with Bernie and Milena but did not take any money from them. After that, each time I made a business move at my office, members of the team would criticize me for practically anything, typographical mistake or for, simply, any trivial. The clock was ticking but I refused to sign.

In December 2008, the general manage did not invite me for her managers' Christmas luncheon (fortunately), just like the first year (2004). In January 2009, I lost my job because of "restructuring," one week after I had been transported to the emergency room for another harsh panic attack that grounded me for two days and for which Ronda sulked at me with immense disdain. Then, again, she had to run her business. My illness had originally started (mildly) in 1995 when I was working under similar corporate pressure and bullying at Le Soleil. What they offered me at the North Side Hotel, was a termination package of one year; which was good.

Justin, the Director of Marketing of the company's hotels in Quebec, came to my office with the Director of Human Resources and Ronda to escort me to the parking lot. I said I had some stuff to pick first.

"No, you move out, and then you tell us if you have anything remaining in your office later. You must get out, now," said Justin.

"No, sir; I will not. I have my wallet, bankcards, car keys and other stuff. Besides, I want to shake the hands of some of the staff members, my friends at the front desk and kitchen."

"No, you cannot shake hands now; you must leave right away!"

"No, I will not, Justin. I believe that after those endless long hours, I deserve to shake the hands of the good ones. Leave me to do it, at least for your own image! After all, you will work with them after I leave, and they will remember that you stopped their professional and hard-working colleague from saying goodbye. It's for you!" I insisted. Of course, I must have been quite reactive and defensive.

Therefore, I simply walked around, shook the hands of a few very young staff, and hugged two of them. I ignored another three, who were mean to me! "Tough cookie," said Allie, one of the nice ones, in front of everyone. "Bless you, Allie," I replied and hugged her. Two others had a couple of tears. As for me, I took my time to collect my belongings. I was not worried because I was very close to retirement age. This meant, a pension check, though quite modest. I knew I had to find a low profile job, somehow to supplement my pension. I waved to the front-desk staff and returned home to have tea with mother. She was 93 years old by then. She was not home, yet, but had gone to the city Shopping Mall at her chosen spot, for cinnamon buns and coffee. (On weekends, she would do the same with her senior friends and I would drop her to the mall and back).

That day a taxi drove her to the mall; I knew this when I called her mobile and found out that she is at the mall. I told her to wait for me and she treated me to lunch and, then, I drove her back home and helped her change her clothes.

After a minute, she looked me in the eye:

"What's wrong, my son?"

"Nothing ma... It is just that I had been working hard for weeks and decided to quit. I meant to tell you. So, I resigned this morning."

"Resign or let go, that is the best thing that happened to you."

"Yes I am so tired and discouraged at human nature."

"You left with grace. I always encouraged you not to shy from doing so, since school, no?"

"Yes"

"But you were let go and you left with grace? That is what happened?"

"Yes ma; that is exactly what happened. I knew you would figure out."

"And you left with grace?" she persisted.

"And authority! ...but I have many holes in my heart together with my stomach pains."

"Fix us a drink and let us talk."

"OK but come to my place (just across the corner) spend the night. I will prepare us supper and then we can watch a nice film."

"As you want my son; I would love to but let your sister know so she does not worry when she returns home." I prepared mom's bag, called my sister and drove mother to my place. Of course, I walked her slowly with her walker to my car and up to my building's elevator on to the fourth floor. It was a typical snowy January evening. In a minute, I had taken her coat off and helped her sit comfortably on the kitchen armchair.

"Are you ready ma for your drink?"

"Yes my love" and I fixed us two drinks and some appetizers. I had a tray of chicken and pasta béchamel in the fridge, which I put in the oven to heat, while we chatted and as I washed some salad; my homemade dressing was ready.

"OK mom; this is to your health my beloved friend!"

"And yours my tender one! Do you want to talk about it?"

"Well, you know mom… Human nature, these days it is all about rivalry as opposed to competition and the usual innuendos, bullying and eternal paradox of cruelty; and it terns personal. I just have to work on my health, for now."

"Yes, my love. However, it is more. I know. I did not forget."

"Had you told anyone in since I told you in 1958, I mean of what they did to me?"

"Never, I never told anyone; not now or even in the recent past. It was then; I told dad so as to get advice from a professional; who said *just let it pass*."

"Was there anyone else in the room when you told dad?"

"I think so; I am almost sure but I made sure to keep my voice down"

"Who was in the room, mom?"

"My son, some relatives but I can't remember who, exactly. This was in 1957 or '58, I guess"

"This can't be a coincidence, ma. Someone is slandering my image; someone is using my life's least of worries to control me through compulsion and coercion while turning me into a punching bag of hurt. I know; I am not stupid. This is a pattern, ma; a pattern- not by one person; not by one group; but by various people in various spots of the hotel industry in Montreal and even a few from our social circle following the plan of a mastermind or several mastermind narcissists. I am sane and I know that these things happen to demolish a person and, perhaps even, to rebuild him or her, to suite the whims of others."

"I never opened my mouth and cannot think of anyone doing it"

"So, maybe it was some of the relatives who were in the room sixty years ago, drilling into something that does not mean anything to me, anymore, only to sensationalize it."

"My son, I wish I knew and I know where you are heading. Now, if you think I had anything to do with this man Zinky's visit to our home, it is not *me* my son; I would never do this. I took your defense that day in 1994 and you hugged me and ran out angry away from the rest of us at home."

"Not you mom; I never, ever suspected you... Therefore, it was them, him…"

"Both, I think"

"Damn it, damn them… Ma, I love you and you have always been a successful businessperson, and loving mom; you are careful. It could not have been you. Each time I stretch my head out of the turbulent ocean of life to gasp for air, they dump me, below, to leave me drown, again; I am not made of rock. …But I will not drown, no way! What is this life so full of rats and worms?" I plunged into her bosom and placed my head on her lap and then broke into tears."

She did the same and wiped my face with her fading hands full of obvious veins; but I could feel her heartbeat and gentle breath, just like a summer breeze loaded with motherly affection.

"What can I do, my son, to undo all this hurt?"

"Calm down ma, you have done everything right and I am alright now. I will strike back, help me God, and may everything work in Divine Order! I am so sorry my love to put you through this; it will be fine. Let us watch the movie, sleep well and have a lengthy breakfast in the morning. Remember; I am not working now… ha ha" I kissed her forehead while stretching my right arm at the back of her frail neck.

"One thing I can tell you, my darling, you have never been a soft-speaker; you speak with a deep, solid and gentle voice and you have deep thinking eyes. You speak five languages, play the piano, write music, you acted on stage and travelled the world; do not be hard on yourself. You can speak of anything. I always told you. Remember how Ms. Abboud spoke highly of you at school?"

"Oh ma….."

"Really, my love" she paused, "it is not you. It is not. It is they; people get jealous and will do anything to break anyone who threatens them. They will pick on you, just like at school fifty years ago"

"Let us sit in the living room ma; wait, I will get you a cover and we can watch the movie." We sat on the sofa eating our supper and stretched on it, for close to an hour until mom went to the guest room while I tidied the kitchen and returned to my bedroom.

For the following few days, I was not at all perceptive of how I had been compromised because I was wiped out. I just treated it for face value, and then by mid-January 2009, it hit me! It hit me very hard to the extent that I started reprimanding myself for not having achieved my childhood objectives, not having risen with courage and independence as many have. Most of all, not having enjoyed and celebrated life, fully, the way I wanted; theatre, music and writing. Never the less, this was my right; my right to take the shape of the life I had survived. I had the right to react to it and interact with it without faking how I was 'shaped' by it, so at to enjoy it- my way. I did not want to be a hotel manager or to lead a team of 50. Five was already good enough for me and I had the wisdom, vision and good will to do it while clinging to the peak of my mountain; no one else's!

Then, the unexpected struck my doorstep! The most beautiful thing happened when I started fiddling with my computer. I browsed the Internet and opened a site known to many as Facebook. This is an electronic vehicle for friends and acquaintances to nurture friendships and to exchange information, news, photos, and other material. It is just like a digest, which links lifetime friends from all over the world. It could go, all the way back to university, school, and childhood days.

That day, I saw a message waiting in my Facebook 'inbox' since early October 2008 (one month after my return from Magog) that I had not noticed or read. The message said: "Hi, Raphy, do you remember me?" It was signed Dahlia.

I replied "Dahlia? American University in Cairo?" and waited for her reply only to know, two days later, that she was the one. She asked me to call her and left me her mobile number.

This was Dahlia, my junior colleague at university, who went on stage after I delivered the Mark Anthony soliloquy in 1977 or 1978. She was the one who climbed the stage after my show, put her hands on my face, and then cuddled my hair. I remember that I blushed like a kid! After that, we studied together for three semesters and developed attraction to each other. We never tried to make it official. I called her the day following her reply and we decided to revert to communicating on Skype, which is another computer program that allows people to talk through the computer's mike and see the other person by means of a built-in Camera. It all came back to me. I was so happy to rekindle the beautiful, energizing past. Then, soon I switched to Skype and called her. She was waiting for my call.

"Hey Dahlia; so good to reconnect after all these years"

"Same here; you haven't changed"

"Are you kidding? I look like a dead duck; and have some health problems; stomach pains; a repetitive pattern that drained me"

"…anything serious?"

"I don't know I am working on it. You look good and you have a tan"

"Yes I just returned from the Red-Sea after a short vacation with my brother and cousins. We were lucky; it was warm. You know Red Sea in Egypt during January, is not that bad".

"Of course, I do! What do you do in life?"

"Working and I play some sports. I have a cat to keep me company and friends surrounding me. I am single, if this is what you meant!"

"Wow, me too and I lost my job, last month, in early January. I do not want to work now. I should be officially retired in a year, (2010). I am just trying to re-energize."

"Then come for a couple of weeks and rest. Do you have a place to stay in?"

"Yes, this can be managed. I have my cousin Marcelle and her family in Heliopolis, not far from where I used to live, before immigration."

"And I live in Zamalek, the other end; not far from university. But it will work"

"Let me think of the logistics, Dahlia. I will call you but must first make sure my aging mom and family will manage without me for a short vacation."

"OK call me when you're ready"

"I will in two days. Good-bye"

"Good-bye"

Then, I decided to take a break from the pressures of my last job, use part of my severance package that the company paid out to me when they let me go, from work, to fly to Egypt. I wanted to meet that girl but also wanted to rekindle the beautiful memories of my childhood. In a sense, I knew I emerged from there and my memories belonged there. This vacation was a break from the mood that overwhelmed me for a while. Moreover, perhaps, this break would ease up my stomach attacks and my panic fits by disassociating me from the recent past. By early April 2009 (Lent and Easter time), I was ready to fly.

Chapter 30
The Break in Egypt—1

Crossing the Atlantic from Montreal to Zurich was not that difficult, despite my state of health, even though it was a full seven-hour flight. My last cross-Atlantic flight was in April of the year before (2008) in which I visited the Monastery of Saint Catherine of Alexandria, in Sinai and that of Saint Anthony the Great Martyr of Egypt fifty kilometers east of Luxor. Earlier, in September 2006, I flew to Greece where I spent most of my vacation in the Island of Rhodes. It is counted as one of the twelve Dodecanese (Twelve) islands of Greece, among which the Island of Patmos, where Saint John the Divine read his book of Revelations to be written by his disciple. Also, just thirty-five minutes by boat from Rhodes, was the Island of Leros (my grandfather's birthplace in 1881; Mother's dad). The three islands, Rhodes, Leros, and Patmos, are members of the Dodecanese Islands (the twelve Greek islands bordering Turkey and not that far from Sicily in Italy). It was from these islands that Greek refugees seeking stability moved to Egypt (Alexandria, Suez, and other cities) in 1883 during the rule of Khedive Emperor Ismail of Egypt and later, another fifty thousand under the leadership of Parissis Bellenis. My great-grandmother Kaliope (Cleopatra) Radiki and her son (Mom's dad), Aristides Nikolaou, were two of the initial crowd of immigrants who settled in Egypt in 1883 and opened their own schools, hospitals, churches, and community centers. They mingled perfectly and were loved by Egyptians. The second phase of fifty thousand Greek immigrants, under Parissis Bellenis, joined them during WW1 and made wonders.

The idea of the book had already started to concretize, then in 2006, throughout my visit to Greece, but I had not started. I wanted to include a chapter or even a few paragraphs on further isolation of my grandparents among many other Greek families and business people that led them to migrate from these twelve islands to Egypt (especially the islands of Leros and Kalimnos), only to settle in Alexandria, Suez, and Cairo, Egypt. These immigrating Greeks settled first in Alexandria around 1883, specifically on the street known as Rue des Sœurs in reference to the sisters of the Sacred Heart of Alexandria, where the ancient Greek Orthodox patriarchate of Alexandria still exists, since the days of popes Theodores1, John 1 and Cyril 1, in the sixth century.

I started writing about Leros and the remaining twelve Greek Islands when I took off from Zurich for Cairo. Leros, (Grandpa's birthplace) is a stunning, small island, so primitive but picturesque, so naïve in its architecture and white houses, so feminine in its gentle and coastal layout and masculine with its lovely little historical hills. Its olive trees surround its white houses, its fields of thyme, basil, rosemary, and oregano shrubs spread all over. They are so natural and revitalizing to one's senses and nostrils. My mother's father, Aristides, left the Greek Islands as a child (at the age of two) with his widowed mother, Kaliope (Cleopatra), to Egypt in 1883, escaping political unrest. He was born in 1881. In fact, the island was under the control and leadership of Italy, though managed by both Turkey and Italy. Moreover, because of the Italian domination of these islands, Grandpa Aristides' birth certificate was Italian, and I still have it, though he was a pure Greek Islander. The Greeks considered, Parissis Bellenis as the *patriarch of justice*; he took it upon himself to liberate thousands of Greeks from the political unrest of these islands. This included Rhodes, Leros, Kalimnos, Patmos, Kos, Castellorizzi, and others.

Statue of Parissis Bellenis in Leros
Erected by the returning Bellenis Greeks from Egypt

He arrived in Egypt and built various schools, hospitals, and churches for them, and they loved him. Then they joined the existing Egyptian Greeks, amid other Egyptian communities: Italians, Muslims, Jews, and Armenians. After WWI, a few returned to the Dodecanese Islands because their islands had acquired their independence. After the 1952 Egyptian Revolution, many of their remaining descendants returned to Greece, as well. My mother and her sisters stayed in Egypt.

Grandfather's baptism church   Leros alley to Waterfront

In Leros, I visited the church were my grandfather was baptized in 1881, and then I went to the city archives and stayed for two hours with my sister, her husband, and friends until we got his register. His register was written in Italian, but the names were Greek. Then the island went back to Greek control (I believe after WWI). However, the Italian and Turkish influence continued, and I could clearly sense it in its architecture and even lifestyle.

It was Easter week and the islanders were ready to celebrate it on Sunday, April 16, 2006. I could sense it all starting Thursday, April 13. The stores, pastry shops chapels and the island's Basilica were ready for the big day. Church bells rang everywhere and Easter pastries filling the display windows. The islanders, I thought, were ready to break their fasting. Perhaps yes; but on midnight on Saturday April 15, thousands were filling the streets of Leros chanting a beautiful old Byzantine Easter song from the year AD 800 that said in Greek *"Christ is risen from the dead, trampling down death by death, and to those in the tombs, granting life."* Of course, they would sing it in Greek with Greek Orthodox pastors dressed in black gowns, marching ahead the crowd and in between, holding a big cross and hundreds of candles. The singing was so powerful, mesmerizing and overwhelming; typical of an ancient 8th century Byzantine chant with the worshipers singing only the main melody, while a male clergy hummed another note- the dominant unchanging note, on a very low bass pitch in a dramatic manner, all the way through. This is the Greek chant in Latin letters, *"…Christos Anesti ek nekron, thanato thanaton patisas, kai tis en tis mnimasi zoin harisamenos."* Celebrations continued until 02:00 am. At 9.00 am, the few churches of that small island were full and I joined some of the Islanders for Sunday brunch with a family I had met during Thursday vigils.

Interestingly, back to Egypt, during the late fifties until the mid sixties, and right in the heart of the district of Heliopolis (in Cairo), I remember vividly how thousands of Christian Egyptians joined by many fellow Muslim citizens of Egypt, doing the same candlelight procession all around six or seven of the Heliopolis churches (of diverse rites). The whole ceremony, in Easter, humbled me and invigorated me. What humbled be most was how the corner bakers of all faiths, surrounded by their neighboring shop owners, would stand out, some with trays of Easter raisin and walnuts brioches to add joy to the celebrants hearts and join them, affectionately, as they broke their fast.

Tale of a Growing Child

The next highlight of my visit to Leros was nothing more than a simple beach that had two or three restaurants. Of course, there were many other private beaches. However, I had chosen that one because it was not far from where I stayed, hardly 1,500 feet to the shore. It was night, and these restaurants were made of white stone and wooden terraces, just six or seven steps higher than the sea level, and less than thirty feet from the actual wet shore. I had my meal on a table by the actual sandy coast on these thirty feet; I ordered a Greek salad, fresh Red Snapper and local white wine, with my slippers soaked in the coastal humid-sand and covered by occasional waves running over my legs. There were two or three cats running between my legs staring at me, every now and then. I cannot describe my feeling of awe and humility. Overall, the restaurant had four wooden tables by the shore, painted in blue, and covered by transparent plastic sheets. It felt quite humid, in view of its closeness to the seashore. The sound of gentle waves added to the impressionistic, portrait and their salty smell, filled my nostrils. On the terrace, there were another five or six tables.

Waterfront in Leros stuffed with restaurants

View from our Leros Motel

Leros beachside restaurants

Halfway between our hotel and where I sat for dinner by the beach was a land which was said to be the one where my grandfather Aristides (my mother's dad) lived as a child, with his widowed mother before moving to Egypt (So was I told; I wonder!).

When my grandfather's dad passed away, his mother, Kaliope, continued her husband's business from home. She made olive oil, Ouzo, and radish preserve, packaged them in jars, and sold them to the houses around her, all the way downhill to the seashore where I sat, and further up toward the old city hall. She would have done the same in Alexandria in 1883; but I never saw her.

All these recent memories ran through my head, halfway from Zurich to Cairo. As the plane flew over Palermo in Sicily on to the clear blue skies of the Mediterranean, I started feeling my heartbeat. It was such a defying moment in which I had fled Canada with my heavy baggage of bullying, over the previous few years, only to return to the land of my childhood passions and roots.

Fortress of Mussolini in Leros WW2 (Italian Occupation)

Finally, the plane slowed down and made a final approach before landing in Cairo. Even though I had visited Egypt in Easter of the year before, I had not experienced this feeling of rising emotions and nostalgia then, as much I felt it now after starting my metamorphosis in Magog. The layers of ambiguity and fear continued to peel off. I was still vulnerable but earnest for the first time in years! I was hopeful and optimistic. We started our descent, and then the flight attendant came to us with warm, wet, scented napkins to wash our faces. She had a basket of Swiss chocolates. I grabbed one, freshened up, and looked through the plane's window.

In the final minutes before touch down, I started to perceive the hazy reddish skies of Cairo. It was that time of the year; it was spring in Egypt, (spring 2009), famous for its few weeks of sandy weather that came from Egypt's Western Sahara Desert and further west from Libya. The portrait was one of red to brownish overcast with hazy skies though not cloudy. By May, usually the skies would clear up, and a hot but beautiful late spring would lead to Egypt's gorgeous though hot summer, followed by its stunning fall; but it was also the time for jasmines, lilies, and pansies. Their smells would fill the gardens of Heliopolis in the older days, and in our garden, in '58, most certainly.

After a few minutes of walking in the airport, I passed through immigration and presented my Canadian passport together with my expired Egyptian passport.

"Welcome home," said the young officer, as he smiled and stamped my expired Egyptian passport. "…you will need to renew it in Cairo or at the consulate in Montreal."

"Thank you," I said. "I am so happy to be home." I smiled and went to pick up my bags and then passed through the customs zone. The whole process from landing until exiting the customs zone hardly took forty-five minutes.

Then I met my cousin Marcelle at the arrival hall. She was the cousin, who had moved to our home in Heliopolis in 1975, during the great civil war of Lebanon, and who witnessed my brother, Camille's departure. Marcelle, her husband (and neighbor from the building behind our villa) and their son, Sherif, were all standing, waiting together. I hugged them, and off we went to their condominium that was not far from the old neighborhood where we all used to live many, many years ago (near the Palace of Baron d'Empain in Heliopolis). As soon as I entered their home and greeted the family, I set the bags aside and asked her for some hot chamomile as I felt my stomach stressing swiftly again. Then I succumbed to a panic attack, for no reason, within one hour of my arrival, took my painkillers, and fell asleep on a couch in their living room. An hour must have passed, and it was already 8:00 p.m. I felt someone wiping my sweat and holding me tight while I experienced the usual chills that hit me during a typical attack. I opened my eyelids slowly and noticed a sweet girl whom I remembered quite well from 1977 or 78. She was holding me and gave me more chamomile tea. She stood next to Marcelle, my cousin. The girl said: "I am Dahlia."

"Oh, Dahlia … Wow, it is so good to see you," I said.

"Shush," she said, "…keep your energy," and she put her arms around me to comfort me from my rising abdominal pains.

"I did not want you to see me like this."

"That is fine, Raphael. Do not mention this. It will be over soon, and I will make sure you have a good vacation. I will make sure all this will go away. You will not be sick again," she said. Her maternal uncle was my physician in 1977 throughout my sinuous problems; and he helped me.

"I hope so, Dahlia. Can we continue our conversation as I lay down on the couch? I am in pain and cannot sit."

"No, I have to go, Raphy. My brother is waiting down in the taxi. We don't drive."

"Have a safe ride"

"Call me in an hour or so to let me know how you feel, Raphy. I do not sleep before 11:00p.m."

"Wait, how did you know my cousin's address?"

"I called Marcelle but she said you were having a panic attack and that you were resting. So she gave me her address, and I rushed to see you."

"You are so kind. Thank you, Dahlia."

Tale of a Growing Child

"Call me, tonight. Will you?"

"Of course I will, and we will meet tomorrow, okay?" I said.

"Sure, but get well first."

"I will. I will call you tonight."

I called her one hour later to reassure her, and the following morning, Marcelle dropped me at her (Marcelle's) place of work. There, I stopped a taxi and continued to a café called Thanos Café, not far from where Dahlia lived and where her cousin Jeanette lived. Soon, I arrived at the café, and Dahlia was waiting for me. We did not sit there but continued to her Cousin Jeanette's home, just around the corner from the café.

Chapter 31
The Break in Egypt—2

Cairo Downtown, *Khedival City*
Built by Egypt's modern Royal Dynasty of Mohamed Ali since 1805

As soon as we arrived at Dahlia's cousin, Jeanette, whom I greeted for the first time. Other family members passed by for some tea. Jeanette was physically challenged; she had two nurses helping her. After a good hour drinking tea, exchanging memories and dropping names of common friends, I asked for a glass of water to take my anti-spasmodic pill, and said, "It was so good to see you all. We must do this again, soon. [I said smiling to Jeanette and then, I turned my face to Dahlia] Dahlia and I will go somewhere where we can sit, chat, and leave you and your family to rest. I am still in pain but not as much as yesterday," I said.

"Yes in half an hour we will go down and cruise the city"

Her cousins brought some more tea and biscuits. My abdominal pains were much more bearable than the previous night.

Then Dahlia and I walked down the street to a Dominican church called *Saint Joseph of Zamalek*, residence of the Comboni brothers of mercy (since 1883) who strived to smuggle victims and refugees of religious intolerance, from Africa to Egypt.

"Let us go in, and pray; I need to pray"

"Of course…" said Dahlia and we entered for a few minutes. I lit a candle for mom.

On the way out of church, I said, "You know, Dahlia, as of this moment in church, my life seems to have turned around, even more than I thought I did in Magog. Something happened to me in this church and I feel human, again; it has grounded with humility by what these brothers are doing to help casualties of violence. I find myself now, ready to engage with the real things of life; feeling happy for children flourishing under Divine mercy; feeling sad for others who are striving to make it to Egypt but still cannot. All this in contrast with loathing myself for what happened to me in the corporate world or the world of injustice, in general. I think this moment snatched me; from one ugly battlefield and dropped me from the sky with intense power to this reality. I know that my progress had already started during my retreat in Magog and continued to do so ever since I stood firm at the hotel for whom I worked last. What happened now, and despite my persisting abdominal attacks, is a turning point because I can think of others now; I started to care for others, again."

"You always did; for your family. Don't be hard on yourself."

Dahlia knew that my priorities were to visit downtown commercial Cairo, which was the district where I used to work (for Switzer-Airlines) prior to immigrating in 1987.

The plan was to spend three full days in Cairo and ten days in Alexandria at Dahlia's family apartment by the resort beach of Agamy, where I had lost my brother in 1975 and where I had almost drowned in 1981.

We walked toward a square by the name of *Soliman Pasha Square* and sat for tea and biscuits at an old and famous teahouse called *J. Groppi* where I used to stop at lunch hour or for delicatessens shopping, with my colleagues and travel partners in the eighties. It was not half as gripping as it was in the late seventies. Alas, it struggled to sustain itself amid the changing political climate with great effort.

Soliman Pasha Square Downtown Cairo

The *J. Groppi* and *À l'Americaine* chain, by the way, was one of those classy Swiss teahouse relics of Egypt between 1910 and 1985. Both teahouses were owned by the same family and were famous for their chocolates, truffles, legendary ice cream, pastries, croissants, bread, coffee, cheeses, and cold cuts, all for in-house consumption, take-away orders or for extended and overseas catering, to Europe. Their products were of such impeccable quality, taste, and reputation that they had become the Egyptian king's number-one choice for his social and tea receptions and even for his overseas catering to King George the Fifth of Great Britain in the forties. We continued walking past many of Egypt's stunning heritage buildings, stores and restaurants that had become half broken in the late sixties until the very early eighties and, almost completely, disfigured in 2009. The *J. Groppi* and *À l'Americaine* chain existed in Alexandria under different names but with the same style. Giacomo Groppi in 1909, a native of Lugano, Switzerland, founded them at the age of forty-six, and handed them over to his son, *Achille Groppi*. Achille had introduced his famous Groppi Vanilla Ice-Cream of Egypt in 1928. While many of the Groppi outlets were bombed during the 1952 Egyptian revolution famous fires, three of them miraculously survived. Now, in April 2009, the Groppi chain still exists but with a different soul. Its remaining owners left Egypt in the eighties after the assassination of President Sadat and following the growth of radicalism. They returned to

Switzerland. I had serviced Giacomo Groppi's grandson (Giovanni) until 1985 while I worked for airlines.

Dahlia and I crossed Soliman Pasha Square and walked all the way past my old office at Switzer-Airlines that had shut down. While walking in one of those alleys, before reaching the old Opera Square, I saw an elderly concierge dressed the old-fashioned Egyptian way. He was wearing Galabeyya, which is a white male-gown that covers a man from neck to feet. He had very dark skin and was in his eighties. He had a big, loving smile, and Dahlia and I could clearly see his golden teeth. I smiled to him and walked closer to him as he sat on a bench at the entrance of this beautiful, old building.

"Hello," he said in English, thinking we were tourists. (Dahlia is of fair complexion, like me).

"Hello," we replied. "We are Egyptians."

"Returning immigrants?" he said.

"You can say so," I said.

"Welcome back to your homeland," he said and stood to greet us.

This was too much for me, and I sensed this continued freedom of thought and soul, again, rekindled after years of isolation.

I gave him a big hug as a son would to his father and could hardly contain my cloudy eyes. "I feel I know you; I don't know why. It is as if I met you before!" I said.

"Maybe," he said, "but you are all my children; you are the children of Egypt."

Her Jasmines, he meant as I thought to myself and at this stage, I went into a state of intense emotions. "Yes, I know, and it is because of people like you that we feel we did not lose our homeland, *Y'abbouya* [which means *my father*]." Of course, this is a typical Egyptian cultural reverence to the old and wise. "*Y'abbouya,* I saw you before; I feel your vibes! I saw you before; I know I did. Where could I have seen you?"

"But I am here from sixty years!" he said in Arabic.

"You mean in this spot—that building?"

"Yes and no," he explained. "I took it over as a concierge from my parents in 1985."

"And where were you before, *Y'abbouya* (father)?"

"...Lappas, not far from Soliman Pasha Square."

"Did you mean Lappas teahouse?"

"Yes," he replied.

"Oh my God, I used to work just across the street from you."

"Which office?" he asked me.

"Switzer-Airlines ... Switzer-Airlines ticketing at the ground floor, and then I moved to sales on the fourth."

"So this is it, then. You used to come to me every morning for your espresso and croissant!"

"God, I did. It makes absolute sense. What is your name, *Y'abbouya*?"

"Gamal."

"God keep you, Am Gamal." Dahlia and I parted with a promise to meet him again one day. Then we walked on to the old Opera site that burned in 1971. We continued further to heritage stores such as Sednaoui Store, behind the old Opera House that was of the same caliber as *Galleries La Fayette* in Paris as well as *Harrods* in London and many more. They, too, were disfigured. Alas, their owners had all left Egypt, under coercion, in the early sixties. I flew backward thirty-seven years to 1971. I remembered the day I stood with other music scholars and surrounded by music professors, singers, Mr. Bellardinelli, the opera's orchestra director in interim, *Professor Decaro, Renzo* and others. To our left, as we tracked back our footsteps, stood the old Azbakeya belly-dancing casino that gave us a hand in salvaging the opera library. Just behind the old Opera Square was the remaining field of Casino Azbakeya, known as Azbakeya Square (in reference to its founder, Prince Azbek (Also, Uzbek) the Mamêluke-Turk in the Middle Ages.

Then, just to our right, I saw one of Cairo's renowned synagogues: *Shaar Hachamaim*, (Gates of Heaven). It is a Sephardic synagogue built in 1904 and has been standing ever since in awesome glory and self-respecting structure. It had survived the 1952 fires and 3 bloody Israeli-Arab wars, miraculously.

I tried to take a few photographs of Shaar Hachamaim Synagogue but the security police stopped me. They thought we were tourists (thank God for that, because if they knew we were Egyptians, we would have wasted hours in interrogations). The armed police were extremely courteous and explained that this was a very special Jewish holy site and that there were prayers, at this time. "We would appreciate your understanding," said the colonel in good English.

"Thank you," we acknowledged. "We fully understand."

On our way back, we walked for a few steps on Adly Street to rest and grab some lunch and made a point to meet at the same place, the following morning at ten to start our trip to old Cairo and its ancient multi faith religious complex. We called Mr. Fares, who was a former retired friend from the tourism industry in Egypt. He had bought himself a taxi to fill his time and make some revenue on contractual trips. We agreed to meet at 10:30 a.m., the following day at the flower shop opposite to the synagogue and that he would take us and bring us back to our homes after having visited the ancient religious sites and the adjacent cemeteries of our families.

This would leave us ample time to have a coffee at ten and to buy some flowers for the cemeteries. Many of the ancient cemeteries of Cairo are located there; Armenian Catholic, Coptic Catholic, Anglican, Greek Orthodox, Greek Catholic and others.

These cemeteries and the churches surrounding them would date as far back as the first century after Christ. The Roman dungeon was built in AD 30, upon which the Greek Orthodox Basilica of Saint George was built in the seventh century. Just next to it, is Saint Mary's Coptic Church (The hanging Church), as well as a few chapels built between AD 30 and 70. Finally, Ben Ezra Synagogue in AD 843 is located in the holy alley of the chapels, next to the well of Moses. The ancient and beautiful mosque of Amr Ibn-el-Assi, conqueror of Egypt, was built around AD 645 just across from the above religious relics. The ancient Jewish cemeteries used to exist in Fustat (*Fussatum*), just as well but were moved to *Basateen* gardens, two kilometers south, around the eighth century to accommodate the post Arab Conquests' Muslim cemeteries. These ancient Muslim cemeteries were built in Fustat, (Fussatum), instead, around and beyond the mosque of Amr Ibn-El-Assi. During the Maméluke rule, they continued to build-up all the way, across eight centuries.

Chapter 32
The Break in Egypt—3

The following day, Mr. Fares passed by us at the flower shop at 10.30 a.m., and off we went with our flowers to visit our dear departed and then, to explore some of Egypt's glorious passions and routes.

Cairo, the old city:

The cemeteries were all situated in Old Cairo—all of them, including the Muslim cemeteries, the Jewish (Basateen), Greek Catholic, Syrian Catholic, Copt Orthodox, Roman Catholic, and a few others. Formerly, after the Arab invasions in the seventh century, Old Cairo was called Al-Fustat (derived from Fussatum in old Demotic Egyptian language, for *city*). It stretched to the city of Basateen (gardens), where the third oldest Jewish cemetery on the planet, was built before Christ).

    Mr. Fares dropped us at the security gate, where we started our primary visits to my brother, father, uncles, aunts and grandparents.

Holy Family second shelter in Old Cairo (Fussatum, Babylonia)

My family's plot was huge and as old as three hundred years. Dahlia did the same with her parents. We entered in one of the scattered modern chapels (1820), lit candles and asked the priest on duty to pray for our beloved ones. After placing our gift of flowers, appropriately, we headed for our tour of the ancient relics, of the adjacent Old Cairo.

They were all out-shadowed by the high and stunning seventh century Byzantine basilica of Saint George, built on top of the Roman dungeon, Babylonia (AD 30), behind which the well of Moses would stand. Two hundred feet later, Christ the infant, the Holy Mother and Saint Joseph, the escort father and mentor of Christ, would seek refuge from King Herod in two of some twenty-seven shelters of the Holy family, in Egypt.

Saint George's Greek Orthodox Basilica was built in the seventh century, and the Hanging Church was built next to it in the early Christian Egypt around AD 70 (Saint Mary's Coptic Church). They were both built on and around the old Fortress of Babylon, which was attributed to Trajan, Roman Emperor in the first century, according to the books of the Coptic clerics. Copts are the early Egyptian pagans, whom, Saint Marc the Evangelist and beloved disciple of Christ had preached to after Christ's ascension to God, thus founding the Church of Alexandria and Africa. The Copts accepted the teachings of Christ through Saint Marc and devotedly embraced them, renouncing the worship of statues, icons and previous gods. This fortress had witnessed the Roman execution of early Egyptian Christian martyrs (Copts and, later, Greeks) under Trajan, Aurelius and others until the sixth century when Emperor Justinian accepted God and believed in Him as unique Creator, giver and redeemer of life and beyond (through Christ) while declining worship of statues, cement and icons. The actual refuge places of the Holy Family in this city, among others, were two: one at the monastery's outdoor chapels just two hundred meters away from the well of Moses and, another, under it, through the ancient Greek Orthodox Cemeteries.

Saint George Greek Orthodox Basilica (AD 720)
Babylonia

Saint Mary Coptic Church. The Hanging Church (AD 30)
Babylonia just behind Saint George Basilica

This first one is known as the Chapel of Saint Sergius the Martyr of Egypt (Saint Serge). It had a grotto two floors below the ground level and had its own well. The second was under the adjacent Greek Orthodox cemetery's chapel of AD 1820 two hundred feet from my family's burial plot.

First we entered the chapel of Saint Sergius, which was basically one of several chapels built at the foot of the Monastery of Saint Georges, in the second century (on its ground level but from outside the monastery; outside the former Roman Dungeon called Babylonia). Then We walked through the chapel's alter (Saint Sergius). One foot below, lay one of the two Holy family's shelters in old Cairo *(Fustat* or *Fussatum)*.

The interior of the historical chapel of Saint Serge (Under renovation.) Holy family's first shelter in old Cairo. Fussatum

To reach the second, we walked further down to the well of the Holy Family (one of the wells of the Holy family used as shelter), on to my brother, dad and family's resting place. I made

my prayers and walked with Dahlia to the other side, doing the same for her parents' gravesite. (See page 181, beginning of Ch. 32)

We took exceptional permission to tour the four floors deep fortress and dungeon of the Romans, in AD30, upon which the 7th century Basilica of Saint George was built and stands until this day. As we stepped down to each floor, restrained by its limited lighting, we were connected to its ceiling because we could look up and see the arcades that had nothing to do with the actual monastery on top of its ceiling; a faint natural light was breaking through the transparent colored glass ceiling, representing the base of the Basilica, above. This was the fortress's dungeon and slaughterhouse under the Roman rule. Then we saw several devices that were used by the Romans to torture early Christians until martyrdom. We even saw the graves of many, their inscriptions and dates in Greek, Roman, and Coptic, dated since a few years after Saint Marc the Evangelist had preached the Gospel to Egypt. We took endless photos and films.

The Dungeon (Babylonia)

Walkway of pilgrims and tourists

Stairway ancient chapels and synagogue

Passage to ancient chapels and synagogue

Only five hundred meters across was the beautiful mosque of Amr Ibn El-Assi, the Arab warrior and conqueror of Egypt in AD 644, by order of Khalif (Successor and disciple) Omar Ibn El-Khattab, second Khalif of Prophet Mohammad, peace be on him. He had built it as his place of worship and residence one street across from the Basilica of Saint George. (See next page)

Rabbi *Abraham Ben Ezra*, who had come from Jerusalem during the reign of Ahmed Ibn-Tulun of the Abbasid Dynasty (followed by Al-Moez Bee Deen-Allah Al-Fatimy), turned one of the historical chapels surrounding the base of Saint George's Basilica into a synagogue.

Mosque of Amr Ibn El-Ass AD 647
Footsteps from the ancient churches of AD70
(Fussatum Babylonia)

    The Christian clerics of the chapels and grottos surrounding the foot of the Roman dungeon and later St. George Basilica ceded it to the Rabbi. In return, he (the Rabbi) paid the high taxes (*Guizieh*) to the ruling party that the financially challenged guardians of these chapels could not afford. *Guizieh* was a tax levied on Christians and Jews who chose to stick to their faith and not convert to Islam. It is an integral part of the *Sharia* law. Across the centuries Egyptian Jews and, later, the Egyptian Board of Antiquities and Historical

Sites, restored this synagogue, repeatedly. The last major restoration was in the eleventh century. The guardians of the synagogue confirmed this to me. We visited it but could only photograph its entrance, while standing in the sacred alley, of chapels.

A few steps up from the back of the temple, lay the well of Moses since more than thirty-two centuries, witnessing an early chapter in the life of Moses in Egypt, before his exodus with the Israelites as described in the biblical book of Exodus.

These Jewish cemeteries of Al-Basateen are considered the third oldest Jewish cemeteries in the world. The second oldest, still in Egypt, are situated in the city of Goshen in Damietta (right axis of the Nile Delta), where Jacob, Abraham's grandson and *Joseph the Tribe*, son of Jacob, lived and where Joseph was buried for four hundred years.

His children (Joseph's), Menasce and Ephraim were born in Goshen Damietta, as well, of their Egyptian mother *Asenath*. Pharaoh had chosen her as wife for Joseph. Joseph remained buried until Moses carried his bones, during the Exodus on to Sachem in the Holy Land (Sachem on Mount Gerizim in historical *Canaan*; now Israel).

Outside of the historical Ben Ezra Mosque

The back of the well overlooks the Jewish Basateen cemeteries
At distance (just a very few kilometers south).
The well of Moses, also seen behind these bars

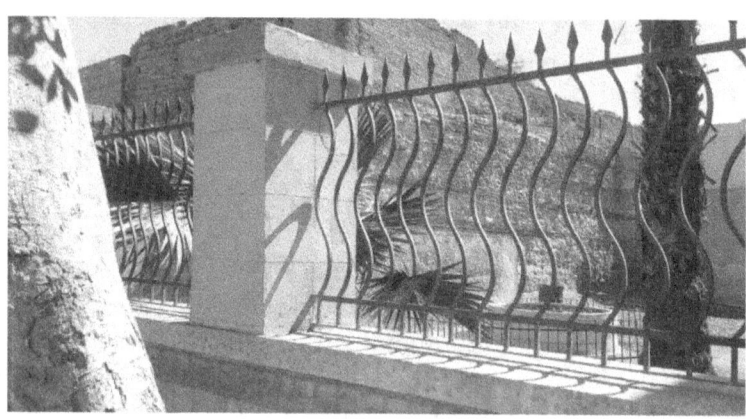

After our religious and commemorative tour, I felt at peace to have visited my family's graves. My visit revitalized my spirit and rekindled part of the Egypt I knew in my heart. My journey of recovery as, gradually, moving forward and so was my love for history and life in general. It was a long day, and I was glad to make it home safe and in one piece. Mr. Fares, dropped

Dahlia to her home, first, and continued with me to my cousins' place.

I was at my cousins' home around 5:30 p.m., before any of them had returned from work. I swallowed two capsules of extra-strength acetaminophens and went for a nice hot shower. These painkillers hurt my stomach, terribly but aborted by pains instantly. I put on my shorts and T-shirt, fixed myself a hot tea, stretched on the sofa, and plunged into a power nap in front of the TV. Marcelle came in first around 8:00 p.m., and her husband followed half an hour later.

Marcelle and I set the dinner table, she warmed the meal, and her husband went for a shower, while I washed some vegetables and made a nice salad. By the time we sat down for dinner, their son came in, and we all sat down by 9:00 p.m.

For the next two days, I stayed with my cousins, visited family and spent some time to reconnect with my friends and blood ties. I called Dahlia and set a date for Wednesday to continue our tour of Cairo and my search for identity, this time in Heliopolis. We made a point of planning to spend a few days in Alexandria with her brother and friends. This would be the following week.

Cairo (Heliopolis) my place of birth

On Wednesday morning, I took a taxi and waited for Dahlia at the gate of Saint Cyril's Church in Heliopolis to attend Sunday service, right in the center of my birthplace on El-Thawra Street (formerly Le Baron Street). This was merely a hundred meters away from my childhood home, and three hundred from Saint Michael's and all Saints chapel. Just in front of me, across the road from Saint Cyril's church, stood all these shops almost identical to how they were twenty-two years before- bakers and grocers, plumbers and butchers. Suddenly, it all came back to me. The original owners had ceded their shops to their children.

Dahlia arrived at 10:50 a.m. and made it for mass at 11:00. On the way out, we met a few good friends, which added joy to my heart. I was ready to escort Dahlia on our journey to the past, the journey into my birthplace neighborhood!

That day, we walked through Ibrahim Street, the extension of Avenue du Baron or, currently, *El-Thawra Street*, on to the *Temple of Vitali Madjar* that was built in 1928 and to which the school of Abraham Betesh was annexed. This temple and school hosted thousands of Jews from Heliopolis. I wanted to take a picture of it and could only do so from outside, given the security around it. It was at this temple where I met many of my Jewish friends after their Sabbath, and we would go for lunch or an excursion to the Cairo zoo with their parents, the following day or two.

Dahlia was ready for a change. She had continued her undergraduate studies and obtained her MA with honors in Mass Communication at the same university I graduated from with a BA. She is eight years younger than I am and always seemed like a baby to me. As for me, I stopped my university studies following my BA in the same major, as hers but I did some extra credits for a minor in Drama and Modern Theatre. Dahlia's parents died in 2000 and 2002. Since then, she was ready for that change; but so was I when I was fit to make such a responsible move. I knew that eventually, we will discuss major decisions and kept it for our luncheon at a neighboring restaurant, after we strolled through the little streets surrounding my childhood home.

Dahlia and I walked through El-Thawra Street (Le Baron) on to the small street where I lived (Osiris Street). We walked for about thirty feet and then, here she was on the left. Our villa half demolished and never rose to a new building.

We learnt that the buyers of our villa could not get permission from the Department of National Heritage to turn it into a six-story condominium building and but stopped halfway after starting to demolish it. Everything stopped for twelve years.

The worst part was that the new owners never restored it to what it was and left it half demolished. But this was their choice.

I tried to peep in its old metal gate and found out that it was still intact and not locked. I grabbed Dahlia's hand and walked in the garden, all around it, and flew back to 1987 and even 1965. The garden was dry, and so were my beautiful mango, vine, orange, and olive trees that yielded such vast and tasty quantities of fruit, before. Unfortunately, they were there but they were all fruitless, and so were the Bougainville and Mimosa bushes. The lilies, pansies, roses and jasmines had vanished. Their bushes were dry but the soil was barely alive and the branches had to be, equally there, but dormant. Then I remembered where my 'brother and I' stacked the fallen jasmines under the mother tree, to continue their remaining days with her. There were no olives, simply dry leaves and dormant branches waiting for someone to nurture them, once more. I felt my late brother passing by in his white sharkskin trousers and smiling at me. My heartbeat was rising and then, Dahlia clutched my shoulder and we headed out of the garden. No more was I able to capture the smell of jasmines or orange blossom flowers.

There was a mango branch, though, half-alive and, most probably, capable of regenerating themselves through its rich soil, if well nurtured. On the way out, we saw auntie Zee's balcony on the ground floor, overlooking the garden. It was still almost intact. Then, I saw myself sitting with her, dad, mom and Camille in 1962, with mom humming Brahms's famous tune from his Symphony number three, while knitting. I even hummed it, a little.

We visited whoever of my friends was at home, in the neighborhood, for hardly a few minutes each, including the Haqqis where we used to spend our Easter Monday brunches just next to our villa and just below the balcony where my brother and I used to stand. Just after this visit, I guided Dahlia through the little streets that had similar gardens as ours, on to our old chapel, Saint Michael's and All Angels, on to its back garden where we used to have our campfires, fifty years before. We continued through, to the old and classy Heliopolis, the Water and Electricity Company and, finally, to the Heliopolis Sporting Club. Soon, I realized that there was something missing, something that meant a lot- not only to me but also to the soul of the land that I knew before I immigrated in 1987. The trees and their branches were there but most of their fruit and jasmines had withered. It seemed to me that the new generation of owners did not realize that buying a new home meant watering its leaves. Gone were the orange blossom flowers and Jasmines bushes that once glittered along this residential area's side streets. Instead, there were Mobile shops, bread stands, cigarette, soda and chips kiosks that masked the beautiful past with thorns of anarchy. I could barely find a few trees that still had some yellow mimosa and red bougainvillea bushes. Their smell was faint and not the same. Something went wrong but I did not want to tell Dahlia!

We went for Lunch at Le Chantilly Restaurant (formerly, in the fifties, Homemade Cakes), minutes from my childhood home. I recognized two faces I remembered from many years; they were thirty years older. One was a woman cashier who used to serve us in the seventies and whose former pastry-shop owner and superior, Signor Polly, was a retired advisor to King Farouk of Egypt in the forties. She smiled to us just as she did across the years but her white hair had covered her head and she had become chubbier than before. The restaurant manager shook our hands; he was Captain and only thirty years old, when we left Egypt in 1987. We shook hands so passionately. Then we sat down, ordered our meal and took a deep breath. For a few seconds I was numb and then we engaged in our discussion until our meals were ready.

"What's on your mind; you are pensive" said Dahlia

"I was disappointed at how the greenery of this strip was compromised'

'Tell me"

"The trees, jasmine trees, orange, olive and mango trees; vines and their grapes; wow; they're gone or almost all gone."

"Yes it is sad; people stopped taking care of their gardens and trees"

"They lost the passion of how to appreciate nature. They just took what there was from their predecessors and did not have the heart to continue planting their trees."

"Don't be hard on yourself. Think of the future."

"Could you help me?"

"Help you how?"

"Think with me; let's think together?"

"You are really something. We could have done this at university but you were not ready"

"I had my reasons; besides my brother had passed away and my ailing dad had started his journey to heaven."

She smiled, caringly.

"I was a wreck then and was not ready; now I am still a wreck but am ready"

"We will take care of your health first and then think together!"

"Can we plan together, also?"

"Yes I would like that" she said.

"Can we start now?"

"She blushed and I did too and then held her hand"

Our meals arrived and for forty-five minutes, we had our lunch discussing each other. She seemed to have had a rich business experience managing and importing meats and agricultural products from Australia. I told her of my successes within the hotel industry in Canada, my health drawbacks and all about the office politics and bullying that I had barely survived. I spoke of Magog but she knew there was more, much more, since childhood.

"Let's continue our planning process next week in Alexandria and perhaps you can come for a vacation to Montreal, this fall, to meet my mother and spend a few days in Magog"

"That sounds like a good plan," she said. I put my hand on her cheek for a few seconds, and then, we left.

Chapter 33
The Break in Egypt 4

My final stretch with Dahlia in Egypt before returning to Montreal was a trip to Agamy Beach of Alexandria with her brother and family friends. Dahlia's family had a home in Agamy resort, and Alexandria was just over two hundred kilometers from Cairo.

Since the departure of my brother in Agamy in 1975, I had only visited it for a day in September 1981. I spent a day at the beach and was about to drown but was saved by that courageous young man. Yet I did not have sufficient courage, then, to visit the beachside where we stayed last in 1975, at the famous Chalet-280 where I had my last warm discussion with Camille. In a sense, I was prepared to try this time, because I needed to rekindle his memory and reinstate him in my life. We had planned to stay four nights and five days.

We arrived in Agamy at 2:00 p.m., freshened up at Dahlia's family condominium, changed our clothes, and headed for the beachside, one kilometer west of the beautiful 1975 Chalet-280.

A friend of Dahlia's family whispered to her, while looking at me, and while catching my eye! He almost looked like he was telling her something about me; something nice. I had told them all about Camille and dad in the car. Then Dahlia looked at me and said:

"Go, Raphy' go and walk to your spot."

"Do you want to join me?" I said.

"No, you go and take your time and do some closure. Remember, dinner at 6:30."

"I'll be back in an hour, Dahlia."

Overall, the metamorphosis that I started in Magog during September 2008 was continuing to roll with ripple effects. My panic attacks would still hit me, ruthlessly, and the painful past of manipulation and mind control had still, not set my mind free. Alas, my heart was still crushed, and I was still, struggling to unlock the vast pain and intense ambiguity that haunted my last twenty years in the hotel industry, in Montreal. If only I could get rid of the stomach and back pains, I could easily deal with the rest. One thing I knew is that I had other aspects of life to enjoy and celebrate.

I walked by the beach, heading east to the chalet. Then I pushed my toes through the immaculate Mediterranean waves, mingled with Alexandria's gentle mud, toward the 1975 relic, just until I found a fence perpendicular to the seashore and blocking my access to where I wanted to go six hundred feet farther (eastward). Since I was not prepared to bypass the fence by jumping over it, I chose another direction. I chose to walk right, down through the first three or four rows of chalets and turn left (parallel to the coast) and then left, again, back to the seafront chalets where my family's 1975 chalet used to stand (leaving that fence behind me). Of course, there was a new apartment building every third chalet as well as dirt, garbage, and broken pavement, mobile shops, cigarette stands and the whole package. I followed my instinct to guide me since I was not sure which one it was. I even came across an empty space where there used to be a restaurant called Darwish Open Terrace. I recognized the surrounding chalets.

Somehow, my left and right turns were almost perfectly accurate. Other than the filthy little streets that once bore figs, grapes, dates trees, rosemary, thyme, and basil leaves, as well as orange blossom and jasmine trees, I could see nothing left than cold and empty summerhouses and some outlets- some, even, half broken. Yet, something pulled me to see the chalet where I had seen my brother last in 1975. I kept moving forward, and my pulse was rising. Then I walked faster and faster almost as if I would see him. I started to sweat and fell short of breath. My footsteps pulled me forward, left, and right until, suddenly, I stopped. The sea was ahead of me. I was once again at the first row of chalets. I turned my head leftwards and there it was ... Cabin-280, or Chalet-280! It was still there, but it was forsaken and half broken down.

Most of its construction (its skeleton) was there, but its edges were falling apart. The once beautiful, white brick balcony with white brick fence was still there but only half-alive and half as beautiful. Nonetheless, I could feel the warmth of the moment. It flew me back to the last evening we spent together, our last brother-to-brother conversation. My parents were inside sleeping while I was contemplating the sea with Camille. My sister was in Cairo preparing to take a few days off from her office with my cousin Marcelle the following weekend. I searched for the wooden deck but did not find it. I stared at the brick fence of the balcony very sharply and bent forward to touch it with my left arm, and then I closed my eyes for a few seconds (having noticed a number of passersby watch me) and made a small prayer. After this, I walked backward to track my earlier footsteps, right to the seashore and then left, again, toward the street that took me to the umbrella where Dahlia, her brother, and our friends were waiting.

That night, I suffered a devastating abdominal attack and had no recourse to any clinic or hospital. This was a public holiday, and the closest hospital was ten kilometers, away. I was in need of a strong painkiller to calm me down but could not find anyone to authorize it or to diagnose me. My acetaminophens would not work. Over the last fourteen ambulatory visits to hospital in Montreal, the ER doctors had to give me Morphine, seven or eight times, to abort the rising and excruciating pain. One of our friends took me in his car, together with Dahlia and her brother, around the resort's pharmacies seeking help without a prescription. Unfortunately, there was nothing open and the intensity of my panic attack was rising to a point where I vomited in the car. I was jumping and throbbing from pain. Just as we prepared to go back home for some primary pain killers, Dahlia spotted a mosque called *Alghofran Mosque* (Forgiveness Mosque) that had a side-sign that mentioned an ER (Emergency Room) for the financially challenged members of its community. Our friend rushed me to the mosque where I filled out a form and wrote my name. I told the veiled woman at the reception, "I am Christian of faith. Can you help me? I am in great pain." (Usually, one has to write her/his faith on government forms and ID documents.)

"What is this, sir? How can you say this? This is a house of God. Please step in," she said. I felt a cold shower on my head and filled the forms with Dahlia, while clearly demonstrating chills and tears from my incessant pains. To my utter joy, the volunteer physician on duty, that night, was a seventy-four-year-old professor of gastroenterology at the University of Alexandria. The physician examined me and saved me with a mild shot of morphine that did the job in two minutes. The nurse asked me to wait for fifteen minutes and our friends waited for us, downstairs, while Dahlia stayed by my side in the clinic. I thanked him and asked if I could donate to the mosque's projects.

"You cannot do this now, but you are welcome, only if you want to do so, next Monday when the administration is open," he said.

The following morning, I returned to sea with the rest. This whole place took me back to the year before my last conversation with Camille, when the music fest (Agamy Sandstock 1974) took place. I had a dip in the sea, swam for over twenty minutes, and then went back to join the rest for an hour, as if nothing had happened, the day before. After that, we all walked down towards home, where I had a nap for an hour, to make up for the night before, after which we went for dinner.

    The following morning on this April day in 2009, we drove toward Alexandria's ravishing downtown district through an old street that was two kilometers south of Agamy Beach and parallel to it. It was a wide but tired historical street that had a sign bearing the name Rue des Sœurs. After a four-kilometer drive eastward, it would reach Alexandria's downtown district. On this fascinating street, there was also the old school of the order of the Sisters of the Sacred Heart, the Franciscan church, various beautiful antique mosques, and Café El-Horreya (formerly Café El-Gezaz) where we stopped for tea.

    This café is special (so were we told by its staff) because it had witnessed the killing of an Egyptian donkey boy, called El-Ajjan, by a non-Egyptian Maltese passenger whom El-Ajjan had given a ride to Café El-Gezaz in 1882. The passenger had scoffed the boy because he (the Maltese) disputed the cost of the ride and stabbed the boy despite the intervention of several passersby. The boy died. Among those who intervened, to stop the killing was an Egyptian, a Greek, and an Italian. It ended with the killing of the Egyptian and the Greek and the wounding of the Italian. We saw several historical little mosques and the Historical Greek Orthodox Monastery that Athanasius and Cyril, early Patriarchs of Alexandria had founded in AD 451. A new trend of Greek migrants, who fled some Greek islands before and during WWI, flooded this same street before and during WW1. Among these were my grandfather and his mother. We drove until we reached the beginning of central Alexandria and the ravishing coast of Alexander the Great and his disciple, Ptolemy the First, all the way to Ptolemy the fourteenth, namely *Cleopatra the Great* or *Cleopatra the Seventh*, last descendent of Ptolemy dynasty in AD 30, who was said to have killed her brother for power.

We drove by the stunning Mediterranean Fortress of Qaitbay, built in 1477 by Maméluke Sultan Al-Ashraf Qaitbay (of Turkish origins) to protect Egypt from foreign invasions. The fortress was severely damaged during the 1882 Egyptian revolution; and was restored in early 1900s. He (the Sultan) built it on top of the ruins of Egypt's legendary lighthouse, once one of the seven wonders. We continued past Alexandria's glamorous *Bibliotheca Alexandrina* and then right through the hottest commercial area in Alexandria built over the last two hundred years. This commercial area faces the romantic Mediterranean shore and covers two-thousand-years-old citterns and remains of the Ptolemaic and Roman ruins since early Christianity, most of which remain unexcavated. Of course, our favorite place was the district of Ramleh, the city that captured my childhood and that of many Egyptians who visited its Mediterranean restaurants in the forties, fifties, and sixties.

Roman fortress of Babylonia in AD 30
Dungeon of Christian martyrs since AD 70

History states that the Roman Emperor Maximus (*Maxentius*) persecuted Saint Catherine of Alexandria until her death during the third century because of her Christian faith. Later, Emperor Justinian canonized her in the sixth century and erected the *Monastery of Saint Catherine, in Sinai.* When Amr Ibn

El-Assi invaded Alexandria in AD 643, he advised Caliph Omar Ibn-Al-Khattab that there were two thousand churches in Alexandria during early Christianity. A few churches remain in Alexandria. Today, over two thousand mosques cover Alexandria. The hardship of Christians continued until, during and after the reign of Sultan Salah-el-Din El-Ayyuby in AD 1174 although his leadership condemned violence.

Earlier, and according to *Ibn Abdel Hakam*, Muslim Historian (born in Egypt, Fustat, in AD803), throughout his work *Futuhat Misr* (Conquests of Egypt) of AD641, Amr Ibn El-Assi, followers applied several levels of pressure to convert Egyptian Copts, Greeks and Jews, by order of Khalif Omar Ibn El-Khattab. *Ibn Abdel Hakam* refers to converting Christians and Jews of Egypt by several progressive means, in the following order 1-*Iqnaa* (Persuasion), failing which, 2-*Ikrah* (coercion), on to 3-*Gizieh* (pay a tax as tribute to refrain from converting to Islam), failing which, and in the event families cannot afford to pay a tax, 4-*Qettal* (killing). Then there was the battle of Babylon (Roman Fortress in Fussatum, *Fustat, ancient-Cairo*) in AD641 between Amr and Patriarch Cyrus, that lasted seven months of heavy fighting and that ended with Amr's prevalence over Cyrus, the Patriarch of Alexandria and Egypt (1st See of Christianity, of five). Amr had offered Cyrus three options: Declare Islam as religion for the Romans in Egypt, pay the Guizieh or War… By orders of Emperor Heraclius in Rome, Cyrus chose war but lost to Amr in this decisive battle of AD641. Cyrus had clearly expressed his desire to be buried at the Patriarchate of the Orthodox Basilica in Alexandria that was founded by Saint Marc the Evangelist. In the seventh century, Copts and Romans were the two predominant Christian groups, which the Arab conquests targeted for conversion. Greeks-Orthodox Christians were quite affluent as well. With the Copts, Muslim rulers reached some consensus, across the years, although many churches were reported burnt, by the state, across the subsequent centuries. In recent years, (2010 onwards until later in 2018, which I witnessed prior to publishing this book), several churches were bombed but by extremist groups or troublemakers, and not the state. The government of Egypt, its army and local security agencies, under pressure, has worked very hard to quell such violent practices. Following two centuries of modern (though fragile) coexistence, since the application of Napoleonic Penal Code and the introduction of the royal rule of Mohamed Ali in 1805, the people of Egypt trained themselves to coexist in fellowship and respect, far more than throughout the previous millennium; …it a divine gift.

Back to my vacation and with Dahlia in my arms for two weeks in Cairo and Alexandria (still in spring of 2009), I felt rejuvenated. On my way home to Montreal, I spend two days in Switzerland (One out and one in) and then three, in North Italy, so as to visit the historical church of *Saint Anthony of Padova* and light a candle for mother. He is her favorite saint and I bought her his statuette from his church in Padova. This was another extension to the enrichment of my broken heart. I was not alone anymore. God sent Dahlia to me after I had accepted His call to worship him in seclusion during my retreat in Magog. In fact, it had to be God who invited me to rest my soul at *Saint Benoit du Lac* in Magog, seven months before (in September 2008) and now in *Padova*. This was not a myth; it was a reality.

A few days later, I flew back to Montreal, determined to remain energized and to take a legal shot at my last place of work, which I regretted deeply, later. In addition, I had to prepare for Dahlia's visit to Montreal that year. I wanted her to meet my family, just as I met her brother and family, in Egypt.

> *Blessed are ye, when men shall hate you, and when they shall separate you from their company, and shall reproach you, and cast out your name as evil, for the Son of man's sake. Saint Luke, Chapter 6, Verse 22*

Part 2

Chapter 34
Return from Vacation

While crossing the Atlantic, I began to trace back my journey to cognitive recovery since it started in Magog last September (2008), the year before I met Dahlia for the first time since university. It also felt that I picked up additional energy and peace during my trip to Egypt. It was all building up. I wanted so much to live again, to think, create music, play the piano, write my articles, finish this paper and to do what I meant to by immigrating to the new world. Many times, I had read books and articles about mind control in the workplace and its roots in warfare. In fact, such tactics are still used to this day; they are executed through psychological control of political prisoners of various countries and institutions. My curiosity led me to seek to understand the basics of this control, through various researches and reviews. I acquired more knowledge of what is known as NLP (Neurological Linguistic Programming), (the principle of control) whether academically studied by researchers or naturally inherent with some psychopaths or sociopaths. However, this was not my purpose and I do not mean to turn it into an academic thesis or discovery in this testimony.

My perception of casualties of office games and undue hardship was a fair premise from which to start my amateur quest as to why I felt overpowered at the workplace and in my own social circles. I needed to do this, in order to put it behind me and to make sure that I was no longer trapped by some recent suggestive mind games. Because this is, really, what controllers do to lay-people, in order to render them helpless and lead them, sometimes, as pawns! For example, a typical psychopath (hunter) would tell his prey "Let me help you be a better person; you can do it" or he/she can look in their prey's in a condescending manner. There, the psychopath could look down at its prey, bend its head forward while posing with some sort of fake pitiful look, claiming affection and a sense of pity for its prey. It could even, turn its face repeatedly with a look of forced compassion. This would condition the prey to accept pity and love from its 'hunter', hence, fall in the trap. Once labeled, it will follow its master, with no defense. Several senior staff whom I met from diverse industries in social gatherings and corporate luncheons agreed that they felt manipulated at their offices or even broken, completely, and beyond. Others experienced it with their spouses, peers, at one time, or another. Hence, manipulation and control tactics had to exist. In fact, it is some form of rigid coercion, different from the violence used in religious or political compulsion, persecution and physical torture. With NLP, one entity can frame the other, quietly and systematically.

In this case, control, bullying, and manipulation in offices, would have at least three principle corporate objectives, 1- stretching a capable person to overachieve and do the impossible, at low cost. 2- To render its life miserable, to have it leave with no compensation. 3- To manipulate its mind with the intention of retaining it to stay, for as long as it took, to accomplish its planned objectives. This means, discourage it from leaving or from seeking career growth elsewhere. This last could mean breaking one's esteem through negative suggestion or the contrary; by multiplying its incentives, dinners, travels and more (positive enforcement) until it was time for it to leave (also known as employee retention programs). All that this needed was a set of invasive psychological tactics to lock its prey and to lead it (*through its peers and even few clients and personal friends*) into doing what it wants, if even it were at the expense of its prey's life aspirations elsewhere and its own health (to the extent of irreversible damage).

Throughout my first assignment at *Le Soleil*, around 1994, I tried repeatedly to leave its dark atmosphere and to search for an opportunity in a calmer set-up (in countryside), seeking income with peace. The General Manager at this countryside hotel knew my current French Manager from Quebec, *Monsieur Legault* (Zinky's partner and friend). Of course, I did not get the job. Soon, Monsieur Legault told me "If you cannot do it here you will not do it in Canada" hence, warning me but also applying *Future Anchoring*, to discourage me from seeking opportunities, elsewhere, to play with my mind, subside my drive for growth and impede my performance in future interviews.

Not only that; but when a career consultant handles a cluster of businesses from the same industry (such as a few hotels in a given district) it would be in the best interest of this consultant to keep trained middle-management-staff of one hotel within their cluster and to move her around within this cluster. In the work field, some refer to it as LMI (Labor Market Information), although it is not quite the same. Of course, the trained staff member cannot aspire to work elsewhere, if it secures an outstanding offer in the marketplace, even after passing an intense series of successful interviews because the references required from the current employer to support his quest for growth, will never go through.

In one of the city center's business luncheons in 1998, a prominent and retired Personnel Development specialist and Career Consultant discussed NLP in the workplace, as mentioned above. He broke down, some of its steps: *Anchoring* (digging into one's *'an employee's'* weaknesses or strengths), *Pacing* (befriending that person while 'rubbing the prey's skin. This is done by repeatedly discussing these anchors), *Leading* (it and pulling it to reach its intended objective), *Calibrating* (stabilizing the situation through rewards and incentives) once the prey is locked, *Reinforcement* (of manipulation and anchoring), and even *Further Leading*. It could also reach cruel stages of future control, known as Future-Anchoring (among others). Such as by telling the staff: 'Next time you go to an interview (or sales presentation) *fake it until you make it, or try to mask your looks and be forceful*. They would say this, just to plant restrictive seeds in the employee's mind. This way, next time one goes to an interview, he or she is impeded by the illusion that he/she may be weak.

Anchoring is when the controller se*eks to surface several life events or character traits within the targeted person so as to bring them to light* (anchor them) and, by doing so, destabilize him. Then keep pounding on them, directly, or with the help of selected team members (such as peers, clients, or even family members) until the controller recognizes which of them ticks the target most. Using peers to do the *anchoring* only destabilizes the target because it confirms the initial controller's accusation of the target. (So now, there is a peer witnessing and confirming the bosses' accusation). Then comes the sequence mentioned just above.

After lengthy thinking (while crossing the Atlantic), the flight attendant passed by and I asked her for a woolen cover and then, I closed my eyes. I managed to sleep for close to two hours before overflying Canada's East Coast.

By 1pm (Montreal time), we had finished our meals, crossed the Atlantic Ocean and were overflying the coast of Nova Scotia. This gave me a chance to close my eyes for another hour and a half. My plane landed at 3pm in Montreal; I took a taxi and was home before 5pm. I called mom, next door, and drove over to visit her, right away, postponing tidying my bags for the following day. My car, easily took off, as my battery was new. I stepped out of the car and she was waiting for me, sitting at the patio's door, all covered up. Mom was almost 93 then and I was almost 58 years old.

"Hello my love. I miss you so much."

"Oh, you have a tan my son. I miss you too". I hugged mom and walked her inside, away from the chilly Montreal April evening in 2009 and then took my coat off.

"I got you this fine silk scarf from the tax free shop as well as your preferred perfume"

"Oh thank you; this is expensive stuff. I love the scarf. Which perfume?"

"Your favorite perfume, in the mid-sixties..."

"...Diorissimo?"

"Yes ma Diorissimo by Christian Dior; your favorite and mine!"

"But of course; the jasmines perfume; your eternal romantic love affair."

"Yes ma…" *This was a classic perfume launched in 1956 by Christian Dior of Paris called Diorissimo and was made of a glorious blend of jasmines, lily of the valley, and ylang-ylang fragrances. Mother opened it and sprayed a little. The scent filled the room, while mother closed her eyes, in ecstasy.*

"Ma…."

"Yes darling"

"I saw everything again, a little different even too different but all the same worth revisiting again and again. I only wish you were with me, in Egypt."

"So, you want to tell me of your lady friend first?" *I had spoken to her about Dahlia on the phone from Egypt.*

"She is coming to meet you mom; she will come in fall for two weeks and I want you to give us your blessings. We were close friends at university but you never saw her. Her name is Dahlia".

"…Blessings? Oh my son; so it is good news? I will wait for her"

"I know you would ma. I told her all good things about you." *Somehow, I did not feel comfortable after mother's comment that she would wait for Dahlia.* I went to the kitchen to fetch a glass of water.

"God keep you for us. You are my angel and have always been!"

"I know; and I will continue to be your angel, my son for many years even after I am gone. Your marriage will add joy to your life and to mine but it will not be void of challenges; of ups and downs."

"Thank you mom; don't say this; we will all go one day and meet again in the Holy Mansion of God."

"I do not doubt that."

"My son; I meant to tell you this a long time ago…."

"Tell me what [I interrupted]; are you alright my love?"

"Yes, yes of course I am, and mean to celebrate your wedding but, when I fly one day, because I just must fly, remember that I will always watch over you, especially in your hard times. I will be there with dad and Camille. If ever it gets too tough, turn your head up or close your eyes and you will feel me flying over you and smiling to you. But I will be watching over you, anyway, in case you are too tired to look."

"Oh ma; and I will look out for you and will find you. If I go first I will be waiting for you" and I threw myself in her lap and hugged her.

"Ma…"

"Yes, my son"

"You remember; back in the fifties, why was Mady (Aunty Helga's daughter), and a few others so harsh towards you. She used to make mean comments about you to me. Why ma…"

"Why do you dwell on the past, my son? Everything changed afterwards and I remember you took my defense and replied to her!"

"They alienated you when you were only new in the family, and then, they picked on me because I took your defense."

"C'est la vie, my son. However, time heals; and by time we all accepted each other, haven't we?"

"Quite so, mom… But it was not genuine; it was false and I was holding your back, always!"

After a few seconds of stretched emotions, we drank some chamomile and I prepared to leave.

"Don't you want to stay for dinner? Your sister will be here later!"

"No dear but I can fix you supper and stay with you as you eat; I am full. They gave us too much food and drink on board!"

"Fine, let us do that. Wait I will move to the kitchen table while you heat some Shepherd Pie for my supper. It's in the fridge." I left after one hour and promised to call her in the morning. Mom would spend a few days at my place the following week and we would have endless chats and laughter.

Tale of a Growing Child

In the meantime, I meant to find a part-time job of a low profile nature before spending my entire severance package.

By the end of May 2009, I had secured a part-time job, in the area, as a department store agent. This was good because I made some money in addition to my remaining severance dollars and subsequent pension checks.

I would spend the remaining time driving mom around and helping her do her shopping or spending some time in shopping malls with a few of her remaining friends. She had started to use a walker but continued to be just as graceful as ever. Mom was aging and started to forget little things. Alas, she was starting Dementia.

In August mom succumbed to a mild stroke and slipped on the floor. I was there that day, next to her. Terrified, I called 911 immediately, for an ambulance that was at our doorstep in seven minutes. The paramedics provided her with first aid and we made it to The West Island General Hospital within less than five more minutes. Mom was a little sad during our ride to hospital, and I was clutching her left hand with my left hand while rubbing her face with my right hand, as she lay on the stretcher in the ambulatory car, until we reached hospital. The ER team was amazing and beyond compassionate. Two hours later, she was stable and I advised my family, accordingly at their place of work, using my mobile phone. We spent the night at the Emergency Room of that hospital and she returned to my place for ten days. I had reduced my hours during those days. She was eager to meet Dahlia in early October and was so strong and determined to do so.

In September, the Chairman of the Chamber of the Commerce invited me for the usual quarterly luncheon. This time, he asked me to give an eight to ten minutes presentation to other longtime friends from the hotel world, neighboring corporations and banks. They were mostly *Baby Boomers* (50 years, plus).

This social function was God sent, and it would help me sum my work experience over the last few years, and present it to past and present colleagues, to clients and members of the chamber, without whining and, most definitely, with the objective of reclaiming my fractured spirit.

In the middle of September, I went for lunch and met many of my *old-timers*. The Chamber of Commerce held the luncheon at the Golf Club of the city of *Le Soleil*. The invitation indicated the names of two guest-speakers that day, one of which was my name, the luncheon menu and the event sponsors. Our host called on me and I went on stage. The theme of my presentation was about corporations, change, violence, coercion and mind control.

Good afternoon everyone

It is so good to be back and see all of you, again. We share so much in common; our years of successes, our challenges and, for a few of us, our disappointments. Many of us managed to cope with our corporate challenges. Many still find it increasingly disappointing how some corporations can crush their experienced staff to reach their aim.

We all remember Eileen… Well I visited her last week and she says Hello to you. She is recovering very well after her seven-year ordeal with her employer. Eileen will return to the work force in another industry, soon, after she has fully recovered. She promises to be present in our next quarterly meeting.

Yes, it is good to be back among you. My presentation this afternoon should not exceed eight to ten minutes. Its title is 'Corporations; the learning curve versus the carving of sculptures', and you know that I am a survivor of corporate hurt. It covers control, manipulation and coercion, both on a corporate level and in our own circles.

Each of us has his (her) own identity; and it is always one that distinguishes us from others. Identity, alas, is the sum of our passions, roots and experiences. As we live our life, interpret its odds and evens, cope with it, react to and interact with it, we develop a pattern of thoughts, actions and habits and, from there, we set our own aspirations; our own character. It is our right. We may even change them as life's cycles hit us. We become at liberty to rise and fall freely and stand-up again with no biased intervention- unless it is by means of some caring help; in our case, transparent coaching, mentoring and training (certainly not by control freaks).

If we are conscious of our habits, we can master them. That is to say, if we realize how we interpret life-cycles, we may, more easily, master our state of mind; refine our thoughts, their subsequent actions and inevitable patterns. Such is the road to conscious character building; to rich identity and to the right to be unique (while respectful of others). It is also the best way to perceive others' social and psychological expectations from us- such as in the work place, within the family, places of worship or social circles. It will help us strive to, both, refrain from outwitting others and from allowing others to outwit us, while achieving our business objectives and social aspirations, interdependently. It is a transparent form of interaction; not a controlled one.

Some may argue that, in business life or in our social circles, intervention through repetitive patterns of Suggestive Remarks is justifiable, in order to push an individual to alter its habits and so that it may achieve its objectives, even far beyond its ability. I beg to differ; suggestion is invasive and indirect. It is not transparent. It is a form of conditioning. It is destabilizing and will not 'push' a person to his or her paradise; it will 'coerce' that person in to a dark cocoon concocted by the suggesting intervener, mostly to his or her own narcissistic portrait of whims.

What is worrisome is that if we are not conscious of our thoughts, actions and reactions, we develop a set of habits that do not emerge from our own will; these habits make us absolutely subject to manipulation by outside forces and life events or the other way around; to be used in order to manipulate others. We must all be alert and conscious of events, opportunities and threats. Otherwise, we will become judgemental as opposed to judicious, snipers or puppets as opposed to facilitators to others and to our business objectives; and even, to our own lives and families.

Worse, still, is that even when we are fully or mostly aware and conscious of our thoughts and actions, we may, still, be target of mind games, manipulation and social programming that are capable of breaking us, reshaping us or, at least, shaking us. And this is the unfortunate reality of lives of prisoners-of-war, of unconscious targets of control or of people who are chosen for research and turned into Gene pigs- whether with or without consent. We fall victims of psychopaths or sociopaths- even at a grocery store, if we are not alert!

We come across these psychopaths, also called gas-lighters or hunters, everyday. Now, when they target us, they may compel us to a battlefield they have concocted for us. They will watch us engage in their battles, social, intimate, and other battles that they have assigned for us. They will scrutinize us as vicious spectators, even judges; they will witness our successes and falls (just as they planned), applauding us with false solidarity, or loathing us with demeaning pity, when we have never asked for these battles, in the first place. They will turn us into grieving pawns, wiping away our energy, our identity, our soul and causing us great pain and undue hardship, most of all, they will derail us from our lives claiming they had the right one, for us. They will leave us stagger even force us to stagger like a slain chicken, each time we gasp for air, just because we dared to have a voice, only to prove their own point, which they may never prove. After that, they will leave us flattened by their demonism and conscious incompetence.

The study of NLP (Neuro-Linguistic Programming) has been researched by masters like Joseph O Conner and John Seymour (amid others) who developed the lives of many of their subject targets, positively. It addresses such issues. Unfortunately, nowadays, it is copied by amateurs who have destroyed many; I mean amateur programmers and business drivers who have no character or taste- simply money-makers, who seek to copy and exercise, ruthlessly, NLP at the expense of their targets, claiming they are team-builders for corporations or motivational speakers for various audiences. They (This type of Neuro-Linguistic Programmers) and their agents (staff in a work place, as an example) seek to rebuild an individual, their way; to reshape it, once they have broken it (through intense scrutiny *and micromanagement). This of course, is not a learning curve; it is a narcissistic means of sculpturing an individual and damaging its identity.*

The problem with some heads of corporations, societies and educational institutions, is that they fail to realize that each time they exercise control over their experienced and knowledgeable managers, their striving citizens, earnest students or faithful subjects, authority resides in those they seek to control; seek to coerce and to accepting violent change, without leaving them space to make their point or to just have a voice.

Now, as we grow older we may, very well, lose our memory, whether because of age, Alzheimer or Dementia. I served in senior homes for years, trying to add joy to the final stages of life, of several seniors. Here is what I found: If, one day, as we grow old, we lose our memory we will, inevitably, lose our identity unless we are provided with dedicated support; support by honorable and caring family members, friends and caregivers, at every single moment of our lives to help us anchor some resourceful moments of our beautiful past. This caring support will render seniors, free from memory failure, and will unchain their prison. But if we are indifferent to the 'aging', we will keep them locked in their state of 'Unconscious Incompetence' and I have seen several in my own circles. Of course, we need not coerce our seniors regain their memories, just help them, refresh them and care for them; but not dump them; in fact, we should nurture and acknowledge them.

Today, there are those who ask you, "Why do you dwell on the past?" claiming that memories do not help. Yes and no, I say! Because if we kill all memories, just as in the case of ailing seniors, we lose identity and, in our current lives, we will become void of character. Remember "Identity like character is the sum of our passions, roots and experiences"; and we need it to make judicious choices throughout our lives; so how can we shut down memories and experience! And, in the workplace, if we shut away our passions, roots and memories, we will not be able to recover from manipulative tactics and could very well, end up victims of daily psychopaths with no recourse to our lifelines and to positive childhood anchors. We will not use our power to build the business and nurture horizontal and vertical relationships. I tell those people who deny their past; you are scared to face life and cope with it and may need to hold on to your own character, if any, without fiddling with the character of others. As for us, today, we are just over thirty business friends. We are a hall of sixty, eyes, sixty ears, thirty hearts, thirty minds and somewhere, if I dare say, in excess of thirty professionals multiplied by fifty years of passions and roots… Think of the mathematics and drop the control freaks…

Thank you for listening to me. It is such a pleasure to come to these luncheons and to see you all.

Bon appétit

The audience seemed enthusiastic and posed some questions, for a few minutes. We promised to meet again soon, for our next luncheon, in the presence of Eileen.

On October 30, 2009, Dahlia arrived in Montreal. I welcomed her at Montreal's Pierre-Elliot Trudeau Airport. Dahlia brought some precious gifts made of Egyptian silver and silk to my mother, sister, nephew, and niece. She did not get a present for my brother-in-law because he had been working in Cairo for several years and because she had already met him the week before in Cairo. He would follow, to Montreal, at Christmas time, for vacation. Dahlia and I were to stay at my family's home during her short visit to Montreal. We arrived at my family's home while everyone was still working or at the gym. Mom was seated and waiting for us at the patio. She was well dressed, stylish and wore some warm clothes. Dahlia rushed to her while I held her bags.

"Hello aunt Laurice; I am Dahlia" and she hugged her.

"Hello my darling, it is so good to see you"

"It is so good to see you, too, aunt Laurice. I heard so much of you. Raphy says you are his best friend"

"And he told me all good things about you, too. Come in my darling it is cold outside; you are not yet used to our cold." Dahlia helped mom with her walker.

"Where do you want to sit, auntie?"

"Here, Dahlia, to the right this is my preferred armchair."

I carried Dahlia's stuff and coat, over to her assigned guestroom on the upper floor and rushed downstairs. "Do you want to use the toilet sweetheart?"

"Yes please" Dahlia went.

"Sweetheart; you just called her sweetheart? This is beautiful my son. You waited a long time."

"Yes ma; it was just not meant to happen before"

Dahlia came down and we had tea until my family returned from work. After this, we all sat for a little meal. By 10 pm, Dahlia went to her room and I stayed in mine at my family's home.

Throughout Dahlia's whole stay, my mother, more than anyone, was absolutely overjoyed and reassured by seeing me, after all these years, reconnect with my old colleague, friend, and soon-to-be wife. It seemed obvious that just as Dad married my mom at the age of sixty, I, too, would do the same—with the difference that mother was twenty-seven years younger than dad, and Dahlia is only eight years younger than I am. Dahlia's parents had passed away twenty years earlier.

My mother's family in Montreal, her nephews and nieces, gave Dahlia abundant love and affection during her short vacation of November 2009.

Dahlia and I had planned a short visit to the city of Magog during her stay in Canada. We would leave in two days and stay at the same motel I had visited the year before, during my retreat of fall, 2008. We told mother about it.

"Ma, in three days we will drive to Magog for our mini retreat. I will get you something nice from the Abbey."

"Can you get me a statue of Saint Anthony of Padova? Don't they have a souvenirs shop?"

"But of course ma and another for the Holy mother." Mother forgot that I had bought her a nice one from the Basilica of Saint Anthony of Padova, itself, earlier this year. Besides, Mom's favorite saints were Saint Anthony and the Holy Mother.

She would pray for their intervention repeatedly, across sixty years of my life.

"Here, take three hundred dollars for your trip"

"No ma I can't"

"Come on take them"

"No ma; that is too much. Just a hundred will be great, if you insist"

"I make more money than you with my two pensions (*Canada and United Nations*). Take them. They are in the second drawer to the left; wrapped in a plastic bag".

"Are you sure ma?"

"Yes, go ahead."

"Alright mom"

"Now go back to your wife and have a good night's sleep"

"Good night my love; thank you" And I hugged her. "Dahlia and I will have breakfast with you in the morning before touring the city."

"Good night my son"

We booked our stay at my favorite motel just overlooking the Lake of Memphre-Magog.

We arrived that evening at five, checked in, rested in our room for an hour and started walking in Magog's main commercial street. We stopped for supper at an Italian restaurant but Dahlia encouraged me not to eat wheat products until we find the underlying cause of my stomach pain.

"Refrain from wheat and excessive milk. Gluten and lactose will only add an unwanted burden to your system which you don't need now," said Dahlia.

"OK, I will have a chicken breast à la Milanese without the cheese and some steamed veggies and roasted potatoes."

"I will go for their Napolitan Spaghetti with shrimps, garlic and roasted tomatoes," said Dahlia.

"Yes, that's a good choice. I had it in 2008 and it's amazing"

"Later on, we will do a comprehensive Bacteria and Parasites test at a tropical disease clinic in Montreal. I am sure there is one," said Dahlia.

When the woman waiter came to greet us, we placed our order and asked for some light Merlot wine of the region. We told her our story.

"It's been 32 years since we left each other at university, in Cairo and now we are reunited"

"Oh my God you will make me cry… Do you love each other?"

I looked at Dahlia and told her "Did I ever tell you?"

"…No, not yet"

I kissed her hand and the waiter offered us the first round of wine on the house.

"Thank you so much, Natalie," said Dahlia

The food was delicious and even easy to digest. We walked back to our motel and had a good night sleep. Dahlia was ready for the motel's delicious morning coffee and breakfast, after which we would go for our walk by the lake. We had to be at the Abbey of Saint Benedict before 11am for Eucharist.

We started our panoramic walk by the lakefront two hundred meters down the road.

"This is where I would end up and do my thinking and I would write my biography on this wooden table."

"It is beautiful"

Dahlia held her takeaway coffee with her and I held my tea, as well as some fresh warm rolls, from a neighboring bakery. After a while we drove uphill for twelve kilometers to the Abbey and she saw it all, live. Mass was solemn as usual and the monks' sermon was serious. On the way out, we bought a little fresh Brie cheese for the day, made by the monks, and returned in the evening for Benedictine chants. We had one more site to visit, which we did. We visited one of Quebec's famous vineyards and visited their wine and sparkling wine cellars. The tasting was delicious and the fifty kilometers drive back and forth was worth it.

Upon our return from Magog in early November 2009, we contacted the Citizenship and Immigration office in Canada for information and procedure in order to start collecting and filling the required forms while Dahlia was in Egypt and while I was in Montreal, preparing for our wedding. Our intention was to apply for civil papers in November to receive clearance by May 2010 and to apply to the Municipal Court to activate our request for a civil marriage.

Dahlia and I continued filling out the extensive immigration forms and collecting the needed copies of fiscal papers, not to mention translating certificates issued in Egypt. For the rest of her stay in Montreal, I drove Dahlia through various hotspots in the city. We spent some valuable time with mother and took her in my car for various similar rides-sometimes by the waterfront and others for some easy shopping, while using her walker. We continued doing so, until Dahlia left for Cairo, late November 2009, with the intention of returning to Montreal for our wedding in July of 2010. I finalized all civil clearances, for our wedding, and was able to set its date at the Montreal Court for July 24, 2010, ten days after Dahlia would arrive.

Chapter 35
The Wedding and the Family

On July 14, the following year, (2010), Dahlia arrived in Montreal's International Airport, for her second visit, where I was waiting for her. I saw Dahlia walking out of customs and rushed forward to hold her in my arms

The date of our civil marriage was set for July 24 at 10:00 a.m., the wedding reception on July 31 at 5 p.m., and the church service on Sunday morning, August 8.

We celebrated the civil marriage at Montreal's Municipal Court, downtown Montreal, with my mother, sister, brother-in-law and their two children together with their sweethearts, as well as many senior and younger cousins, my other cousin (Marcelle's elder brother) and his lovely wife, who did not live far from the courthouse. After the civil celebration, these last two, threw a rich and classy early afternoon high tea and Champaign reception. There were about eighteen adults and youth at the courthouse and, later, at my cousin's home that day.

The size of the court assigned for our civil ceremony was about twenty-thousand square feet (40 * 40 m), enough to seat eighty visitors. It had two sets of seat-columns and eight or ten rows. Mom was sitting on the right column's first row, surrounded by her elder nephew (Kaliope's first son, ten years older than I was. This was Antoine. He had assisted me on the eve of Camille's departure in 1975) and my cousin Marcelle's elder brother and his wife who would throw their reception after the ceremony. My sister sat to the other side of mom with her husband. Her children sat on the left column's first row. The rest of the guests sat further down. The hall was well ventilated and was clearly richer than others used for legal matters.

Dahlia and I sat facing each other at two sides of a modest rectangular table on a slightly elevated platform at the extreme left end of the hall (The head table). We would turn our heads to the joyful audience and join the 'funky' jokes. Mother was ecstatic clapping and throwing kisses from her lips to us and, of course, celebrating one of the final chapters of her life on earth, victoriously. Mom would do the same whenever I invited her to attend my graduation from university, watch me act in one of my theatre performances or as Master of various Ceremonies at university, many years before. The youth was jumping left and right taking pictures of us. Suddenly we heard a bell and the courtroom's door, situated on the extreme right end, opened. The magistrate, a young beautiful Canadian of Haitian descent, stepped in, smiling and raising her right hand modestly to great the audience, while holding her register with her left hand. She walked through the court's aisle all the way up to our table. We all stood up to greet her. She greeted everyone and then asked us to take our seats.

"Bonjour, the session has started. It is my pleasure to run the civil union ceremony of the newlywed in accordance with the rules and by-laws of *L'État Civil du Québec (*(Quebec's Register of Civil Status) and with the guidelines of the Supreme Court of Canada. Please refrain from clapping or talking during this short ceremony. Will the groom please mention his full name?"

I mentioned mine

"And the bride…"

Dahlia mentioned hers

The magistrate opened her book to compare her register's data with that on the copy of the marriage certificate that we had submitted to the government, the year before. The information corresponded. Then she said:

"Before we go further let me read to you some basic guidelines that the civil-union law of Quebec, commits you to. These guidelines explain your dues and rights toward each other. If you are not satisfied with any of its contents, please say so now, and we will annul the union. If you agree you are asked to sign and will be subject to all laws and by-laws set herein. This is an original of your legal commitment to these laws. Please go through it again."

Dahlia and I read it and nodded, approving of its content.

"Then please sign below, each of you"

We did and she gave each of us a temporary copy of her legal statement.

"And now we move to the final part of our ceremony. Are your vows ready?"

"Yes, your honor" said Dahlia

"Yes your grace" I said

"Then, please state your vows to each other. We start with the bride"

"Raphy, I promise to love you and to cherish you with all my heart and mind during our lifetime union"

"And the groom, please…!"

"Dahlia, I promise to do the same and to make up for all the wasted years since university"

"I declare the union legal and official. Congratulations. You will each receive a certified testimony of this union, by mail, within two weeks. The groom may kiss the bride"

We did for a few lengthy seconds and the audience shared the moment with its applause and clapping. Mom was waving to me to walk to her so that she could hug Dahlia and me. However, so did every one until we proceeded in our cars and taxis to our cousins' neighboring place for their truly classy mid-day Champaign reception. Within twenty minutes, we were all having a toast and mother was excited!

"I want to live; I want to live and see you both together for as long as I can" she said.

"Yes mom, of course you will", I said.

After this delightful family celebration, we drove to our neighboring church to pray and to light a candle, just until we performed the official church ceremony (after two weeks) at my beautiful church in Ottawa, where I had sung with its Senior Choir for four years. We lit a candle and drove back to my apartment, to officially, move in together as husband and wife. I had moved Dahlia's belongings, gradually over the previous few days, from my family's home, to my apartment.

Dahlia commented on my apartment's artistic set-up, its modern furniture but in particular, about my rosewood tea table.

"What a beautiful piece of furniture; the piano, too... Did you buy them in Montreal?"

"No, my love; most of the furniture here is from Montreal but there are just a few items that my mother wanted me to keep from the bulk of my family's furniture which I had shipped over from Egypt, in 1987, with the help of my travel network in Cairo. Mother wanted me to keep the piano and this table and a few more souvenirs. Everything else is in the family's home, next door. It is mom's furniture and her property. If she goes, my sister can have it; she already does since 1997. We had two small rosewood tables; mother kept one and gave me this one. It has a story."

"What? Tell me!"

"Well, in 1959, if my memory does not fail me, a friend of mother's called auntie Lucie, of Jewish faith, came to our home to let us know that the Egyptian authorities asked her and her family to leave Egypt on the weekend together with many other Egyptian Jews, in view of the Suez Canal crisis. She insisted mom took them, as she did not want to leave them behind. Mom reluctantly accepted them because she could not pay for them. Auntie Lucie did not want mother to pay for them, either. Mom accepted two tables and one bronze statue. We got them here amongst the rest of our belongings; she kept one at my family's home, I kept the other. I took care of mine and plugged a humidifier at six feet distance from it and the piano to protect the wood from cracking, if the heater was on."

"It's beautiful, such decoration and taste."

"Yes, a true masterpiece. Mom loved auntie Lucie for many other reasons."

Dahlia was tearing. "Very sad story"

"Yes, such a waste of Egyptians; of life, in General!"

"When President Sadat took over, twelve years later, he wanted to bring Egypt's children back, and he worked hard on it!"

After sometime, tidying up, we settled down, rested and went out for a quick bite.

On July 31, we held a dinner and dance reception at the City's Community Hall overlooking Montreal's beautiful Canal Lachine (also known as Lac Saint Louis). There were over eighty adults and youth that day, and the atmosphere was truly warm, jovial, and spectacular. My lifetime friends from Toronto and Ottawa came, all the way with their children, which had to have cost them substantial travel expenses in addition to hotel accommodations in Montreal. My best man, Zarif, an old university colleague and close friend gave a warm speech before dinner. I remember some of his words, to this day, as I write these lines: "With a life of over fifty years of giving love, affection, and care to his family, friends, and strangers, God has rewarded him with this tender and intelligent lifetime friend of his, Dahlia." He looked straight to my eyes, smiling but firmly and proudly, acknowledging our friendship. His wife came with him. I nodded with appreciation and love. My other friend (Camille's old best friend) and his wife, Elaine, told me during the wedding, "Raphael, you deserve this break. It is about time you enjoyed life with your college friend and lifetime companion."

The church celebration took place, the following week, at the Southminster United Church in Ottawa. On August 8, we drove to Ottawa for one hundred and sixty kilometers (Ninety minutes). This was my church for four years, and its congregation was and still is my extended family. I had sung with its Senior Choir for four years. They blessed our marriage and prayed for it.

"This devout son of our church has served its senior choir and its Mission and Service committee for close to four years. He was searching for love, and he found it in this girl, Dahlia, his college sweetheart thirty-three years ago. They both stand in front of you as their extended family to perform their vows. Do you accept their matrimony, today, under God?" said the reverend to the congregation, who responded with a loud applause. An hour later, the reverend held our heads in her arms to bless us and then opened the register, which we signed.. A few of my friends from Ottawa (only) were able to join. The church was 75 percent full of fellow parishioners and true human beings. I will always love them with all my heart, mind, and soul. Two weeks, later, I received the Christian Marriage Certificate by mail.

We returned to Montreal for another dinner with other family members and their children at the home of my other cousin, Marcelle's younger brother and wife (returning for his summer vacation from Dubai).

Across the three ceremonies between July 14 and August 8 and many more, my sweet mother glittered with happiness and joy. She would clap as we sat together, when we said a joke or if we listened to a preferred song. Mom loved Dahlia and she showered her with vast affection and respect. Dahlia loved Mom and would throw her head into her arms; she would cook her some of her favorite Mediterranean dishes and carry them over to her home, just *for her eyes*. She would peel her grapes.

In between the three ceremonies, family and friends threw endless parties, and mother was always present.

Our festive mood continued throughout the remaining months of August and September with nephews, nieces, and friends of my nephew and niece passing by to greet us or joining parties here and there. As for me, I was in another world, so happy and yet a little nervous!

Dahlia was to return to Cairo on September 29 and I would follow on December 17. This gave us sufficient time to file for her immigration from within Canada but first for a romantic retreat in the city of *Charlevoix*, in Quebec, Canada, offered by Marcelle's elder brother.

There was a lot of thinking and planning as to how we would start our lives, at our age, where we would live, and how we would split our time between Canada and Egypt. This was a very difficult task given my aging mother and her growing dementia. Of course, I needed to go to Egypt for a month or two because my rising abdominal pains were excruciating and I had reached a point where I had to reverse things and have a life of my own, before I regretted it forever. My life was at stake; real stake. Moreover, I wanted to spend time with Dahlia's family. Besides, I had to find the right way to tell mother. Therefore, that Friday, Dahlia and I passed by mom for our daily tea.

"My love, I need to go to Egypt, when we return from *Charlevoix*. We will need to go for two months in order for me to rest and to give myself a chance to recover from my endless pains. I am very optimistic I can do it or at least start my journey to recovery. I want to leave in the second week of December and will be back in early March of next year (2011). Ma, I will not abandon you, ever. I will call you every day, at least once, and you will be happy to see me fit, when I return. Do you trust me? I am tired from my painful attacks and…"

"Stop Raphy. Go! Go my love and be happy. I am not worried; besides you suffered enough for fifteen years and you deserve a break. I will wait for you; I will see you again in 2011!"

"Really ma… You are OK with that?"

"Of course my love, go! Will you be back in spring?"

"Yes ma, March 4, 2011, I promise"

"Then go and rest. Call me every two or three days, that's more than enough!"

"Every day mom, every single day of my life away from you…"

"Fine my tender one. Now go with your wife and spend the rest of the evening together… Are we all having brunch on Sunday?"

"Yes but tomorrow we will watch Saturday *Matiné* movie together (You, Dahlia and I) and we will have popcorn and soda."

That week passed, peacefully but the following week, my health broke down to a point where I was taken by ambulance to a renown Montreal hospital for excruciatingly painful abdominal attacks that made me shake as if I were epileptic.

In the ambulance car, Dahlia soaked some medical cloth with her cold bottle of water and wiped my forehead repeatedly.

"Don't be afraid. I am with you and it will be over soon." Dahlia never twitched or complained from all this drama and seemed far more solid than I thought. She deserved more.

The paramedics would not give me anything to abort the pain, such as morphine or Voltaren, before I had done all my tests.

We arrived to the hospital's ER (Emergency Room) while my mood was swinging unbearably, my violent vomiting, stomach, gallbladder and back pains induced me to short moments of unconsciousness. I felt daggers piercing my body for ninety full minutes until the physician authorized morphine; and then, after three minutes, everything subsided and my heartbeat stabilized. I flunked on my stretcher for twenty-four hours and was home, next day, drenched. Dahlia was with me all the way. She slept at the hospital next to me until I was strong to return. We took a taxi home and we called my family to re-assure them that everything was all right and back to normal.

"It will soon be over", she reassured me.

"Dahlia, I want to see a psychologist to see if any of this is neurological. I cannot believe I will continue living like this. This must stop."

"Do you know one?"

"Yes, two blocks away from our place. His name is Paul Feldman"

"So, when do you want to see him?"

"Before flying to Egypt"

"Alright, if you want to; though I think a comprehensive parasites and bacteria test can help you, too. Like I said, we need to make all sorts of tropical diseases tests."

"I need your help and also want professional advice. I will do both."

"Fine love, call him and fix something"

I passed by the doctor's office, two blocks away, and his assistant, Rosie, said, "I can only fix appointments with a prescription."

"I don't have one and was hoping Doctor Feldman could forego this."

She paused and then "Wait he goes out any minute now and will leave immediately for his clinic downtown Montreal. However, there is someone in his office now. I will ask him when his patient leaves." In a minute or two, the patient left and Rosie went to the doctor's office; and then returned, "He will see you for a minute"

"Good morning doctor Feldman; my name is Raphy. Thank you for seeing me"

"How can I help you Raphy. I must leave right away to my clinic at university"

"I am having intense recurring abdominal attacks, followed by chills, tears, bloating and back pains. I tried all sorts of MRIs, Cats-Scans, blood and urine tests, gastroscopies, colonoscopies, endoscopies- everything for fifteen years; but found absolutely nothing. I even ran gluten and lactose intolerance tests; but found nothing and I am tiered"

"What did your doctors say?"

"Between my doctors and recurring ER ambulance visits; they could not find anything. They said I might have IBS or Crones disease; or maybe a stone. A few told me '…it is between my ears', but I found nothing and decided to let go. Now I want to visit this road and see if it is neurological."

"You mean psychological? …well, can you come next week?"

"Yes, when?"

He looked in his calendar "Like today next week. We will have an introductory session for one hour and then I will tell you if it is the right approach to take."

"Thank you, doctor Feldman. What time?"

"11.00"

"I will be here"

"By the way to you have insurance?"

"No, sir"

"Then don't waste your money, if there is no point. I will let you know, then and will charge you one session, only. Before I do anything, I want you to run a comprehensive parasites and bacteria test to make sure that we will start on the right foot. Do this and send me a copy of all results until we meet next week."

Dahlia's hint was judicious and I told her. We immediately went to my family doctor and asked him for a prescription to present to a neighboring laboratory. He gave it to us but the laboratory gave me homework to do for three weeks before running my tests. They wanted me to abstain from all proton pumps, acid blockers and anti-reflux drugs, for three weeks that could impede the lab results.

The following week, mother had a second stroke that grounded her. I had to postpone my appointment with doctor Feldman to the following month. We called the ambulance who asked us to keep her lying flat on her back and in less than seven minutes they were at my family's doorstep. It was miraculous that mother would have her stroke in our presence. At no time was the mercy of God distant from us. The ambulance brought mom back in the evening with Dahlia, alone, next to her. I drove behind the ambulance as it moved with her from the hospital. We had been with her at hospital all the time until we returned home. We stayed until midnight just until my family returned home.

The day after, I had another panic attack and I vomited violently. Interestingly, several relatives told me to "shape-up" from my health problems to help my mother, "shape up and be responsible", while seated with their expensive whiskey. Their indifference to my health crushed me and I wondered why people found it so easy to preach instead of care.

"How can I shape-up if I am sick? And why have you done nothing to help me, for fifteen years?"

"Well maybe you just didn't listen enough at work; maybe this is an accumulation of your grief caused by your stubbornness"

"What stubbornness, me, stubborn… How do you know? Tell me… How would you know? How dare you ask me, this? Do you work with me? Did you know that I worked seventy hours a week and was not even allowed to delegate to my junior staff?"

"Well perhaps you should have started by listening to Dr. Zinky!"

"Oh…. That is what it is all about, to you! Come; come, really!" I replied "…I am heart-broken at your insensitivity. I am not supposed to be discussing my work with you; this should remain between my employer and me only! You are my blood relative not my coworker! And how about you; why did you never make it in the hotel industry in Canada for the thirty years following your immigration?"

"That's none of your business. I hope you learnt something!"

"Learnt? Come-on let us not be hypocrites… Some close blood relative! Spare me your sermons; will you. I am not supposed to be having this conversation with you; it is only between my superior, *your friend* and me! Besides, yes, I do; I learn every day and I allow myself to be transformed, by the will of God and not by pressure."

He smiled, mockingly!

"That's enough…. ", Dahlia stopped me and we both stepped out of my family's living room. Our voice was high and mom was resting up in her room. We went up and pretended there was nothing. Luckily, she thought we were having fun. We hugged her and went home.

Across the last ten years, members of my family would set me up with single women, who were either divorced, exerted or out of my moral league.

"What is stopping you? …ask her for marriage and settle down" one of them said, one day.

"What do you mean settle down [I'd reply]. You do not choose for me and if I do not find the girl of my choice, who responds to my soul's desire; I will stick to prayer, music, reading, writing, theatre and meditation. That is what makes me happy and I am not weak because of it! Besides, you send me exerted girls; women, divorced or extra liberal candidates; I don't like that; I know what I am looking for!"

"And you like how miserable you look? Go… Go and watch yourself in the mirror!"

"You're not my doctor and we should not be having this conversation. It is totally invasive!"

"We cannot help you anymore; we did all we could for you. Do what you want! You just crave approval and bring muffins to your staff so that they would love you; you see what I mean?"

"…How arrogant and pretentious! How petty and immoral! Hey, stop this, right now [I would shout], if it does not add one inch of joy to my life, to hell with it. You choose such liberal women for me and I… just do not accept! Give me a break… Give me a break for God's sake, besides, yes, I bring an occasional tray of muffins and tea to the office because it feels good."

This would go on and on, for years, adding unwanted fuel to my rising anxiety and to my fading soul, when I knew very well, that my substitute for marriage was always reading, writing and theatre until I found someone like Dahlia. I would spend hours at the library interacting with fellow writers reading from world classics; that was so simply my joyful zone. No one had any right to choose for me…

Dahlia and I continued to visit Mother at her home, where she lived with my sister (behind our apartment block), until she left to Cairo on September 29, 2010. The plan was for me to join her on December 17, 2010 but under the circumstances and, given my health breakdown, she decided to return to Montreal by the end of November, so as to fly with me back to Cairo and in order not to leave me alone, should I feel tired or faint, on the way to Cairo. Dahlia never preached; she only took action and, it worked, ultimately! During that time, Dahlia would always cuddle Mother and prepare her favorite drink. Dahlia would then hug Mother while sitting next to her and even join her for a Single Malt, Mom's favorite. She would peel pistachios for mom since mom's arthritis did not permit her to use her slightly twisted fingers. Mom was in utter joy and so was I, because she saw me happy, at last. Mom's joy will remain in my heart until my last breath.

    Mother fell again a few days later (still in October), as I was helping her to her room with my sister. She had fallen several times over the past six years, but this time, Mom's fall was not good. While my sister and I were struggling to overcome the challenges of mother's mobility, we realized that she deserved much more; she deserved professional care. What she really needed was a ten-hour daily nurse, at home, or a full time nursing home, and there were several of them in Montreal. However, no one could imagine that Divine intervention would continue to guide us to such hights that it would lead us to one of the most distinguished and capable nursing homes on the island of Montreal, just across the street from where I lived and only two blocks away from where my mother used to live with my sister. This residence was a place that had exceeded all levels of care, comfort, compassion, and well-being for its residents. Its name is Summer-Breeze Senior Living. Mom's years of work for the Royal Air Force during the war and later for the United Nations served her well. We found out that her benefits covered over 85 percent of her costs. This was a stroke of good fortune. It helped us address Mom's declining memory and rising dementia by taking the harshest decision of our life, though with an unimaginable sense of grief. It was unconceivable that we should, finally, send her away from her home, but we had to for her own sake!

Chapter 36
Cutting the Umbilical Cord

Mom's last fall left her with two broken fingers, bruises on her cheek and forehead, as well as a swollen left shoulder. She was standing facing the mirror at home while leaning with her elbows on the sink and rinsing her mouth when, in a fraction of a second, she slipped to the left and fell on the towel hanger that was fixed to the wall under the window frame. This happened on Sunday night, October 17, 2010.

Before this incident, Mother had been receiving daily intermittent nursing care at home for three years but had to wait alone, in the living room, watching TV, for at least two hours between 3 and 5 p.m.. She would also sleep on her sofa until someone returned home. After the incident, she was graceful, courageous, and capable of hiding her obvious pain. Finding the amazing nursing home just across from our homes seemed a valuable early Christmas gift. The confirmation of her insurance that it would cover most of her new residence costs was priceless. The residence was attractive and colorful.

The most difficult part was the part where we had to move Mother and find her a gentle and convincing reason for doing so, without alarming her, especially after her years of grace, love, and candor as a mother, wife, daughter, and RAF veteran. We decided to lie a little in the beginning, so as not to scare her; we told her that she would move for a transitory period for convalescence. She would do so, just as she did in 1983, following her knees operations in Switzerland and through which I stood by her, all the way from arranging for the hospital in Bern, choosing the surgeon, right through to her return home, in Heliopolis, Cairo. She and I had flown out and come in together, endlessly. She was extremely cooperative and was happy to do so, knowing that we lived only one minute, away.

To do things right, we chose her a room on the ground floor of this four-floor operation and set the room up in such a way that it would look exactly like her twenty-year-old bedroom at home in Montreal. We moved her small TV in her new residence and placed it on a brown piece of furniture, just like her former room, and placed all her family memorabilia as well as the statue of the Virgin Mary and Saint Anthony of Padua, her favorite saints. To the left of her bed, we brought her a side table where we placed her paper towels, caramel mints, crackers, and cashew nuts, just like she had them for twenty years. The room had its own mini-fridge, so we did not bring hers.

On November 5, 2010, my sister and I explained to Mother that we were going for her check-ups next door so that she could stay for convalescence, which would only take a few weeks. We drove her across to Summer-Breeze Senior Living and entered from the main gate. This gate led to a small area called the sunroom, closed by solid windows and exposed to the well-kept green entrance with sun pouring in from everywhere. There was a second door leading to the main lobby that stretched all around from the extreme left where there was the first main TV lounge and more windows, on to the right where there was a lovely warm bistro-café and several tables and chairs. The bistro offered cakes, cookies, and fresh fruit. Behind the bistro was a huge five stars restaurant.

If we looked ahead between the bistro on the right and the TV lounge to the left, we could see the reception desk, in the center, with a cheering lady receiving guests and, behind her, a corridor leading to the bedrooms of the ground floor. Mother's room was behind the reception desk, only several feet from all the action but overlooking the backside of the building where there were some enchanting plants, trees, and herbs, as well as a very large patio and a piano, leading to the backside garden..

The staff and some caregivers greeted us and escorted Mom to her room while we followed. Her clothes, pajamas, and gadgets were all in the room, and within minutes, we were all out again for tea and some cookies. We sat for an hour with Mother at the bistro where she met a few people and where we explained to her that she would have lunch and that we would return later, after her check-up, to see how she was doing. We asked her if she wanted to return to her room after lunch or lie down on a couch in front of the living room's TV where she could have a little nap; this way, we could advise her nurse.

    The first day went extremely well. By night time, we returned for some tea and TV watching, as we always did, at home, before she went up to her room to sleep. Of course, over the past three years at home, it was extremely difficult for her to struggle up the high wooden staircase to her bedroom, but in this residence, her bedroom was on the main floor. Holding on to her, going toward her room with her caregiver on the first night, was no less endearing than clinging to her dress when I was six. What a feeling I had that night, and what mixed emotions entangled me—one with a commitment to give her infinite support and love, while, at the same time, another seeking her affection and absolution for having had to place her at this great home. After her caregiver helped her freshen up and change into her pajamas, I helped her to her bed and sat next to her for fifteen minutes, watching the TV.

"Go home, now, my love. Go and rest," said Mom.

"Okay, my love. Sleep tight. God bless you." I stepped out of her bedroom, on her first night away from home. I looked back while holding the door and whispered, "We'll have breakfast together, my love?"

She nodded, while still a little distraught. I returned to her bed, bowed, kissed her forehead, and said, "I'll keep the TV on, Ma, and will turn the volume down, as you always liked to."

"God keep you, my son."

"Always Ma, always next to you"

"You are my tender one. Go, go."

Across the years, especially after Camille, mom would always tell me "you are my unique tender child," because I never wasted a moment to stand by her in time if need and sorrow.

"Breakfast in the morning, ma?"

"Yes" And she closed her eyes with a peace of mind.

I dimmed the light a little and stepped outside of the room to the Resident's lobby, past its reception, heading to the sunroom. I continued, past the reception and through the lobby.

The TV lounge was now to my right while the bistro was on my left. I walked straight through to the door leading to the sunroom, on to the main gate, and then to the parking lot. There were hardly three people sitting in the TV lounge, when I left.

It was raining, so I rushed across Saint Patrick's boulevard straight to my apartment building. Three minutes later, I was up in my apartment's living room that overlooked mother's Residence. I looked down through my balcony's glass door and saw Summer-Breeze faint evening lights. I smiled, opened the fridge, and grabbed a beer and some crackers. I put my pajamas on, threw myself on the couch, turned my TV on, and prepared to unwind for the night, but with a heavy heart.

The following day, I woke up and rushed to the laboratory to undergo the tests that Doctor Feldman had asked me to do. Then I returned home, prepared myself a tea and a small bite. After this, I called Dahlia in Cairo, on Skype. We chatted for thirty minutes. She told me she had seen many of our university friends at the neighboring social club with friends of hers. Even through computer conferencing, Dahlia continued to glitter with immense love and warmth.

At 9:30 am, I put my coat on and crossed over to have breakfast with Mom. I entered Summer-Breeze Senior Living, greeted the receptionist, Maria, and then went to Mother's room. She was already out of bed, assisted by her morning caregiver in the bathroom, freshening up and preparing to have her breakfast at the huge restaurant (behind the bistro-café). I greeted her, "Good morning, Mommy. Take your time. I am waiting for you outside while reading my papers."

"Raphy…? Good morning, love… I will not be long now."

A fancy set of her clothes, which my sister had chosen for her the night before, her makeup, and preferred perfume lay on the bed ready for her. Just like her evening caregivers, the morning nurse acted and thought like an angel of mercy. Her level of professionalism, concern, and commitment to giving love was remarkably high. I waited in a small lounge area that was situated between the two hallways featuring bedrooms, until mother came out with one of her kind nurses, Andrea. We walked to the breakfast room (using her walker) and sat at a table to the far right, by the window, one that overlooked the colorful entrance, parking lot, and Saint Patrick's boulevard. It was my thought that for the first week, until mom had absorbed the physical separation from her home environment, I would not force her to mingle with new friends. Meanwhile, the table we sat at also overlooked my apartment building across the street, and Mother's chair was ideally placed for her to recognize its closeness. I pointed to it.

    I wanted to make it clear to her that she was only footsteps away from my familiar apartment building and a block or two from where she lived with my sister's family. Within less than a week, my sister and I transported all the remaining valuable props she had in her former bedroom to her new but similar bedroom at Summer-Breeze.

    Soon, I received my lab tests and they clearly indicated that I had acute acidity, reflux and some vicious bacteria called H. Pylori that had been nesting in my stomach for many years. They yielded severe legions that were about to turn to ulcers. The Family Doctor ordered me a three months cure of several drugs that would cure me from any bacteria and ordered a diet that would help heal the stomach wounds over a period of eighteen months. I advised Doctor Feldman who asked me to call him back upon my return from Egypt. However, for now I had a ray of hope. Had it not been for Dahlia, my fifteen years of suffering would have continued, until it was too late.

    It took Mother two weeks to feel a little less anxious than when she first moved, and so did this fortnight help us cope with the harsh change.

    To me, Mom was still my lifetime legend and icon who swept RAF (Royal Air Force) Egypt and, later, the United Nations in Europe and Egypt with her candor, dignity, grace, and beauty for so many years. Her transition was just as dignified, and was even surrounded by four RCAF WWII (Royal

Canadian Air Force) veterans at Summer-Breeze. Gradually, I made friends with all her caregivers, nurses, residents and staff members while confiding in them with my trust and hope for their continued genuine care and support to Mother. This meant that when I left for Egypt in December, with Dahlia, I would have nurtured sufficient mutual respect to put my mind at ease while I was away for three months. During these three months, Dahlia would resolve her pending business challenges, and I would have a chance to recover, while following my prescribed diet.

For now, I continued to visit Mother every day thereafter in November and December until Dahlia returned from Cairo towards the end of November. My sister and my cousins continued without me for the three months while I was away with Dahlia in Egypt. Before I left, I made a point of encouraging Mom to join little groups of residents at other tables for her meals, starting with her third week at Summer-Breeze. I would continue visiting her during breakfast, and teatime. After this, I would return to give her a late morning hug while promising to return in three hours, just after her lunch and again later after dinner, until she had stabilized and, in fact, until we all did.

Just until I took off with Dahlia to Cairo on December 17, 2010, I never ceased to visit mother three times a day. I would even take my afternoon nap with her after she finished her lunch. I wrapped her shoulder with my left arm, sitting to her right, in the sunroom, and looking straight through the glass gate to my apartment building on the other side of the street, hence reinforcing her sense of security. This is where she would feel most comfortable after lunch for the next three years.

By the fourth week in November, Mom had her own circle of friends and was always in action with Social Tea, in-house piano or guitar concerts, and bingo games.

My finances where not getting better because I was no longer generating any income while incapable, of assuming regular hours whether on a fulltime or part-time basis. At least, I could see some light at the end of the tunnel. I knew for sure that there was no way that my last two hotel experiences were not directly involved with my state of mind, soul, and independence- it provoked my stomach legions that were already *carved* by H. Pylori. I just did not want to let them win. But I knew now, that every single moment of our lives, every single thought and every direction we take, is governed by divine order, despite the indifference or judgment of those we counted so much on.

On Sunday, November 22, 2010, one week before Dahlia's return from Cairo, my sister prepared the usual Sunday dinner at her home, inviting Mother to come from Summer-Breeze, for the first time since her move. This very risky move would destabilize mom's earlier difficult settling. I was to pick up mother at 4:30 from Summer-Breeze in a daring mission to bring her out for this family reunion and to take her back around eight o'clock, terribly distraught. Mother had already missed three of those Sunday family dinners since she moved to Summer-Breeze. Of course, everyone linked my sister's dinners to Mother's own Sunday dinners in the sixties, seventies and early eighties at our family's lovely villa in Heliopolis some forty years earlier.

Soon, on Sunday, November 22, I drove across to Summer-Breeze at 4:15 to make sure that Mother was ready. Mother was well dressed, ready and seated at the bistro on her wheelchair so that I would walk her out to my car. (She had started using a wheelchair, only if her knees would hurt her). She needed to pay one last visit to the bathroom, and I preferred that she did so at Summer-Breeze since their bathrooms were equipped for residents with walkers or wheelchairs, in excess of 28 inches of width. The bathroom at my sister's home would have been too narrow for Mom. Another of Mother's beloved caregivers, Chrisla, helped her as I waited for her at the bistro with a tea. When she was out, we were ready to move slowly to my car, on to the driveway of her former home. Previously (at Mom's home), Mom and I would sit for long hours in the driveway with our favorite drinks, watching people walk their dogs and socializing with neighbors.

    Incidentally, evenings were the epic part of mom's day. It was when my sister would return from work and join us for drinks and later, Dahlia, when she added joy to my life. Mom did not recall the driveway memoires entirely, that night; yet she knew she was heading to a familiar and favorite place of hers. My nephew came outside to help me move Mother out of the car, through the driveway, into her old home, and then to the living room. Then we encouraged her to walk out of the wheelchair and sit on her favorite love seat, the one she sat on for so long to watch TV. She was subdued at first, and then she let go while enjoying some appetizers, though in a distant world.

    "You see, my love; it took us only one minute to drive from Summer-Breeze!" I said.

    "I want to stay here. Why can't I do that?" said our mom.

    "Well it will not be long. Your convalescence is progressing well, and soon we will be together, here or at Summer-Breeze," I continued making my innocent lie, cautiously.

    In a few minutes, Mom was reflective but content as we all sat down for about one hour before we moved to the dinner table. Mother sat on her usual chair as graceful as always. We insisted that she had the right to eat with dignity, far from her wheelchair, so we helped her sit on an elevated chair with a cushion for her back. The purpose of the wheelchair, we thought, was only to move out and in of the nursing home. Even within the nursing home, she would only use her walker. At dinner, we spent another ninety minutes enjoying our meal that was made of boneless chicken breasts in orange and light garlic sauce and rosemary, steamed potatoes in butter sauce, and steamed asparagus tossed in melted blue cheese. In view of my financial restraints, I was only able to contribute with some delicious éclairs filled with custard-cream, covered by a rich mixture of hazelnuts, chocolate, and sprinkled with crunchy caramel. I used to bake these forty years ago, in Bath, England.

The clock was running fast, and before it was 7:45 p.m., we found ourselves entering into one of the most difficult experiences we could have ever imagined; it was the hard task of moving mother back to her wheelchair and further to her Residence. It seemed that my mother had instantly recaptured her earlier memories of her home and was eager to sit by the TV for a while, as she always did, before she moved up to her old bedroom. This is how it all went.

"Mom, love, we should prepare to move in about ten minutes," I said.

"Okay, honey," she said, thinking we were moving back to the living room.

Ten minutes later, I said, "Okay, Mom, did you want to stand now and let me help you with your coat?" I was bringing her wheelchair and coat close to the dinner table.

"Where are you taking me?" she shouted.

"Back to your room, my love, just next door." I did not want to lie to her.

"No, no, no. Take me upstairs. Take me to my room, this room."

"Light of my eyes," I said, "we are all with you tonight, tomorrow morning, and always. You will go to your own room, just next door, and I will stay with you as I have always done, until you sleep. Then I will return tomorrow for breakfast, and we will all be with you, every single day. Just give them a chance to give you some physiotherapy for a few more days so we can finish with this convalescence. Didn't you tell me it was like a five-star hotel in Switzerland?"

"What will you all do after I go there?"

"You mean tonight, Ma?"

"Yes, tonight!"

"The guests will go home and we will go to sleep. You will sleep in your room, and I in mine, just across. Tomorrow, we will have breakfast, and spend the day together. Do you not feel sleepy, my love? Everyone is!"

"Do what you want!" she replied.

"I want you to be here, Ma; you must believe me. But I am happy that we are only ten steps away; besides, I will pass by you each time I make a visit to the toilet (suggesting that I would be in the neighboring bedroom). Come on; remember when I sprained my back in Christmas of 1996? Do you remember when I went to emergency and how you took a taxi every day to visit me; until I recovered? Now look, my love, you are not downtown, and you are not alone. We are all here, just a few seconds walk from each other! I will stay with you until you sleep. I will kiss you and return for breakfast in the morning. In the meantime, I will check over you, as I said" I was lowering my volume and pace to calm her anxiety and to have this difficult moment subside; it worked.

"We're coming too," said my niece, nephew and his fiancée.

All the youth helped move Mom. We rolled the wheelchair slowly to my car and to the passenger door. We carefully moved her to the passenger seat, with no hitches. My nephew made a joke to ease up the mood. We all drove to Summer-Breeze Senior Living in three cars and made it there, five minutes, later. It was past 8:30pm, and the residence had locked all its gates. Therefore, I used the electronic password to open the main gate, and we pushed mom's chair to her room. The young ones hugged Mom and left in tears, while I remained with her until Chrisla, her night caregiver, came. She helped her through her needs in the bathroom, changed her clothes, and walked her to bed. I remained next to her.

"I am right here, Ma, waiting outside until you go to bed!" I said and turned the TV on. In a few minutes, she was in her pajamas, ready for bed.

"Let's watch some TV together," I said and kissed her forehead. "Shall we have one of your favorite caramel-mints?"

"Yes, let's do that."

Mom's caregiver left the room, and we stayed for a few minutes until she felt sleepy and started shutting her eyes. "Do you want to sleep now, Ma?" I whispered.

"Yes, my son, go join them and have some fun."

"Okay, I will go just to my room next door to sleep, my love (*referring to my apartment building*). They all went home."

"So they are not continuing their party?"

"No, my love, we spent four hours already together. We are all sleepy, just like you. The party is over and we will have many more in the future."

"Okay, my tender son. Go, go home, but leave me one light in the hallway."

"Sure, my love, and I will keep the TV on the weather network, at a low volume, just as you like it."

"Thank you. Good night, my darling."

"Good night, love. See you for breakfast, early morning!"

"Really...?"

"Yes, Ma, I promised you to do so before you went to bed. Now I will do the same and be right here when you wake up." I hugged her lovingly and left while whispering, "See you!"

"God bless you, my son."

"I love you, Ma, and bless you too."

Ma was clearly happy; her mind was rested and peaceful again.

I was home in less than five minutes, had a shower, chamomile tea, and stretched on my couch to watch some TV. I slept soundly all the way until 3:00 a.m., and then I moved to bed.

Somehow, that night, I felt that I assumed my role as a child of God.

Chapter 37
Four Weeks to Go
A Shade from Sixty Years

The following morning, November 23 (2010), I dressed up and put my coat on. It felt a little cold, and I saw some grizzles of snow, gently covering the streets. That day, the dark clouds covered the sky. I entered Mother's room, and found her almost ready. I greeted her and waited outside of her room again, until her morning caregiver brought her to the tiny lounge at the doorstep of her room. We all walked to the breakfast room, where Mom and I had a warm talk.

"Guess who is coming back on the twenty-ninth of November, five days from now, Ma?"

"Your wife ... really, is she coming?" She could not remember her name.

"Yes, my love, Dahlia, my wife, and we will spend two weeks together. We may go for a few days after that, but we will be returning soon." I did not want to remind her of the whole truth about my leaving with Dahlia to Egypt for three months. The truth was that, amidst other health priorities, my family had a property in Cairo that a few acquaintances had vandalized and which I wanted to reclaim, while there.

"This is wonderful news."

"Yes Ma, really wonderful. She loves you so much."

"And I love her too."

After a good hour of chatting over tea and cake, I said, "Ma, while you go with your friends for your *move and groove* exercises, I will go to make my usual teeth check-up but will be back in the early afternoon."

"Of course, my love... Thank you for passing by!"

Ma's physiotherapist was passing by, and I told her that Mother was ready for her exercises. She helped Mom stand, and I left saying, "See you after lunch, Ma."

"See you, my son."

Over the remaining few days before Dahlia's return from Cairo to Montreal and another four weeks before our heading back to Cairo (on December 17, 2010), the mood in my circle of family and friends was reaching high levels of emotions, sadness, and affection for the physical separation involved with our travel. This was due to the rising fear of change, surrounding my marriage and because of my separation from the family at the age of sixty, but most of all because Mother was not getting younger and because we were not comfortable enough to accept her *aging*.

In addition to how I could hardly bear the anguish that followed my decision to marry at the age of sixty and under my present financial circumstances, I started understanding the horror of my move—that of leaving Mother when she needed me most. This was the moment of harsh separation; one that I always feared as a child. Since the age of seven, I made a commitment to be next to her and dad during their journey to heaven. Dad left in my arms, in 1978. Right now, there was no point in being so apprehensive; I had no dark premonitions.

Gradually, I fought my way to analyzing the situation pragmatically and to finding solid and indisputable logic for all these changes. Mom had to move to a medical care-giving institution, a nursing home where she could be observed by professionals every minute of the day while, never having to be left alone on a couch for two or three hours anymore. At Summer-Breeze, she was never alone, and even though it took a good two or three weeks for her to stabilize, she managed to accept the illusion that Summer-Breeze was an extension of her own home's living room, while surrounded by so many nurses, peers, and even dear friends.

On Sunday, November 28, I had dinner with Mother at Summer-Breeze and announced the great news that Dahlia was coming back to Montreal the following day to spend three weeks with us and that we would both leave on December 17, to finalize our pending family business and then come back after a few weeks. I promised her to heal my ailing abdomen, by then.

"Tomorrow?" said mother?

"Yes, my love, tomorrow."

We shared a bottle of beer and Seven-Up, nibbled on some crackers and chatted for an hour and a half until she was ready to go to bed. The following day, my better half arrived and visited mom for a few minutes, promising to return after she (Dahlia) had changed her clothes and Mom had finished her supper. Mother was all bubbled up with her makeup, French perfume, and hairstyle. She wrapped her arms around Dahlia, and Dahlia threw herself in them for a few minutes. Mom was beyond joyful and happy, and so were we all. As for Dahlia, she never ceased to inspire me with her giving nature. We returned to Mother after had finished supper and after we had freshened up. We also returned the following morning after breakfast and went for a Canadian grocery-shopping experience to fill up our fridge.

Dahlia seemed more and more of a beautiful woman but the time to nurture our spousal friendship, had not reached the so longed for heights. We continued to visit Mother all through Dahlia's stay in Montreal, until December 17, at least twice if not three times a day. However, we made sure not to visit her during her daily social event, which usually featured fruits, cakes, cookies, and fresh juice, cheese and crackers or chips, dips, and wine. The reason we chose to avoid visiting her at that time was to leave her sufficient space to mingle with her friends, especially if there was a visiting singer with a guitar or on the house piano. Soon, mom had secured herself a circle of friends and she became, independent, once more, though certainly more vulnerable. This per bondage would help when we were away.

One day, before flying back to Cairo on December 17, I told Dahlia the following: "My love, I know I have been distant from you and have been putting such a load on you for my mother and for my health. Now, I feel that you read me and that you know that I do not want to lose a chance to stand by Mom before we leave tomorrow; a chance that may never come back."

"Don't mention it, my sweet friend." She blushed, interrupting me, and her eyes turned wet.

"Thank *you* for being so supportive! I know what you are doing for me. I know the sacrifice you have done for me and keep doing. It is because you know that I was hurt and that I am unable to stand up, but you also know that I love you and that we will have ample chance to make up for the lost time. We will have fun in Egypt; I am sure."

"Shh, I told you it is not your mistake, and I knew what kind of person you were when I fell for you first in 1977 at university, especially on that stage. You pierced my heart, and I will bring you to exactly who you were and to where you always were; no more, no less. Just don't feel betrayed by life because these are petty people and you know it!"

"My darling, I love you so much and want to take a break with you when we go to Egypt. I want to spend a few days in Alexandria to put all this behind us. I want to hug you and be romantic, imagining us thirty years younger!"

"I'd love that..."

On Tuesday December 14, 2010, we had finished most of our shopping and decided to buy chicken-salad sandwiches and some takeaway tea for an open-door mid-December lunch at the neighboring Centennial Park, (right in a semi-open hut). It was also the Jewish feast of Hanukkah. We dressed well, since a few flurries of snow had already fallen and the winter cold was pressing. We planned to spend an hour in order to return home and prepare ourselves, on time, for a seasonal Dinner Gala with mom and her senior friends, at the Residence.

The executive committee of Summer-Breeze, its middle managers, nurses, caregivers, waiters, and some staff's children were holding a Mid-December party for residents on this Jewish feast. They were to do another on Boxing Day, that month, after we had flown to Egypt.

We were not the only ones at the park. As we parked our car and paved our way to the snowy walkway and on to one of its semi-open huts, we met a few people walking their dogs and others sitting and reading. The sky was clear and sunny but chilly. Snow flurries and frost covered the green grass, everywhere, the night before. We settled down and started our picnic. Dahlia had brought a disposable Christmassy tablecloth so that we may enjoy our little chilly picnic.

As has been the habit of visitors of this park, we would greet each other to maximize our enjoyment and to add cheer to our pre-Christmas *Panoramic Adventure*.

After a few minutes of chatting, I saw a passer-by walking with his lady-friend or wife approaching us, face to face. He would have had to be sixty years old and so was his companion. She was of a small and thin posture, had curly and dyed hair, lovely smile and deep expressive eyes flooded with shades and stories. She seemed familiar to me. The man was six feet high (a little less than two meters). He was bald, thin and had a boney face; deep dark eyes, and one we could easily call a solid survivor of life. He kept his head high. As he walked towards us, he bent forward, slightly, as if he was analyzing me, with a shrewd smile. He turned his head slightly and said something to his companion, and then gazed back at us. His eyes caught mine and it pierced them. He had deep, deep looks, searching eyes and seemed a little perplexed; and so was I.

I smiled to them and so did Dahlia.

"I know you…" he said in a subdued emotional voice.

I lost my breath and was about to have a heart failure; I sweat and searched in his eyes, too!

"Are you from Egypt?"

"Yes" I replied

"…AMC Anglican Mission of Cairo?"

"Yes; I am Raphy, Raphy Politis"

"Roland, *Raphy*; I am Roland Levy!"

"…Soccer team?"

"You got it!"

"Untie Lucie's son?"

"Yes"

"Oh my God Roland; Oh my sweet Lord"

He stood firm, as always, and clutched my shoulders and broke into tears. We hugged each other, while Dahlia was completely stunned.

I looked at Dahlia and said, "This is Roland my best lifeline from the soccer team. He is one of those who restored my self-esteem at school.... auntie Lucie's son, mom's friend"

"Hello Roland; he speaks very highly of you...." said Dahlia.

"Yes... You had a tough start of life, my friend" turning his head to me!

"And it isn't any easier, Roland. Besides, so did you, Auntie Lucie, Uncle Joachim and Davido, have it tough in the late fifties; it was undue hardship"

I looked at his friend and explored her, politely.... "I think I know you, too," I said.

"I am Karina, Stavros' baby-sister, from the girl's college"

"Stavros the goal-keeper...?"

"Yes"

"Oh, Karina; I remember you so well; sit down folks; sit down" and I hugged Karina.

They sat down.

"How is Stavros? Your family left in 1963 or so, right?"

"Yes, '63"

"Is he here? Stavros..."

"We lost him in a car accident in Athens in 1974. We were never the same since we left Egypt. My parents died in 1978 and 1979, subsequently. They could not handle Stavros' departure. Roland and I married in 1979, just after mother's departure. Roland came to Athens and took me with him to Montreal. We have two twin girls; one is married."

"And we still have a few members of the soccer team around, living in North America- even in Montreal" said Roland. "We have Haitham, Mustafa and Vahan; and of course, their families"

"I am awfully sorry; that is too much for the soul to handle. I have such a heavy heart for Stavros' departure. My brother, too, left us in 1975 at seventeen. Yet, I am overwhelmed to know that you two connected. I am so touched"

"Is this your wife?" asked Karina.

"Yes we recently married. I am a late bloomer just like dad; remember he used to pick me up from school after the mathematics class?"

Dahlia intervened and said; "If you have nothing to do, we live just a few blocks away on Saint Patrick Boulevard. Please come for some drinks at our place and then join us for supper, tonight, with Raphy's mother at the Senior Home: *Summer Breeze*! The day after tomorrow we will fly to Egypt for two or three months. And when we return, we should spend more time together!"

"Roland?" looked at Karina.

"What time is the supper?" asked Roland.

"5 pm."

"Alright, if this is fine with you Karina, we will pass just before 5 pm for some tea at Raphy and Dahlia's place and then we will cross to say hello to Raphy's mom and stay with her for a few minutes. She was my mother's friend and I would love to see her. When you come back from Cairo for spring we will spend more time with your mom. Until then, we will visit her, every week."

We all agreed.

"How are your parents?" I asked almost sure to hear the inevitable.

"Dad died in Paris in 1967. Mother, Davido and I arrived in Montreal in 1974 where mother died in 1991. In Paris, we were accommodated by friends of our community, for the first few years after leaving Egypt."

"…and Davido…?"

"He is married and is living in Israel since 1993"

"You have some lovely parents. I loved your mom; she was very kind to my mother"

"You haven't changed," he said and nodded his head, respectfully.

"So it's good or bad?"

"It's the best thing anyone can have. I always told you not to change, so as to please others."

I blushed and we made a point of meeting at our place at 4 pm"

On the way home, Dahlia and I bought some English Cake and then we passed by mom at Summer Breeze Senior Living and made sure she was aware that there was a seasonal event that evening.

"Mom, we will be back at 4.30 pm to make sure if you need anything and we will all move to our table. We have a table booked for us with your friends Phyllis and Achilles."

"Fine my darling. I will see you then."

"Guess who we met today?"

"Whom did you meet?"

"Auntie Lucie Najjar's son, Roland"

"Lucie Najjar?"

"Yes ma, Lucie from Egypt. Remember, she gave you her rosewood tables and bronze lady?"

«Lucie Najjar? Oh my darling, is she in Montreal?"

"No ma, she lives in Israel with her young son. But Roland, the elder one, is here." I did not want to break her heart and mention auntie Lucie's departure. "He will pass by you, with his wife, for a few minutes, this afternoon, and will continue visiting you every week until our return in spring. After that, we will all spend quality time with you."

At 4 pm, Roland and Karina passed; we had prepared some, cake, tea biscuits and hot water for them. "Let me have your coats... There is boiling water folks; would you like tea or coffee?"

"Tea," they both mumbled "but can only stay for fifteen minutes as we are invited for a Hanukkah celebration". Soon, we started chatting and discussing the beautiful past...

"Here... [I said] mother's home is just across the road; right through the balcony window."

"That's quite a relief," said Karina

"Quite right" said Dahlia

"So you studied at university, together?" Roland asked.

"Yes, at the American University in Cairo; many years ago; to be specific between 1975 and 1980".

I offered them a plate of biscuits and then placed it back on the side table. Roland was staring, nervously and eagerly, at the table. He went into a trance... It was one of his mother's rosewood tables, which she had given to my mom in 1959.

"Have a look at it" I said "Here, Roland, please, feel it" I removed the biscuits and the vase.

Suddenly, Roland turned the rosewood table, slightly to the right and we could see the bottom. It said *Lucie, Levi-Najjar*.... "I wrote mom's name on it, in 1959 and showed it to her," said Roland, "I told mother, one day we will all reunite again, even with our valuable belongings"

Dahlia broke in tears, while I could not pick-up my breath. It was very difficult to restrain our emotions.

"Take it down with you. I'll put it in your car," I said breathlessly.

"No way; no way; I mean it." Shouted Roland, hysterically "Oh my dear mom...and dad! Oh I miss you, so much"

"Roland, fifty years ago your mother implored my mother to take you tables and mom accepted. God bless you, please! Please take it.... my childhood friend. This is Egyptian wood from Egyptian trees, branches and roots.....Don't break my heart; take it" And I hugged him, hysterically.

Eventually, he took it and we crossed to visit mom at the Senior Home.

It was a celebration for all ages, charged with fellowship and affection, and understandably, tears inducing! It was a dancing ball for whoever could dance and a clapping hall for those who could not. Roland and Karina squeezed mother in their arms and kissed her hand; while she felt so overwhelmed. She was relatively alert and remembered Roland's parents. Roland and Karina left after fifteen minutes.

"We promise to visit you every week, aunt Laurice, while Raphy and Dahlia are on vacation; and then we will spend spring together," he whispered to mom's ears. We bid each other farewell after having exchanged e-mail addresses and phone numbers, overseas. I played a few songs on the piano and mom was in ecstasy.

On December 16, we felt the clock ticking as I walked with Dahlia through the neighborhood for last minute shopping (for mom's Christmas gift) before we returned one last time to visit her for our final but dark farewell. I bought some finger food to consume onboard in case the cabin staff did not have sufficient appetizers to accompany our drinks. I really bought pretzels, nuts, and mini dills. We returned to our apartment, filled four post-dated checks for our rent and gave them to our building janitor.

By 9:00 am, December 17, all our bags were ready, and so were our handbags, ready to go.

At 11:45, we visited Mom, for what I found to be one of life's most difficult and shaky farewells. Mom was waiting for us in the sunroom. We sank next to her on the big couch. We all had a tea and some fresh cookies, and we left our dear mother knowing that she would be surrounded by her friends and family until we returned in March of the following year (2011). We gave mom her early Christmas gift.

"Ma this is for you, a small CD player and four CD albums containing over two hundred of our preferred lifetime hymns. I ordered them from USA and Adel, Auntie Kaliope's son mailed them to me from Washington, just for you. The nurses will help you turn them on whenever you want. I will set it up now, next to your bed. Ma, here is a small wooden cross which you are free to hang wherever you want. Just let us know. It will protect you and remind you that God will be always with you.

"Oh what a lovely gift my children; I love it and I remember those hymns. The cross too is beautiful. Keep it on my side-table."

"OK my love, we will do. Merry Christmas"

"Merry Christmas my children… When will I see you again?"

"…In a few weeks, Ma. At the most, by March 4, and we will call you every single day."

"God bless you, my children. Do not worry about me. Your sister and my nephews will take care of me. In addition, I have all these friends with me, now. I will wait for you so we can all be together again!"

"God keep you for us, Ma." Then we walked out slowly, drove to my sister's place to bid her and her husband farewell, and then we drove our car to a public garage, where we left it and removed its battery. We took a taxi back to our apartment to shower and change our clothes. We called the taxi company one hour in advance and ordered the taxi-van to drive us to the airport. I called my nephew and niece from the airport to say good-bye and sat down with Dahlia after the security checkpoint with some hot tea, and for some moments of reflection before our departure.

Chapter 38
Return to Egypt for winter and the Unbelievable

The plane took off from Montreal to Paris at 8:20 p.m. on December 17, 2010. Dahlia sat on my right next to the window, and I sat on the left seat, by the aisle. We fastened our seatbelts, sat upright, and tidied all our belongings in the rack above, except for my pretzels, nuts, fresh mini-dills, my copybook (to continue this testimony), and our eyeglasses. These, we placed between our seats and then we held each other's hand and shut our eyes. My state of anxiety was at its highest level, and it did not take me much to fall into deep sleep even before take-off while the plane moved slowly through the airport's taxiway.

Soon I could feel Dahlia's tiny and loving hand around my neck, cuddling it in reassuring affection. After this, I felt nothing for close to forty minutes. Suddenly, I woke up at the voices of cabin crew talking to passengers. They were distributing drinks to the row just ahead of me. I turned my head and saw Dahlia smiling at me.

"How are you, my love?" I asked her.

"Drowsy, but I can certainly do with a drink. And you, my love?" she asked.

"Same." I stretched my neck forward. "How long have I been sleeping?"

"...A little over forty minutes."

"I am so thirsty. I could do with a beer, as well."

The flight flight attendant overheard me as she approached our row. "What beer do you prefer?" she said in a French accent.

"A lager, please, and a big glass of water" She gave me my water and two cans of beer. (There would be no second round of drinks before supper; so she gave me two cans) Dahlia had red wine, and we started nibbling from our nuts and crackers. It would take another forty-five minutes before we receive our meal. The plane was full; I could easily count over three hundred passengers in the cabin. There was time to wait for the meal and to relax from the previous rocky and emotionally charged few weeks. Somehow I felt, for the first time, that we were man and wife leading our life, as we should.

After dinner service, we slept again and only woke up for coffee and croissants ninety minutes before landing in Paris, where we waited two hours to board our connecting flight to Cairo. We arrived in Cairo at 6:15 p.m. on December 18, 2010. My heart was heavy, the air was thick, and we barely caught sunset as we rode the cab that took us to Dahlia's apartment in the suburb of Cairo, called Zamalek. It was footsteps away from Saint Joseph's Church, where we had made our vows in March 2009, and two months after I lost my job, still in 2009. I did not feel the rich emotional moments of souvenirs when we approached landing, as I had when I landed in Cairo to meet Dahlia in 2009, or even 2008. Of course, I called my dear mother to let her know we were safe.

The taxi driver seemed just over fifty years of age. He was well dressed, gray-haired, professional, but distant. It was interesting how he commented on Egypt's "thrifty lifestyles of a recent few" that seemed obvious on the huge commercial buildings we drove past. Many of the small and medium villas that once existed with the 1912 reforms of Cairo's modern sector of Heliopolis, under the leadership of the Baron Édouard d'Empain, where I was raised and grew up, had clearly been neglected. Every now and then, after the sixties, a new villa was erected with a modern but dull avant-garde look, void of the character and soul that once existed in modern Heliopolis. Each street of each major heritage sector in Cairo had its own clear and distinct style, whether beautiful Islamic ornamented architecture, Fatimid streets and mosques, Maméluke structures, colonial English, or romantic French. However, this driver's comments were far from reassuring. He seemed to condemn the character that once existed between 1800 and 1960, even though it displayed the sum of the previous fifty centuries of character and culture in a clear and definitive manner. He called it a "waste of national wealth," the very wealth that many condoned because it nurtured the image and character of the homeland, one of a rich, giving and loving soil of Egypt, across so many centuries.

This land lost its identity because of continued, conflicting foreign rulers, whether under Persian, Roman, Arab, and Maméluke invasions of Egypt. In fact, the conflicts between ruling parties of Egypt during the medieval ages alienated it from world renaissance, while the thrust of its growth focused on religious matters. During this period, Egypt bounced and survived various feuds, conflicts, and struggle of powers between its rulers. These would bounce to Baghdad, Iraq and return to Cairo, Egypt. Such a period witnessed the killings of several Arab rulers who lost power to each other, alternately.

For example, after the Arab Conquest of Egypt in AD 644, under Amr Ibn El-Assi, several foreign Arab rulers governed Egypt, starting with the First Fatimid, Islamic Rule of Egypt in AD 976, followed by the Abbasids and, later, the Second Fatimid reign. Egypt bounced and survived various battles between its Arab rulers who burnt and destroyed the city of Al-Fustat (Fussatum), the former name of Old Cairo, because one ruler lost a battle to another. However, following each feud and urban destruction, Fustat was able to stand and rebuild itself; it remains just as stunning, beautiful, and nostalgic as ever.

Then, following several confrontations with the Crusaders and, following the sixth and last Crusader invasion, a wise, intelligent and tolerant leader of Kurdish origins from Tikrit in Iraq (Sultan Saladin Al-Ayyuby), arose and founded the Ayyuby rule. He ruled Egypt and Syria between AD 1173 and 1194. Following his reign, foreign rulers continued to govern Egypt, first under the Ottoman Mamélukes (in the thirteenth century) and, later, under the Ottoman reign, for close to four centuries, just until the Napoleonic invasion of Egypt in 1798 and later, the British rule..

It is important to mention that many scholars of Egyptology regard Sultan Ayyuby as master of urban planning. It was only after his reign that Egypt isolated itself, grievously, from world renaissance, as mentioned, above but flourished under its own umbrella of Turkish and religious secular rule. This continued until the time of the French revolution and just prior to Napoleon's marine assault on Egypt in 1798, followed by Britain's conquest of Egypt in 1803 and the conquering of French troops. Britain continued to rule Egypt throughout the glorious Royal governance of Sultan Mohamed Ali's Dynasty between 1805 and 1952. Then, Egypt claimed independence of Britain in 1954, under Nasser. It (the new government of Egypt, in 1952) abolished Egypt's most flourishing and glorious rule of Mohamed Ali's one hundred and fifty years dynasty; it broke a sovereign state and promised to rebuild it. In the end, setting aside the rise of this new Pan Arabism of the fifties, Egypt still had to reclaim its glory again. It had to rebuild what 1952 had destroyed; it had to reinstate what Mohamed Ali's Dynasty had founded since AD 1803. Egyptians had to overcome their egos and false expectations. They had to give, again. Give to Egypt.

When Napoleon attempted to conquer Egypt in 1798, it was a time where Egyptians had little direction or inclination to open up to the West's evolution. This is because Egyptians had been reclusive and governed by non-Egyptian people who were Mamėluke-Ottomans since the thirteenth century and for several centuries. They were mostly from Turkey. The medieval age flow of immigration from the Arab Peninsula, Yemen, Afghanistan, and Pakistan that confined Egypt's state of mind, mostly to religion, religious architecture, and some modest trade, influenced the character of Egypt, grievously, and crippled it. It confined Egypt's state of mind to a cocoon of norms and traditions, from the Asian Subcontinent, while delaying it from seeking knowledge from the flourishing West. Of course, Al-Azhar University shined as one of the world's oldest citadels of culture, knowledge, research, and Muslim governance. But when Egypt fell into the hands of Britain in 1805, the great ruler of Egypt, Mohammad Ali (once a Mamėluke himself), turned Turkey's Grande-Porte (or Ottoman Headquarters) down and founded a productive and fair modern dynasty of royal rulers for 150 years, ending in 1952 with the rise of social-idealism under President Nasser.

The taxi driver's attitude reminded me of the days following Egypt's coup d'état of 1952 that toppled the king because he (the driver) preached a lot.

Frankly, Egypt's people were already a complex of intertwining roots and a casualty of several foreign invasions. For example, in 572 BC, Persia invaded Egypt and ruled it for more than two centuries, until Alexander the Great freed Egypt in 332 BC. After the death of Alexander, the Great, came the Byzantine Ptolemaic rule (under Ptolemy II). The first was a disciple of Alexander the Great and left the Egyptians space to rule their land. Therefore, the Byzantine Ptolemaic rule ended the last of the Pharaohs (Neqtaneb II in 341 BC) under Alexander the Great (consensually). It seized power, all the way until the thirteenth Ptolemaic descendent in 30 BC, 'Cleopatra the Great or Cleopatra the Seventh'. She married her younger brother to save Egypt (but later killed him in pursuit of power) while courting Marc Anthony of the Roman Republic, to gain more power. After Octavius of the Roman Republic defeated Marc Anthony, the Roman Republic took over the reign of Egypt for five hundred years, and Cleopatra, the last of the thirteen descendants of Ptolemy, died with her lover, Marc Anthony.

The Roman rule under Octavius (who took the title of Augustus the Great) and others who followed him continued for five centuries (despite another attempt to invade Egypt by Persia). The Roman rulers vandalized Egypt's riches of wheat and cotton and sent its profits to the coffers of Rome, let alone persecuting Christians of Egypt until the Arab conquest of Egypt in AD 644 under Arab Warrior Amr Ibn El-Assi. He defeated Cyrus of Alexandria (by consent from Arab Khalif Omar Ibn Al-Khattab) during the reign of Trajan of the new Roman Empire (previously, the Roman Republic). Then, in the middle ages, the Ottoman rule of Egypt continued the sucking of its wealth for four centuries, leaving the people of Egypt undermined in their own country.

So really, the most stable identity for Egyptians (despite its various short-sighted fallbacks but infallible achievements) was that new identity that was revealed but not necessarily defined during the reign of the great Royal Family of Mohammad Ali (in 1803) for one hundred and fifty years. It was the sum of all previous conflicting but yet enriching identities, Pharaohs, Jews, Persians, Hellenic (Greek), Coptic, Roman, Islamic, Ottoman, art, culture, science, agriculture and architecture, as well as the recent French and English marks of colonialism and intermarriage, that shaped modern Egypt. In the 1880s French, English, Italian, Greek, Armenian and American missionaries and boarding schools added to Egypt's glittering mosaic.

The Napoleonic invasion of Egypt soon applied the Napoleonic Penal Code. It refined the Egyptian penal system, and streamlined the application of the Muslim Legal Code, Sharia law, without compromising the rights of Muslim families to run their civil matters, through Sharia Law. Already, Cairo was a complex city of multiple cultures in the Medieval Ages and was recognized as the richest canvass of cultures on the planet. *Meshullam Menachem (A jeweler living in Florence, Italy and collector of precious gems),* wrote in 1481: "If it were possible to place all the Italian cities of Rome, Milan, Padua, and Florence with four other cities, they would not contain the wealth and population of half of Cairo." We drove through Cairo, considerably tired from our flight, until we reached Zamalek. A few minutes before Dahlia's apartment, we drove past a beautiful giant hotel that was once a castle owned by a rich Egyptian Greek Orthodox by the name of Michel Loutfallah and his mother. This Palace hosted Empress Eugenie in 1869 during the inauguration of *l'Opéra du Caire.*

"Another of the remains of the abusive Royal Family," said the driver, pointing to the hotel.

"... Why so?" I said. "Why?" Dahlia pinched my leg as we sat in the backseat. Finally, discouraged as I was, I decided not to argue with him because I love Egypt with all its successes and failures and did not want someone like him, criticize it. He was probably an ideologist, a passive one!

Ten days later, it was December 29, 2010. We had tidied our belongings and called some friends and relatives to greet them. After this, Dahlia and I crossed over Zamalek Main Street to the Gezira Sporting Club. This is a huge and posh social, sports, and leisure outlet, similar to the Heliopolis Sporting Club, where I grew as a child. We were to meet her brother and friends for tea and some winter sun. That day, we made plans to spend New Year's Eve at the club. This was good enough for me; it was a breath of fresh air for a change.

Soon it was Friday morning, December 31, 2010. Dahlia and I walked to the club and did some soft jogging around its main track. We had a light lunch and then a tea and decided to walk back to rest before we returned for our New Year's dinner.

By 7:00 p.m., we were all dressed for the dinner-show at Gezira Club. We took a taxi to avoid walking through the small but rugged streets by night. At 7:30, we met Dahlia's brother and some friends at the club's main hall, where I called mother with my cell phone and gave her my love as she gave us her blessings.

By 10:00 p.m., the show started, and it was lovely. Our host was an Egyptian comedy and drama diva whom I recall since my childhood as an amazing entertainer. *Samir Sabry* is his name. He must have been seventy years old, that night. Other performers joined, and we continued to enjoy the celebration. By midnight, I stepped out to call Mother, again. (She had just finished her supper, as it was 6 p.m., in Montreal). Luckily, I made it through to her and was able to exchange a few precious moments. Mom asked me when I would return, and I explained that I would fly back a few weeks after the New Year (without scaring her) but that I would call her to confirm it within the week. I promised to call her next day anyway, once or twice, and she was satisfied and happy. I felt good and gratified. I called my sister, as well, and wished her and the family well.

By 1:00, I was ready to go home to sleep and looked at Dahlia to start moving. She agreed and was ready to walk back home in the dark hours. On the way home, I noticed some strange action happening on the small streets of Zamalek. Dahlia and I saw various security cars driving past us. They were heading to the bridge that crossed over the ravishing River Nile by night, on to the other side of the river. I saw several security and army cars running across to downtown Cairo: *Maspero* (National Radio and Television Headquarters) and Tahrir Square. Tahrir Square is adjacent to the National Museum, Home Office, the American University in Cairo, and the Science and Research Institute. This last had hosted hundreds of priceless references, not to mention the *Description of Egypt* (Description de l'Égypte) that was compiled between 1798 and 1805 by 160 civilian scholars and scientists, including a chosen sixty or seventy, known popularly as the *savants* of Napoleon Bonaparte. They had accompanied Bonaparte during his attempt to conquer Egypt. Tahrir Square is also adjacent to the Ministry of Internal Affairs.

The vehicles were running quickly, and on our side of the Nile River, we saw all the luxurious waterfront restaurants, ships, cruisers. Both sides of the Nile River glowed with glare, colors, and lights. It was clearly New Year's Eve. However, the streets of Zamalek were empty and unlike streets during a typical New Year's Eve. While there was a clear sense of hidden celebration, I captured a different mood of gloomy vibes, one that evoked mystery and a sense of the unknown.

"Oh, no... God, please!" I said to myself, feeling the worst and clutching Dahlia's hands as we walked. "Not again... Another presentiment," I said in a loud voice.

"What's going on? What presentiment?" said Dahlia!

"Something is wrong, honey. I smell turbulence and blood in the air!"

"How so, my love"

"Let's rush home, honey. Dahlia, I know that something is wrong."

We rushed home, drank some hot chocolate and went to bed.

Next morning, on January 1, 2011, I woke up with a heavy heart. I could smell fresh coffee in our apartment. Dahlia had already woken up, so I rushed to the bathroom to brush my teeth and grab a coffee before I turned the TV on for any news. Dahlia had it already turned on, and she looked deadly pale and restrained. Alas, my presentiments had not failed me. The news anchor mentioned that a church was bombed during midnight service in Alexandria on New Year's Eve. The news talked of eighty deaths and many more wounded. I was dumbfounded but could not believe it until I saw the news clip pictured by some amateur hand-phone.

Minutes later, I saw professional photographers rushing to the scene and documenting what had happened. The church that was bombed was the All Saints Church in downtown Alexandria. Yes, there were about eighty deaths and sixty severely injured. By 6:00 p.m., this tragedy was broadcasted all across the world. Within days, the mood in the streets was shifting toward apprehension and fear. The same déjà-vu of the early fifties haunted me again, only this time I was not nine years old; I was sixty! Ideological fury and anarchy was imminent.

Within weeks, demonstrations filled the streets of Cairo demanding explanations from the government and requiring reforms. Suddenly, these honorable demonstrations turned to violent riots and religious confrontations. By January 25, 2011, hell broke loose in Egypt's main cities. First, in Tahrir Square in downtown Cairo, demonstrators insisted on explanations and some reform schedule from the government, but the government did not give, any.

As for me, I questioned myself whether being with the love of my life in a land I once belonged to and under the present circumstances is really what we both wanted! I could not handle seeing Egypt, hurt all over again! Besides, Dahlia had not

Tale of a Growing Child

received her Permanent Residence Card yet (Canadian Green Card), and so she was most definitely unable to move back to Canada, should something grievous take place. Not only were her papers not ready, but their progress had frozen under the circumstances. In addition, I could not leave her. To top it, my health progress, although obvious, was very slow. There was so much thinking to engage with and much pain to witness; and yes there was pain, killings, deaths and the usual silent worldwide witnesses that stood indifferent to Egypt's tragedies, previously, continued to stand still. Interestingly but not strangely, despite all odds, Egypt and its people, remained strong, united and unshakeable.

"And fear not them which kill the body, but are not able to kill the soul: but rather fear him which is able to destroy both soul and body in hell." Words of Christ, the Saviour, according to Saint Matthew 10:28

Chapter 39
The Following Three Months in a Turbulent Egypt

We booked our return flight to Montreal for March 4, 2011. I had received notice that my application to sponsor Dahlia as spouse, for her PR in Canada (Permanent Residence), conformed to all requirements by CIC (Citizenship and Immigration Canada). The CIC took its positive decision, regardless of my reduce income in 2009 and of the loss of my job; but also in view of my average income for the three previous years and, of course, of my high compensation package. However, it was the Canadian Embassy in Cairo that would have to handle it for final approval, following which we could apply for the PR card, in Canada. I was hoping to finalize it in Canada, since I had started in Canada. This would take place after a total of six months, as of the date in which the Canadian authorities approved her request and transferred it to Cairo. The situation in Cairo and other neighboring cities (part of the infamous Arab Spring) impeded the operations of various consulates, including the one in Cairo. The world superpowers were on an edge because of what was happening in Syria, Iraq, Yemen, Sudan, Liberia, Algeria, Tunis, Egypt and Gaza. This meant that Dahlia would only receive her PR in May or June of 2011 (in Cairo), just after we returned to Montreal on March 4, and not before; this was very difficult to manage; but we did.

This week, (early January 2011), thousands of young demonstrators demanded President Mubarak's impeachment, but he stayed put, waiting for the storm to settle. He warned his people from the repercussions of stepping down. He outlined how dangerous it would be, given the circumstances of rising violence in the region, but he promised to step down in September, once he had arranged for a safe transition of power. He meant what he said. After all, this peaceful revolution *seemed* to have been triggered by honest students, and they were. Unfortunately, it was hijacked and derailed by some vicious masterminds. Finally, on February 11, 2010, some emerging Egyptian media scrutinized and assaulted President Mubarak and members of his Cabinet to the point where he chose to give-up his responsibilities as President. (He did not abdicate). The military regime in interim forced Mr. Mubarak and members of his cabinet into custody. Food supplies were scarce; Dahlia and I picked groceries in bits and pieces from various stores. Many of the supplies we bought had expired, but we had no choice. I also bought powdered milk, crackers, and biscuits because bread was quite scarce.

    Violence in the streets was rising, and we had to stay in our homes. Looters vandalized many shopping centers, apartment houses with no intervention from the police or the military. A déjà-Vu of the years between 1950 and 1954 was recurring. (See chapter 4) Some looters headed to the National Science and Research Center in Tahrir Square and bombarded it with machine guns; they were about to destroy the priceless Five Volumes describing modern Egypt that Napoleon's *Savants* had researched for years. They almost broke into the Cairo Ancient Museum in Tahrir Square but lay Egyptians pushed them back, in a fierce battle. At this stage, Egyptians adopted a new form of civil defense. We saw that every block of four or five neighboring buildings appointed a team of eight to ten of its youth to repel street gangs from invading them. They held metal pipes and stones all night, for more than two months. They banged the streets with these pipes, warning imposters, every time they heard a strange vehicle pass by or a rowdy motorcycle drive in the neighborhood. I heard all this with my wife but was too old and weak to join our block's youth. To top it, the worst thing anyone could imagine, under the circumstances, happened. Someone forced hundreds of jails open, and freed more than twenty thousand felons, criminals, and political prisoners. They were loose all over Egypt. They had been jailed for many long years and were, inevitably, charged with anger. Soon, they filled the streets of Cairo and Alexandria. All Egyptians knew that this was no Arab Spring. It was a concocted demonic plan to break the soul of Egypt. Even if worldwide networks underplayed this chaos and despite the questionable display of solidarity of many members of the American Administration, at that time, in the heart of Tahrir Square, Egyptians knew something was not right. The déjà-Vu of the 1956 crisis was recurring in 2011 until 2013 but with no more Legendary Lester B. Pearson from Canada or Eisenhower from America to call for peace and justice.

At this stage, the violence became unbearable.

All through this ordeal, I could still call Mother to greet her without referring to the unrest, which she obviously knew nothing about. Of course, she could no longer remember why I was outside of Canada and asked me repeatedly when she would see me. "At the end of this week, I'll let you know, my love. I will let you know. It should not be long now. I promise you."

"All right, my son; let me know when, as soon as you have an idea."

My calls to Mom persisted, lovingly, day after day. They were hard, truly tearful, and difficult to cope with but absolutely reassuring and stabilizing to me, if only for a few hours after the call. Other than that, there was nothing to do than to walk (carefully) to the Gezira Club, to meet friends and have some late winter sun. Dahlia's brother and their lifetime friend would join us.

Ironically, at night, the streets of Cairo were flooded with sounds, smell and images of crowded cafes, giant screens, TVs, tea glasses, water pipes, backgammon, motorcycles, sirens, bullets, radio announcements and passers-by, as if nothing was wrong. Meanwhile, hundreds of Christians and Muslims were killed, only adding fresh fuel to citizens' rising apprehensions. Shops and commercial centers were burned. Looters filled the streets and people with strange clothes, talking in clearly foreign and even strange non-Egyptian tribal accents, roamed Cairo squares; people who were definitely not Egyptians; infiltrators. The smell and sight of smoke filled the air, everywhere! Amidst all this drama, hundreds of Muslims defended Christians from anarchists and the other way round, slowing down any chance of further civil violence. It worked and Divine mercy, prevailed!

By late February, things were easing-up a little, though not too much. On Sunday, February 13, we went next door for prayer at the Roman Catholic Diocese of Saint Joseph. It is the residence of the Comboni Missionaries.

The Roman Catholic Church in Rome, was founded it in 1881 in homage to Saint Daniel Comboni of Khartoum, Sudan, who fought so much for social justice in Central Africa. He was born in Rome 1831 and died in 1881. The Comboni Missionaries helped and sheltered thousands of Sudanese refugees from the self-declared Mahdi (*Messenger-of-God*) of Sudan as well as many other thousands of persecuted Africans. The Comboni Missionaries also promoted dialogue between people of diverse views, faiths and beliefs. In the meantime, Egypt had become a citadel of culture, social justice, tolerance and religious cohesion at the turn of the nineteenth century. They stool do, at this Parish, that offers housing, charity, schooling, conferences and much more.

We made a point of visiting Dahlia's elderly but mentally challenged cousin Jeanette to cheer her and to buy her some pastries, as we did following each Sunday service and throughout the week. She was well off but could not manage herself or her finances without help. Dahlia made sure she had twenty-four-hour rotating nurses at home. She arranged to have two lovely nurses that slept at Jeanette's apartment, one alternating every two weeks with the other. Personally, it made me feel good to be able to cheer Jeanette; after all, someone might be doing the same with Mother in Montreal. Jeanette lived three blocks away from the church and six from our home.

We continued to hear bullets and motorcycles on The 26th of July Avenue. As we entered the church, two National Security guards greeted us with respect and made us feel comfortable. Inside the church, there were at least two hundred worshippers of all ages and all roots.

We sat at our favorite place in the second row; just six feet away from the church's alter. The brilliant priest had cut, clipped, and hung pictures of several martyrs. These were pictures of youth from all faiths, Muslim and Christian, hung at the altar. There was not one dry eye that day in church. This was just another act of divine intervention that was comforting and that kept coming through to me, all across my life, repeatedly, during moments of despair. It felt good to be human and surrounded by humans. It felt good to live in a world that continued to bind humans of all shades, seeking comfort, dignity and fellowship.

As we prepared to receive Communion, I walked forward and, to my left, I noticed a very tall, white-haired, elderly man, who was dressed in a dark suit. He was about eighty-five years old. His face was quite familiar to me, and so was his thick, white, twisted moustache. Suddenly, I remembered where I saw him! I had seen him in 1971 at the Cairo Opera House, standing next to Maestro Bellardinelli, Music Director in Interim of the Opera, then, and to Professor Decaro who was composer and violin virtuoso. Both Bellardinelli and Decaro were friends of my piano teacher, Mrs. Rossi. I looked at the man, and I think that he noticed me. He stood ahead of me in line for Communion but to my left. When I took my Communion, I turned back to my seat, and saw him already seated in the first row. He was staring at me, as I returned, as if he was analyzing me. After service, I introduced myself to him as Olympia Rossi's student and an admirer of Professor Decaro. I mentioned that I had seen him during the tragic burning of the old and beautiful Cairo Opera in 1971. He confirmed that he was the one and that he knew Mrs. Rossi and the Cairo Opera Orchestra team. It was *Mr. Renzo*. He spoke faintly, with low volume and with a classy smile of rich mannerism. He bowed his head as he spoke. Suddenly I realized that he had undergone the same operation my father had undergone in 1959 when he discovered he had throat cancer. The man had extracted his larynx and spoke with no vocal chords. "Can you understand what I say?" he asked me.

"Yes, of course, with no question. Fifty years ago, my father had the same operation, and I heard him for twenty years.

He sat next to me at home, for my homework through primary and secondary stages," I said while smiling, respectfully.

He smiled and clutched my shoulder with grace and pride! "But I think I also met you later at the airport when you worked for Switzer-Airlines and while you were checking-in my friends Olga and Xaven Katchadourian on their way to Geneva. I think you had a question about playing a piano piece for Franz List." (As mentioned earlier, Olga and Xaven Katchadourian were first cousins of Aram Katchadourian, composer of one of the world's most sublime ballets, *Ballet Spartacus*). Both Xaven and Olga had four-hand piano concerts in Alexandria, that week in the seventies. They had started presenting their concerts within the Armenian Community in Egypt since the fifties.

"Yes, you are right," I said. "It was the *Impromptu of Chopin* in C sharp minor, rather than Lizt. I needed their help with it, and they did help me. Wow, I am touched! You remember that, sir!"

"Of course, I do." He smiled gracefully.

As for me, I had managed to rekindle another shade of the beautiful past.

So, Dahlia and I walked a few blocks south to '26th July' Avenue, to visit her cousin Jeanette. I crossed to the opposite side of Jeanette's apartment building to buy her favorite fresh pastries from *Patisserie Simonds* that its original owners had founded in 1893, but who left Egypt in the sixties.

Jeanette is fifty-eight years old; she walks, while bending herself to the side. She sits with her legs crossed over each other on the sofa, just like a schoolchild. She wears one of two nightgowns, alternatively, all the time; they are worn-out but clean. She smiles earnestly and carries a heartfelt load of souvenirs. Her eyes carry deep hurt; her hair is all died and untidy. Of course, she looks like she is sixty-five years old. Jeanette suffers from muscular dystrophy. Her speech is slow, unarticulated, and many times distraught by an anguish that she keeps reliving and cannot overcome. Jeanette sees every one as a kind parent to her. She calls Dahlia "Mama" and calls me "Uncle

Farid," who was her favorite uncle until he died in Italy several years earlier. When she talks, she raises her right hand and slightly backward, pointing it to the ceiling. She moves it in a circular motion as she passionately recounts her better years like a typical *femme-fatale*. She loves pastries and she keeps recounting the better days when she used to live with her family on *Raousha Beach*, in Beirut before the devastating 1975-war. Dahlia and I would visit Jeanette on a daily basis with her preferred French Mini-Pastries, if even for twenty minutes.

One day, in mid-February, just before we arrived at the street leading to Saint Joseph's Church, we found congestion and could not even walk peacefully on its narrow and dusty pavement, let alone the burden of our heavy load of groceries. Instead, Dahlia and I walked through a parallel side street that led, all the same, to our apartment building. Suddenly, I noticed another déjà-vu! A scent I loved; a scent I recalled from the beautiful past. This time it was the smell of real jasmines, both Egyptian and Indian jasmines. I looked to the right and found a villa with a big garden and two jasmine trees overflowing from its metal fence. *A garden with jasmine trees… My God, there were Jasmines in Zamalek, two minutes away from our apartment…* I thought. I moved forward to smell them. It occurred to me that I was still guided, even teased by Camille. Dahlia looked at me and smiled. She knew exactly what was running in my mind. It was refreshing!

The following day, we continued to see strangely dressed people walking in *Tahrir Square* and other parts of Egypt. They joined the celebrations; they were people that had done nothing to boast about; they did not build our homeland; where did they come from; who were they to claim all that questionable joy, amidst all the suffering of so many youth, why did they come now? Who recruited them! Where were those true Egyptians who had nurtured its branches for centuries, why did we allow them to leave their homeland in the sixties? One thing I was sure of, the roots of these Egyptians, are still all around Egypt, breading jasmines and flowers; and now these new illegal comers in the streets of Egypt meant nothing to me! During the riots and the killing of Egyptian youth, the same was happening in Syria and Iraq but I chose not to find answers for these persistent questionable tragedies that many networks called Arab Spring. I chose to weep at how some heartless perpetrators inflicted violence to de-stabilize the area (from the back scenes) and how some other world-leaders stood silent.

There was a lot of action, that day, so Dahlia and I chose to rush back home. We made it in a few minutes. Several helicopters hovered in the skies. I smelt both rotten garbage, burnt garbage almost everywhere.

On Sunday, February 27, 2011, we meant to go to church for the 8:30 a.m. service instead of the usual 11:00 service so that we could meet friends at the Gezira Sporting Club, after mass, and then visit Jeanette for tea before we headed home for lunch and start packing of our bags. That morning, it was very cold, and I turned two heaters on. Unfortunately, the electric meter's wires melted, and we smelt a very unpleasant and suspicious smell of burning wires.

So we turned the master electric power off and rushed to Cairo's *Compagnie des Eaux et D'électricité*, which is situated in one of Cairo's oldest residential and commercial areas, called *El-Sabtia*. Although it was only three kilometers away, this whole environment of violence was dark and risky. We managed to find a taxi and asked the driver to drop us a couple of blocks before our destination. I wanted to enjoy the walk through this historical suburb. As usual, for such areas, they revealed vast history and an intriguingly rich artisanal life that once existed in the eighteen hundreds, and that turned to a place for plumbers, electricians, and other small successful businesses for homes and car accessories. The streets were dirty but manageable; they recounted such rich history! The Egyptian worker who guided us to the electric company was quite cordial. This was a place where Italian Egyptians, French Egyptians, and Egyptian Jews once lived together.

One end of this city (facing the River Nile and almost opposite to our side of the River Nile in Zamalek), was called Boulak or Beau-Lac (Beautiful Lake). The French engineer Gustave Eiffel (of Eiffel Tower in Paris) had chosen it as his domicile while constructing Cairo's adjacent two glorious bridges starting from the Cairo suburb of Beau-Lac to the other side of the Nile in Zamalek, where we live. The other end of the city led to Shubra, an equally old corner of Cairo, filled with history (the birthplace of the famous singer and my beloved diva, Dalida). *Oh what history*, I thought. We walked through the gates of an impressive modern building, and there it was Cairo's Central Water and Electricity headquarters. People who guided us were humble and professional; in fact, they were eager and earnest to do so. By the time, we explained our problem, they asked us to pay an amount of money to change the electric meter for a stronger one. They also promised to have it done that very day, while it usually took five days to change the meter, and it was.

"You are such good people," said one of them. "Are you Egyptian, Greeks, Italians, Jews?"

"Egyptians with Syrian roots, why?" We did not want to explain more.

"You are so blonde," he said, looking at my wife.

"Well, this is Egypt, my friend," I said.

"We miss the good old people!"

"We were all Egyptians. Our planet is one country, my friend, and its people are one family! Is it too difficult now?" I asked.

"It is not like before. The last few years have been difficult and we needed some change."

"We were all one family, one striving nation - Muslims, Christians, and Jews!" I replied.

He took us to the technicians' room where they had set a breakfast table for their team, covered with fresh hot Egyptian bagels called (*semeet*) and *Stengel* rolls (another Yiddish Egyptian tradition that has outlived all odds)! They got both from a neighboring old bakery. They were all extremely nice and insisted we join them for breakfast. I said, "Thank you so much; we just had breakfast, but I cannot ignore these delicious rolls." Dahlia and I cut a small piece of *semeet* each and we ate it in front of them. It was warm, crunchy, and covered with sesame, seeds, and the technicians appreciated our gesture of ease. A stout, fifty-year-old man, sitting in the middle of their office, spoke to us in perfect French and mentioned that he was a graduate of *College des Frères de la Salle*. He was proud to engage in a French conversation with us, while his team kept applauding him and smiling at him, humorously. He was their boss and seemed to me an extremely modest and good man. The whole ambience was refreshing, and they all promised to resolve our problem between 2p.m.and 3p.m. that day. Were these some of the remaining roots of the mother tree? All this happened at a moment everyone was tired of violence and hate; therefore, it was a natural moment of camaraderie. We thanked them deeply and rushed to take a cab to Saint Joseph's parish, next to our home, for the 11:00 a.m. service. We actually made it ten minutes ahead of time. We were home at 2 pm, to welcome the electricity technician.

The taxi driver who took us to church was seventy years old, another relic of the day! He was a kind and professional, silent man. Suddenly, he flashed back like a fireball, talking about how we reminded him of the *beautiful past* when Egypt was a thick canvass of rich layers of cultures. We saw tears in his eyes as he overflowed with love. He kept telling us rich stories from the past and was so emotional about it. Later, at church, the priest talked of fellowship and the importance of leaning on one another in these violent and hard days. By God, I thought! This testimony was one of the most enriching diaries I had ever written, before I returned to Montreal.

The problem is that there are more than ninety million Egyptians, standing with their brushes and paints; with their needles and threads, searching for the renewed canvass, a social canvass, waiting to make their point on it and to leave their mark, their shades, views, hopes and aspirations. The canvass was missing.

By 4:00 p.m., the electricity was up and running with a brand-new strong meter! In the afternoon, we passed by Jeanette for half an hour and got her some raisin-filled chocolates muffins from *Patisserie Simonds*. Alas, Jeanette looked very tired. Her muscular dystrophy was taking hold of her mood, speech, and movements. She said she wanted to die and looked so sad. I hugged her, saying, "I know what you feel, Jeanette. There was a time I felt just as you do, but do me a favor and let me hug you and reassure you that it passes away. I promise you it will and that we will always be with you, and so will these lovely nurses and friends remain with you!" Dahlia told me that Jeanette's two brothers had the same sickness and that they passed away at the same age as Jeanette, soon after they had experienced these symptoms, many years ago; her parents followed within two years, out of grief, leaving her all by herself. I called mother that night and explained that we would be back in Montreal in less than one week.

Saint George Basilica and fortress seen from Hanging Church

Chapter 40

Reflections and Resolutions — Across the Atlantic

On March 1, we scheduled a private taxi to pick us at 3.30 am for March 4, 2011. It was to drop us no later than 4.30 am at Cairo airport for check-in and for our flight departure. The taxi was timely and all travel procedures went well. In no time, we were on board stretching on our seats. We closed our eyes until the plane took off to Paris where we connected to our trans-Atlantic flight, heading west. Somehow, I felt my abdominal pains were decreasing significantly but Dahlia insisted I should stick to the diet. Six months later, I repeated the cure, to be safe.

We landed in Montreal on schedule. We cleared all immigration and customs formalities within forty minutes and took a taxi back home. On the way, we made a quick stop at Summer-Breeze Senior Living to greet Mother, first, and then continued home, just across the road. Mother had already started her dinner and saw us rushing in the restaurant with our coats to hug her, while the taxi driver waited outside for a few minutes. Dahlia and I kept our purses with us as we entered to greet Mother. Even the driver, was overwhelmed at this moment and waited anxiously to hear that we had met her.

The receptionist spotted us walking inside the lobby, waving at Mom, as we turned right, past the bistro to the restaurant. Suddenly, there she was, looking at us, all dressed up, made up, and absolutely vibrant; she was doing a little dance in her chair. Two of the care managers and the restaurant servers were waiting to watch that moment, and so were most of the residents that sat in the restaurant. Mother was all bubbly and spiraling with joy, ready for us in her dark-blue outfit covered with her classy, silk, burgundy shawl and gold broche. She was waiting with grace and pride. Our Royal Air Force girl from Egypt was as stunning as always! I threw myself in her lap and wrapped her with my right arm. I had to kneel because she was already seated. I kissed her hand, and Dahlia took over, smothering her with love and kisses.

"Oh, Ma, I missed you so much, my love! You are so beautiful!" I said. *"You kept your promise and waited for me,"* I said to myself. I noticed that mom's friends Florence, Shirley, and Phyllis were almost in tears. After all, they were in their third age cycle and must have reflected about themselves and their own families. So were the neighboring tables happy for us, and so were the caregivers (who had become our friends). A few clapped, so I threw kisses at them with my hands. One of her friends, Adornina, said in her warm Italian accent, *"You …very good children. She knew how'a to raise you."*

The staff had prepared juice, wine, beer, and cookies for us, and we had to change our plan with the taxi. I left Dahlia behind, rushed outside to the taxi and continued to our apartment building, just across. The driver helped me with the bags up to the elevator while I opened the apartment door and then, paid the driver, put my boots on, brought Dahlia's boots with me, and crossed back, on foot, through the snow to Summer-Breeze, across Saint Patrick Boulevard. It took me fifteen minutes before I returned to join them.

The staff had also prepared us an adjacent table and squeezed two dinner sets for Dahlia and me to join Mother and her circle of friends. Of course, we were very tired but managed to pull ourselves to stay until it was time for Mother to go to sleep. We had a lot of fun gossiping and chitchatting with Mom. She was never alone during our absence. As always, my sister and her family were always surrounding her, and so were cousins and friends like Roland and Karina. After that, we left, promising Mom to return for breakfast and making sure she was comfortable in bed, once her caregiver had refreshed her and helped her with her pajamas. I made sure to turn the TV on very low volume, kissed her good night, and said: "See you in the morning, my love," hence starting a new chapter in Montreal with a good and endearing moment of reunion with Mother and my family, within a new life cycle and, most of all, together with Dahlia, in better health. By 11:00 p.m., we had unpacked most of our belongings, showered, and prepared to go to sleep. We had already set our bed the day of our departure to Cairo in 2010.

Chapter 41

A Breath of Fresh Air ... Gentle Breezes from the Past
The day following our return to Montreal

In the morning, we made a few telephone calls to friends and relatives and then crossed over to visit Mother for breakfast. She had not forgotten that we arrived the night before and that we had dinner together. In fact, I got the feeling that she had forgotten that we were away for three months and that she was under the impression that we had kept the family routine as before. Even more, she was very stable at Summer-Breeze and did not display any feelings of anguish or nostalgia for her home next door. We left Mom before lunch and promised to be back at suppertime. Luckily, that day, Summer-Breeze was organizing a piano recital of some oldies, while offering fruit, juice, tea, coffee, and cakes. Therefore, neither Dahlia nor I felt uncomfortable leaving her. She prepared herself for the afternoon event with her new friends, until we met that evening. My sister and her husband would join us at Summer-Breeze that evening for tea. After joining her for breakfast that morning, we took a taxi to our garage to pick up our car and reconnect the battery. We drove along the highway for half an hour until both the battery and the car ran perfectly well.

Dahlia had bought Mom a linen shawl from the transit area at Paris airport, and I bought her another flask of a classy Eau de Toilette, which she loved and which she used to enjoy in the early nineties. This time, it was not the same as my earlier gift to her, Diorissimo by Christian Dior. Instead, it was another perfume by Crab Tree and Evelyn, called Summer Hill, which, had a little scent of Orange Blossom mixed with lily, clover flowers (I think) and peach. It was as expensive as last year's perfume. On the other hand, I bought Dahlia the same Jasmines perfume (Diorissimo) which I had bought mom, the year before. Dahlia laughed because of my choice of fragrance that had to include jasmine and lilies, but she loved it and, of course, I did, too. Like me, she has always had a taste for older scents and styles.

  We went to see Mother around 5:50 p.m., but she was still having her dinner. Therefore, we waited in the bistro within her sight and drank some tea. She kept waving to us and smiling like a child. I did have a heavy heart and wanted to close the earlier chapter of mind games, finally. Moreover, even though it had not completely sunk into me, I think I had reached a threshold of intellectual security and effective judgment for the first time in twenty-four years. My journey that started in September 2008, searching for reasons for all my hurt, was almost ending. With Dahlia in my arms, the truth did not matter to me anymore! Incidentally, we heard that Mr. Zinky's business in Montreal collapsed and that he returned to Egypt, with his wife, while operating from home, in a Cairo suburb.

  After a warm hour and a half exchanging gifts with Mother, my sister, and her two wonderful children, Dahlia and I showed her pictures of the family and of the brighter side of Cairo and Alexandria. We left her with her friends at Summer-Breeze and drove to a neighboring soup house where we had a mild dinner and then returned home for a well-deserved night of rest.

  It was too cold to have our walks by Centennial Park's lake, a few blocks away and next to the Marché, so we stayed indoors within shopping malls while continuing to visit Mother two or three times a day; sometimes for as little as fifteen minutes. We promised that we would take her out in the special assistance van to the Marché (Farmers Market) by the end of April or in early May. In the meantime, I continued to give thanks to God and told Dahlia that I wanted to spend two days in our favorite motel in Magog to visit Saint Benedict's Abbey and to light him a candle. We did so, toward the end of April. In between, I solicited opportunities to work as a freelance photographer for Real Estate and Corporate Luncheons. Soon, I started generating some money to supplement my two pensions.

Tale of a Growing Child

By the time we went to Magog, on the following weekend, the weather was a little milder though damp and chilly. We made it to our motel, safely, and with a lot of eagerness and joy. On the first night, we drove up to the abbey for ten minutes to listen to the chanting. After this, we cuddled up in our favorite restaurant, next-door to our motel, for a steak sandwich. My stomach was clearly healing and I felt my appetite was gradually coming back, although I still had to be cautious with mustard and dills.

In the morning, it was sunny, so we drove up again for the 11:00 o'clock prayers. We lit a candle for Saint Benedict, received Eucharist, and drove back next to the lake opposite to our motel. Then we walked in the muddy ground, still half-frozen, in our coats with our heads and necks covered. I saw the bench where I had sat for hours and where I started writing my testimony, in 2008. "It was here where I sensed the beginning of my metamorphosis," I told Dahlia.

"It was here where God heard your prayers, my love, and made you rest," responded Dahlia.

"It was here that He invited me to pray and rest; you are so right, and He got me out of jail."

We drove back to Montreal after our second night and then spent some time with Mother. When we got home, I called my friend Bernard Malvoun to tell him I was back.

"We are back at home, Bernie! Dahlia and I want to see you and Milena," I said.

"Let us do it on Saturday afternoon. They say it will be a perfect spring day," said Bernie.

We met at the park and talked of the changes in Egypt and my shifting state of mind. I asked them about their children, their studies and their general growth. They seemed impressed by the change that they noticed in my attitude and loved Dahlia.

By mid-June, the weather was spectacular. We planned to spend a few hours at Centennial Park and chose Friday, June 24, 2011, to do so. Dahlia and I made some sandwiches that day and we were ready to celebrate spring after our several-month ordeal with the violence in Egypt and after my anguish away from Mother. It was a beautiful setting for a glorious picnic. We passed by Mother before noon and got her some of her favorite cinnamon-raisin buns that had just come out of the oven of a German bakery next door. Of course, at Summer-Breeze, there was never a dull moment in the bistro, which, incidentally, was always loaded with goodies, fruit, pastries, and other surprises.

It was such a lovely day especially that it coincided with the feast of Saint John the Baptist, which is a revered National *Quebec Holiday*. It is the most widely celebrated day in Quebec. On that day, Summer-Breeze had so many activities running for its residents. Mom was ecstatic, and we managed to walk her out with her walker, well covered, through the front gate, where red, white and yellow tulips, trees, and benches surrounded her. Many other residents were outside with their caregivers helping them or showing them to their seats. The atmosphere was jovial, and the music could be heard everywhere. There was a keyboard outside, and we saw Gregg, the musician, sitting by his electric keyboard singing some lovely oldies, while the waiters were setting up an outdoor buffet and BBQ for the residents, for a change. Mom acted like a child, holding her friends' hands. They seemed like a blessed group of peers and friends, as they sang along, with Gregg.

Dahlia and I were happy for Mom and felt comfortable leaving her on such a glorious day to her activities and friends.

"Okay, Mom, you should start your buffet in thirty minutes. Have fun, my love; we will do the same. We prepared some sandwiches and will go to the park, for lunch. But we will see you in the late afternoon."

"Okay, my darlings," said Mom. "God bless you, and I will see you later." She was clearly busy with her friends, so we headed to our car and drove off to Centennial Park for our two-hour nature retreat. I never knew if mother was really at peace with the new set-up or if she held some hurt, in her heart, for having had to leave her home. But she knew she was my queen.

We parked the car in the busy lot, walked through its front gate heading toward the spot by the lake where we usually sit and found that there were two benches still available. My energy levels were high and my stomach was now healing very fast. I was ready to live again. Squirrels were hopping on the damp ground in between the busy tables, while families scattered around them, everywhere. They continued hopping between the children and their friends, right up to the branches of the happy trees, the branches that trembled with a cheerful dance generated by the joyful, visiting birds. They had immigrated down, south of the border, to USA in winter, and just returned to Canada for spring, summer and fall, to join the feast. Both birds and squirrels watched over the celebrating mob of diverse ages, looks, roots, sounds, and accents on this sunny and bright *Saint John the Baptist* weekend. Barbeques were sizzling with the smell of their charcoal-grilled medley of marinated meats or corn. Sandwiches, crudités, coolers, warm flasks of coffee and tea, cups, glasses, forks, and plates, covered the tables. They glittered with a lively mosaic of colors.

As we walked through the tables to the two vacant benches, the smell of wet grass, fresh trees and the greasy lake water, at distance, almost completed the canvass much before we sat down on one of the two remaining benches by the lake. We saw ducks and geese flying in between our legs and all over the graceful water ripples that moved from inside the lake outwards, and then, receded. As they did, flickers of sunrays turned the ripples' sides to patterns of rich diamonds necklaces, until they subsided. The lake's reserve of live fish joined the celebration and intercepted the water ripples every now and then, with each fish generating a smaller circle and turning the whole scene into a water ballet presented by fish and applauded by the flapping wings of flying ducks and pigeons. The proud, long-necked white geese preferred to rest on the water and to swing with its ripples, occasionally flapping their wings to acknowledge their presence and to contribute to the celebration. The geese nibbled on some weeds, cleverly, as the rest danced their dance and as the families and friends around us sang their song. An occasional disk-player added depth of field to the sounds as it played music of diverse passions and different styles.

    The smell of the BBQ reached a point where I was drooling and ready for my sandwiches. I clutched Dahlia's hands, just until we came across a set of two tables clearly occupied by a group of close families and friends. There were over twenty people around the tables, apart from the prams and children, all giggling, munching, and crunching chips and teasers.

"Come on in! Jump in and join us, folks!" shouted a gray-haired, cheerful adult with an Asian accent, around fifty-five years of age, and quite thin. He was busy turning the hamburgers on the barbeque while several kids were stretching their hands, holding their plates for a cut from the tasty burgers. The man's accent sounded like it was from India, Pakistan, or their surrounding nations. He had a small chin-beard. He was almost dancing while managing his barbeque.

"Thank you, thank you!" said Dahlia.

"Where are you going?" shouted the man in a jovial manner.

"We will have a walk, sit by the lake, and leave you to your space," I said.

"You sit right here and share our table. Really, what space? Where are you from?" he asked in a loud but positive voice.

"Egypt!" said Dahlia.

"Hey, come join us! We have Egyptians, Indians, Pakistanis, Italians, Greeks, and Canadians, both French and English. Come sit down for half an hour; we have a lot of food and drink. Keep your sandwiches for later. If you drink beer, grab one each from the cooler and relax. If you don't, we have lots of soft drinks, as well. This is a democratic table."

We sat down with appreciation but we laughed at his positive and forthcoming tone of command. I jumped on some sliced carrots and a drink while Dahlia stuck to chips for a start.

"Have you lost any family members in the current violent events in Egypt?" asked one woman.

"No, we haven't. Thank you for asking," said Dahlia.

"We were there for three months and only came back last month!" I added.

We talked under interesting pressure because of the crazy but lively and jovial atmosphere with people giggling and talking in diverse accents, while surrounded by kids jumping all around us. I looked at the man who invited us and told him that what he did was "so kind and hospitable." I added, "We appreciate this family ambience and missed it after months of ambiguity and memories of the beautiful past."

"Hey, you are more than welcome. Come again every two weeks," said a man who was from Egypt who had immigrated to Canada with his family in 1991.

We both smiled at this moment of celebration, a true moment of life, the way it should be, the way it was in Egypt in the fifties, sixties and seventies!

This was an organized picnic by neighbors, families and work-friends. It took place every other weekend during spring and summer. To top it, it was Saint John the Baptist's weekend, and the mood was, by far, the most energizing I had witnessed for a while. We paid our reverences to all of them, raised a toast with whatever was remaining in our cans, and moved to the lakeside. For me, it was a meal shared with love—truly, my daily bread!

"Truly refreshing," I told Dahlia and we went to sit by the lake to watch the birds. "This is life, for a change, Dahlia. It takes me back to 1956 when I was five and my sister was six ... the Japanese Gardens in Helwan-Cairo, its lake and ducks; St. Michael's and All Saints Bible studies and campfires; Heliopolis Club. It reminds me of Alexandria and later with my sister and Camille in Agamy and other beaches in Alexandria and Ras-El-Bar (Damietta) by the sea front, in the morning, and the Nile-front in the evening, always with ducks and geese! This is what I see today in the park; it is happening again! It is so beautiful! I see images from the past, at Ras-El-Bar café, when we were kids, and I still smell the Nile water, too, through this lake!"

She smiled and said, "Do you want to walk with me around the lake."

"No, no, Dahlia, thank you. Not yet; I need to sit and reflect, one more time; please."

"Fine, I will walk alone, and you can do some dreaming while waiting for me. However, I need you to do something, for me. Make your resolutions and remember that you are free, now; you are free both because you got rid of your primary source of abdominal pains and, second, because you mind is no longer conditioned by the negative environment that has been haunting you for so long. Now, you are the boss; you are in control of your life again. So go have fun, dream but no more digging in unwanted puzzles. You had sufficient time to meditate during your retreats in Magog and Egypt."

"Okay, love. Go and walk."

"Close your eyes," she said in a very low tone… "…and breathe."

In a few seconds, I started shuffling the maple leaves with my eyes but did not find any mimosa bushes or bougainvillea flowers. Of course, I still missed their scent but I found other scents in these trees. …and when I sat down on that bench, I looked around and found those squirrels coming forward to me to greet me, with several birds hovering over my legs. The squirrels sat on their backs and held their hands toward their mouths, most probably to eat a crumb of something that *Mother Nature* had left for them. Anyway, they lifted their two hands to their mouth while sitting on their bottoms and staring at their prey, to devour it, without paying attention to me; …or had they noticed me but just wanted to have their meal next to me, as I ate mine. So too did the birds move around me and then tease me as I ate my sandwich. They, too, wanted company, or did they just want to keep me company? I think that they cared and wanted to include me in their world, which I loved; and I think they liked me, too. I even came across a few frogs

Tale of a Growing Child

hopping at the edge of the lake, in between and out of its weeds. I missed the jasmines and the lilies but, at second thought, I asked myself, did I really need them around me? They were already inherent in my veins.

With the squirrels next to me and the birds around me, I sensed another sign—a new scent, a scent of fellowship and inclusion. Hence, I became earnest and content, sharing my lunch with the birds and with the rest of my friends, the squirrels. Then, I became one of them! I was no longer loathing myself as a prisoner.

Therefore, unlike a ladder of career growth or religious and social rivalry, which I was never too keen to yield my soul to, I found today another ladder. I found a ladder of humility and penitence to which I belonged, for a while. It was Saint Benedict's ladder, as he called it, one of obedience and acceptance and I found myself climbing it, closer to my God the Creator. Of course, I knew I had already passed the desert of corporate slavery and outlived it, but could this park, be my second desert, to eternal freedom, the second passing. Could this bench be my ultimate ladder to God? *I think so; I believe so. I could be at the first step of the ladder. Now, I am free to climb it!* I closed my eyes and went to a distant; very distant journey of peace, acceptance and closure, one in which I felt pulled on the ladder by God to His Glory!

Chapter 42
Reflections and Resolutions by the Lake

We are born in a world we did not choose. We grow within an environment of affection, love, justice and peace if it is our fortune, until we stand up on our feet to face life. Or else, we are born in a heartless surrounding and struggle to identify our own paradise, sometimes not even knowing what options are available and what we really want to achieve. We lead our lives through childhood, adolescence on to adulthood. We find ourselves in an educational surrounding, school or college, and later, in a work environment, or social network; these could be nurturing or destructive, but society expects us to cope with both. We do, we cope with both, we manage to stand up and build ourselves. Then we face change, and we cope with it. We encounter more change, and we struggle to cope with it. Yet, we engage with further change, and we struggle desperately to hold on to our identity before it slips away for good with ruthless change.

We rise and fall; we succeed, we fail. We meet the good and face the bad. Often, we rise and manage to turnover a new leaf. Frequently, we lose patience and succumb to despair. We work hard to improve ourselves or, at least, to overcome the painful past and sustain the hurtful present; we do so from one side—ours! The ugliness of intense scrutiny may confine us to a cocoon that our societies' selective perceptions have pushed us into, to a circle of thought, which could often be cold and too dark, to the extent that we feel alienated. The ugliness and coldness of such societal indifference drags us to a concocted battlefield that that we have not chosen and that we are not eager to fight. However, hurt persists, and a few will succeed to shape us, for good, if we do not stand up for our space and push them away. Others push us back; they manage to exclude us because of how they enforce their own whims and lack of vision. They will call us fools or crazy, if we dare to have a voice. They do so with no respect to our own aspirations, claiming they know what is best for us or for their societies, as if they knew it all! People will continue to marginalize us by words, looks, or even by omission and indifference. They will continue, forever, trying to extinguish our spirit. Some of them succeed in separating us from our lands, homes, workplace, and even our own bodies, minds or souls. Little do perpetrators of intolerance, violence, and injustice come to their senses and recognize their acts, so that we can acknowledge the painful past, turn the page, and move on! However, at all times we have the option to seek Divine intervention; and when we do so it drives us to one of the houses of our Creator with a sense of peace and Divine strength, before we return to the battlefield, once more.

If only it were possible to wipe away years of exile and mental anguish and to undo the past! If only we could pretend that there was nothing wrong and shield ourselves, sufficiently, in order to enjoy what we love, in whichever time remains, we could still be leading our lives, or at least a part of it, the way we choose. However, how can we taste joy in a complete and genuine manner if we mask our pain with false pretense? Now, more than seventy years after WW2 (World War 2), many are still isolated or scattered in their cocoons, in their margins and their tents around the world, because others have not changed their ways and their habits of defining the world and labeling the helpless! Many have overcome their fears and confronted change; many have not. Have I?

If dad (amongst others) could survive the harsh socialist and agriculture reforms introduced, in Egypt, during the early sixties, at the age of seventy, struck by throat-cancer, years after he was an honorable lawyer, government employee, and graceful landlord, but still manage to sell his land at half its value and stand up strong, why can't I do like him? If he was barely able to use the underrated income from his land to buy a small property so as to make some money in order to raise his family, without his voice, only to see it swindled by a new socialist regime and continue to stand, half broken but graceful, why can't I do like him? If he could walk in the streets of Cairo to manage his fiscal papers, buy groceries, attend church, and help me with my homework until the age of eighteen, not swayed by the reaction of those who could not understand his voice, who am I to complain of my health? If Jeanette could revitalize her spirits with a word of comfort or some French pastries when she is bedridden with muscular dystrophy and limited intelligence, then why do I not celebrate life without complaining? If I know that some owners of businesses were nationalized by the same socialist regime of the fifties and the sixties that hit my father, aunts, uncles, and friends- owners who found themselves ransacked of their money, equipment, and inventories but still managed to continue, then why don't I? If half of these managed to flee the mother tree and to cope with the hardships of immigration, starting all over again overseas, while the remaining half were paralyzed or succumbed to some heart seizure or brain tumor, leaving their families, behind, to survive the human and material losses, gracefully, then why don't I learn?

If Dad and Mother could both lose a son at eighteen and promise my sister and me that, everything will be alright because *God would stand by us*; why can't I accept Him, when He actually stood by us, across the years. If hundreds of thousands of Egyptians of all shades struggled, across the centuries, to sustain systematic hurt and cruel coercive treatment, but still clung to hope and stuck to their mother tree, gracefully, then why can't I do like them? If so many families have lost their dear ones, their homes and businesses during the recent events of the invented *Arab Spring* because of inexplicable induced violence, conflicting pressure groups, world indifference and weak governments but still manage to wait in anticipation for some light, then why can't I be like them?

If across the years, life has challenged the Church of God and its followers, ever since the first century, in Egypt and elsewhere; challenged it in the very land that the angel of God had chosen as refuge for the Holy Family but could still flourish miraculously, why do I worry? If its followers were turned targets of such harsh discriminatory taxes, coercion, killing and treatment for so many centuries, but were able to uphold their faith, why do I not learn! If this church struggled to escape retribution, despite all means of coercion, quelling and compulsion, to deny its faith, but could still stand firm without the use of one single weapon, why can I not do the same? If a little child was born two thousand years ago in Bethlehem, if He was crucified and killed for His Godly message but could rise and shine for twenty centuries, what more do I want! If despite all these challenges, His covenant still stands out as one of the world's indisputably most affluent, influential and nurturing of the Covenants of God, one that never used one single bullet or sword to spread His word, then why can't corporations and societies drive their businesses and nations without crushing their flock? Why do they stretch their members to the point of slavery, torture or loss of identity?

If Egypt could survive the loss of its ancient library in Alexandria more than fifteen centuries ago, and the damaging of other heritage and cultural institutions, such as the opera house and science research center, but still continue to shine, then why can't we start rebuilding what we lost and why do we continue destroying what we built? If among all of Egypt's recent sectarian and religious violence, my Muslim friend rushes me to the emergency room of a public clinic in a mosque in Agamy (Alexandria), during one of my painful panic attacks to receive free merciful health care, while my ID states that I am Christian, then why do we continue fighting? If Muslims died defending Christians targeted by a few imposters and agents of violence, during the recent ordeal in Egypt between 2011 and 2013, and the other way around, then why do we question the will of God and why don't we live in fellowship?

If a teacher scoffs his pupil in class because he reads poetry with intense passion, why do we write poetry, and why do we teach it? If the eternal struggle for power could split the world into two groups- preachers and listeners, than who will account for the needs of the listeners who do not have the chance to talk, and who will push back the idol preachers who choose not to listen.

If Egypt could devote huge public resources to rekindle the footsteps of the Holy Family despite the cultural and religious dissonance; if it could do the same to restore synagogues in Egypt when there are no more local Jews remaining to take care of them, why can't I see the goodness in people? If a more than a million Jews were forced out of their homes in the Arab lands, Jews whose ancestors lived and flourished in these lands over the last six thousand years, but still manage to stand up firm and help lead the world in art, music, science, and health research, then why can't I move on with my music? If millions of Christians, Jews, Armenians, Assyrians, Yazidis, Iraqis, Syrians and other nations were target of crushing genocide and abuse across the last century (and before) but could lead their lives despite all odds, why do I not learn from them! If four and a half million Palestinians were forced out of their homes in the Holy Land for seventy years, surviving violence and marginalization but can still sustain the burden of alienation and continue to be earnest and to cling to life, why can't I do like them? If the sun continues to rise every morning, then why do I lose hope and why do I worry about injustice.

If I was able to fall five times during my life but managed to stand up six, firmer, stronger, and hopeful, then when will I smile and be thankful? If amid the dumps, smoke, and sewage of some streets of Cairo, during its recent trampled uprising, I could still smell some lilies and jasmines, who cares about the dry gardens, when we could plant them again. If I could sustain the last twenty years of corporate bullying, struggling with hurt by management snipers, if I could withhold my character when I was scoffed during these long recent years by some cruel social innuendos that were inflicted on me by peers and management, why do I let my mind spin about the past? Why do I not fight back! If I have survived all that and still manage to find the will to write this testimony and to play my repertoire of favorite songs, then why do I lose faith? If, despite all the mind games, control, and manipulation I was subjected to, I was still able do one thing, I could still remember to worship God and seek rest in *Magog*, then God was with me, and I was not alone, never alone—so why am I afraid? If I could find myself forced to live in a world that others have chosen to confine me to, claiming they wanted to help me, but could still cling to the one I always wanted to have, than why do I need to continue holding so many grudges and not just do what I love best?

  Here is what I will do; I will make a difference. I will keep giving out my hands and heart to people in need, just as I did with my parents, Jeanette, aging citizens, exploited colleagues and others around me. I will continue, whenever and wherever I can; I will not stop; I will forget the rest; I will celebrate life; I will prevail, under God.

Chapter 43
The Day the Sun Came Back

It must have been a long, deep sleep and a moment of extended reflection that I fell into because I felt something poking my shoelace. I looked down and found a pair of birds and a duck plucking my lace with their beaks while looking up at me, shrewdly, to catch my attention. One of them was turning her head gently in a full circle, gazing with her eyes down at my lace and then up at face. As for me, I had started eating one of my two sandwiches before I fell into sleep but had not finished it. The rest remained in my hand as I dropped my head and slept. The birds continued biting my shoelace, and then the duck stretched her head upward towards me.

The duck was about to shout at me and say, "Hey, pal, give me something to eat!" Eventually, I cut whatever remained from my sandwiches into small pieces and spread them over my two hands and around me. The birds kept snatching a piece or two, each, while tickling my palms each time, they did, and then they fled. Other birds reached out to my palms and the ground, below me, and many more hovered over my head until they had eaten all of my two sandwiches. Each time they snatched a bite, they flew over the lake and around it. I smiled and was thrilled. As I did, some thick clouds passed over my head, and then the sun broke them apart while its rays pierced me glamorously. Suddenly, I smelled jasmines and lilies, right under my nose, here in this Montreal Park.

"How are we doing?" I heard a voice from the left. It was Dahlia.

"I went into a trance, and the strangest thing happened!" I said.

"I know you did. I was here all the time, and you were rambling … even snoring!"

"You did not walk?"

"No."

"Okay, I will tell you about the trance later, but did you know what happened?"

"You mean the birds on your shoes?"

"Yes, the birds, Dahlia. I gave them my sandwiches because they were hungry."

"Do you want mine? I still did not eat them!" she said.

"No, no, thanks, I already received my bread for the day, at that festive table of friends, in the park. It is not that, it is just that …" I stalled.

"Come on! Say it!"

When I gave food to the birds, the clouds split into two, and the sun broke through them while glowing on my face, and then the birds followed the sunlight. I felt Camille was here!"

"Quite possible"

"At that instant, I smelled jasmines and lilies."

"That is because I wore your favorite French *jasmine and lilies* perfume, the one you bought for me, on Mother's Day; remember. I had it on since the morning, but you only noticed it now—I mean when you opened your eyes, right now. You are back, my friend."

"…Really?"

"Of course" said Dahlia.

"Did you know that Egypt exported jasmine oil to France, and from there to the world, in the fifties, sixties, and seventies?"

"Yes, yes, yes, you told me that, many times. You told me also that you overlooked shipping many of them when you worked for airlines. But Egypt never stopped to produce jasmines."

"You mean never stopped exporting jasmine oil?"

"No, I am using your metaphor. I do not know about jasmine oil; I meant jasmines, other jasmines, just as we found them around the table that invited us for a snack and all across the last sixty years: Karina, Roland, your friends and others. It never stopped. Look at us talking about it by the lake and watching the birds in Montreal. It confirms the point. You see, there were a few more jasmine trees that remained in Egypt; we passed by them, but you did not notice them, just as you failed to smell my jasmine perfume this morning. Now you do. It is because you were distraught by your worries and with your stomach and back pains, let alone the bullying. Now your stomach is healing very well. You were not alone…"

"Of course"

"I know that. Of course, I am right; because you sought, God's help in Magog; because, as you said, they had locked you in your cocoon of fear and ambiguity and fastened the jail's lock with intended hurtful slurs, to make you stagger. Camille loves you, Raphy. Just let go and start resting. Rest and let him rest, as well; let him fly back home. Just relax, my friend! Are you ready to let go? Are you ready to accept God's gift through the good people around us, His nature and blessings? Doesn't it make sense to you?"

"Of course it does, but then, I am drained and want to fly, again, so much; just like these birds; I want to fly again, but with you, just like we did at university!"

"Well, do it! Fly!"

"With what; I have no wings. I lost my wings and I want theirs!"

"No, you don't! You did it before, five times, with no wings! Do it again. Fly!"

"Will you fly with me?"

"Yes, I will."

The Lord is my Shepherd, I shall not want!"

Chapter 44
Egypt 2013-2016 the Eternal Cradle of Civilization

The Immoral Struggle for Power

The following year, 2012, Egyptians withstood various waves of harsh and violent attacks on civilians, households, cultural sites, and government offices, from within the homeland and from the Eastern Sinai and Western Sahara, Desert. It had all started with the burning of the Church of All Saints in Alexandria on December 31, 2010. After this, Egypt's jails broke loose with thousands of escaping felons, everywhere. They and others almost brought several institutions to rubbles; some vicious terrorists or enemies of Egypt, must have incited them! Others attacked the children's palliative hospital and ransacked part of its equipment. The riots and unexplained violence subsided for a few weeks and then restarted in November of 2011, almost eight months after Dahlia and I had returned to Montreal. They reached their climax in April of 2012, throughout the rule of the interim religious party that, for many Egyptians, had forced itself through to power.

    The whole ambience of violence did not represent the January 25, 2011's initial call for change. It was a call that had been in progress ever since President Nasser died in 1970 and continued to boil, with rising expectations, under President Sadat, who was struggling to shade his predecessor's overoptimistic promises. To top it, he had to cope with corrupt members of a ruling cabinet that he inherited from the sixties and a fractured public-relations agenda with the West.

    My family and I immigrated to Canada under Mubarak's rule (in 1987). For the following twenty-five years (under Mubarak), Egypt quelled many extremist groups while, to a few citizens of Egypt, some members of the Mubarak's ruling party flourished through corporate greed. After President Mubarak stepped down in 2011, under pressure, the violence continued while various US political heads stood in Tahrir Square, right in the middle of riots, violence and tragedy, in an act of unexplained, Wagnerian and, rather, pretentious solidarity, to many. Egyptians knew, very well, that this was not an Arab Spring but a failed attempt to break Egypt.

It continued but, so too did we continue to see people standing in the midst of violence and killing, wearing strange clothes, gowns and apparels. They spoke in Arabic but with a strange non-Mainstream Egyptian accent. They were not Egyptians and seemed to have come from other places *from within the region*. How did they infiltrate in my motherland? Many wondered! The persistence of people walking around with strange gowns, in the streets of Egypt, asking for a bite of crumbling Egypt, continued, while Egypt's real builders were cast out overseas in the sixties or locked, then, in their present houses in various cities of Egypt. They were afraid to buy their groceries and to shop, devastated by fear and tears.

The Egyptian National Research Center that contained priceless research and description of Historical and Modern Egypt, authored by so many of its children, let alone, the *Sixty Savants* of Napoleon Bonaparte's intellectual team, was severely fractured. Some fifteen-year old kids bombed it, during the so-called *Arab-Spring* uprising in Egypt, just as we saw them in the early fifties. These strangely dressed people tried to do the same with the Cairo Historical National Museum but lay Egyptian people quelled it. Most of the content of the National Science Center were saved just as music scholars had salvaged the Library of the beautiful old Opera House, in October 1971. Were these looters, Egyptians thinking on their own, of course not! Did they mean well? Definitely not. We saw it and lived it and the world stood silent as it did during the 1956 tripartite aggression on Suez and Egypt, until Hon. Lester B. Pearson took a stand at the UN Supreme Concil..

All this violence had nothing to do with the spark of hope that Egyptians had ignited on January 25, 2011, one that, among others, had called for the protection of places of worship (churches) and the abolishing of corporate corruption; search for hope for the young generation and dignity for the aging one. Some mastermind had hijacked this spark and ceded it to criminals and agents of war.

After several failed attempts for fictitious democratic elections and several corrupt reshuffles of parliament within a staggering Egypt (under the interim religious ruling party) and despite continued concocted coercive hate messages through social media inciting Muslims against Christians and Christians against Muslims; the people of Egypt stood still, unshakeable; and they spoke. They set their foot on the ground. The people claimed for their country before it broke by those who hate her. On June 30, 2013, thirty-five million Egyptians, Muslims and Christians, stormed the streets of several Egyptian cities and asked the Brigadier General Abdul Fattah El-Sissy to bring their country back to them. He did, thanks to his determination and wit, to their flame of love for Egypt and to Divine order; a new era of hope emerged.

A ray of hope was blinking over Egypt that night when several million earnest Egyptians were ready for real change. The world was stunned and world media was numb. Within a few weeks, the endless acts of violence subsided, but the aspect of law and order was only starting to prevail. Over the last few years, and even much before, Egyptians were hurt by foreign invasions and coercive politics as well as by internal dissonance and opportunists seeking to break them. Now, the opportunity arose for Egypt's children to assume their roles and to rebuild it again; to reclaim its heritage; norms and traditions, to rekindle its identity, before it slips away, for good, to the hands of some imposters. This was possible, even if it took five or ten years to reverse crumbling indicators. It was no longer an option to count on the president. He had so much on his plate. There was no time to lose, because external and internal politics would not cease to destabilize Strategic and Glorious Egypt. Largely, the Egyptians had been hurt so much by such persisting and destabilizing tactics that they, almost all, succumbed to some sort of Divine Fellowship. It took them centuries of suffering to realize that such fellowship was the only way out, and they attained it. It was beautiful, to say the least.

To me, dad's code of ethics was revealing itself, naturally: *Mercy*, while fellow Egyptians of all faiths strived to protect each other; *Truth* (the whole truth), which was the realization of the duty of all citizens to respect each other's faiths; and *Love*, by sending caring messages to casualties of terror when initiated by a few looters. *Justice* and P*eace* were looming in the air and a new horizon was shining over Egypt.

In early October of 2013, Summer-Breeze Senior Living, of Montreal, asked me to contribute to a talent show for its senior residents (among other volunteer musicians). I managed to deliver my dream piece of music, the Second Movement from Rachmaninoff's piano concerto Number 2 (*Adagio Sostenuto*) to an audience of about thirty residents and their families, including mother. Mother was ecstatic, though getting wiser, more loving, far more distant and in a world of her own. However, she seemed so content. As for me, I had achieved my dream of playing this movement, in her presence, despite the few finger-slips. I remember playing it with such passion, rekindling its author's profound impressionistic and melancholic mood through its cadences to the extent that my eyes turned wet as I looked at mother. By the end of the show, most residents were humming the tunes played by another musician, Demis, a volunteer guitarist who added joy and gave hope to their lives four times a week, from three to five in the afternoon. Some were even singing with him. All of the residents were swinging in their chairs and clapping with the songs, joyfully, including poor ninety-year-old Florence who lost her son in a car accident but did not know it. He used to visit her twice a day, until he lost his life the week before. However, she was already part of this tree of love and hope, in a dimension of beatitudes. She did not notice it. Other volunteer musicians and comedians such as Demis, Richard, and Gregg, just as well, gave meaning to her life and to the lives of other residents with their music. The neighboring parish of Saint Thomas would raise half the cost of

Florence's monthly bill, and the government of Quebec would raise part of the balance using her remaining pensions. After all, her son was once an active member of its congregation. On this day, I decided to devote many hours of my life to assist seniors and to add joy and dignity to their lives, whether here at Summer Breeze or in another residence.

Soon, I showed mother how far I reached with this book, in hard copy. It was close to eighty percent of this final manuscript. I made a point of showing her my dedication, on the first page. The earlier dedication outlined my gratitude to her for making it possible for me to write this book; a book that I presented to her. She understood and smiled to me and I kissed her forehead.

Finally, I decided to study the first movement of Rachmaninoff's same piano concerto (Number 2). Our soccer team's remaining members agreed to visit the Montreal Granby Zoo, a few months later. There were six of us, Roland, Karina, Haitham, his wife (Manal), the love of my life, my wife, Dahlia and I. We all planned to visit the green Montreal Granby Zoo, in spring, (during the last week of the following May, in 2014) when it would reopen for the public. All this planning was during the last week of November 2013. Haitham and his family moved from New York and settled in Montreal. They visited mother but she could barely remember them. In the meantime, we received news from Egypt. Jeanette returned to God, on Boxing Day. I was heartbroken for her and clung to mother more, during these holidays.

On Christmas week of 2013, Dahlia and I bought mother a small Christmas tree that turned around itself with the sound of chimes. We turned it on, in her room, in view of the season. Mother, was in a very distant world and I would not waste a moment to shower her with, but a fraction of what she had given me across the years. My Panic was starting, for the inevitable.

Chapter 45

A dark dawn in mid-January
Mother, my eternal angel

At 3 am, on a cold and snowy January 14, 2014, I woke up in bed troubled and pensive. I thought I smelt mom's Jasmine perfume, and looked around but she was not in my room. Dahlia was still sleeping. I said the Lord's Prayer and found myself grabbing my clothes, coat, keys and mobile telephone. I rushed to my car and drove to Summer Breeze Senior Living in the midst of the deep piling snow. I was there at 3.30 am. I opened mom's door and there she was gasping for air and clearly, restless. I held her left hand and put my right one on her forehead and cheeks.

"Mom, I am here my love; Raphy, sitting by your side and will not leave you. Christ is with us and He will tell us what to do. You are fine my love and I love you so much. She was clearly dehydrated."

I tried to give mom some water, to drink, with a straw; it did not work. I tried a swab and was barely fortunate to wet her lips and mouth walls. I continued to wipe here forehead with a wet cloth, and sing to her in a low voice, the theme from Brahms' Symphony No. 3. I held-up myself so hard, so as not to break. I kept hugging her and gently throwing my head in her lap. I kept kissing her hand as she kept gasping for air. I wanted her to rest but she had already started a journey she was finally ready for; one I could not halt; one I found so hard to deal with.

The nurse on duty could not offer any help but she looked me straight in the eyes, in an extremely decisive manner, passing a message of support and advice, urging me not to fight the will of God. She was compassionate and expected me to understand. By 7 a.m., I called my sister and her family and asked them to come over, which they did. I telephoned our priest, who came within forty-five minutes. He sprinkled mother with holy water and anointed her forehead with blessed oil. Mother, barely, managed to taste a small piece of the body of Christ, with a little water on her tongue.

    The new shift arrived with a new nurse; my family arrived too. By 8.30 am, mom was looking to her bedroom's ceiling, smiling and turning her eyes upwards, to something only she could see, but we could, clearly, imagine. She screamed twice, in a faint voice. My heartbeat was rising, dramatically. The day I apprehended most when I was seven was drawing closer. We continued to moist mom's mouth with water while her rate of breath slowed down, her lips closed, halfway, with a gentle smile. Her hands crisscrossed each other as she placed them on her stomach, her eyelids half shut, and her head leaned leftwards, and a little forward. Her breathing continued to slow down, and then, it stopped... It stopped for good, at 09.27 am. There was silence in the room and my soul went with hers. My sister stared in my eyes with assurance, bowed to mother's forehead, and kissed her. I froze for a while, and kissed her hands, in utter defeat and then threw myself in her bosom. I stayed next to mom until the coroner's team arrived at 10.15 am. My Nephew and Niece arrived shortly after.

    "Good bye my love, we will meet again in His great Mansion." I told her, while kissing her forehead. "Good night my angel, my lifetime friend; I will see you in the morning." The world seemed so still and I felt myself in another zone, a different era, one that I yet had to discover and cope with.

    For the following week, I would visit mother's resting place, every day for at least twenty minutes of intense prayer and singing. I would fill a small bottle with Holy water, from our church, and sprinkle it over her resting place. On the third day, almost fifteen minutes after I had started to pray while singing for her, and sprinkling Holy water, I broke out in tears. This helped me a lot. After a few seconds, I smelled a beautiful whiff of burning incense, just as the one the pastor holds in a church altar. I turned my head left, right and backwards; there was no one else visiting that day. I was the only one standing in this snow-covered graveyard, on that cold January morning. Then I knew that the smell was genuine and that its source was, precisely, from where I stood! The smell flew from the ground, over my head and around my face and then rose to the infinite skies. I looked upwards and gave praise; I blessed mom and said, "Thank you my angel".

Two weeks later, I accepted an offer at a senior home, next to where Dahlia and I lived. I joined its team as receptionist, working twenty to thirty hours a week, seeking solace and closure, hoping to add meaning to its residents' lives. After all, they reminded me of my parents. They were residents who could no longer engage with others, as they did before.

In spring 2016, Dahlia and I spent some time in Magog and then we returned during December 2016, to stay in Cairo, until spring, 2017.

Today, on June 24, 2017, Dahlia and I visited mother's former Senior Home. We met few of her friends but she was no longer there. It was not the same. She was in our hearts, forever. Besides, I no longer had a house big enough, to contain a piano. Alas, we had to move to a smaller house, with one room less and I sold my piano. Of course, I kept an electric keyboard but could no longer practice my scales or study major works. I never finished the first movement from Rachmaninoff's Piano-Concerto number 2, which had always been my dream, and I had to reduce my music hours to an insignificant minimum. Of course, I never made it to real theatre, classic concerts or fame, as I had promised Camille and, which was the life I would have had to lead. Intense scrutiny and invasive bigots had derailed me. Nevertheless, I changed, a little, to the better; to what I wanted to do with my life; I took the shape of the years that life had confined me to, just as water takes the shape of the pipe it runs through. Most important of all, I took that shape while keeping my initiative, independence and identity. I clung to my faith; I continued reading Arabic and English poetry, from my heart, at the City Library, with no fear of scrutiny or hurt, to the best I could, which was better than not doing much.

As I look back, I can easily state that across the years, I was broken, repeatedly and fiercely, but would always rebuild myself using my own God-given ingredients and tools, always within Divine order, no more, no less- with no need for some miserable psychopath to re-shape me and mould me, crush me or scoff me, privately or publicly.

It felt beautiful and, thankfully, I finished this manuscript in good health and state of mind; I wrote it for mother who, in all fairness, was the source of its priceless stories, since my childhood. I did it in appreciation of all she did for my family and, certainly, me. She witnessed its growth since the first chapter. I did it for other creations of God targeted for alienation from their lands, homes or souls. I did it for all parents and their distant children yearning for each other, for the sake of all flowers and jasmines, hurting, far away from their mother trees and for branches and homelands, ailing at distance, at their departing fruit.

To eternal Egypt, my mother, thank you!

Rafik G. Baladi   Jasmines from Egypt Branches Forever   2018

Rafik G. Baladi   Jasmines from Egypt Branches Forever   2018

www.ingramcontent.com/pod-product-compliance
Lightning Source LLC
Chambersburg PA
CBHW072141100526
44589CB00015B/2028